OPEN SECRETS

OPEN SECRETS

WIKILEAKS, WAR AND AMERICAN DIPLOMACY

Complete and Updated Coverage
by The New York Times

Introduction by Bill Keller
Edited by Alexander Star

Grove Press
New York

Printed in the United States of America

ISBN-13: 978-0-8021-4576-5

Grove Press
an imprint of Grove/Atlantic, Inc.
841 Broadway
New York, NY 10003

Distributed by Publishers Group West

www.groveatlantic.com

11 12 13 14 15   10 9 8 7 6 5 4 3 2 1

CONTENTS

PART FIVE
AFTERMATH

PART SIX
OPINIONS

OPEN SECRETS

PART ONE

INTRODUCTION

"An air of intrigue verging on paranoia permeated the project,
perhaps understandably, given that we were dealing with a mass
of classified material and a source who acted like a fugitive—changing crash pads,
e-mail addresses and cellphones frequently."

—from "The Boy Who Kicked the Hornet's Nest"
By Bill Keller

THE BOY WHO KICKED
THE HORNET'S NEST

By BILL KELLER

In June 2010, Alan Rusbridger, the editor of the London daily newspaper The Guardian, phoned me and asked, mysteriously, whether I had any idea how to arrange a secure communication. Not really, I confessed. The Times doesn't have encrypted phone lines, or a Cone of Silence. Well then, Alan said, he would try to speak circumspectly. In a roundabout way, he laid out an unusual proposition: An organization called WikiLeaks, a secretive cadre of anti-secrecy vigilantes, had come into possession of an enormous amount of classified U.S. government communications. WikiLeaks's leader, an eccentric former computer hacker of Australian birth and no fixed residence, had offered The Guardian half a million military dispatches from the battlefields of Afghanistan and Iraq. There might be more after that, including an immense bundle of confidential diplomatic cables. The Guardian had suggested—both to increase the impact and to share the labor of handling such a trove—that The New York Times be invited to share this exclusive bounty. The source had agreed. Was I interested?

I was interested.

The adventure that ensued over the next six months combined the cloak-and-dagger intrigue of handling a vast secret archive with the more mundane feat of sorting, searching and understanding a mountain of data. As if that was not complicated enough, the project also entailed a source who was elusive, manipulative and volatile (and ultimately openly hostile to both The Times and The Guardian), an international cast of journalists, company lawyers committed to keeping us within the bounds of the law, editors wrestling with some potent ethical questions and an array of government officials who sometimes seemed as though they couldn't decide whether they wanted to engage us or arrest us. By the end of the year, the story of this wholesale security breach had outgrown the story of the actual contents of the secret documents, and had generated much breathless speculation that something—journalism, diplomacy, life as we knew it—had profoundly changed forever.

The fruits of this endeavor—the scores of articles produced by The Times and the documents that support them, along with the commentary published in our opinion pages—are compiled in this volume, in the belief that they will be of interest to anyone who follows America's relationship with the rest of the world. We have included an expanded profile by our London bureau chief, John Burns, and his collaborator Ravi Somaiya of Julian Assange, the man who set this curious story in motion. We have also included a summary of the feverish reactions, pro and con, and essays by some of the correspondents involved on what it all means. In this introduction I will lay out in some detail what we did and why we did it.

Soon after Alan Rusbridger's call, we sent Eric Schmitt from our Washington bureau to London. Eric has covered military affairs expertly for years, has read his share of classified military dispatches, and has excellent judgment and an unflappable demeanor. His main assignment was to get a sense of the material. Was it genuine? Was it of public interest? He would also report back on the proposed mechanics of our collaboration with The Guardian and the German magazine Der Spiegel, which Assange had invited in as a third consumer of his secret smorgasbord. Eric would also meet the WikiLeaks leader, who was known to a few Guardian journalists but not to us.

Eric's first phone call home was encouraging. There was no question in his mind that the Afghanistan dispatches were genuine. They were fascinating, a ground-up diary of a troubled war. And there were intimations of more to come—especially classified cables from the entire constellation of American diplomatic outposts. WikiLeaks was holding those back for now, presumably to see how this venture in dealing with the establishment media worked out. Over the next few days, Eric huddled in a discreet office at The Guardian, sampling the trove of war dispatches and discussing the complexities of this project: how to organize and study such a voluminous cache of information; how to securely transport, store and share it; how journalists from three very different publications would work together without compromising their independence; how to publish responsibly material laden with risks; and how we would ensure an appropriate distance from Julian Assange. We regarded Assange throughout as a source, not as a partner or collaborator, but he was a man who clearly had his own agenda.

By the time of the meetings in London, WikiLeaks had already acquired a measure of international fame, or, depending on your point of view, notoriety. Shortly before I got the call from The Guardian, The New Yorker had published a rich and colorful profile of Assange by Raffi Khatchadourian, who had embedded with the group. WikiLeaks's biggest coup to that point had been the release, in April 2010, of video footage taken from one of two U.S. helicopters involved in firing down on a crowd and a building in Baghdad in 2007, killing at least 18 people. While some of the people in the video were armed, others gave no indication of menace; two were in fact journalists for the Reuters news agency. The video, with its soundtrack of callous banter, was horrifying to watch, and was an embarrassment to the U.S. military. But WikiLeaks, in its zeal to make the video a work of antiwar propaganda, also released a version that didn't call attention to an Iraqi who was toting a rocket-propelled grenade and packaged the manipulated version under the tendentious rubric "Collateral Murder."

Assange was, throughout our dealings, coy about where he had obtained his secret cache. But the suspected source of the video, as well as the military dispatches and the diplomatic cables to come, was a disillusioned Army private first class named Bradley Manning, who had been arrested and was being kept in solitary confinement.

On the fourth day of the London meeting, Julian Assange slouched into The Guardian's office, a day late. Eric took his first measure of the man who would be a large presence in our lives: "He's tall—probably 6-2 or 6-3—and lanky, with pale skin, gray eyes and a shock of white hair that seizes your attention," Eric wrote to me later. "He was alert but disheveled, like a bag lady walking in off the street, wearing a dingy, light colored sports coat and cargo pants, dirty white shirt, beat-up sneakers and filthy white socks that collapsed around his ankles. He smelled as if he hadn't bathed in days."

Assange shrugged a huge backpack off his shoulders and pulled out a stockpile of laptops, cords, cellphones, thumb drives and memory sticks that held the WikiLeaks secrets.

The reporters had begun preliminary work on the Afghanistan field reports, using a large Excel spreadsheet to organize the material, then plugging in search terms and combing the documents for newsworthy content. They had run into a puzzling incongruity. Assange had said the data included dispatches from the beginning of 2004 through the end of 2009. But the material on the spreadsheet ended abruptly in April 2009. A considerable amount of material was missing. Assange, slipping naturally into the role of office geek, explained that they had hit the limits of Excel. Open a second spreadsheet, he instructed. They did, and the rest of the data materialized—a total of 92,000 reports from the battlefields of Afghanistan.

The reporters came to think of Assange as smart and well-educated, extremely adept technologically, but arrogant, thin-skinned, conspiratorial and oddly credulous. At lunch one day in The Guardian's cafeteria, Assange recounted with an air of great conviction a story about the archive in Germany that contains the files of the former Communist secret police, the Stasi. This office, Assange asserted, had been thoroughly infiltrated by former Stasi agents who were quietly destroying the documents they were entrusted with protecting. The Der Spiegel reporter in the group, John Goetz, who has reported extensively on the Stasi, listened in amazement. That's utter nonsense, he said. Some former Stasi personnel were hired as security guards in the office, but the records were well protected.

Assange was openly contemptuous of the American government, and certain that he was a hunted man. He told the reporters that he had prepared a kind of doomsday option. He had, he said, distributed highly encrypted copies of his entire secret archive to a multitude of supporters, and if WikiLeaks was shut down, or if he was arrested, he would disseminate the key to make the information public.

Eric told me that for all his bombast and dark conspiracy theories, Assange had a bit of Peter Pan in him. One night, when they were all walking home from dinner, Assange suddenly started skipping down the sidewalk. Eric and John Goetz stared, speechless. Then, just as suddenly, Assange stopped, got back in step with the group and returned to the conversation he had interrupted.

For the rest of the week, Eric worked with David Leigh, The Guardian's investigations editor, Nick Davies, an investigative reporter for the paper, and Goetz, of Der Spiegel, to organize and sort the material. With help from two of The Times's best computer minds—Andy Lehren and Aron Pilhofer—they figured out how to assemble the material into a conveniently searchable and secure database.

Journalists are characteristically competitive, but the group worked well together. They brainstormed topics to explore and exchanged search results. Der Spiegel offered to check the logs against incident reports submitted by the German Army to its Parliament—partly as story research, partly as an additional check on authenticity.

Assange had provided us the data on the condition that we not write about it before specific dates when WikiLeaks planned to post the documents on a publicly accessible Web site. The Afghanistan documents would go first, after we had had a few weeks to search the material and write our articles. The larger cache of Iraq-related documents would go later. Such embargoes—agreements not to publish information before a set date—are a commonplace in journalism. Everything from studies in medical journals to the annual U.S. budget is released with embargoes. They are a constraint with benefits, the principle benefit being the chance to actually read and reflect on the material before launching it into public view. Embargoes also, as Assange surely knew, tend to build suspense and amplify a story, especially when multiple news outlets broadcast it at once. The embargo was the only condition WikiLeaks would try to impose on us. What we wrote about the material was entirely up to us. Much later, some American news outlets reported that they were offered last-minute access to the WikiLeaks documents if they signed contracts with financial penalties for early disclosure. The Times was never asked to sign anything or to pay anything. For WikiLeaks, at least in this first big venture, exposure was its own reward.

Back in New York we assembled a team of reporters, data experts and editors and quartered them in an out-of-the-way office. Andy Lehren, of our computer-assisted reporting unit, did the first cut, searching terms on his own or those suggested by other reporters, compiling batches of relevant documents and summarizing the contents. We assigned reporters to specific areas where they had expertise and gave them password access to rummage in the data themselves. This became the routine we would follow with subsequent archives.

An air of intrigue verging on paranoia permeated the project, perhaps understandably, given that we were dealing with a mass of classified material and a source who acted like a fugitive—changing crash pads, e-mail addresses and cellphones frequently. We used encrypted Web sites. Reporters exchanged notes via Skype, believing it to be somewhat less vulnerable to eavesdropping. On our periodic conference calls, we spoke in amateurish code. Assange was always "the source." The latest data drop was "the package." When I left New York for two weeks to visit bureaus in Pakistan and Afghanistan, where we assume communications may be monitored, I was not to be copied on message traffic about the project. I never imagined that any of this would defeat a curious snoop from the National Security Agency or Pakistani intelligence. And I was never entirely sure whether that prospect made me more nervous than the cyberwiles of WikiLeaks itself. At a point when relations between the news organizations and WikiLeaks were rocky, at least three people associated with this project had inexplicable activity on their e-mail that suggested someone had been hacking into our accounts.

From consultations with our lawyers we were confident that reporting on the secret documents could be done within the law, but we speculated about what the government—or some other government—might do to impede our work or exact recriminations. And, the law aside, we felt an enormous moral and ethical responsibility to use the material responsibly. While we assumed we had little or no ability to influence what WikiLeaks did, let alone what would happen once this material was loosed in the echo chamber of the blogosphere, that did not free us from the obligation to exercise care in our own journalism. From the beginning, we agreed that in our articles and in any documents we published from the secret archive we would excise material that could put lives at risk.

Guided by reporters with extensive experience in the field, we redacted names of ordinary citizens, local officials, activists, academics and others who had spoken to American soldiers or diplomats. We edited out any details that might reveal continuing intelligence-gathering operations, military tactics or locations of material that could be used to fashion terrorist weapons. Three reporters with considerable experience of handling military secrets—Eric Schmitt, Michael Gordon and C. J. Chivers—went over the documents we considered posting. Chris Chivers, a former Marine who has reported for us from several battlefields, brought a practiced eye and cautious judgment to the business of redaction. If a dispatch noted that Aircraft A left Location B at a certain time and arrived at Location C at a certain time, Chris edited it out on the off chance that this could teach enemy forces something useful about the capabilities of that aircraft.

*   *   *

The first articles in the project, which we called the war logs, were scheduled to go up on the Web sites of The Times, The Guardian and Der Spiegel at 5 p.m. on Sunday, July 25. We had approached the White House days before that to get its reaction to the huge breach of secrecy as well as to specific articles we planned to write—including a major one about Pakistan's ambiguous role as an American ally. On July 24, the day before the war logs went live, I attended a farewell party for Roger Cohen, a columnist for The Times and The International Herald Tribune, that was given by Richard Holbrooke, the Obama administration's special representative for Afghanistan and Pakistan. A voracious consumer of inside information, Holbrooke had a decent idea of what was coming, and he pulled me away from the crowd to show me the fusillade of cabinet-level e-mails ricocheting through his BlackBerry, thus demonstrating both the frantic anxiety in the administration and, not incidentally, the fact that he was very much in the loop. The Pakistan article, in particular, would complicate his life. But one of Holbrooke's many gifts was his ability to make pretty good lemonade out of the bitterest lemons; he was already spinning the reports of Pakistani duplicity as leverage he could use to pull the Pakistanis back into closer alignment with American interests. Five months later, when Holbrooke—just 69, and seemingly indestructible—died of a torn aorta, I remembered that evening. And what I remembered best was that he was as excited to be on the cusp of a big story as I was.

We posted the articles on nytimes.com the next day at 5 p.m.—a time picked to reconcile the different publishing schedules of the three publications. I was proud of what a crew of great journalists had done to fashion coherent and instructive reporting from a jumble of raw field reports, mostly composed in a clunky patois of military jargon and acronyms. The reporters supplied context, nuance and skepticism. There is much in this collection worth reading, but my favorite single piece in the first round of war logs was one of the simplest. Chris Chivers gathered all of the dispatches related to a single, remote, beleaguered American military outpost and stitched them together into a heartbreaking narrative. (see p. 276) The dispatches from this outpost represent in miniature the audacious ambitions, gradual disillusionment and ultimate disappointment that Afghanistan has dealt to occupiers over the centuries.

If anyone doubted that the three publications operated independently, the articles we posted that day made it clear that we had followed our separate muses. The Guardian, which is an openly left-leaning newspaper, used

the first war logs to emphasize civilian casualties in Afghanistan, claiming
that the documents disclosed that coalition forces killed "hundreds of civilians in unreported incidents," underscoring the cost of what the paper called
a "failing war." Our reporters studied the same material, but determined
that all of the major episodes of civilian deaths we found in the war logs had
been reported in The Times, many of them on the front page. (In fact, two
of our journalists, Stephen Farrell and Sultan Munadi, were kidnapped by
the Taliban while investigating one major episode near Kunduz. Munadi
was killed during an ensuing rescue by British paratroopers.) The civilian
deaths that had not been previously reported came in ones and twos, and
did not add up to anywhere near "hundreds." Moreover, since several were
either duplicated or missing from the reports, we concluded that an overall
tally would be little better than a guess.

Another example: The Times gave prominence to the dispatches
reflecting American suspicions that Pakistani intelligence was playing a
double game in Afghanistan—nodding to American interests while abetting
the Taliban. We buttressed the interesting anecdotal material of Pakistani
double-dealing with additional reporting. The Guardian was unimpressed
by those dispatches and treated them more dismissively.

Three months later, with the French daily Le Monde added to the
group, we published Round 2, the Iraq war logs, including articles on how
the United States turned a blind eye to the torture of prisoners by Iraqi
forces working with the U.S., how Iraq spawned an extraordinary American military reliance on private contractors and how extensively Iran had
meddled in the conflict.

By this time my paper's relationship with our source had gone from
wary to hostile. I talked to Assange by phone a few times, and heard out
his complaints. He was angry that we declined to link our online coverage
of the war logs to the WikiLeaks Web site, a decision we made because
we feared—rightly, as it turned out—that their trove would contain the
names of low-level informants and make them Taliban targets. "Where's the
respect?" he demanded. "Where's the respect?" Another time he called to tell
me how much he disliked our profile of Bradley Manning, the Army private
suspected of being the source of WikiLeaks's most startling revelations. The
article traced Manning's childhood as an outsider and his distress as a gay
man in the military. Assange complained that we had "psychologicalized"
Manning and given short shrift to his "political awakening."

The final straw was a front-page profile of Assange by John Burns and Ravi Somaiya, published Oct. 24, that revealed fractures within WikiLeaks, attributed by Assange's critics to his imperious management style. Assange denounced the article to me, and in various public forums, as "a smear."

Assange had been transformed by his outlaw celebrity. The derelict with the backpack and sagging socks now wore his hair dyed and styled, and favored fashionably skinny suits and ties. He had become a kind of cult figure for the European young and leftish, and was evidently a magnet for women. Two Swedish women had filed police complaints alleging that Assange had insisted on having sex without a condom; Sweden's strict laws on nonconsensual sex categorize such behavior as rape, and a prosecutor had issued a warrant to question Assange, who initially described it as a plot concocted to silence or discredit WikiLeaks.

I had come to think of Julian Assange as a character from a Stieg Larsson thriller—a man who could figure either as hero or villain in one of the mega-selling Swedish novels that mix hacker counterculture, high-level conspiracy and sex as both recreation and violation.

In October, WikiLeaks gave The Guardian its third archive, a quarter of a million communications between the State Department and its outposts around the globe. This time, Assange imposed a new condition: The Guardian was not to share the material with The New York Times. Indeed, he told Guardian journalists, he had opened discussions with two other American news organizations, The Washington Post and the McClatchy chain, and intended to invite them in as replacements for The Times. He also enlarged his recipient list to include El País, the leading Spanish-language newspaper.

The Guardian was uncomfortable with Assange's condition. By now journalists from the Times and The Guardian had a good working relationship. The Times provided a large American audience for the revelations and access to the U.S. government for comment and context. And, given the potential legal issues and public criticism, it was good to have company in the trenches. Besides, we had come to believe that Assange was losing control of his stockpile of secrets. An independent journalist, Heather Brooke, had obtained material from a WikiLeaks dissident, and had joined in a loose alliance with The Guardian. Over the following weeks, batches of cables would pop up in newspapers in Lebanon, Australia and Norway.

David Leigh, the Guardian investigations editor, concluded that these rogue leaks released The Guardian from any pledge, and he gave us the cables.

On Nov. 1, Assange and two of his lawyers burst into Alan Rusbridger's office, furious that The Guardian was asserting greater independence and suspicious that The Times might be in possession of the embassy cables. Over the course of an eight-hour meeting, Assange raged intermittently against The Times—especially over the front-page profile we published— while the Guardian journalists tried to calm him. In midstorm, Rusbridger called me to report on Assange's grievances and relay his demand for a front-page apology in The Times. Alan knew that was a nonstarter, but like a good diplomat he was buying time for the tantrum to subside. In the end, both Alan and Georg Mascolo, editor in chief of Der Spiegel, made clear that they intended to continue their collaboration with The Times. Assange could take it or leave it. Given that we already had all of the documents, he had little choice. Over the next two days the news organizations agreed on a timetable for publication.

The following week we sent Ian Fisher, a deputy foreign editor who was a principal coordinator on our processing of the embassy cables, to London to work out the final details. The meeting went smoothly, even after Assange arrived. "Freakishly good behavior," Ian e-mailed me afterward. "No yelling or crazy mood swings." But after dinner, as Ian was leaving, Assange smirked and offered a parting threat: "Tell me, are you in contact with your legal counsel?" Ian replied that he was. "You had better be," Assange said.

Ian left London with an understanding that we would continue to have access to the material. But just in case, we took out a competitive insurance policy. We had Scott Shane, a Washington correspondent, pull together a long, just-in-case article summing up highlights of the cables, that we could quickly post on our Web site. If WikiLeaks sprung another leak, we would be ready.

Because of the range of the material and the very nature of diplomacy, the embassy cables were bound to be more explosive than the war logs. Dean Baquet, our Washington bureau chief, gave the White House an early warning on Nov. 19. The following Tuesday, two days before Thanksgiving, Dean and two colleagues were invited to a windowless room in the State Department, where they encountered an unsmiling crowd: representatives of the White

House, the State Department, the office of the director of national intelligence, the C.I.A., the Defense Intelligence Agency, the F.B.I. and the Pentagon, gathered around a conference table. Others, who never identified themselves, lined the walls, and a solitary note-taker tapped away on a computer.

The meeting was off the record, but it is fair to say the mood was tense. Scott Shane, one reporter who participated in the meeting, described "an undertone of suppressed outrage and frustration."

Subsequent meetings, which soon gave way to daily conference calls, were more businesslike. Before each discussion, our Washington bureau sent over a batch of specific cables we intended to use in the coming days. They were circulated to regional specialists, who funneled their reaction to a small group at State, who came to our daily conversations with a list of priorities and arguments to back them up. We relayed the government's concerns, and our own decisions regarding them, to the other news outlets.

The administration's concerns generally fell into three categories. First was the importance of protecting individuals who had spoken candidly to American diplomats in oppressive countries. We almost always agreed on those, and were grateful to the government for pointing out some we had overlooked.

"We were all aware of dire stakes for some of the people named in the cables if we failed to obscure their identities," Scott wrote to me later, recalling the nature of the meetings. Like many of us, Scott has worked in countries where dissent can mean prison or worse. "That sometimes meant not just removing the name, but also references to institutions that might give a clue to an identity and sometimes even the dates of conversations, which might be compared with surveillance tapes of an American embassy to reveal who was visiting the diplomats that day."

The second category included sensitive American programs, usually related to intelligence. We agreed to withhold some of this information, like a cable describing an intelligence-sharing program that had taken years to arrange and might be lost if exposed. In other cases, we went away convinced that publication would cause some embarrassment but no real harm.

The third category consisted of cables that disclosed candid comments by and about foreign officials, including heads of state. The State Department feared publication would strain relations with those countries. We were mostly unconvinced.

The embassy cables were a different kind of treasure from the war logs. For one thing, they covered the entire globe—virtually every embassy, consulate and interest section the United States maintains. They contained the makings of many dozens of stories: unvarnished American appraisals of foreign leaders, narratives of complicated negotiations, allegations of corruption and duplicity, countless behind-the-scenes insights. Some of the material was of narrow local interest, some of it had global implications. Some provided authoritative versions of events not previously fully understood. Some consisted of rumor and flimsy speculation.

Unlike most of the military dispatches, the embassy cables were written in clear English—sometimes with wit, color and an ear for dialogue. ("Who knew," one of our English colleagues marveled, "that American diplomats could write?")

Even more than the military logs, the diplomatic cables called for context and analysis. It was important to know, for example, that cables sent from an embassy are routinely dispatched over the signature of the ambassador, and those from Washington are signed by the secretary of state—regardless of whether the ambassador or secretary had actually seen the material. It was important to know that much of the communication between Washington and its outposts is given even more restrictive classification—top secret, or higher—and was thus missing from this trove. We searched in vain, for example, for military or diplomatic reports on the fate of Pat Tillman, the former football star and Army Ranger who was killed by friendly fire in Afghanistan. We found no reports on how Osama bin Laden eluded American forces in the mountains of Tora Bora. (In fact, we found nothing but second- and third-hand rumors about bin Laden.) If such cables exist, they were presumably classified top secret or higher.

And it was important to remember that diplomatic cables are versions of events. They can be speculative. They can be ambiguous. They can be wrong.

One of our first articles drawn from the diplomatic cables, for example, reported on a secret intelligence assessment that Iran had obtained a supply of advanced missiles from North Korea, missiles that could reach European capitals. Outside experts had long suspected that Iran had obtained missile parts, but not the entire weapons, so this glimpse of the official view was revealing. The Washington Post fired back with a different take, casting doubt on whether the missile in question had been transferred to Iran, or whether it was even a workable weapon. We went back to the cables—and the experts—and concluded in a subsequent article that the evidence presented "a murkier picture."

The tension between newspapers' obligation to inform and governments' responsibility to protect is hardly new. At least until this year, nothing The Times had done on my watch had caused nearly so much agitation as two articles we published about tactics employed by the Bush administration after the attacks of Sept. 11, 2001. One article, which was published in 2005 and won a Pulitzer Prize, revealed that the National Security Agency was eavesdropping on domestic phone conversations and e-mail without the legal courtesy of a warrant. The other, published in 2006, described a vast Treasury Department program to screen international banking records.

I have vivid memories of sitting in the Oval Office as President George W. Bush tried to persuade me and the paper's publisher to withhold the eavesdropping story, saying that if we published it, we should share the blame for the next terrorist attack. We were unconvinced by his argument and published the story, and the reaction from the government—and conservative commentators in particular—was vociferous.

This time around, the Obama administration's reaction was different. It was, for the most part, sober and professional. The Obama White House, while strongly condemning WikiLeaks for making the documents public, did not seek an injunction to halt publication. There was no Oval Office lecture. On the contrary, in our discussions before the publication of our articles, White House officials, while challenging some of the conclusions we drew from the material, thanked us for handling the documents with care. The secretaries of state and defense and the attorney general resisted the opportunity for a crowd-pleasing orgy of press-bashing. There has been no serious official talk—unless you count an ambiguous hint by Senator Joseph Lieberman—of pursuing news organizations in the courts. Though the release of these documents was certainly embarrassing, the relevant government agencies actually engaged with us in an attempt to prevent the release of material genuinely damaging to innocent individuals or the national interest.

The broader public reaction was mixed—more critical in the first days, more sympathetic as readers absorbed the articles and as the sky did not fall; more hostile to WikiLeaks in the United States than in Europe, where there is often a certain smug pleasure in seeing the last superpower brought down a peg.

In the days after we began publishing our respective series based on the embassy cables, Alan Rusbridger of The Guardian and I went online to answer questions from readers. The Guardian, whose readership is more sympathetic to the guerrilla sensibilities of WikiLeaks, was attacked for being too fastidious about redacting the documents: How dare you censor this material? What are you hiding? Post everything now! The mail sent to The Times, at least in the first day or two, came from the opposite field. Many readers were indignant and alarmed. Who needs this? How dare you? What gives you the right?

Much of the concern was heartfelt, reflecting a genuine conviction that particularly in perilous times like ours governments need wide latitude and a measure of secrecy to do their job of keeping us safe. That is compounded by a popular sense that the elite media has become too big for their britches and by the fact that our national conversation has become more polarized and strident.

Although it is our aim to be impartial in our presentation of the news, our attitude toward these issues is far from indifferent. The journalists at The Times have a large and personal stake in the country's security. We live and work in a city that has been tragically marked as a favorite terrorist target, and in the wake of 9/11 our journalists plunged into the ruins to tell the story of what happened there. Moreover, The Times has nine staff correspondents assigned to the two wars still being waged in the wake of that attack—plus a rotating cast of photographers, visiting writers and scores of local stringers and support staff. They work in this high-risk environment because, while there are lots of places you can go for opinions about the war, there are few places, and fewer by the day, where you can go to find honest, on-the-scene reporting about what is happening. We take extraordinary precautions to keep them safe, but we have had two of our Iraqi journalists murdered for doing their jobs. We have had four journalists held hostage by the Taliban—two of them for seven months. We had one Afghan journalist killed in a rescue attempt. Last October, while I was in Kabul, we got word that a photographer embedded for us with troops near Kandahar had stepped on an improvised mine and lost both his legs.

We are invested in the struggle against murderous extremism in another sense. The virulent hatred espoused by terrorists, judging by their literature, is directed not just against our people and our buildings. It is also aimed at our values, and at our faith in the self-government of an informed electorate. If the freedom of the press makes some Americans uneasy, it is anathema to the ideologists of terror.

So we have no doubts about where our sympathies lie in this clash of values. And yet we cannot let those sympathies transform us into minions, even of a system we respect.

I'm the first to admit that news organizations, including this one, sometimes get things wrong. We can be overly credulous (as in some of the prewar reporting about Iraq's weapons of mass destruction) or overly cynical about official claims and motives. We may err on the side of keeping secrets (President Kennedy reportedly wished, after the fact, that The Times had published what it knew about the planned Bay of Pigs invasion, which possibly would have helped avert a bloody debacle) or on the side of exposing them. We make the best judgments we can. When we get things wrong, we try to correct the record. A free press in a democracy can be messy. But the alternative is to give the government a veto over what its citizens are allowed to know. Anyone who has worked in countries where the news diet is controlled by the government can sympathize with Thomas Jefferson's oft-quoted remark that he would rather have newspapers without government than government without newspapers.

The intentions of our founders have rarely been as well articulated as they were by Justice Hugo Black 40 years ago, concurring with the Supreme Court ruling that stopped the government from suppressing the secret Vietnam War history called the Pentagon Papers: "The government's power to censor the press was abolished so that the press would remain forever free to censure the government. The press was protected so that it could bare the secrets of government and inform the people."

There is no neat formula for maintaining this balance. In practice, the tension between our obligation to inform and the government's obligation to protect plays out in a set of rituals. As one of my predecessors, Max Frankel, then the Washington bureau chief, wrote in a wise affidavit filed during the Pentagon Papers case: "For the vast majority of 'secrets,' there has developed between the government and the press (and Congress) a rather simple rule of thumb: The government hides what it can, pleading necessity as long as it can, and the press pries out what it can, pleading a need and a right to know. Each side in this 'game' regularly 'wins' and 'loses' a round or two. Each fights with the weapons at its command. When the government loses a secret or two, it simply adjusts to a new reality."

In fact, leaks of classified material—sometimes authorized—are part of the way business is conducted in Washington, as one wing of the bureaucracy tries to one-up another, or officials try to shift blame, claim credit, advance or confound a particular policy. For further evidence that our government is highly selective in its approach to secrets, look no further than Bob Woodward's all-but-authorized accounts of the innermost deliberations of our government.

The government surely cheapens secrecy by deploying it so promiscuously. According to the Pentagon, about 500,000 people have clearance to use the database from which the secret cables were pilfered. Weighing in on the WikiLeaks case in The Guardian, Max Frankel remarked that secrets shared with such a legion of "cleared" officials, including low-level army clerks, "are not secret." Governments, he wrote, "must decide that the random rubber-stamping of millions of papers and computer files each year does not a security system make."

Beyond the basic question of whether the press should publish secrets, criticism of the publication of the documents obtained by WikiLeaks generally fell into three themes: 1. That the documents were of dubious value because they told us nothing we didn't already know. 2. That the disclosures put lives at risk—either directly, by identifying confidential informants, or indirectly by complicating our ability to build alliances against terror. 3. That by doing business with an organization like WikiLeaks, The Times and other news organizations compromised their impartiality and independence.

I'm a little puzzled by the complaint that most of the embassy traffic we disclosed did not profoundly change our understanding of how the world works. Ninety-nine percent of what you read or hear on the news does not profoundly change our understanding of how the world works. News mostly advances by inches and feet, not in great leaps. The value of these documents—and I believe they have immense value—is not that they expose some deep, unsuspected perfidy in high places or that they upend your whole view of the world. For those who pay close attention to foreign policy, these documents provide texture, nuance and drama. They deepen and correct your understanding of how things unfold, they raise or lower your estimation of world leaders. For those who do not follow these subjects as closely, the stories are an opportunity to learn more. If a project like this makes readers pay attention, think harder, understand more clearly what is being done in their name, then we have performed a public service. And that does not count the impact of the revelations on those most touched by them. WikiLeaks cables in which American diplomats recount the extravagant corruption of Tunisia's rulers helped fuel a popular uprising that overthrew the government.

As for the risks posed by these releases, they are real. WikiLeaks's first data dump, the publication of the Afghanistan war logs, included the names of scores of Afghans that The Times and other news organizations had carefully purged from our own coverage. Several news organizations, including ours, reported this dangerous lapse, and months later a Taliban spokesman claimed that Afghan insurgents had been perusing the Wiki-Leaks site and making a list. I anticipate, with dread, the day we learn that someone identified in those documents has been killed.

For its seeming indifference to the safety of those informants, Wiki-Leaks was roundly criticized, and in its subsequent postings it has largely followed the example of the news organizations and redacted material that could get people jailed or killed. Assange described it as a "harm-minimization policy." In the case of the Iraq war documents, WikiLeaks applied a kind of robo-redaction software that stripped away names (and rendered the documents almost illegible). With the embassy cables, Wiki-Leaks posted mostly cables that had already been redacted by The Times or its fellow news organizations. And there were instances in which WikiLeaks volunteers suggested measures to enhance the protection of innocents. For example, someone at WikiLeaks noticed that if the redaction of a phrase revealed the exact length of the words, an alert foreign security service might match the number of letters to a name and affiliation and thus identify the source. WikiLeaks advised everyone to substitute a dozen upper-case Xs for each redacted passage, no matter how long or short.

Whether WikiLeaks's "harm-minimization" is adequate, and whether it will continue, is beyond my power to predict or influence. WikiLeaks does not take guidance from The New York Times. In the end, I can only answer for what my own paper has done, and I believe we have behaved responsibly.

The idea that the mere publication of such a wholesale collection of secrets will make other countries less willing to do business with our diplomats seems to me questionable. Even Defense Secretary Robert Gates called this concern "overwrought." Foreign governments cooperate with us, he pointed out, not because they necessarily love us, not because they trust us to keep their secrets, but because they need us. It may be that for a time diplomats will choose their words more carefully—or circulate their views more narrowly—but WikiLeaks has not repealed the laws of self-interest. A few weeks after we began publishing articles about the embassy cables, David E. Sanger, our chief Washington correspondent, told me: "At least so far, the evidence that foreign leaders are no longer talking to American diplomats is scarce. I've heard about nervous jokes at the beginning of meetings, along the lines of 'when will I be reading about this conversation?' But the conversations are happening . . . American diplomacy has hardly screeched to a halt."

As for our relationship with WikiLeaks, Julian Assange has been heard to boast that he was a kind of puppet master, who recruited several news organizations, forced them to work in concert, and choreographed their work. This is characteristic braggadocio—or, as my Guardian colleagues would say, bollocks. Throughout this experience we have treated Julian Assange and his merry band as a source. I will not say "a source, pure and simple," because as any reporter or editor can attest, sources are rarely pure or simple, and Assange was no exception. But the relationship with sources is straightforward: You don't necessarily endorse their agenda, echo their rhetoric, take anything they say at face value, applaud their methods or, most important, allow them to shape or censor your journalism. Your obligation, as an independent news organization, is to verify the material, to supply context, to exercise responsible judgment about what to publish and what not, and to make sense of it. That is what we did.

But while I do not regard Julian Assange as a partner, and I would hesitate to describe what WikiLeaks does as journalism, it is chilling to contemplate the possible government prosecution of WikiLeaks for making secrets public, let alone the passage of new laws to punish the dissemination of classified information, as some have advocated. Taking legal recourse against a government official who violates his trust by divulging secrets he is sworn to protect is one thing. But criminalizing the publication of such secrets by someone who has no official obligation seems to me to run up against the First Amendment and the best traditions of this country. As one of my colleagues asks, if Assange was an understated professorial type rather than a character from a missing Stieg Larsson novel, and if WikiLeaks was not suffused with such glib antipathy toward the United States, would the reaction to the leaks be quite so ferocious? And would more Americans be speaking up against the threat of reprisals?

Whether the arrival of WikiLeaks has fundamentally changed the way journalism is made I will leave to others, and to history. Frankly, I think the impact of WikiLeaks on the culture has probably been overblown. Long before WikiLeaks was born, the Internet had transformed the landscape of journalism, creating a wide-open and global market with easier access to audiences and sources, a quicker metabolism, a new infrastructure for sharing and vetting information, and a diminished respect for notions of privacy and secrecy. Assange has claimed credit on several occasions for creating something he calls "scientific journalism," meaning that readers are given the raw material to judge for themselves whether the journalistic write-ups are trustworthy. But newspapers have been publishing texts of documents almost as long as newspapers have existed—and ever since the Internet eliminated space restrictions, we have done so copiously.

Nor is it clear to me that WikiLeaks represents some kind of cosmic triumph of transparency. If the official allegations are to be believed, most of WikiLeaks's great revelations came from a single anguished Army private—anguished enough to risk many years in prison. It's possible that the creation of online information brokers like WikiLeaks and OpenLeaks, a breakaway site announced in December by a former Assange colleague named Daniel Domscheit-Berg, will be a lure for whistle-blowers and malcontents who fear being caught consorting directly with a news organization like mine. But I suspect we have not reached a state of information anarchy. At least, not yet.

As 2010 wound down, The Times and its news partners had a conference call to discuss where we go from here. The initial surge of stories drawn from the secret cables was over. More articles would trickle out, but without a fixed schedule. We agreed to continue the redaction process, and we agreed we would all urge WikiLeaks to do the same. But this period of intense collaboration, and of regular contact with our source, was coming to a close.

Just before Christmas, Ian Katz, The Guardian's deputy editor, went to see Assange, who had been arrested in London on the Swedish warrant, briefly jailed, and bailed out by wealthy admirers, and was living under house arrest in a country manor in East Anglia while he fought Sweden's attempt to extradite him. The flow of donations to WikiLeaks, which he claimed had hit 100,000 euros a day at its peak, had been curtailed when Visa, MasterCard and PayPal refused to be a conduit for contributors—prompting a concerted assault on the Web sites of those companies by Assange's hacker-sympathizers. He would soon sign a lucrative book deal to finance his legal struggles.

The Guardian seemed to have joined The Times on Assange's enemies list, first for sharing the diplomatic cables with us, then for obtaining and reporting on the unredacted record of the Swedish police complaints against Assange. (Live by the leak . . .) In his fury at this perceived betrayal, Assange granted an interview to The Times of London, in which he vented his displeasure with our little media consortium. If he thought this would ingratiate him with The Guardian's rival, he was naïve. The paper happily splashed its exclusive interview, then followed it with an editorial calling Assange a fool and a hypocrite.

At the mansion in East Anglia, Assange seated Katz before a roaring fire in the drawing room and ruminated for four hours about the Swedish case, his financial troubles and his plan for a next phase of releases. He talked vaguely about secrets still in his quiver, including what he regards as a damning cache of e-mails from inside an American bank.

He spun out an elaborate version of a U.S. Justice Department effort to exact punishment for his assault on American secrecy. If he was somehow extradited to the United States, he said, "I would still have a high chance of being killed in the U.S. prison system, Jack Ruby style, given the continual calls for my murder by senior and influential U.S. politicians."

While Assange mused darkly in his exile, one of his lawyers sent out a mock Christmas card that suggested at least someone on the WikiLeaks team was not lacking a sense of the absurd.

The message:
"Dear kids,
Santa is Mum & Dad.
Love,
Wikileaks."

PART TWO

BACKGROUND

"Within WikiLeaks, and perhaps even within Assange himself,
a tension was emerging. He had spoken, and written,
of pioneering a new era of 'scientific journalism'. . . .
But from the start, this concept was cast in an uneasy alliance
with what Assange referred to in WikiLeaks's earliest days
as a fight against global injustice—the judgment of which,
it seemed clear, would be rendered primarily by himself."

—from "Who Is Julian Assange?"
by John F. Burns and Ravi Somaiya

Julian Assange, the founder of WikiLeaks.

WHO IS JULIAN ASSANGE?

By JOHN F. BURNS and RAVI SOMAIYA

As 2011 began, Julian Assange found himself a cosseted houseguest in a stately British country house, dressed for the part in an expensive brown herringbone tweed jacket and V-neck cashmere sweater. With studied nonchalance, he posed sitting atop farm gates; on other occasions he tossed snowballs, sipped martinis and hosted lengthy exchanges with selected journalists and admirers in a "drawing room" nearly the size of a basketball court, warmed by a roaring log fire. A Hollywood scriptwriter would have struggled to find a more incongruously opulent location for Assange, the embattled, live-out-of-a-backpack founder of WikiLeaks, to mark the arrival of the new year, and to revel in his sojourn from the globalized turmoil he generated in the departing year.

Ellingham Hall, 100 miles from London in the manicured East Anglian countryside memorialized by the 19th-century landscape paintings of Thomas Gainsborough and John Constable, is a three-story Georgian mansion set beside a graceful man-made lake. It anchors 650 acres of private pasture and woodland that can be rented out for weddings and country-house shooting parties hunting pheasant and grouse. The estate's owner, Vaughan Smith, is a former officer in one of Britain's most aristocratic regiments, the Grenadier Guards, a sometime combat cameraman of distinction, and currently the wealthy proprietor of the Frontline Club, a cozy journalists' hangout that has been Assange's London redoubt for long periods in the past year.

Before Assange arrived at Ellingham Hall, he had been released by a British judge after 10 days in a segregation unit at Wandsworth Prison in London, and vouchsafed into the safekeeping of Smith, one of a group of friends and celebrities who posted $370,000 bail. Awaiting possible transfer to Sweden to face criminal investigation in a sexual abuse case, Assange indignantly denied allegations of the "rape, sexual molestation and forceful coercion" of two women who had relationships with him during a visit to

Sweden in the summer of 2010—a journey, ironically, that he had undertaken with a view to gaining legal sanctuary in Sweden from the risk of American prosecution. In Assange's reckoning, the allegations were the product of a "smear campaign," possibly orchestrated by hostile government agencies and abetted by the punitive legal climate for sexual abuse cases in Sweden, which he described as "the Saudi Arabia of feminism."

With his British lawyers vowing to fight the extradition case all the way to Britain's highest courts and, if necessary, to the European Court of Human Rights in Strasbourg, France, which has intervened in the past to strike down British deportation rulings, the legal battle seemed likely to run well into 2011, and perhaps beyond. Along the way, Assange's lawyers planned to argue that sending their client to Sweden would open the way for the United States to subject him to "illegal rendition" to the prison at Guantánamo Bay, Cuba, or even to the death penalty. When The Guardian and The New York Times published portions of the 68-page Swedish police report on his case, the man responsible for the largest leak of official documents in history complained to the BBC that the Swedish prosecutors had been "deliberately, and illegally, selectively taking bits of material and giving them to newspapers." He called it "an abuse of power" and denied any conflict with WikiLeaks's practices. "We are an organization that does not promote leaking," he said. "We're an organization that promotes justice."

Beyond the legal drama lay the serious questions at the heart of the political intrigue that has unfolded around Assange and his brainchild, WikiLeaks, since it released troves of classified American documents onto the Internet: Was he, as he claimed, the harbinger of a new world order in which nations and generals and corporations and the rich and powerful will no longer be able to hide their peccadilloes and wrongdoing—their crimes, even—behind walls of law-enforced confidentiality and secrecy? Or was he an egomaniacal, crypto-anarchic destroyer of diplomatic traditions that have served for centuries, of the secrecy basic to Western security and military operations and of the privacy essential to democratic life and civil society?

All those are questions that have cast angry divisions among the millions who have followed the WikiLeaks story—especially, but by no means only, in America. It is an epic clash that has drawn impassioned support for Assange from many on the liberal left and libertarian right, from human rights activists and those grown tired of America's wars and the superpower shadow the United States has cast across the globe, as well as from legions of anarchists and dissidents and back-room computer hackers. On the opposing side, there has been a tide of indignation and recrimination, most prominently from top officials of the Obama administration, who have identified in WikiLeaks a new and menacing threat to American national security, and impaneled a task force to review possible criminal prosecution of Assange.

For his part, Assange had little difficulty claiming a place in history. In a BBC interview at Ellingham Hall, he compared his importance to that of Martin Luther King Jr. when he recounted how a black guard at Wandsworth had handed him a card saying he had "only two heroes in the world—Martin Luther King and you"; without any apparent sense of unease at the grandiosity of the idea, Assange added, "That is representative of 50 percent of people." John Humphrys, one of Britain's best-known television and radio presenters, picked up the theme, asking if Assange saw himself as a martyr or as "some sort of messianic figure," unflattering characterizations made by some disaffected WikiLeaks associates. Assange responded with reflection on his "feeling of betrayal"—by the Swedish women who had accused him of sexual improprieties, as well as by his detractors within WikiLeaks, then added: "The world is a very ungrateful place. Why should I continue to suffer simply to do some good in the world?"

Over 6 feet tall with naturally ice-white hair, Assange has an ambivalent personality, charming some and alienating others; admirers who have met him compare him to a comic-book hero, while detractors say he could more readily be cast as a supervillain. Often dressed in elegant suits—but insisting that they are borrowed, consistent with the austere personal habits of his past—he has a style that is both serene and laconic. Weighing his thoughts for a few beats, he then speaks in long, carefully structured sentences in the style of a practiced polemicist. His friends describe him as funny, loyal and kind. But those who have displeased him have found that his calm, deep voice is also quick to rise to righteous anger.

He seems to revel in his rootlessness, changing his cellphones and e-mail addresses like other men change their shirts. He continued to sleep on the floors and couches of friends long after he became a celebrity figure. A New York Times reporter who spent days with him in London in the summer of 2010, Eric Schmitt, said he appeared to be carrying all his worldly belongings on his back. "He sloughed off a huge backpack from his shoulder from which disgorged a couple of laps, cords, cellphones and other gear," Schmitt told colleagues later. "His nomadic life seemed to tumble out of this unassuming rucksack."

Julian Paul Assange was born on July 3, 1971, in Townsville, a small tropical city on Australia's northeastern coast. Little is publicly known of his biological father, but after Julian's first birthday his mother married a theater director, Brett Assange, the man who gave Julian his last name, and the two founded a traveling puppet theater. His childhood, Assange told The New Yorker magazine, was spent on the move, a propensity he has suggested could be genetic. When she was 17, around the time Assange was born, his mother, Christine, burned her schoolbooks and left home on a motorcycle. The two of them, he has said, had decamped 37 times by the time he was 14.

If any one place can be described as his childhood home, it is perhaps Magnetic Island, a tiny, mountainous mass off the coast of Townsville in a protected marine national park. The island's legend is that its magnetism skewed the compass readings of early seafarers; by the 1970s, it was home to a community of proud nonconformists who donned hats made of coconut-palm leaves to ward off the fierce sun. The editor of the island's newspaper Magnetic Times, George Hirst, has described it as "a place you came to when you didn't fit in anywhere else."

Christine and her son, according to the newspaper The Australian, lived there three times before his 11th birthday. His mother wrote of their experiences on the island in the guestbook at a visitor center when she returned in 2009, according to The Australian. "I lived in a bikini, 'going native' with my baby and other mums on the island," she wrote, recalling how she lived in an "old abandoned pineapple farm." She recalled slashing her "way to the front door with [a] machete," and shooting Taipan snakes— 12-foot predators that have the most deadly venom on land—"in the water tank and on son's bed." Food had to be suspended from the ceilings "to protect from possums."

Assange was mostly home-schooled, he has said, and his mother has explained that she felt formal education would lead her children to an unhealthy respect for authority. His stepfather, Brett, told reporters that in any interactions with other children Assange "always stood up for the underdog," and was "always very angry about people ganging up on other people." In 1979, when Julian was 8, his mother, who had separated from Brett and remarried, had another child, Julian's half brother. Her new partner was reportedly a musician with links to a new-age cult called The Family that experimented with LSD and sometimes persuaded mothers to give their children up to its leader, Anne Hamilton-Byrne.

As the new couple traveled, according to The Australian, Julian briefly attended a small school in an east-coast village called Goolmangar. Classmates there told the newspaper that they remembered a shy boy whose parents' alternative lifestyle was well known. One of them, Peter Graham, recalled his compassion. "He was the sort of kid who moved a spider and let it free when the others wanted to kill it," Graham said. "He was always a nurturing sort of fellow." When he was not in school, Assange told The New Yorker, he took correspondence classes and studied informally with university professors. But he was also an avid reader, drawn to science, devouring one library book and then pulling similar texts from the shelves, following the trail of footnotes.

In 1982, Mrs. Assange's new relationship, too, deteriorated. Fearing for her safety when her husband turned abusive, she has told reporters, she went on the run for five years while Julian was between 11 and 16. "'Now we need to disappear,'" Assange remembered his mother saying. The young boy suspected that her estranged husband had moles in the government, and cult connections, and could track them. By the time he was a teenager, Assange, the perpetual wanderer, had grown to embrace his outsider status. He and a friend, he wrote later, "were bright sensitive kids who didn't fit into the dominant subculture and fiercely castigated those who did as irredeemable boneheads."

In the late 1980s he found computers when the family lived across the street from a store selling a Commodore 64, a rudimentary machine. Assange was fascinated, and eventually his mother bought it for him. A fast learner, he graduated quickly, he has said, to hacking into networks, including those of the U.S. Department of Defense, on a primitive precursor to the Internet. And he found love. When he was 18, his son, Daniel, was born to a girlfriend, who quickly became his wife. But the couple split in 1991 and fought a custody battle that his mother says put him in the hospital for a few days—exhausted and depressed, he was so stressed that the pigmentation leached from his hair. The couple eventually reached a custody agreement eight years later. Yet the inconstancy of Assange's life, and long periods of absence from Daniel, left the two with an arms-length relationship by the time the boy reached adulthood.

Prompted by Assange's increasingly bold hacking with a group called the International Subversives, the police raided his home at around the same time he split with his wife. When the case came to court five years later, he pleaded guilty to 24 charges of computer crimes. In sentencing him, the Australian judge, Leslie Ross, was lenient, noting that Assange had done no harm to the networks he had entered. In court the judge spoke of the "unstable personal background that you have had to endure," and referenced "the rather nomadic existence that your mother and yourself were forced to follow and also the personal disruption that occurred within your household." He avoided a 10-year jail sentence and was fined $2,100. Still, Assange railed at "a great misjustice" he felt had been done.

He was burned out, The New Yorker reported, and spent the next years motorcycling across Vietnam, trying to start a computer security consulting firm and supporting his son as best he could. He attended the University of Melbourne, where he studied physics. It was a lifestyle that those who knew him best saw as engendered by an upbringing that encouraged him to think of himself as an innate rebel against an unjust establishment. In 2006, the year Assange founded WikiLeaks, his son, now a computer programmer in Melbourne, wrote online that his father "just has a tendency to follow the path of highest resistance simply for the sake of defiance."

Assange's own reasons for starting an organization that would lead him into conflict with the most powerful government in the world are partly documented on a sprawling blog he maintained at that time. A picture he posted shows a smiling and rumpled figure, standing in bright sunlight as the wind takes his long, white hair. Writing eclectically, in a scientifically rendered prolix style, he expounded on the social difficulties faced by brilliant children, presenting graphs and statistics to back up his points about maladjustment. He wrote of carbon offsetting and of Kurt Vonnegut, and he quoted the science fiction writer Douglas Adams.

But as the blog developed, his attentions turned to injustice and action, conspiracies and leaks, peppered with mathematical phrases and an underlying sense of his own mission. On New Year's Eve 2006 he posted what is now seen by many as WikiLeaks's founding manifesto. "The more secretive or unjust an organization is, the more leaks induce fear and paranoia in its leadership and planning coterie," he wrote. "This must result in minimization of efficient internal communications mechanisms (an increase in cognitive 'secrecy tax') and consequent system-wide cognitive decline resulting in decreased ability to hold onto power as the environment demands adaption.

"Hence in a world where leaking is easy, secretive or unjust systems are nonlinearly hit relative to open, just systems," he continued. "Since unjust systems, by their nature induce opponents, and in many places barely have the upper hand, mass leaking leaves them exquisitely vulnerable to those who seek to replace them with more open forms of governance. Only revealed injustice can be answered; for man to do anything intelligent he has to know what's actually going on."

A few days later he simplified his views in a statement that seemed to come from the withdrawn little boy who gently saved spiders while on the run from a fearsome stepfather, the hacker who believed that entering closed systems was his right and the young father who fought bitterly for custody of his child. "Every time we witness an injustice and do not act," he said, "we train our character to be passive in its presence and thereby eventually lose all ability to defend ourselves and those we love." He stopped maintaining the blog shortly afterward and turned his full attention to his new project, WikiLeaks.

By early 2006, Assange had barricaded himself inside his Melbourne house, near the university, drawing diagrams of WikiLeaks's structure on the walls and doors in fits of creativity. It was the realization of his years of theorizing, planning and rehearsing for what amounted to the hacking world's equivalent of breaking into Fort Knox.

His vision for WikiLeaks was of an elaborate network of computer servers, globally distributed, that could be used as dead drops for leaks, and for encrypting, storing and releasing material on the Internet, supported by an opaque financial infrastructure dependent on anonymous donors. Like Jules Verne's Nautilus for a new age, this high-tech vessel was to be run under the iron hand of its inventor, Assange, and crewed by activist volunteers possessed with what he would later describe as "quasi-religious zeal." By 2010, he told Times reporters in the lengthy interview in London, there were 800 volunteers, led by 40 core members, with only a handful drawing salaries, Assange's own a reported $86,000 in 2010.

That figure was reportedly two-thirds of all the money paid by
WikiLeaks in salaries in 2010—a point dear to many in the organization's
inner circle, who have an almost monastic vision of their commitment. Like
other closed communities embarked on visionary endeavors, WikiLeaks,
from the outset, was founded on the principle that it would survive and
prosper on the enthusiasms of a worldwide network of activists, hackers
and left-wing campaigners, their reward to be taken from the new, more
just world that would be forged by their efforts.

While acknowledging Assange's high-intensity intelligence, reck-
oned by many who have met him to be in the genius range, denizens of
the cyberworld have argued about the credit he can claim for the technological breakthrough represented by WikiLeaks, if not about the impact of
the purloined documents he would come to post. Many have argued that
his place in the pantheon should allow him to be recognized not for the
kind of intellectual leap that had Archimedes leaping from his bath, but
for his grasping, sooner than others, the possibilities for a new generation
of superhacking that came with the computer age and the storage of vast
amounts of secret, or at least confidential, information. From this perspective, Assange has been less the nonpareil innovator than the Henry Ford
among hackers, a man who exploited, brilliantly, the technologies, and the
ideas, pioneered by others.

Some have identified the man who paved the way: an American engineer named Timothy C. May, whose "Crypto-Anarchist Manifesto," written
in 1992, explored the possibilities of the nascent Internet, data storage and
encryption, and the anonymity of the accomplished cybersubversive to
engage in all manner of high-tech mischief, including the outing of national
secrets. May called his imaginary vehicle for this, a sort of prototype for
WikiLeaks, BlackNet, though nobody at the time did much of anything to
realize the idea's potential.

The classified documents that would be WikiLeaks's lifeblood came,
at first, from siphoning material as it passed across the Internet. But soon, a
steady stream of whistle-blowers and hackers were proffering secrets, and a
series of widely lauded coups followed. WikiLeaks made news as it posted
documents on the Guantánamo Bay detention operation, the contents of
Sarah Palin's personal Yahoo e-mail account, reports of extrajudicial killings in Kenya and East Timor and the membership rolls of the neo-Nazi
British National Party. Praised for providing a window through which a

cleansing sun could shine, Assange named the umbrella organization that shielded WikiLeaks the Sunshine Press.

But within WikiLeaks, and perhaps even within Assange himself, a tension was emerging. He had spoken, and written, of pioneering a new era of "scientific journalism"—presenting raw documents drawn from the darkest recesses of power and allowing a global audience to judge the facts for itself. In this vision, WikiLeaks's mission was to be impartial. Birgitta Jonsdottir, a crucial WikiLeaks volunteer in its early days, told The New York Times that many of its members understood it to be a sort of black box into which whistle-blowers of every stripe and nationality, and whatever their cause, could drop their material without fear of reprisal.

But from the start, this concept was cast in an uneasy alliance with what Assange referred to in WikiLeaks's earliest days as a fight against global "injustice," the judgment of which, it seemed clear, would be rendered primarily by himself. At times, the new world he was intent on creating seemed borrowed from other millennial visions, from Plato to Thomas More and Karl Marx, where evil would be banished and repressive authority dismantled by a new, "scientific" process that would transcend the imperfect human endeavors of the past and replace flawed governing conducted in smoke-filled rooms with a brighter, purer form of democracy. In this new Utopia, he told the Frontline Club in London, the nation state and its laws would recede before a new, global community liberated by the dismantling of all barriers to knowledge. "The right of all people to know what is happening transcends all others," he said.

In 2010, WikiLeaks turned to exploiting its biggest leak of all—a vast cache of Pentagon and State Department documents downloaded by an equally idealist—and solitary—Army private in Iraq named Bradley Manning, then 22, onto what he said was a Lady Gaga CD. As he prepared to release the files, Assange increasingly focused on the perfidy of the U.S. government. At the Frontline Club and elsewhere, he spoke of the United States' having abandoned the principles of the founding fathers, to the point that it had become "the greatest threat to democracy," with a government and society dominated by the military, its people cowed into conformity by what he called "the security state," its principal newspapers serving as "stenographers of power," and its people denied the "knowledge" they needed to countervail. Pressed to explain why so much of his energy was directed at America, instead of China, Russia or other repressive states, he told the Times reporters in the October interview that covert American power, as represented by its intelligence agencies, "is equivalent to the rest of the world combined."

In the spring of 2010, WikiLeaks took its first high-profile swipe at the American military. It published a classified 2007 combat video showing American Apache helicopters in Baghdad killing at least 12 people, including two employees of the Reuters news agency. Assange unveiled the video, which he had entitled "Collateral Murder," at the National Press Club in Washington. It was one of the last times he would step foot in the United States. He told reporters he had published "the full source material"—an unedited 40-minute video—in an effort to help "keep journalism honest." But five times as many people, more than 10 million by early 2011, had viewed an 18-minute version, edited to emphasize the crimes Assange judged to have taken place. Some claimed that the edited video misrepresented events to score a political point. Assange himself argued that posting the unedited footage allowed him leeway in presenting his version, but that he hoped the material would "result not simply in the prosecution of those pilots or their immediate commanders, but some higher-level reform."

By June 2010, Assange was preparing even more explosive materials, related to the wars in Afghanistan and Iraq, and secret State Department cables. This time, he planned to reach a still wider audience by creating an uneasy alliance with what he called his "media partners," initially the British newspaper The Guardian, The New York Times and the German news magazine Der Spiegel. Eric Schmitt of The New York Times recalled that he was particularly disdainful of the American military. Later, he would tell Der Spiegel, referring to a release of classified U.S. material, that he loved "crushing bastards." And when reporters pressed him to review the classified Afghan material and remove the names of Afghans working for U.S. forces, or acting as informants, he was defensive, insisting initially, against the evidence, that all the redaction had already been done. The next day he recanted, and promised to do the redacting before it was released.

Several weeks later, he held a copy of The Guardian aloft at a news conference to announce the leak of 77,000 classified U.S. documents on the war in Afghanistan. At the time, he sounded almost indifferent to Bradley Manning's prospects, predicting that the soldier would get a sentence of no more than 20 years, and would serve no more than 10. When the issue was

pressed later on, he shifted to saying that WikiLeaks had made a "significant contribution" to Manning's defense fund, a statement he would repeat
in interviews through the winter. (Jeff Paterson, the project director for
the defense fund, said in December that no donation had arrived, despite
promises made in July. As a controversy began to brew, WikiLeaks finally
made a $15,000 transfer in early January.)

As ever, Assange's political aim was paramount. "This material,"
he told Der Spiegel in July, "shines light on the everyday brutality and
squalor of war. The archive will change public opinion and it will change
the opinion of people in positions of political and diplomatic influence."
Later, it emerged that the release contained hundreds of Afghan names
after all, and that Assange alone had made the decision not to remove
them. In the October interview he told the reporters from The Times
that he had judged that a greater good was served by airing the documents
promptly, saving the time it would have taken to remove all potentially
harmful details.

It was an issue that would continue to dog him in the following months,
with his critics, particularly in Washington, saying he was careless of threats
to human life. Adm. Mike Mullen, chairman of the Joint Chiefs of Staff,
told a Washington news conference, "Mr. Assange can say whatever he likes
about the greater good he thinks he and his source are doing, but the truth
is they might already have on their hands the blood of some young soldier
or that of an Afghan family." While a Taliban spokesman in Afghanistan
said that the insurgents had formed a nine-member commission to "find
about people who are spying," Assange challenged the Pentagon to name
anybody who had been harmed. No clear evidence of harm to any of those
named has yet emerged.

The spotlight turned on Assange after the Afghan documents were released
gave him a new level of international celebrity, his public appearances
attracting intense media overage and legions of fans. He unveiled a new,
more dapper self, and his self-assurance, never lacking but hitherto more
carefully veiled, seemed to grow in bounds; he talked of "tremendous success," and of seismic changes he felt WikiLeaks, and the documents, would
effect in the way the world was governed. Under attack from critics, he
referred repeatedly to his millennial mission, or what he called his "duty to
history." And he began to talk of himself as a likely casualty to his mission,

predicting that the United States would not rest until it had found a legal formula for putting him, and WikiLeaks, out of business.

For millions, Assange became a blank slate onto which they could project their hopes for a brighter and more open future, and for a world in which American power, at least in its more arbitrary forms, could be reined in. WikiLeaks volunteers, many of them drawn from Britain, Iceland, Sweden, the Netherlands, Germany and Switzerland, have said that their resolve to carry on has been steeled by the pressure the U.S. government has applied to the group and its leader in the wake of the publication of its secrets. Kristin Hrafnsson, a steely haired Icelandic journalist who has become WikiLeaks's effective second-in-command—a man as tough and acerbic as Assange, and frequently encountered at his side—has said that donations to the organization and offers to volunteer began "pouring in" as the confrontation with the United States sharpened.

Any effort to categorize the principal players faces an inherent problem in the organization's emphasis on secrecy, including a deliberate obscurity about who its most important figures are. What is known is that WikiLeaks's core members, the 40 or so who run the operation, are drawn from overt hacking communities like the Chaos Computer Club in Berlin, a large organization that has dedicated itself to using the tools of hacking and cryptography to undermine the powerful. At the club's conference in December last year, an undisguised glee surfaced whenever establishment figures were seen to have been brought low by superior programming skills—speakers were met with cheers and whoops by audiences of hundreds as they revealed loopholes in the banking and mobile telephone systems. The club has developed so-called cryptophones, theoretically immune to interception, which for a short time Assange would insist that his core leaders use.

In Iceland, many of WikiLeaks's activists have been campaigners for the Icelandic Modern Media Initiative, which propagates legal measures that would make Iceland a haven for unfettered journalism and freedom of information—a safe harbor, for those intent on obtaining and publishing secrets, of the kind that Switzerland provided over many decades for banking. At lower levels, WikiLeaks's volunteers are usually young, left-leaning idealists who see in Assange a rebel leader fashioned for the cyber age, someone who can fight oppression by breaking open the secret world of the powerful, without the clash of arms that insurgency demanded in an earlier age, including people like Angel Spasov, 30, an unemployed college graduate in London, who has attended some of Assange's public appearances. "Someone is finally fighting the governments," Spasov said as he balanced precariously on a crowd-control barrier in London, a red bandanna tied over his nose and mouth, to catch a glimpse of Assange as he left a hearing on the Swedish extradition bid in late 2010. "He's exposing their secrets," he said. "He's the man."

But for all the adulation, the tide of success for Assange did not take long to turn. Two weeks after the Afghan documents were released, he flew to Stockholm at the expense of the Swedish Association of Christian Social Democrats, a political group, to give a keynote speech on his work the following Saturday. When he arrived, he told The New York Times, he was celebrated by many as a hero. Rick Falkvinge, a friend of Assange's who spent time with him in Stockholm, described a new swagger in the Australian—"the charisma of a star." This, he said, had "an effect" on those he met.

Ten days later, the bubble burst when the two Swedish women went to the police with their allegations of sexual abuse. Assange has repeatedly denied any wrongdoing, saying that the sex he had with the women was entirely consensual and dismissing the allegations as an attempt to discredit him, and by extension his work. No evidence of such a vendetta has emerged, but many details of the allegations have been revealed in Swedish police documents obtained by The Times and other media organizations, in court testimony and in interviews with Assange, his associates in Sweden and a lawyer for the two women.

When Assange arrived in Stockholm his liaison with the political group was a blonde, left-wing, feminist activist in her early 30s who has not been officially named, but who has been referred to in legal proceedings as Ms. A. The two had built a rapport by telephone and e-mail and had agreed that Assange would stay at her comfortable Stockholm apartment, with soft lighting and modern art on its white walls, as she would be away until the day of the speech. Meanwhile, in Enkoping, a town 30 miles north of Stockholm, another woman, known as Ms. W, a sometime artist in her mid-20s, had been following Assange avidly in the media. While Googling him one evening, she said, she discovered that he was to speak in Stockholm and immediately contacted Ms. A, who was listed as his liaison, to volunteer her help. She heard nothing.

Two days after Assange arrived in Stockholm, Ms. A returned a day earlier than planned and agreed, over dinner and tea with her guest, that he would stay on with her. According to The Guardian, which obtained an unredacted version of the police document, she told the police that that night, Assange began stroking her leg before pulling off her clothes and snapping her necklace. The Guardian quoted her as having told the police that she realized that he was trying to have unprotected sex with her when he pinned her arms and legs to stop her from reaching for a condom. Eventually one was used but, she told her police interviewer, he appeared to have "done something" with it, resulting in its tearing. She said he ejaculated without withdrawing. In his own interview with the police, Assange refused to discuss details of the encounter, though he insisted that he had done no wrong.

The next morning Ms. W, who had not received a response to her offer to help with Assange's speech, decided to take the day off work and attend the lecture anyway. After the speech, she joined a group dinner for the guest of honor and sat next to Assange, who fed her bread and cheese, she said, and put his arm around her. Two days later, they took a train together to her small apartment in Enkoping. He could not use a credit card to buy his ticket, he told Ms. W, "because it could be traced," leaving her to buy both their fares. She was upset, she said, when he ignored her on the journey and instead used his smartphone to read about himself online.

The unredacted police report obtained by The Guardian says that after arriving at her apartment the two had sex using a condom. In the report, she described waking up to find him having sex with her again, without a condom. Under Sweden's strict sex laws, the claim that he had sex with Ms. W without a condom, and while she slept, led prosecutors to list rape among the possible charges against him. Later that morning, Ms. W told the police, Assange ordered her to get some water and orange juice for him, and later demanded breakfast, which she left the apartment to buy. She told the police that "she didn't like being ordered around in her own home but got it anyway." Worried about leaving him alone in her apartment, she said, "Be good." His answer, she said, was "Don't worry, I'm always bad."

From Enkoping, Assange returned to Ms. A's apartment in Stockholm, despite what she describes as growing tension between them after their previous sexual encounter. Then, the following day, according to statements given later in court, Assange tried to initiate sex again by rubbing "his erect penis" against her. This, lawyers for the Swedish government have said, is the grounds for one of the allegations of "sexual molestation."

Later the same week, according to the police report, Ms. W got in touch with Ms. A to try to find Assange after he had failed to call her, and the women realized that both had had sex with Assange without a condom. A friend of Ms. A's said in an interview this summer that the two women resolved to insist that Assange have a test for sexually transmitted diseases. At around this time, Ms. A asked Assange to leave her apartment, according to a friend. Later that day, when he had not taken the test, the two women went to Stockholm's Klara police station, where they "wanted to get some advice" and were "unsure of how they should proceed." Prosecutors promptly issued an arrest warrant for Assange, prompting him to complain to reporters that his accusers were unknown to him. "Their identities have been made anonymous so even I have no idea who they are," he told the Swedish newspaper Aftonbladet.

When Assange spoke to investigators in Stockholm, he declined to answer almost all of their questions about sexual details. "I had no reason to suspect that I would be accused of something like this," he said. The complaints made against him to the police, and repeated in the Swedish press, he added, included "a number of false statements" and "a bunch of incredible lies."

Assange's suspicions of political interference in the case were aroused, he said later, by a series of reversals in the prosecution process. A day after the initial arrest warrant, another prosecutor decided to downgrade the investigation to one of "molestation," a minor offense, and to revoke a warrant for Assange's arrest. The decision was again changed in late August when a senior state prosecutor, Marianne Ny, who specializes in sexual crimes, overruled subordinates in Stockholm and restored the original allegations, saying rape was the appropriate charge for the evidence on file.

To press home Assange's claims of political interference, Mark Stephens, Assange's lead lawyer in London, has repeatedly said that "a senior political figure" worked to have the case reopened, without identifying him. The reference appears to have been to Claes Borgstrom, the lawyer for the two Swedish women, who is Sweden's former equal opportunities ombudsman, and the spokesman on gender equality issues for the Social Democratic Party, the main opposition group in the Swedish Parliament. In an interview in Stockholm, Borgstrom, 66, said it was common under Sweden's rape laws for men who force sex on women without a condom to face prosecution. "It's a violation of sexual integrity, and it can be seen as rape," he said.

Borgstrom said that by presenting the allegations against him as part of a political conspiracy, Assange had made "victims" of the two women, who now faced vilification on the Internet and regular death threats. "There are three persons who know for a fact that this has nothing to do with Wiki-Leaks, the C.I.A. or the Obama administration, and they are Julian Assange and my two clients," he said.

Assange was asked to appear for questioning again, according to prosecution documents obtained by The Guardian, but he left Sweden instead and headed for London after, he has said, seeking permission from the prosecutor. Shortly afterward, his application for a Swedish residence permit was rejected, and he refused to return to Stockholm. Iceland, another country with generous press freedoms and a strong WikiLeaks base, had also lost its appeal, with Assange concluding that its government, like Britain's, is too easily influenced by Washington. In his native Australia, the authorities had signaled their intent, too. Assange told The Times that a senior Australian official had told him, "You play outside the rules, and you will be dealt with outside the rules." Under British law his Australian passport entitled him to remain for only six months. His options, it seemed, were rapidly dwindling.

In mid-October Assange agreed to a sit-down interview with The Times, his first with the paper. When he arrived at a noisy Ethiopian restaurant in London's rundown Paddington district for what would be a four-hour lunch, he moved like a hunted man, back in his nomadic mode. Although he sported an expensive brown leather Belstaff jacket—borrowed, as he insisted—he had a woolen beanie pulled down low over his brow. He trailed a youthful, largely silent, entourage that included a filmmaker assigned to document any unpleasant surprises, and insisted on pitching his voice barely above a whisper, saying it was a ploy to foil the Western intelligence agencies he presumed were listening. He spoke of cyberattacks on WikiLeaks's servers, saying alarms on its computers had been triggered, and he spoke of his fears of being prosecuted by the United States.

Over lamb skewers and hot flatbreads he said that WikiLeaks, then preparing to release nearly 400,000 documents on the Iraq war, was entering its most hazardous time yet. "By being determined to be on this path, and not to compromise, I've wound up in an extraordinary situation," he said. "When it comes to the point where you occasionally look forward to being in prison on the basis that you might be able to spend a day reading a book, the realization dawns that perhaps the situation has become a little more stressful than you would like."

Despite the risks, he said, he was convinced that his work would "produce justice and save lives." He spoke of his determination to "right wrongs" and said that his leaks would "provide a guide for all our decisions, civilization's decisions." He had expected WikiLeaks to change the world by 2008, he said, and was surprised that it had taken much longer—four years from WikiLeaks's founding—to make such a widespread impact. At times, he sounded resigned to an unhappy ending to his venture, suggesting that others might have to carry his legacy forward. "I have no illusions about it being a path that's not easy," he said. But "retiring on some sunlit upland for some 15 years of pleasant decline is not in my nature." He added, with a hint of a valedictory, "If we are victorious, then many others will follow my lead."

His problems in Sweden, and the threats of prosecution by the United States, were not the only challenges. As the sex scandal broke, he began to face growing restiveness within WikiLeaks, too. Smari McCarthy, a WikiLeaks insider who eventually left the organization, said that "about a dozen" disillusioned volunteers had left in late summer, in the face of what many characterized as Assange's imperious and dictatorial leadership style. Some of these departures were hastened by a discontent over what seemed to be Assange's determination to conflate his private problems in Sweden with the wider worldwide struggle for which his WikiLeaks associates had signed on.

In August, Assange suspended Daniel Domscheit-Berg, a German who had been the WikiLeaks spokesman under the pseudonym Daniel Schmitt, accusing him of unspecified "bad behavior." And when Herbert Snorrason, a 25-year-old political activist in Iceland, questioned Assange's judgment over a number of issues in an online exchange in September, Assange was uncompromising. "I don't like your tone," he said, according to a transcript. "If it continues, you're out." He also complained that his associates had abandoned him during his troubles in Sweden. "No legal help, no $, no accommodation, passports, positive press spins, private investigators, hacking those with information," he wrote. He added, "Wake up and stop being a jerk."

A core WikiLeaks volunteer, who requested anonymity, pleaded with Assange to temper his imperiousness. Forty-two seconds later, according to the transcript of an online conversation obtained by The Times, he responded with one crisp, dismissive paragraph: "I am the heart and soul of this organization, its founder, philosopher, spokesperson, original coder, organizer, financier and all the rest. If you have a problem with me, piss off."

When asked about reports of dissent over the lunch, Assange, who had been affable, raised his voice. "Who has told you that?" he asked, repeatedly demanding a list of names as his rapt entourage fell silent beside him. Assange denied that any important volunteers had quit, apart from Domscheit-Berg. The rest, he said, were "not consequential people." He also responded testily to questions about WikiLeaks's opaque finances, the fate of Manning, the Army private accused of leaking the documents to the group, and what appeared to be WikiLeaks's lack of accountability to anybody but himself, calling the questions "cretinous," "facile" and reminiscent of "kindergarten." Asked about his anger, he embraced it. "I've been angry for a while," he said. "I like my anger. It's directed effectively."

In late November and early December, WikiLeaks' release of American embassy cables dominated news reports. But for Assange, the celebrations were quickly stifled. On Dec. 6, Ny, the Swedish prosecutor who had wanted to question Assange on the allegations of sexual misconduct in Stockholm, issued European and Interpol arrest warrants, seeking his extradition to Sweden. Assange's lawyer, Stephens, effectively declared legal war, comparing Ny in public statements to Lavrenti Beria, chief of Stalin's secret police, and arguing that his client should be allowed to give answers by telephone or at the Swedish Embassy in London instead of returning to Sweden.

Many of Assange's supporters, including some prominent public figures, like the filmmaker Michael Moore, hinted that the Swedish charges were a thinly veiled conspiracy to silence him. The socialite Bianca Jagger, who frequently appeared to support Assange in London, told reporters that she was "very concerned that this case is becoming politicized," adding that justice and freedom of expression were at stake. Ms. A and Ms. W, the women who had accused him of sexual crimes, quickly became reviled figures for many WikiLeaks supporters, their names and addresses posted online, their lives pored over by those determined to discredit them.

It was to little effect. On a dark, cold Tuesday morning, Assange, his lawyers and close supporters, gathered at a nondescript cafe for a final meal before he turned himself in to the British police at a north London police station. There, he made a show of his defiance, telling officers he would not submit to the standard procedures. He would not give a British residential address, fingerprints or a DNA sample, and he would not submit to a picture. After he repeated his refusal to give an address at his initial bail hearing in court, he was sent to Wandsworth Prison as a flight risk, sweeping out of a London courthouse in an armored police van as his fans shouted, "We love you, Julian!"

The day the thick door of his solitary confinement cell slammed shut, legions of online supporters rose up in what many of the world's newspapers quickly dubbed a cyberwar. There was a tenfold increase in downloads of software used by the online activist group Anonymous to attack the Web sites of companies like MasterCard, Visa and PayPal, who had refused to process donations to WikiLeaks, saying that the organization had flouted their commercial rules. Later, the Web sites of the Swedish prosecutor's office and of Claes Borgtstrom, the lawyer for the two Swedish women, were brought down, too, collapsing under mass "attacks" when thousands of activists bombarded the sites simultaneously.

The cyberattacks, which WikiLeaks has said it was not involved with, were a blow for freedom of speech, according to one Anonymous activist in the United States, Gregg Housh, who saw no gap between the sexual allegations and Assange's work. "To all of us," said Housh, who disavows any illegal activity on the Internet himself, "there is no distinction. He is a political prisoner, and the two things are completely entwined."

When Assange was granted bail, he emerged from his cell into an explosion of photographers' flashbulbs and spotlights under the grand arch of the Royal Courts of Justice. Pictures of his face, stylized to resemble the iconic image of Che Guevara, bobbed above the crowd on placards. "Exposing War Crimes Is No Crime," said one. As the cheers subsided, he stood defiant, backed by his entourage and flickering lights within the courthouse, and raised his release papers. "Well, it's great to feel the fresh air of London again," he said before thanking his supporters and railing against his "time in solitary confinement in the bottom of a Victorian prison."

Later, as he walked through a bitterly cold London evening, fluffy snowflakes landing silently on the shoulders of the suit he had worn in court, a reporter asked Assange how he felt. "I have enough anger to last me 100 years," he said. "But I will channel that into my work."

Bradley Manning is accused of leaking
classified documents to WikiLeaks.

WHO IS BRADLEY MANNING?

By GINGER THOMPSON

He spent part of his childhood with his father in the arid plains of Central Oklahoma where classmates made fun of him for being a geek. He spent another part with his mother in a small, hardscrabble corner of southwest Wales, where classmates made fun of him for being gay. Then he joined the Army, where his social life was defined by the need to conceal his sexuality under the "don't ask, don't tell" policy, and he wasted brainpower fetching coffee for officers.

But it was two years ago, when Private First Class Bradley Manning visited Cambridge, Mass., to see a man with whom he had fallen in love, that he finally seemed to have found a place where he fit in, joining a circle that included politically motivated computer hackers and his boyfriend, a self-described drag queen. So when Manning's military career seemed headed nowhere good, the private turned increasingly to those friends for moral support. Today, some of those friends wonder whether his desperation for acceptance and recognition, together with a deepening disenchantment with the war in Iraq, may have played a role in leading him to disclose the largest trove of government secrets since the Pentagon Papers—a disclosure that would land him in solitary confinement in a military prison.

"I would always try to make clear to Brad that he had a promising future ahead of him," said Daniel J. Clark, who is starting his own computer business and became a friend to Manning. "But when you're young, and you're in his situation, it's hard to tell yourself things are going to get better, especially in Brad's case, because in his past, things didn't always get better."

Much remains unknown about Manning's journey to prison from the small Oklahoma town where he was born. However, interviews with those who know him, along with e-mail exchanges between Manning and the computer hacker who eventually turned him in, offer some insights into how he grew up, why he joined the Army and why his last several months before the document leaks seemed so troubled.

"I've been isolated so long," Manning wrote in May 2010 to Adrian Lamo, a computer hacker who later turned the chat logs over to the authorities and the media. "But events kept forcing me to figure out ways to survive."

Survival was something Manning began learning as a child in Crescent, Okla. His father, Brian Manning, was also a soldier and spent a lot of time away from home, former neighbors recalled. And his mother, Susan Manning, drank to help cope with the culture shock of having moved to the United States from her native Britain. Jacqueline Radford, a former neighbor, recalled that when students at Manning's elementary school went on field trips, she would send additional food or money to make sure Manning had something to eat. "I've always tried to be supportive of him because of his home life," Radford recalled about Manning. "I know it was bad, to where he was left to his own, and had to fend for himself."

At school, little Bradley Manning was clearly different from most of his peers. He preferred hacking computer games rather than playing them. And he seemed opinionated beyond his years about politics and religion, and even about keeping religion out of politics. In a hometown that he once mockingly described in an e-mail as having "more pews than people," Manning refused to recite the parts of the Pledge of Allegiance that referred to God, or to turn in any homework that had to do with the Scriptures. And if a teacher challenged his views, he was quick to push back. "He would get upset, slam books on the desk if people wouldn't listen to him or understand his point of view," said Chera Moore, who attended elementary and junior high school with Manning. "He would get really mad, and the teacher would say, 'O.K., Bradley, get out.'"

It was something he would hear a lot throughout his life.

After Manning's parents split up, Manning, then a teenager, moved with his mother to Haverfordwest, her hometown in Wales, and began a new chapter of isolation. Haverfordwest is several times bigger than Crescent. It is centuries older, with traditions that run much deeper. And as a bustling market town, life there moved at a significantly faster pace.

Former students at his school, Tasker Milward, recalled that Manning got teased about his accent. He got teased because he loved Dr Pepper. He got teased because he spent most of his time huddled in front of a computer. And then, students began to suspect that he was gay.

Manning's reactions were all over the place, his classmates said. At times, he idly boasted about stealing other students' girlfriends. Other times, he openly flirted with boys. Often, with only the slightest provocation, he would fly into fits of rage. "It was probably the worst experience anybody could go through," said Rowan John, a former classmate who was openly gay in high school. "Being different like me, or Bradley, in the middle of nowhere is like going back in time to the Dark Ages."

Life ahead did not get immediately brighter for Manning. People who know him said his mother sent him back to live with his father and older sister in Oklahoma because of his troubles at school. He was hired and quickly fired from a small software company, where his employer recalled him as a clean-cut, highly intelligent and well-spoken young man with an almost innate sense of programming, and the personality of a bull in a china shop. Then he was kicked out of the house, friends said, after his father learned he was gay. Clark, the Cambridge computer businessman, said Manning told him he had spent a short period of time living out of his car, working a series of minimum-wage retail jobs and secretly showering at a gym.

Later, Manning moved to Potomac, Md., to live with an aunt. In 2007, he enlisted in the Army, friends said, to try to give his life some direction and earn money for college. He was granted a security clearance as an intelligence analyst, trained at Fort Huachuca, Ariz., and then assigned to the Second Brigade, 10th Mountain Division at Fort Drum, N.Y.

Before being deployed to Iraq, Manning met a young, eccentric classical musician named Tyler Watkins. The student and the soldier had little in common, a friend said, but Manning fell deeply in love. Watkins, who did not respond to interview requests, was a student at Brandeis University, near Cambridge. On trips to visit him in Massachusetts, Manning got to know many people in Watkins's broad network of friends, including some who were part of the tight-knit hacker community.

Friends said Manning found the atmosphere in Cambridge to be everything the Army was not: openly accepting of his geeky side, his liberal political opinions, his relationship with Watkins and his ambition to do something that would get attention. Although hacking has come to mean a lot of different things, at its core, say those who do it, is the philosophy that information should be free and accessible to all. And Manning had access to some of the most secret information on the planet.

In computer chats with Lamo, the hacker, Manning wrote that he wanted people to see the truth "because without information, you cannot make informed decisions as a public."

Those chat logs, published by Wired magazine, provide the clearest insight into Manning's thinking and motivations. They chronicle his growing disillusionment with the Iraq war, his disdain for the military, how easy it was for him to gain access to hundreds of thousands of classified documents and his sense that exposing the government's secrets would do more good than harm. In one passage from the chat logs, Manning described being ordered to investigate 15 Iraqi detainees who had been charged with hostile acts against the government.

Manning wrote that his investigation found that the men had written a "benign political critique" of Prime Minister Nuri Kamal al-Maliki of Iraq and posed no serious security threat to the government. But, he wrote, his commanding officer refused to accept that finding. "He didn't want to hear any of it," Manning wrote. "He told me to shut up and explain how we could assist the [federal police] in finding MORE detainees."

Later, Manning wrote that he had always questioned the way things worked and investigated to find the truth. "But that was a point where I was a PART of something," he wrote. "I was actively involved in something that I was completely against."

In another passage from the logs, Manning wrote further about his motivations for leaking the classified material. "What if I were someone more malicious," he wrote. "I could've sold to Russia or China, and made bank?" When Lamo asked why he didn't sell the material, Manning responded: "Another state would just take advantage of the information . . . try and get some edge. If it's out in the open it should be a public good."

Even as he worked as an intelligence analyst in a unit stationed east of Baghdad, his military career was anything but stellar. He had been reprimanded twice, including once for assaulting a soldier. He wrote that he felt "regularly ignored" by his superiors, "except when I had something essential, then it was back to 'Bring me coffee, then sweep the floor.'" And it seems the more isolated he felt in the military—he wore custom dog tags that said "Humanist," and friends said he kept a toy fairy wand on his desk in Iraq—the more he clung to his hacker friends.

According to Wired, Manning told Watkins last January that he had gotten his hands on a secret video showing an American military helicopter attack in 2007 that killed 12 people, including two employees of the Reuters news agency. In a computer chat with Lamo, Manning said he gave the video to WikiLeaks in February. Then after WikiLeaks released it in April, Manning hounded Watkins about whether there had been any public reaction.

"He would message me, 'Are people talking about it?'" Watkins told *Wired*. "That was one of his major concerns once he'd done this. Was it really going to make a difference?"

In his chats with Lamo, Manning described how he downloaded the video and lip-synched to Lady Gaga as he copied hundreds of thousands of diplomatic cables. "Hillary Clinton and several thousand diplomats around the world are going to have a heart attack," he boasted. "Everywhere there's a U.S. post, there's a diplomatic scandal that will be revealed." But even as he professed an inflated sense of purpose, he called himself "emotionally fractured," and "a wreck," and he said he was "self-medicating like crazy."

Today, Manning awaits trial in the Quantico Confinement Facility in Virginia. His lawyer, David E. Coombs, wrote a blog post in December about the conditions under which he was being detained. Coombs said Manning was confined 23 hours a day to his cell, 6-feet wide by 12-feet long, where he eats all his meals. Coombs said that Manning was prohibited from doing any exercises—including situps or push-ups—in the cell, had no conversations with guards or other inmates and was allowed to receive visitors for only three hours on weekends and holidays.

Coombs wrote that guards had never "tried to bully, harass or embarrass" Manning. But, he wrote, to make sure Manning did not try to hurt himself, the guards checked on him every five minutes, asking whether he was O.K., and requiring him to answer. "At night, if the guards cannot see PFC Manning clearly because he has a blanket over his head or is curled up towards the wall," Coombs wrote on his blog, "they will wake him to make sure he is okay."

Dozens of antiwar activists and friends of Manning's have staged protests in New York, Oklahoma City and Quantico to demand the soldier's release, arguing that his exposure of war crimes makes him a hero, not an outlaw. Those supporters have raised tens of thousands of dollars to help pay for his legal defense. Their cause has won the support of the filmmaker Michael Moore and of Daniel Ellsberg, who leaked the Pentagon Papers. However, the City Council in Berkeley, Calif., tabled a resolution to honor

Manning for releasing the video of a laughing United States Apache helicopter crew shooting a group of men in Baghdad.

As Manning faces the possibility of a lengthy prison term if convicted, some of his remarks now seem somewhat prophetic. "I wouldn't mind going to prison for the rest of my life, or being executed so much," he wrote, "if it wasn't for the possibility of having pictures of me plastered all over the world press."

PART THREE
STATE'S SECRETS

A cache of diplomatic cables provides a chronicle
of the United States' relations with the world.

President Bashar al-Assad of Syria, left,
and William Burns, a State Department official.

Somali pirates released the Faina for a $3.2 million ransom in 2009.
The ship's cargo included 32 Soviet-era tanks

LEAKED CABLES OFFER RAW LOOK AT U.S. DIPLOMACY

By SCOTT SHANE and ANDREW W. LEHREN

WASHINGTON—A cache of a quarter-million confidential American diplomatic cables, most of them from the past three years, provides an unprecedented look at back-room bargaining by embassies around the world, brutally candid views of foreign leaders and frank assessments of nuclear and terrorist threats.

Some of the cables, made available to The New York Times and several other news organizations, were written as recently as late February, revealing the Obama administration's exchanges over crises and conflicts. The material was originally obtained by WikiLeaks, an organization devoted to revealing secret documents. WikiLeaks posted 220 cables, some redacted to protect diplomatic sources, in the first installment of the archive on its Web site on Sunday.

The disclosure of the cables is sending shudders through the diplomatic establishment, and could strain relations with some countries, influencing international affairs in ways that are impossible to predict.

Secretary of State Hillary Rodham Clinton and American ambassadors around the world have been contacting foreign officials in recent days to alert them to the expected disclosures. A statement from the White House on Sunday said: "We condemn in the strongest terms the unauthorized disclosure of classified documents and sensitive national security information."

The White House said the release of what it called "stolen cables" to several publications was a "reckless and dangerous action" and warned that some cables, if released in full, could disrupt American operations abroad and put the work and even lives of confidential sources of American diplomats at risk. The statement noted that reports often include "candid and often incomplete information" whose disclosure could "deeply impact not only U.S. foreign policy interests, but those of our allies and friends around the world."

The cables, a huge sampling of the daily traffic between the State Department and some 270 embassies and consulates, amount to a secret chronicle of the United States' relations with the world in an age of war and terrorism. Among their revelations, to be detailed in The Times in coming days:

• A dangerous standoff with Pakistan over nuclear fuel: Since 2007, the United States has mounted a highly secret effort, so far unsuccessful, to remove from a Pakistani research reactor highly enriched uranium that American officials fear could be diverted for use in an illicit nuclear device. In May 2009, Ambassador Anne W. Patterson reported that Pakistan was refusing to schedule a visit by American technical experts because, as a Pakistani official said, "if the local media got word of the fuel removal, 'they certainly would portray it as the United States taking Pakistan's nuclear weapons,' he argued."

• Thinking about an eventual collapse of North Korea: American and South Korean officials have discussed the prospects for a unified Korea, should the North's economic troubles and political transition lead the state to implode. The South Koreans even considered commercial inducements to China, according to the American ambassador to Seoul. She told Washington in February that South Korean officials believe that the right business deals would "help salve" China's "concerns about living with a reunified Korea" that is in a "benign alliance" with the United States.

• Bargaining to empty the Guantánamo Bay prison: When American diplomats pressed other countries to resettle detainees, they became reluctant players in a State Department version of "Let's Make a Deal." Slovenia was told to take a prisoner if it wanted to meet with President Obama, while the island nation of Kiribati was offered incentives worth millions of dollars to take in Chinese Muslim detainees, cables from diplomats recounted. The Americans, meanwhile, suggested that accepting more prisoners would be "a low-cost way for Belgium to attain prominence in Europe."

• Suspicions of corruption in the Afghan government: When one of Afghanistan's two vice presidents visited the United Arab Emirates last year, local authorities working with the Drug Enforcement Administration discovered that he was carrying $52 million in cash. With wry understatement, a cable from the American Embassy in Kabul called the money "a significant amount" that the official, Ahmed Zia Massoud, "was ultimately allowed to keep without revealing the money's origin or destination." (Mr. Massoud denies taking any money out of Afghanistan.)

• A global computer hacking effort: China's Politburo directed the intrusion into Google's computer systems in that country, a Chinese contact told the American Embassy in Beijing in January, one cable reported. The Google hacking was part of a coordinated campaign of computer sabotage carried out by government operatives, private security experts and Internet outlaws recruited by the Chinese government. They have broken into American government computers and those of Western allies, the Dalai Lama and American businesses since 2002, cables said.

• Mixed records against terrorism: Saudi donors remain the chief financiers of Sunni militant groups like Al Qaeda, and the tiny Persian Gulf state of Qatar, a generous host to the American military for years, was the "worst in the region" in counterterrorism efforts, according to a State Department cable last December. Qatar's security service was "hesitant to act against known terrorists out of concern for appearing to be aligned with the U.S. and provoking reprisals," the cable said.

• An intriguing alliance: American diplomats in Rome reported in 2009 on what their Italian contacts described as an extraordinarily close relationship between Vladimir V. Putin, the Russian prime minister, and Silvio Berlusconi, the Italian prime minister and business magnate, including "lavish gifts," lucrative energy contracts and a "shadowy" Russian-speaking Italian go-between. They wrote that Mr. Berlusconi "appears increasingly to be the mouthpiece of Putin" in Europe. The diplomats also noted that while Mr. Putin enjoyed supremacy over all other public figures in Russia, he was undermined by an unmanageable bureaucracy that often ignored his edicts.

• Arms deliveries to militants: Cables describe the United States' failing struggle to prevent Syria from supplying arms to Hezbollah in Lebanon, which has amassed a huge stockpile since its 2006 war with Israel. One week after President Bashar al-Assad promised a top State Department official that he would not send "new" arms to Hezbollah, the United States complained that it had information that Syria was providing increasingly sophisticated weapons to the group.

• Clashes with Europe over human rights: American officials sharply warned Germany in 2007 not to enforce arrest warrants for Central Intelligence Agency officers involved in a bungled operation in which an innocent

German citizen with the same name as a suspected militant was mistakenly
kidnapped and held for months in Afghanistan. A senior American diplomat
told a German official "that our intention was not to threaten Germany, but
rather to urge that the German government weigh carefully at every step
of the way the implications for relations with the U.S."

The 251,287 cables, first acquired by WikiLeaks, were provided to The
Times by an intermediary on the condition of anonymity. Many are unclassified, and none are marked "top secret," the government's most secure communications status. But some 11,000 are classified "secret," 9,000 are labeled
"noforn," shorthand for material considered too delicate to be shared with
any foreign government, and 4,000 are designated both secret and noforn.

Many more cables name diplomats' confidential sources, from foreign
legislators and military officers to human rights activists and journalists,
often with a warning to Washington: "Please protect" or "Strictly protect."

The Times, after consultations with the State Department, has withheld from articles and removed from documents it is posting online the
names of some people who spoke privately to diplomats and might be at
risk if they were publicly identified. The Times is also withholding some
passages or entire cables whose disclosure could compromise American
intelligence efforts. While the White House said it anticipated WikiLeaks
would make public "several hundred thousand" cables Sunday night, the
organization posted only 220 released and redacted by The Times and
several European publications.

The cables show that nearly a decade after the attacks of Sept. 11,
2001, the dark shadow of terrorism still dominates the United States' relations with the world. They depict the Obama administration struggling to
sort out which Pakistanis are trustworthy partners against Al Qaeda, adding
Australians who have disappeared in the Middle East to terrorist watch
lists, and assessing whether a lurking rickshaw driver in Lahore, Pakistan,
was awaiting fares or conducting surveillance of the road to the American
Consulate.

They show officials managing relations with a China on the rise and a
Russia retreating from democracy. They document years of effort to prevent
Iran from building a nuclear weapon—and of worry about a possible Israeli
strike on Iran with the same goal.

Even when they recount events that are already known, the cables
offer remarkable details.

For instance, it has been previously reported that the Yemeni government has sought to cover up the American role in missile strikes against the local branch of Al Qaeda. But a cable's fly-on-the-wall account of a January meeting between the Yemeni president, Ali Abdullah Saleh, and Gen. David H. Petraeus, then the American commander in the Middle East, is breathtaking.

"We'll continue saying the bombs are ours, not yours," Mr. Saleh said, according to the cable sent by the American ambassador, prompting one of Yemen's deputy prime ministers to "joke that he had just 'lied' by telling Parliament" that Yemen had carried out the strikes.

Mr. Saleh, who at other times resisted American counterterrorism requests, was in a lighthearted mood. The authoritarian ruler of a conservative Muslim country, Mr. Saleh complains of smuggling from nearby Djibouti, but tells General Petraeus that his concerns are drugs and weapons, not whiskey, "provided it's good whiskey."

Likewise, press reports detailed the unhappiness of the Libyan leader, Col. Muammar el-Qaddafi, when he was not permitted to set up his tent in Manhattan or to visit ground zero during a United Nations session last year.

But the cables add a touch of scandal and alarm to the tale. They describe the volatile Libyan leader as rarely without the companionship of "his senior Ukrainian nurse," described as "a voluptuous blonde." They reveal that Colonel Qaddafi was so upset by his reception in New York that he balked at carrying out a promise to return dangerous enriched uranium to Russia. The American ambassador to Libya told Colonel Qaddafi's son "that the Libyan government had chosen a very dangerous venue to express its pique," a cable reported to Washington.

The cables also disclose frank comments behind closed doors. Dispatches from early this year, for instance, quote the aging monarch of Saudi Arabia, King Abdullah, as speaking scathingly about the leaders of Iraq and Pakistan.

Speaking to another Iraqi official about Nuri Kamal al-Maliki, the Iraqi prime minister, King Abdullah said, "You and Iraq are in my heart, but that man is not." The king called President Asif Ali Zardari of Pakistan the greatest obstacle to that country's progress. "When the head is rotten," he said, "it affects the whole body."

The American ambassador to Eritrea reported last year that "Eritrean officials are ignorant or lying" in denying that they were supporting the

Shabab, a militant Islamist group in Somalia. The cable then mused about which seemed more likely.

As he left Zimbabwe in 2007 after three years as ambassador, Christopher W. Dell wrote a sardonic account of Robert Mugabe, that country's aging and erratic leader. The cable called him "a brilliant tactician" but mocked "his deep ignorance on economic issues (coupled with the belief that his 18 doctorates give him the authority to suspend the laws of economics)."

The possibility that a large number of diplomatic cables might become public has been discussed in government and media circles since May. That was when, in an online chat, an Army intelligence analyst, Pfc. Bradley Manning, described having downloaded from a military computer system many classified documents, including "260,000 State Department cables from embassies and consulates all over the world." In an online discussion with Adrian Lamo, a computer hacker, Private Manning said he had delivered the cables and other documents to WikiLeaks.

Mr. Lamo reported Private Manning's disclosures to federal authorities, and Private Manning was arrested. He has been charged with illegally leaking classified information and faces a possible court-martial and, if convicted, a lengthy prison term.

In July and October, The Times, the British newspaper The Guardian and the German magazine Der Spiegel published articles based on documents about Afghanistan and Iraq. Those collections were placed online by WikiLeaks, with selective redactions of the Afghan documents and much heavier redactions of the Iraq reports.

Fodder for Historians

Traditionally, most diplomatic cables remain secret for decades, providing fodder for historians only when the participants are long retired or dead. The State Department's unclassified history series, titled "Foreign Relations of the United States," has reached only 1976.

While an overwhelming majority of the quarter-million cables provided to The Times are from the post-9/11 era, several hundred date from 1966 to the 1990s. Some show diplomats struggling to make sense of major events whose future course they could not guess.

In a 1979 cable to Washington, Bruce Laingen, an American diplomat in Tehran, mused with a knowing tone about the Iranian revolution that had just occurred: "Perhaps the single dominant aspect of the Persian psyche is an overriding egoism," Mr. Laingen wrote, offering tips on exploiting this psyche in negotiations with the new government. Less than three months later, Mr. Laingen and his colleagues would be taken hostage by radical Iranian students, hurling the Carter administration into crisis and, perhaps, demonstrating the hazards of diplomatic hubris.

In 1989, an American diplomat in Panama City mulled over the options open to Gen. Manuel Noriega, the Panamanian leader, who was facing narcotics charges in the United States and intense domestic and international political pressure to step down. The cable called General Noriega "a master of survival"; its author appeared to have no inkling that one week later, the United States would invade Panama to unseat General Noriega and arrest him.

In 1990, an American diplomat sent an excited dispatch from Cape Town: he had just learned from a lawyer for Nelson Mandela that Mr. Mandela's 27-year imprisonment was to end. The cable conveys the momentous changes about to begin for South Africa, even as it discusses preparations for an impending visit from the Rev. Jesse L. Jackson.

The voluminous traffic of more recent years—well over half of the quarter-million cables date from 2007 or later—show American officials struggling with events whose outcomes are far from sure. To read through them is to become a global voyeur, immersed in the jawboning, inducements and penalties the United States wields in trying to have its way with a recalcitrant world.

In an era of satellites and fiber-optic links, the cable retains the archaic name of an earlier technological era. It has long been the tool for the secretary of state to send orders to the field and for ambassadors and political officers to send their analyses to Washington.

The cables have their own lexicon: "codel," for a Congressional delegation; "visas viper," for a report on a person considered dangerous; "démarche," an official message to a foreign government, often a protest or warning.

But the drama in the cables often comes from diplomats' narratives of meetings with foreign figures, games of diplomatic poker in which each side is sizing up the other and neither is showing all its cards.

Among the most fascinating examples recount American officials' meetings in September 2009 and February 2010 with Ahmed Wali Karzai, the half brother of the Afghan president and a power broker in the Taliban's home turf of Kandahar.

They describe Mr. Karzai, "dressed in a crisp white shalwar kameez," the traditional dress of loose tunic and trousers, appearing "nervous, though eager to express his views on the international presence in Kandahar," and trying to win over the Americans with nostalgic tales about his years running a Chicago restaurant near Wrigley Field.

But in midnarrative there is a stark alert for anyone reading the cable in Washington: "Note: While we must deal with AWK as the head of the Provincial Council, he is widely understood to be corrupt and a narcotics trafficker." (Mr. Karzai has denied such charges.) And the cables note statements by Mr. Karzai that the Americans, informed by a steady flow of eavesdropping and agents' reports, believe to be false.

A cable written after the February meeting coolly took note of the deceit on both sides.

Mr. Karzai "demonstrated that he will dissemble when it suits his needs," the cable said. "He appears not to understand the level of our knowledge of his activities. We will need to monitor his activity closely, and deliver a recurring, transparent message to him" about the limits of American tolerance.

Not All Business

Even in places far from war zones and international crises, where the stakes for the United States are not as high, curious diplomats can turn out to be accomplished reporters, sending vivid dispatches to deepen the government's understanding of exotic places.

In a 2006 account, a wide-eyed American diplomat describes the lavish wedding of a well-connected couple in Dagestan, in Russia's Caucasus, where one guest is the strongman who runs the war-ravaged Russian republic of Chechnya, Ramzan Kadyrov.

The diplomat tells of drunken guests throwing $100 bills at child dancers, and nighttime water-scooter jaunts on the Caspian Sea.

"The dancers probably picked upwards of USD 5000 off the cobblestones," the diplomat wrote. The host later tells him that Ramzan Kadyrov "had brought the happy couple 'a five-kilo lump of gold' as his wedding present."

"After the dancing and a quick tour of the premises, Ramzan and his army drove off back to Chechnya," the diplomat reported to Washington. "We asked why Ramzan did not spend the night in Makhachkala, and were told, 'Ramzan never spends the night anywhere.'"

Scott Shane reported from Washington, and Andrew W. Lehren from New York.
Reporting was contributed by Jo Becker, C. J. Chivers and James Glanz from New York; Eric Lichtblau, Michael R. Gordon, David E. Sanger, Charlie Savage, Eric Schmitt and Ginger Thompson from Washington; and Jane Perlez from Islamabad, Pakistan.

—This article was originally published on November 28, 2010

AROUND THE WORLD, DISTRESS OVER IRAN

By DAVID E. SANGER, JAMES GLANZ and JO BECKER

In late May 2009, Israel's defense minister, Ehud Barak, used a visit from a Congressional delegation to send a pointed message to the new American president.

In a secret cable sent back to Washington, the American ambassador to Israel, James B. Cunningham, reported that Mr. Barak had argued that the world had 6 to 18 months "in which stopping Iran from acquiring nuclear weapons might still be viable." After that, Mr. Barak said, "any military solution would result in unacceptable collateral damage."

There was little surprising in Mr. Barak's implicit threat that Israel might attack Iran's nuclear facilities. As a pressure tactic, Israeli officials have been setting such deadlines, and extending them, for years. But six months later it was an Arab leader, the king of Bahrain, who provides the base for the American Fifth Fleet, telling the Americans that the Iranian nuclear program "must be stopped," according to another cable. "The danger of letting it go on is greater than the danger of stopping it," he said.

His plea was shared by many of America's Arab allies, including the powerful King Abdullah of Saudi Arabia, who according to another cable repeatedly implored Washington to "cut off the head of the snake" while there was still time.

These warnings are part of a trove of diplomatic cables reaching back to the genesis of the Iranian nuclear standoff in which leaders from around the world offer their unvarnished opinions about how to negotiate with, threaten and perhaps force Iran's leaders to renounce their atomic ambitions.

The cables also contain a fresh American intelligence assessment of Iran's missile program. They reveal for the first time that the United States believes that Iran has obtained advanced missiles from North Korea that could let it strike at Western European capitals and Moscow and help it develop more formidable long-range ballistic missiles.

In day-by-day detail, the cables, obtained by WikiLeaks and made available to a number of news organizations, tell the disparate diplomatic back stories of two administrations pressed from all sides to confront Tehran. They show how President George W. Bush, hamstrung by the complexities of Iraq and suspicions that he might attack Iran, struggled to put together even modest sanctions.

They also offer new insights into how President Obama, determined to merge his promise of "engagement" with his vow to raise the pressure on the Iranians, assembled a coalition that agreed to impose an array of sanctions considerably harsher than any before attempted.

When Mr. Obama took office, many allies feared that his offers of engagement would make him appear weak to the Iranians. But the cables show how Mr. Obama's aides quickly countered those worries by rolling out a plan to encircle Iran with economic sanctions and antimissile defenses. In essence, the administration expected its outreach to fail, but believed that it had to make a bona fide attempt in order to build support for tougher measures.

A Sense of Urgency

Feeding the administration's urgency was the intelligence about Iran's missile program. As it weighed the implications of those findings, the administration maneuvered to win Russian support for sanctions. It killed a Bush-era plan for a missile defense site in Poland—which Moscow's leaders feared was directed at them, not Tehran—and replaced it with one floating closer to Iran's coast. While the cables leave unclear whether there was an explicit quid pro quo, the move seems to have paid off.

There is also an American-inspired plan to get the Saudis to offer China a steady oil supply, to wean it from energy dependence on Iran. The Saudis agreed, and insisted on ironclad commitments from Beijing to join in sanctions against Tehran.

At the same time, the cables reveal how Iran's ascent has unified Israel and many longtime Arab adversaries—notably the Saudis—in a common cause. Publicly, these Arab states held their tongues, for fear of a domestic uproar and the retributions of a powerful neighbor. Privately, they clamored for strong action—by someone else.

If they seemed obsessed with Iran, though, they also seemed deeply conflicted about how to deal with it—with diplomacy, covert action or force. In one typical cable, a senior Omani military officer is described as unable to decide what is worse: "a strike against Iran's nuclear capability and the resulting turmoil it would cause in the Gulf, or inaction and having to live with a nuclear-capable Iran."

Still, running beneath the cables is a belief among many leaders that unless the current government in Tehran falls, Iran will have a bomb sooner or later. And the Obama administration appears doubtful that a military strike would change that.

One of the final cables, on Feb. 12 of this year, recounts a lunch meeting in Paris between Hervé Morin, then the French defense minister, and Secretary of Defense Robert M. Gates. Mr. Morin raised the delicate topic of whether Israel could strike Iran without American support.

Mr. Gates responded "that he didn't know if they would be successful, but that Israel could carry out the operation."

Then he added a stark assessment: any strike "would only delay Iranian plans by one to three years, while unifying the Iranian people to be forever embittered against the attacker."

In 2005, Iran abruptly abandoned an agreement with the Europeans and announced that it would resume uranium enrichment activities. As its program grew, beginning with a handful of centrifuges, so, too, did many Arab states' fears of an Iranian bomb and exasperation over American inability to block Tehran's progress.

To some extent, this Arab obsession with Iran was rooted in the uneasy sectarian division of the Muslim world, between the Shiites who rule Iran, and the Sunnis, who dominate most of the region. Those strains had been drawn tauter with the invasion of Iraq, which effectively transferred control of the government there from Sunni to Shiite leaders, many close to Iran.

In December 2005, the Saudi king expressed his anger that the Bush administration had ignored his advice against going to war. According to a cable from the American Embassy in Riyadh, the king argued "that whereas in the past the U.S., Saudi Arabia and Saddam Hussein had agreed on the need to contain Iran, U.S. policy had now given Iraq to Iran as a 'gift on a golden platter.'"

Regional distrust had only deepened with the election that year of a hard-line Iranian president, Mahmoud Ahmadinejad.

During a meeting on Dec. 27, 2005, with the commander of the United States Central Command, Gen. John P. Abizaid, military leaders from the United Arab Emirates "all agreed with Abizaid that Iran's new President Ahmadinejad seemed unbalanced, crazy even," one cable reports. A few months later, the Emirates' defense chief, Crown Prince Mohammed bin Zayed of Abu Dhabi, told General Abizaid that the United States needed to take action against Iran "this year or next."

The question was what kind of action.

Previously, the crown prince had relayed the Emirates' fear that "it was only a matter of time before Israel or the U.S. would strike Iranian nuclear facility targets." That could provoke an outcome that the Emirates' leadership considered "catastrophic": Iranian missile strikes on American military installations in nearby countries like the Emirates.

Now, with Iran boasting in the spring of 2006 that it had successfully accomplished low-level uranium enrichment, the crown prince began to argue less equivocally, cables show. He stressed "that he wasn't suggesting that the first option was 'bombing' Iran," but also warned, "They have to be dealt with before they do something tragic."

The Saudis, too, increased the pressure. In an April 2008 meeting with Gen. David H. Petraeus, then the incoming Central Command chief, the Saudi ambassador to Washington recalled the king's "frequent exhortations to the U.S. to attack Iran," and the foreign minister said that while he preferred economic pressure, the "use of military pressure against Iran should not be ruled out."

Yet if the Persian Gulf allies were frustrated by American inaction, American officials were equally frustrated by the Arabs' unwillingness to speak out against Iran. "We need our friends to say that they stand with the Americans," General Abizaid told Emirates officials, according to one cable.

By the time Mr. Bush left office in January 2009, Iran had installed 8,000 centrifuges (though only half were running) and was enriching uranium at a rate that, with further processing, would let it produce a bomb's worth of fuel a year. With that progress came increased Israeli pressure.

After the Israeli defense minister issued his ultimatum in May 2009, the chief of staff, Lt. Gen. Gabi Ashkenazi, followed up in November.

"There is still time for diplomacy, but we should not forget that Iran's centrifuges are working day and night," he told a delegation led by

Representative Ike Skelton, the Democratic chairman of the House Armed Services Committee.

That, in turn, led Arab leaders to press even more forcefully for the United States to act—before Israel did. Crown Prince bin Zayed, predicting in July 2009 that an Israeli attack could come by year's end, suggested the danger of appeasing Iran. "Ahmadinejad is Hitler," he declared.

Seemingly taken aback, a State Department official replied, "We do not anticipate military confrontation with Iran before the end of 2009."

So it was that the United States had put together a largely silent front of Arab states whose positions on sanctions and a potential attack looked much like Israel's.

Banks and Businesses

Despite an American trade embargo and several rounds of United Nations sanctions, the Bush administration had never forged the global coalition needed to impose truly painful international penalties on Iran. While France and Britain were supportive, countries like Germany, Russia and China that traded extensively with Iran were reluctant, at best.

In the breach, the United States embarked on a campaign to convince foreign banks and companies that it was in their interest to stop doing business with Iran, by demonstrating how Tehran used its banks, ships, planes and front companies to evade existing sanctions and feed its nuclear and missile programs.

The cables show some notable moments of success, particularly with the banks. But they also make it clear that stopping Iran from obtaining needed technology was a maddening endeavor, with spies and money-laundering experts chasing shipments and transactions in whack-a-mole fashion, often to be stymied by recalcitrant foreign diplomats.

One cable details how the United States asked the Italians to stop the planned export to Iran of 12 fast boats, which could attack American warships in the gulf. Italy did so only after months of "foot-dragging, during which the initial eleven boats were shipped," the embassy in Rome reported.

Another cable recounts China's repeated refusal to act on detailed information about shipments of missile parts from North Korea to Beijing, where they were loaded aboard Iran Air flights to Tehran.

The election of Mr. Obama, at least initially, left some countries wondering whether the sanctions push was about to end. Shortly after taking office, in a videotaped message timed to the Persian New Year, he reiterated his campaign offer of a "new beginning"—the first sustained talks in three decades with Tehran.

The United Arab Emirates called Mr. Obama's message "confusing." The American Embassy in Saudi Arabia reported that the talk about engaging Iran had "fueled Saudi fears that a new U.S. administration might strike a 'grand bargain' without prior consultations."

In Europe, Germany and others discerned an effort to grab market share. "According to the British, other EU Member states fear the U.S. is preparing to take commercial advantage of a new relationship with Iran and subsequently are slowing the EU sanctions process," the American Embassy in London reported.

The administration, though, had a different strategy in mind.

The man chosen to begin wiping out the confusion was Daniel Glaser, a little-known official with a title that took two breaths to enunciate in full: acting assistant secretary of the Treasury for terrorist financing and financial crimes.

The first big rollout of his message appears to have come in Brussels on March 2 and 3, 2009, during what the cables called "an unprecedented classified briefing" to more than 70 Middle East experts from European governments.

Mr. Glaser got right to the point. Yes, engagement was part of the administration's overall strategy. "However, 'engagement' alone is unlikely to succeed," Mr. Glaser said. And to those concerned that the offer of reconciliation was open-ended, one cable said, he replied curtly that "time was not on our side."

The relief among countries supporting sanctions was palpable enough to pierce the cables' smooth diplomatese. "Iran needs to fear the stick and feel a light 'tap' now," said Robert Cooper, a senior European Union official.

"Glaser agreed, noting the stick could escalate beyond financial measures under a worst case scenario," a cable said.

The Czechs were identified as surprisingly enthusiastic behind-the-scenes allies. Another section of the same cable was titled "Single Out but Understand the E.U. Foot-Draggers": Sweden, considered something of a ringleader, followed by Cyprus, Greece, Luxembourg, Spain, Austria, Portugal and Romania.

The decoding of Mr. Obama's plan was apparently all the Europeans needed, and by year's end, even Germany, with its suspicions and longstanding trading ties with Iran, appeared to be on board.

China's Concerns

Still, there could be little meaningful action without Russia and China. Both are permanent members of the United Nations Security Council, where multilateral action would have to pass, and both possess a global reach that could effectively scuttle much of what the United States tried on its own.

The cables indicate that the administration undertook multilayered diplomatic moves to help ensure that neither would cast a Council veto to protect Iran.

As of early 2010, China imported nearly 12 percent of its oil from Iran and worried that supporting sanctions would imperil that supply. Obama administration officials have previously said that the year before, a senior adviser on Iran, Dennis B. Ross, traveled to Saudi Arabia to seek a guarantee that it would supply the lost oil if China were cut off.

The cables show that Mr. Ross had indeed been in Riyadh, the Saudi capital, in April 2009. While there is no direct account of those meetings, a suggestion of dazzling success turns up later, in cables describing meetings between Saudi and Chinese officials.

The offer may have come during a Jan. 13 meeting in Riyadh between Foreign Minister Yang Jiechi of China and King Abdullah and other senior Saudi officials, one of whom told Mr. Yang, "Saudi Arabia understood China was concerned about having access to energy supplies, which could be cut off by Iran," according to one cable.

The conversation, evidently shaped by Mr. Ross's request, developed from there, the cable indicated. A later cable noted simply, "Saudi Arabia has told the Chinese that it is willing to effectively trade a guaranteed oil supply in return for Chinese pressure on Iran not to develop nuclear weapons."

That left Russia.

Dealing With Russia

Throughout 2009, the cables show, the Russians vehemently objected to American plans for a ballistic missile defense site in Poland and the Czech Republic. Conceived under President Bush and billed as a shield against long-range Iranian missiles that American intelligence said were under development, the site was an irritant to Russia, which contended that it was really designed to shoot down Russian missiles.

In talks with the United States, the Russians insisted that there would be no cooperation on other issues until the Eastern Europe site was scrapped. Those demands crested on July 29, when a senior Russian official repeatedly disrupted a meeting with Russia's objections, according to one cable.

Six weeks later, Mr. Obama gave the Russians what they wanted: he abruptly replaced the Eastern Europe site with a ship-borne system. That system, at least in its present form, is engineered to protect specific areas against short- and medium-range missiles, not pulverize long-range missiles soaring above the atmosphere. Mr. Obama explained the shift by saying that intelligence assessments had changed, and that the long-range missile threat appeared to be growing more slowly than previously thought.

The cables are silent on whether at some higher level, Russia hinted that Security Council action against Iran would be easier with the site gone. But another secret meeting with the Russians last December, recounted in the cables, may help explain why Mr. Obama was willing to shift focus to the short- and medium-range threat, at least in the near term.

In the meeting, American officials said nothing about a slowing of the long-range threat, as cited by Mr. Obama. In fact, they insisted that North Korea had sent Iran 19 advanced missiles, based on a Russian design, that could clear a path toward the development of long-range missiles. According to unclassified estimates of their range, though, they would also immediately allow Iran to strike Western Europe or easily reach Moscow—essentially the threat the revamped system was designed for.

Russia is deeply skeptical that Iran has obtained the advanced missiles, or that their North Korean version, called the BM-25, even exists. "For Russia, the BM-25 is a mysterious missile," a Russian official said. (That argument was dealt a blow last month, when North Korea rolled out what some experts identified as those very missiles in a military parade.)

Whatever the dynamic, Mr. Obama had removed the burr under the Russians' saddle, and in January 2010, one cable reported, a senior Russian official "indicated Russia's willingness to move to the pressure track."

The cables obtained by WikiLeaks end in February 2010, before the last-minute maneuvering that led to a fourth round of Security Council sanctions and even stiffer measures—imposed by the United States, the Europeans, Australia and Japan—that experts say are beginning to pinch Iran's economy. But while Mr. Ahmadinejad has recently offered to resume nuclear negotiations, the cables underscore the extent to which Iran's true intentions remain a mystery.

As Crown Prince bin Zayed of Abu Dhabi put it in one cable: "Any culture that is patient and focused enough to spend years working on a single carpet is capable of waiting years and even decades to achieve even greater goals." His greatest worry, he said, "is not how much we know about Iran, but how much we don't."

William J. Broad and Andrew W. Lehren contributed reporting.

—This article was originally published on November 28, 2010
See diplomatic cable on p. 473.

WIDER WINDOW INTO IRAN'S MISSILE CAPABILITIES OFFERS A MURKIER VIEW

By MARK MAZZETTI and WILLIAM J. BROAD

WASHINGTON—It was one of the most provocative assertions to emerge from the WikiLeaks cache—a diplomatic cable from this past February confidently describing the sale of 19 missiles to Iran by North Korea that could give Tehran the ability to strike Western Europe and Russia.

But a review of a dozen other State Department cables made available by WikiLeaks and interviews with American government officials offer a murkier picture of Iran's missile capabilities. Despite the tone of the February cable, it shows there are disagreements among officials about the missiles, and scant evidence that they are close to being deployed.

The conflicting portraits illustrate how the batch of diplomatic documents made available by WikiLeaks can be glimpses of the American government's views, sometimes reflecting only part of the story, rather than concrete assertions of fact.

While there are a range of opinions about the details of the weapons sale and the readiness of the missiles, what most American officials appear to agree on is that at the very least North Korea sold a number of ballistic missile parts to Tehran in 2005.

The sale set off alarms in Washington, because the parts were for BM-25 missiles, a weapon with powerful engines that—if deployed by Iran—could bolster Tehran's ability to strike far beyond the Middle East, State Department cables show.

But five years later, American officials in interviews said that they had no evidence that Iran had used the parts or technology to actually construct a BM-25, let alone begin the years of flight testing necessary before it could reliably add the missile to its arsenal.

It is unclear why Iran appears to have had trouble with the BM-25. According to one American official, it is possible that Iran did not get complete "missile kits" from the North Koreans in 2005, or that Iranian scientists have had difficulty mastering the technology.

Both American officials and outside experts appear to agree, however, that Iran did use some of the BM-25 technology to launch a satellite into space last year, and that Iranian scientists probably used data from that launching for its military program.

"Just because the BM-25 program hasn't progressed as far as the Iranians hoped it would, the concern remains," said one official, who spoke on the condition of anonymity because assessments about Iran's missile program are classified.

The dozen cables provide a glimpse of secret discussions between the United States and a number of foreign governments about the BM-25, described earlier this week in an article in The New York Times. Their views are colored by their relationships with Iran.

The Israelis, for instance, take a more alarmist stance than the United States because Israel regards Iran as its greatest threat. Russia, on the other hand, denies that the BM-25 even exists.

In the cables, American officials argue that North Korea developed the medium-range weapon based on a Russian design, the R-27, once used on Soviet submarines to carry nuclear warheads.

The cables describe how the North Koreans, in turn, transferred "missiles" or "missile systems" to Iran. The cables do not refer to missile parts or "kits."

But the cables, written over four years, vary in the certainty with which Americans make the claim about the technology transfer, with one cable saying Iran "has probably acquired" BM-25s and another discussing "substantial data indicating Iranian possession of a missile system."

The public release of the cables has stirred debate among experts outside the government on the existence of the BM-25 and whether, if Iran has the weapon, it poses an immediate threat to Western Europe.

Many experts say the BM-25 has undergone no flight testing either by North Korea or Iran, and they note that traditionally it takes a dozen or so tests over several years to perfect a missile and prepare it for military deployment.

On the other hand, NATO last month agreed to establish an antimissile shield and has invited Russia to take part, suggesting growing concern in Europe of an Iranian missile threat.

One of the most knowledgeable public analysts of Tehran's endeavors in rocketry is Michael Elleman, a missile engineer who contributed to a report on Iran's program issued in May by the International Institute for Strategic Studies, an arms analysis group in London.

That report was skeptical of Iran's having obtained the BM-25 from North Korea. Now, Mr. Elleman said, he is less certain.

"It is possible that the BM-25 does not exist," he said in an e-mail message. "However, it is more likely that it does, in some fashion. We just do not know, precisely, because it has never been tested."

The first cable in the WikiLeaks cache that refers to the BM-25 came from the American Embassy in Tel Aviv, sent to Washington on May 5, 2006. The cable discusses a meeting a month earlier between Senator Joseph I. Lieberman, the Connecticut independent, and Meir Dagan, director of Mossad, Israel's main spy agency.

According to the cable, Mr. Dagan talked of Iran's having a medium-range missile, the Shahab-3, that "can currently carry nuclear material, and reported that Iran is also trying to adapt the BM-25 missile, which already has a longer range, for this purpose."

American intelligence officials do not believe that Iran has yet mastered the technology to put a nuclear warhead on top of a missile.

But the most detailed discussion about the missile is contained in a cable from Feb. 24 of this year, which describes the disagreements between American and Russian officials about the missile.

The cable shows that American officials firmly believed that Iran had obtained 19 of the missiles from North Korea, and that there was direct evidence of the weapons transfer. But it goes on to indicate that the Russians dismiss that claim as a myth driven by politics.

Mark Mazzetti reported from Washington, and William J. Broad from New York.

—This article was originally published on December 3, 2010

MEDDLING NEIGHBORS UNDERCUT IRAQ STABILITY

By MICHAEL R. GORDON

Iraq's police and security forces preparing for
the planned withdrawal of American troops in 2011.

WASHINGTON—Saddam Hussein's Iraq was a regional menace that
sent shudders through its neighbors. Today's Iraqi leaders are struggling
to restrain the ambitions of the countries that share Iraq's porous borders,
eye the country's rich resources and vie for influence.

"All Iraq's neighbors were interfering, albeit in different ways, the Gulf
and Saudi Arabia with money, Iran with money and political influence, and
the Syrians by all means," Jalal Talabani, Iraq's president and the senior

Kurdish official in the government, told Defense Secretary Robert M. Gates in a Dec. 10, 2009, meeting, according to a diplomatic cable. "The Turks are 'polite' in their interference, but continue their attempts to influence Iraq's Turkmen community and Sunnis in Mosul."

With American troops preparing to withdraw from Iraq by the end of 2011, the meddling threatens to aggravate the sectarian divisions in the country and undermine efforts by Iraq's leaders to get beyond bitter rivalries and build a stable government. It also shows how deeply Iraq's leaders depend on the United States to manage that meddling, even as it exposes the increasing limits on America's ability to do so.

Cables obtained by the anti-secrecy organization WikiLeaks and made available to several news organizations describe flustered Iraqi leaders complaining of interference by manipulative neighbors, some of whom—in the view of the United States—do not want it to regain its previous position of power.

"The challenge for us is to convince Iraq neighbors, particularly the Sunni Arab governments, that relations with a new Iraq are not a zero-sum game, where if Iraq wins, they lose," noted a Sept. 24, 2009, cable from Ambassador Christopher R. Hill, which was aptly titled "The Great Game, in Mesopotamia." American diplomatic cables disclosed by WikiLeaks show that Prime Minister Nuri Kamal al-Maliki's fears about outside interference are so great that he asked President Obama during a July 2009 visit to Washington to stop the Saudis from intervening. Saudi Arabia's efforts to rally the Sunnis, the Iraqi leader complained, were heightening sectarian tensions and providing Iran with an excuse to intervene in Iraqi politics, according to an account of the Oval Office session Mr. Maliki shared with Ambassador Hill.

The suspicions have often been mutual. "I don't trust this man," King Abdullah of Saudi Arabia told John O. Brennan, Mr. Obama's top counterterrorism adviser, according to a cable about a March 15, 2009, meeting at the king's private palace in Saudi Arabia. "He is an Iranian agent."

Jockeying for influence in Iraq by outside countries has been going on ever since Mr. Hussein was ousted, hardly surprising given Iraq's strategic position in the Middle East, its vast oil reserves, its multisectarian population and the fact that it is a nascent, if unsteady, democracy largely surrounded by undemocratic neighbors.

The Iranians, who waged a bloody eight-year war with Mr. Hussein, have no desire to see a strong Iraq emerge from the ashes of his regime, especially one that has ties with the United States.

So they have sought to influence its politics by funneling cash to Iraqi political factions, ordering assassinations and shipping arms to militants, some of which an Oct. 23, 2008, cable from Dubai warned might be disguised as medical supplies. The Saudis, who see Iran as the chief threat in the region, have used their satellite television stations and deep pockets to support Sunni groups. Syria, which Iraqi leaders have repeatedly complained to American diplomats is dominated by a Baathist regime sympathetic to the ousted Baathists in Iraq, has allowed insurgent fighters to sneak into Iraq. Even Turkey, which has good relations with the Iraqi government, has secretly financed nationalist and anti-Kurdish Sunni political parties.

Some top Iraqi politicians have tried to cast themselves as the right ones to resist Iranian influence and help Iraq improve ties with its Arab neighbors.

Ayad Allawi, who leads the Iraqiya Party, has emphasized his relationship with Arab leaders while his supporters have cast Mr. Maliki's Dawa Party supporters as fearful of interacting with the Arab world, the cables show. Mr. Maliki's aides have presented themselves and their boss as being more savvy about resisting Iranian pressure than many of their rivals—if only the Americans can keep the Saudis in line.

Iran, by the United States' reckoning, has done the most to try to shape Iraqi politics. A Nov. 13, 2009, cable sent by Ambassador Hill, which called Iran "a dominant player in Iraq's electoral politics," estimated that Iran's annual support to political groups in Iraq was $100 million to $200 million. Some $70 million of that, the cable asserts, is directed to the Islamic Supreme Council in Iraq, a leading Shiite party that has also worked closely with American officials, and its former militia, the Badr Corps.

Using an acronym for the Iranian government, the ambassador acknowledged Iran's pragmatism: "The IRIG recognizes that influence in Iraq requires operational (and at times ideological) flexibility. As a result, it is not uncommon for the IRIG to finance and support competing Shia, Kurdish, and to some extent, Sunni entities, with the aim of developing the Iraqi body politic's dependency on Tehran's largesse."

In a Sept. 24, 2009, cable titled "Prime Minister Accuses Iran of Trying to DeStabilize Iraq," Ambassador Hill reported that Mr. Maliki had told him that Iran was trying to use its money and influence to try to "control" the Iraqi Parliament and was prepared to provide military support to Shiite militants if political efforts failed. Iran, Ambassador Hill quoted Mr. Maliki as saying, was trying to rally the Shiites to counter the "Saudi project to align the Sunni states."

Some cables nonetheless reflect American concern that Dawa Party officials inserted into government posts by Mr. Maliki may have close ties to Iran. A February cable prepared by the embassy's political officer notes that Mr. Maliki has moved to replace intelligence officers accused of having Baathists ties with Dawa Party loyalists. After pushback from Iraqi officials, and, apparently, interventions by American officials, the number of suspected Baathists who were to be fired was reduced. But a military intelligence headquarters was forced to hire 47 Dawa political officers who had been in exile in Iran, "where they may have received intelligence training," the cable notes.

American diplomats and generals have told Arab leaders in the region that the best way to counter Iran's ambitions is to establish a good working relationship with Mr. Maliki, which means sending ambassadors to Baghdad and refraining from financing and mobilizing opposition groups or insurgents that seek to undermine him. But as Ambassador Hill acknowledged in his cable on the "Great Game," American diplomats "still have work to do to convince them that a strong, stable, democratic (and inevitably Shia-led) Iraq is the best guarantee that Iraq will be able to shake Iranian manipulations and see its future bound up with that of the West and its moderate Arab neighbors."

Of all the Arab leaders in the region, President Hosni Mubarak of Egypt, the cables suggest, was the most sympathetic to the American approach, a policy that reflects Egypt's deep suspicions of Iran. Omar Suleiman, Egypt's intelligence chief, told Gen. David H. Petraeus in a June 2009 meeting that Egypt's goal was "to bring Iraq back to the Arab World."

Toward this end, Egypt promised to send a new ambassador to Baghdad, a noteworthy move given that the previous Egyptian ambassador was kidnapped by insurgents and killed in 2005. In a conversation with King Abdullah, President Mubarak advised the Saudi monarch "not to search for another man," but instead to accept Mr. Maliki, Mr. Suleiman confided.

The Saudis, on the other hand, have good ties with Mr. Maliki's principal rival. They may have been unwilling to deal with Mr. Maliki or send an ambassador to Baghdad, but a Feb. 23, 2010, American Embassy cable from Riyadh notes that King Abdullah rolled out the red carpet for Mr. Allawi.

Like the Iranians, the Saudis have not hesitated to use their money and political influence inside Iraq, according to American diplomats. "For now the Saudis are using their money and media power (al-Arabiyya, al-Sharqiya satellite channels, and other various media they control or influence) to support Sunni political aspirations, exert influence over Sunni tribal groups, and undercut the Shia-led Islamic Supreme Council of Iraq (ISCI) and Iraqi National Alliance (INA)," Ambassador Hill's "Great Game" cable noted.

And Mr. Talabani complained in a Dec. 14, 2009, meeting with a senior State Department official that the Saudis "had pressured Kuwait to backtrack on initial agreements with Iraq on issues dating to the Saddam-era," a cable noted. (The cable quoted Mr. Talabani as saying that Qatar and Bahrain were seeking better ties with Iraq "despite Saudi opposition.")

Syria has been another difficult neighbor. It has long been accused by the Iraqis of harboring senior Iraq Baath Party members aligned with the former regime, and allowing foreign fighters to sneak into Iraq. The Obama administration sought to improve ties with President Bashar al-Assad of Syria and even sent a team from the United States Central Command to Syria to discuss ways to better control the border. But after a series of bombings in Baghdad in August 2009, which Mr. Maliki attributed to Syria, the Iraqis refused to take part in the talks.

In a December 2009 meeting with Jeffrey D. Feltman, an assistant secretary of state, Mr. Maliki, who lived in Syria for 16 years during Mr. Hussein's rule, described the Syrians as more difficult to deal with than the Iranians and recounted that the Syrians had boasted to him during his years in exile that they were skilled in negotiating with the Americans, a cable said.

Of all Iraq's neighbors, Turkey has forged one of the best relationships with the Iraqi government and with Kurdish officials in northern Iraq. Turkey, the cables note, also played an important role in helping the United States and Iraq negotiate the security agreement that provides for the withdrawal of American troops by the end of 2011.

But Turkey has been unable to resist the temptation to intervene in Iraqi politics. Turkey, an April 2009 cable noted, "played an unhelpful role in recent Iraqi provincial elections through its clandestine financial support of the anti-Kurd al Hadba Gathering," a Sunni-led political group that prevailed in provincial elections in Nineveh Province in Iraq.

According to a Jan. 31, 2010, cable from Ambassador Hill, Turkey's ambassador to Baghdad, Murat Ozcelik, also opposed Mr. Maliki's bid to win re-election in his talks with American diplomats. While Turkey had supported Mr. Maliki in the past, Mr. Ozcelik said it was backing his rivals now because the Turks believed that if Mr. Maliki was re-elected he "would focus on increasing his own power and would not be cooperative in resolving outstanding issues," Ambassador Hill reported.

—This article was originally published on December 5, 2010

See war log on p. 515.

YEMEN SETS TERMS OF
A WAR ON AL QEADA

By SCOTT SHANE

WASHINGTON—One Obama administration security official after another was visiting to talk about terrorism, and Yemen's redoubtable president, Ali Abdullah Saleh, seemed to be savoring his newfound leverage.

The Americans are "hot-blooded and hasty when you need us," Mr. Saleh chided one visitor, Daniel Benjamin, the State Department's counterterrorism chief, but "cold-blooded and British when we need you."

It was Jan. 31, just a few weeks after a young Nigerian trained and equipped in Yemen had tried to blow up an airliner as it approached Detroit. The wave of attention to Al Qaeda's Yemen branch and its American-born propagandist, Anwar al-Awlaki, might not do much for tourism, but paradoxically it did give the Yemeni leader more influence.

Mr. Saleh said coyly that while he was "satisfied" with the military equipment the United States was supplying, he "would like to be more satisfied in the future," according to an account of the meeting sent to Washington.

Diplomatic cables obtained by WikiLeaks and made available to several news organizations offer the most intimate view to date of the wily, irreverent and sometimes erratic Yemeni autocrat, who over the past year has become steadily more aggressive against Al Qaeda. But he appears determined to join the fight on his own terms, sometimes accommodating and other times rebuffing American requests on counterterrrorism.

The cables do not substantially alter the public picture of Mr. Saleh (pronounced SAH-leh), 68, a former military officer who has led Yemen for three decades. But with direct quotations from private meetings, the cables are like crisp color photographs of what was previously in fuzzy black and white.

Yemen, long an arid, impoverished afterthought for the United States, now draws high-level American attention far out of proportion to its size. In

October, militants in Yemen sent off printer cartridges packed with explosives to Chicago addresses. The bombs were intercepted, but the plot set off a furor and prompted the latest in a series of phone calls between President Obama and his Yemeni counterpart about counterterrorism and aid.

At times, the cables show, Mr. Saleh has not hesitated to use his country's daunting problems as a kind of threat.

"Referencing the high poverty rate and illicit arms flows into both Yemen and Somalia, Saleh concluded by saying, 'If you don't help, this country will become worse than Somalia,' " said a September 2009 cable from the American ambassador, Stephen A. Seche, describing Mr. Saleh as being in "vintage form."

The cables portray Yemen, a land of 23 million people that is nearly the size of Texas, as a beleaguered, often baffling place, bristling with arms and riven by tribal conflict, where shoulder-launched missiles go missing and the jihad-curious arrive from all over the world. The Americans are seen coaxing the Yemenis to go after Al Qaeda, working out the rules for American missile strikes, seeking a safe way to send Yemeni prisoners home from the Guantánamo Bay prison and sizing up Americans caught in Yemeni security sweeps.

Always at the center of the diplomatic traffic is Mr. Saleh, who first appears seeking a half-million tons of wheat in a 1990 meeting with James A. Baker III, then the secretary of state. These days, his most pressing requests are for heavy weapons and military training. But he also has become more cooperative with the American campaign against Al Qaeda.

In a 2009 meeting with John O. Brennan, President Obama's top counterterrorism adviser, Mr. Saleh offered an unusual bargain. He "insisted that Yemen's national territory is available for unilateral CT operations by the U.S."—but with a catch. If there were to be an attack on a Western target, Mr. Saleh said, it would not be his fault.

"I have given you an open door on terrorism," he said, "so I am not responsible."

In fact, despite such rhetoric, Mr. Saleh has imposed strict limits over American operations in his country, even as he has helped disguise them as his own.

When the first two American missile strikes against Qaeda camps in Yemen took place in December 2009, Mr. Saleh publicly claimed that they were Yemeni strikes to avert any anti-American backlash. Gen. David H.

Petraeus flew to Yemen to thank the president, who promised to keep up the ruse. "We'll continue saying the bombs are ours, not yours," Mr. Saleh said, according to a cable.

A deputy prime minister, Rashad al-Alimi, had already assured the Americans that "U.S. munitions found at the sites" of strikes "could be explained away as equipment purchased from the U.S."

Moreover, Mr. Alimi implied that Yemeni officials accepted as inevitable that the missiles had killed civilians along with militants. They were Bedouin families—"poor people selling food and supplies to the terrorists" and thus "acting in collusion with the terrorists and benefiting financially," he said.

Still, Mr. Saleh told General Petraeus that "mistakes were made" in the killing of civilians. He agreed to the American commander's proposal that to improve accuracy, future strikes would be carried out by American aircraft rather than by cruise missiles fired from distant ships.

But he firmly denied General Petraeus's request to send American advisers along on Yemeni counterterrorism operations. For his part, General Petraeus put off Mr. Saleh's request for 12 armed helicopters, even though the president promised to use them "only against Al Qaeda." The United States has been wary of fueling the Yemeni government's long-running conflicts with the so-called Houthi rebels in the north and secessionists in the south.

The two sides also sparred over Yemen's restrictions on material the United States shipped to its embassy in the diplomatic pouch, which the Yemenis evidently suspected was being used to import eavesdropping equipment. The Americans have complained about poor security at the airport in Sana, Yemen's capital, including X-ray screeners who do not watch their monitors, and also security officers who "harass" American diplomats.

Beyond such testy bargaining, emptying the Guantánamo Bay prison, where Yemenis are the single largest group remaining, has been a regular source of tension. When Mr. Saleh rejected an American plan to send the Yemenis to a Saudi rehabilitation program in March 2009, a cable described him as "dismissive, bored and impatient" and said he had "missed a good chance to engage the new administration on one of its key foreign policy priorities."

At the same time, the embassy was tracking the growing number of Yemeni arrests of expatriate Americans suspected of having links to militants. By last February, such arrests were occurring about once a week, and Mr. Seche wrote to Washington that the embassy's "sharply increased workload" urgently required more personnel.

"In the past two years, the Muslim convert community of Amcits living in Yemen," Mr. Seche wrote, using shorthand for American citizens, "has been increasingly linked to extremist activities." Sorting out such cases was difficult, a February cable said, citing an American woman who had reported the midnight arrest of her husband but appeared to be "omitting or manipulating critical details."

Yemen had become a magnet for would-be jihadists from around the globe, and a January cable listed 23 Australian citizens and residents to be added to terrorism watch lists because of activities in Yemen or connections to Mr. Awlaki, the radical cleric hiding there. Many of the Australians were women, and Qaeda operatives in Yemen were seeking "to identify a female for a future attack," the cable said.

The cables report on American and Yemeni attempts to track down and destroy stocks of the shoulder-fired missiles known as "manpads," for man-portable air-defense systems. Their lethality against aircraft make them a major counterterrorism concern.

Yemen's Defense Ministry insisted that it had no stocks of such missiles, but Yemen's National Security Bureau—a newer agency that works closely with the United States—told the Americans that the Defense Ministry "does indeed have MANPADS, but would never speak of them because they are considered a state secret."

A close ally in the counterterrorism efforts, the cables make clear, is Prince Muhammad bin Nayef, the deputy interior minister in neighboring Saudi Arabia, who in October tipped off American officials about the parcel bomb plot. Shortly after the attempted bombing of the airliner bound for Detroit, Prince Nayef told Gen. James L. Jones, then President Obama's national security adviser, that the only way to combat Al Qaeda in Yemen was to "keep them on the run" and that Yemeni and American strikes on Al Qaeda were proving effective.

Saudi authorities "have been monitoring conversations of Al Qaeda operatives in Yemen very closely, and whereas before the attack they were hearing relaxed 20-minute phone conversations over cellphones, after the attack the phones went virtually silent," Prince Nayef said, according to a cable. That showed that Qaeda operatives "are more focused on their own security rather than on planning operations," he said.

Andrew W. Lehren contributed reporting from New York.

—This article was originally published on December 3, 2010

See diplomatic cable on p. 463.

LIBYA DELAYED
NUCLEAR FUEL DISPOSAL DEAL

By ERIC SCHMITT

WASHINGTON—In the early morning of Nov. 25, 2009, a large Russian cargo plane left the Libyan capital, Tripoli, on a secret mission without its intended cargo.

A small stockpile of spent nuclear fuel destined for disposal in Russia remained behind in a lightly guarded research center, apparently because of a fit of pique by Libya's mercurial leader, Col. Muammar el-Qaddafi. In a frantic cable back to Washington, American officials in Tripoli warned of dire consequences unless the carefully brokered deal to remove the 5.2 kilograms (11.4 pounds) of highly enriched uranium stored in seven five-ton casks was quickly resurrected.

If the enriched uranium "is not removed from the casks within three months, its rising temperature could cause the casks to crack and to release radioactive nuclear material," the American Embassy in Tripoli reported, according to cables made public by WikiLeaks. "Security concerns alone dictate that we must employ all of our resources to find a timely solution to this problem, and to keep any mention of it out of the press."

The seeds of what appeared to be the demise of the secret deal were planted weeks earlier in New York, when Colonel Qaddafi expressed unhappiness that he was not permitted to set up his tent in Manhattan or to visit ground zero during a United Nations session.

But the scope of the colonel's anger was not fully realized until Nov. 20, 2009, when the Libyan government unexpectedly ordered a team of visiting American and Russian scientists to halt preparations to ship the spent nuclear fuel to Russia, despite separate agreements Libya had reached with the United States and Russia.

The Libyans, in fact, had already agreed to pay $30,000 to have the Russians remove the material and bury it in a secure location. The episode was first reported by The Atlantic on Nov. 27, before WikiLeaks posted the cables.

Colonel Qaddafi's son Seif al-Islam el-Qaddafi told the American ambassador on Nov. 27 that Libya balked at its promise to ship its final enriched uranium stockpile because it was "fed up" with the slow pace of improved relations with Washington. Libya had agreed in 2003 to dismantle its unconventional weapons program in exchange for greater military, security and economic cooperation.

"The Libyan Government has chosen a very dangerous issue on which to express its apparent pique about perceived problems in the bilateral relationship," the American ambassador, Gene A. Cretz, wrote to Washington.

Diplomats warned that if the enriched uranium was not sent to Russia soon, Russian scientists would be required to develop entirely new and risky technology to remove the spent fuel from the casks in Libya itself.

In the next few weeks, the cables revealed, American and Russian officials prevailed upon the Libyans to disengage the research center's loading crane to prevent an intruder from moving the casks. Extra security guards were sent to the site. (Before that, diplomats noted that they had seen only one guard with a gun and they raised doubts whether that was even loaded.)

American and Russian officials successfully smoothed Colonel Qaddafi's ruffled feathers.

By late December, the Russian aircraft was back on the tarmac in Tripoli. Visiting United States Energy Department officials reported that the loading of the casks overnight on Dec. 20-2 1 was carried out without a hitch. Libyan officials at the Tajoura Nuclear Center offered no insights into the reasons behind the government's about-face.

At 5:15 a.m. on Dec. 21, the Russian-chartered plane took off. Energy Department officials confirmed several hours later that the flight—and its secret cargo—had arrived in Russia.

—This article was originally published on December 3, 2010

CASH FLOW TO TERRORISTS EVADES U.S. EFFORTS

By ERIC LICHTBLAU and ERIC SCHMITT

WASHINGTON—Nine years after the United States vowed to shut down the money pipeline that finances terrorism, senior Obama administration officials say they believe that many millions of dollars are flowing largely unimpeded to extremist groups worldwide, and they have grown frustrated by frequent resistance from allies in the Middle East, according to secret diplomatic dispatches.

The government cables, sent by Secretary of State Hillary Rodham Clinton and senior State Department officials, catalog a list of methods that American officials suspect terrorist financiers are using, including a brazen bank robbery in Yemen last year, kidnappings for ransom, the harvesting of drug proceeds in Afghanistan and fund-raising at religious pilgrimages to Mecca, where millions of riyals or other forms of currency change hands.

While American officials have publicly been relatively upbeat about their progress in disrupting terrorist financing, the internal State Department cables, obtained by WikiLeaks and made available to several news organizations, offer a more pessimistic account, with blunt assessments of the threats to the United States from money flowing to militants affiliated with Al Qaeda, the Taliban, Hamas, Lashkar-e-Taiba and other groups.

A classified memo sent by Mrs. Clinton last December made it clear that residents of Saudi Arabia and its neighbors, all allies of the United States, are the chief financial supporters of many extremist activities. "It has been an ongoing challenge to persuade Saudi officials to treat terrorist financing emanating from Saudi Arabia as a strategic priority," the cable said, concluding that "donors in Saudi Arabia constitute the most significant source of funding to Sunni terrorist groups worldwide."

The dispatch and others offered similarly grim views about the United Arab Emirates ("a strategic gap" that terrorists can exploit), Qatar ("the worst in the region" on counterterrorism) and Kuwait ("a key transit point"). The cable stressed the need to "generate the political will necessary" to block money to terrorist networks—groups that she said were "threatening stability in Pakistan and Afghanistan and targeting coalition soldiers."

While President George W. Bush frequently vowed to cut off financing for militants and pledged to make financiers as culpable as terrorists who carried out plots, President Obama has been far less vocal on the issue publicly as he has sought to adopt a more conciliatory tone with Arab nations. But his administration has used many of the same covert diplomatic, intelligence and law enforcement tools as his predecessor and set up a special task force in the summer of 2009 to deal with the growing problem.

While federal officials can point to some successes—prosecutions, seizures of money and tightened money-laundering regulations in foreign countries—the results have often been frustrating, the cables show. As the United States has pushed for more aggressive crackdowns on suspected supporters of terrorism, foreign leaders have pushed back. In private meetings, they have accused American officials of heavy-handedness and of presenting thin evidence of wrongdoing by Arab charities or individuals, according to numerous cables.

Kuwaiti officials, for example, resisted what they called "draconian" measures sought by the United States against a prominent charity and dismissed allegations against it as "unconvincing," according to one cable.

The documents are filled with government intelligence on possible terrorist-financing plots, like the case of a Somali preacher who was reportedly touring Sweden, Finland and Norway last year to look for money and recruits for the Shabab, a militant group in Somalia, or that of a Pakistani driver caught with about $240,000 worth of Saudi riyals stuffed behind his seat. One memo even reported on a possible plot by the Iranians to launder $5 billion to $10 billion in cash through the Emirates' banks as part of a broader effort to "stir up trouble" among the Persian Gulf states, though it was not clear how much of the money might be channeled to militants.

One episode that set off particular concern occurred in August 2009 in Yemen, when armed robbers stormed a bank truck on a busy downtown street in Aden during daylight hours and stole 100 million Yemeni riyals, or about $500,000. American diplomats said the sophistication of the robbery and other indicators had all the markings of a Qaeda mission. "This bold, unusual operation" could provide Al Qaeda "with a substantial financing infusion at a time when it is thought to be short of cash," a dispatch summarizing the episode said.

Al Qaeda's branch in Yemen, known as Al Qaeda in the Arabian Peninsula, is seen as a rising threat by the United States and was blamed for a parcel bomb plot in October and the failed attempt to blow up a jetliner last Dec. 25. The cables do not make clear whether the finances of the Yemen group are tied to Osama bin Laden's network.

American officials appear to have divided views on the bin Laden group's fund-raising abilities. A February cable to Richard C. Holbrooke, the administration's special representative for Afghanistan and Pakistan, said that "sensitive reporting indicates that al-Qaida's ability to raise funds has deteriorated substantially, and that it is now in its weakest state since 9/11."

But many other cables draw the opposite conclusion and cite the group's ability to generate money almost at will from wealthy individuals and sympathetic groups throughout the Middle East while often staying a step ahead of counterterrorism officials.

"Terrorists avoid money transfer controls by transferring amounts below reporting thresholds and using reliable cash couriers, hawala, and money grams," a recent cable warned. "Emerging trends include mobile banking, pre-paid cards, and Internet banking."

The documents suggest that there is little evidence of significant financial support in the United States or Europe for terrorist groups in Afghanistan and Pakistan, despite a string of deadly but largely low-budget attacks in London and other European cities in recent years, according to the documents.

"U.K. financing is important, but the real money is in the Gulf," a senior British counterterrorism official told a Treasury Department official, according to a cable last year from the American Embassy in London.

In hundreds of cables focusing on terrorist financing, the problem takes on an air of intractability, as American officials speak of the seeming ease with which terrorists are able to move money, the low cost of carrying out deadly attacks, and the difficulty of stopping it. Interdictions are few, and resistance is frequent.

In Kuwait, for instance, American officials have voiced repeated concerns that Islamic charities—largely unregulated by the government there—are using philanthropic donations to finance terrorism abroad. But a Kuwaiti minister, in a meeting last year with the United States ambassador, "was as frank and pessimistic as ever when it came to the subject of apprehending and detaining terror financiers and facilitators under Kuwait's current legal and political framework," a memo summarizing the meeting said.

Saudi Arabia, a critical military and diplomatic ally, emerges in the cables as the most vexing of problems. Intelligence officials there have stepped up their spying on militants in neighboring Yemen, and they provided the tip that helped uncover the recent parcel bombs. But while the Saudis have made some progress, "terrorist funding emanating from Saudi Arabia remains a serious concern," according to a cable in February. Mrs. Clinton's memo two months earlier said Al Qaeda, the Taliban, Lashkar-e-Taiba and other groups "probably raise millions of dollars annually from Saudi sources, often during Hajj and Ramadan." Officials said they believed that fund-raisers for extremist groups had often descended on the pilgrims to seek money for their causes.

The American Embassy in Riyadh, Saudi Arabia, reported in February that the Saudis remained "almost completely dependent on the C.I.A." for leads and direction on terrorist financing.

So it was not surprising that a month earlier, the embassy reported in a separate cable that Treasury Department officials had provided information to the Saudi domestic intelligence service, the Mabahith, on three senior Taliban leaders—Tayyeb Agha, Mullah Jalil and Khalil Haqqani—who had made several fund-raising trips to the kingdom, the cable said. (Like a number of other suspected financiers identified in the cables, the three Taliban leaders do not appear on the Treasury Department's list of "banned" entities suspected of terrorism financing connections.)

The Americans shared phone numbers, e-mail addresses and passport information for the three men with the Saudis to cross check against Saudi customs databases. Saudi authorities said they were not familiar with the Taliban leaders but promised to pursue the tips.

Last week, American officials said steady pressure from the Bush and Obama administrations had led to significant improvements in fighting terrorist financing. They said, for example, Saudi Arabia was now taking actions that they had long hesitated to take or had resisted, including holding financiers accountable through prosecutions and making terrorist financing a higher priority. A leading Saudi religious scholar has issued an edict against terrorist financing, and the Saudis have created new financial intelligence unit.

"The U.S. government has been relentless in pursuing sources and methods of terrorist financing, including prioritizing this issue with all countries in the gulf region," said Stuart A. Levey, a senior Treasury official, who was speaking generally about American policy and not about anything in the leaked cables. "As a result, we have put Al Qaeda under significant financial pressure."

Behind the scenes at diplomatic encounters, tensions have occasionally flared. In 2007, a senior Bush administration official, Frances Fragos Townsend, told her Saudi counterparts in Riyadh that Mr. Bush was "quite concerned" about the level of cooperation from the Saudis, and she brought a personal letter on the subject from the president to King Abdullah, according to a cable summarizing the exchange.

Ms. Townsend questioned whether the kingdom's ambassador to the Philippines, Mohammed Ameen Wali, might be involved in supporting terrorism because of his involvement with two people suspected of being financiers, the summary said.

Prince Saud al-Faisal, the Saudi foreign minister, challenged the assertion, however, saying the ambassador might be guilty of "bad judgment rather than intentional support for terrorism," and he countered with an assertion of his own: an unnamed American bank handling the Saudi Embassy's money in Washington was performing unnecessary audits and asking "inappropriate and aggressive questions."

American diplomats said that while the Saudis appeared earnest in wanting to stanch the flow of terrorist money, they often lacked the training and expertise to do it. "Their capabilities often fall short of their aspirations," a cable last November said.

Saudi leaders appear equally resigned to the situation, according to the cables. "We are trying to do our best," Prince Mohammed bin Nayef, who leads the Saudis' anti-terrorism activities, was quoted as telling Mr. Holbrooke, the special representative to the region, in a May 2009 meeting.

But, he said, "if money wants to go" to terrorist causes, "it will go."

Andrew W. Lehren contributed reporting from New York.

—This article was originally published on December 5, 2010

CABLES FROM AMERICAN DIPLOMATS PORTRAY U.S. AMBIVALENCE ON TUNISIA

By SCOTT SHANE

Tunisians from the country's south joined protests
in Tunis on Jan. 23, 2011.

Moises Saman for The New York Times

Cables from American diplomats in Tunisia portray a deepening ambivalence toward the rule of President Zine el-Abidine Ben Ali, expressing alarm about popular resentment of the blatant corruption of the country's first family but also gratitude for Mr. Ben Ali's cooperation against terrorism and the stability he long imposed.

Those cables, from the cache obtained by the anti-secrecy organization WikiLeaks and made public in recent weeks, helped fuel the anger on the streets that culminated Friday with Mr. Ben Ali's flight after 23 years in power. Posted on a site created last month called TuniLeaks, the diplomats' disgusted and lurid accounts of the kleptocratic ways of the president's extended family helped tip the scales, according to many Tunisian commentators.

"What's Yours Is Mine" was the wry title of a June 2008 cable reporting the brazen habits of the president's clan.

"Corruption in Tunisia is getting worse," the cable said. "Whether it's cash, services, land, property, or yes, even your yacht, President Ben Ali's family is rumored to covet it and reportedly gets what it wants," the cable said, reporting that two nephews of Mr. Ben Ali's had seized the yacht of a French businessman in 2006.

While the cable recounted routine demands for bribes by low-ranking government workers (the cost of a traffic stop, one Tunisian said, was up from 20 dinars to 40 or 50, or about $28 to $34), it said the flagrant thievery at the highest levels was most worrisome.

"Although the petty corruption rankles, it is the excesses of President Ben Ali's family that inspire outrage among Tunisians," the cable said. "With Tunisians facing rising inflation and high unemployment, the conspicuous displays of wealth and persistent rumors of corruption have added fuel to the fire."

Another cable, from July 2009, reported a "lavish" dinner of the American ambassador, Robert F. Godec, with Mr. Ben Ali's son-in-law, Mohamed Sakher el-Materi, in his beachfront home in Hammamet. There was "staff everywhere" and "ancient artifacts everywhere: Roman columns, frescoes and even a lion's head from which water pours into the pool," the cable said. The dinner included a dozen dishes, including ice cream and yogurt flown in from St. Tropez on the French Riviera.

"El Materi has a large tiger ('Pasha') on his compound, living in a cage," the ambassador reported. "He acquired it when it was a few weeks old. The tiger consumes four chickens a day. (Comment: The situation reminded the ambassador of Uday Hussein's lion cage in Baghdad.)," the cable added, referring to a son of Saddam Hussein.

The ambassador called the opulence of the evening "over the top," saying that his hosts' "behavior make clear why they and other members of Ben Ali's family are disliked and even hated by some Tunisians."

"The excesses of the Ben Ali family are growing," he added.

Some cables report how the "quasi mafia" of the country's ruling family muscled its way into the management of Tunisia's most profitable bank and how Mr. Ben Ali demanded a 50 percent share of a private university.

Others, however, make it clear just how much United States officials, preoccupied with the threat of terrorism in many other Muslim countries, valued Mr. Ben Ali's cooperation and ability to maintain order.

An upbeat August 2008 cable giving Condoleezza Rice, then the secretary of state, a survey of Tunisia before a visit reported that "Tunisia styles itself 'a country that works'." The writer added, "While Tunisians grumble privately about corruption by the first lady's family, there is an abiding appreciation for Ben Ali's success in steering his country clear of the instability and violence that have plagued Tunisia's neighbors."

The cable reported not only Tunisia's successes against terrorists but also its progressive social ways, calling it "a model for the region on women's rights."

Tunisian activists associated with the independent blog Nawaat.org (the core, in Arabic) created the TuniLeaks site on Nov. 28, the same day WikiLeaks, along with The New York Times and other news organizations, began posting the first of 251,287 confidential diplomatic cables the organization had obtained.

The Tunisian government subsequently tried to block access to the site, but the striking details of the cables circulated on Tunisian Web sites, adding to the ferment against Mr. Ben Ali.

On its Twitter feed, WikiLeaks has highlighted reports of its reported role in encouraging the Tunisian uprising. Foreign Policy magazine tagged the end of Mr. Ben Ali's rule "the first WikiLeaks revolution," and while that may be an overstatement, the cables' role in what President Obama lauded Friday as "this brave and determined struggle for the universal rights" underscores the awkward dilemma the WikiLeaks cables have posed for the administration.

Secretary of State Hillary Rodham Clinton has been pressing an "Internet Freedom" initiative, emphasizing the power of the Web to expose injustice and promote democracy. But at the same time, the Justice Department is conducting a criminal investigation of WikiLeaks and its founder,

Julian Assange, including using subpoenas to try to obtain the private Internet activity, credit card numbers and bank account details of Mr. Assange and his associates.

—This article was originally published on January 15, 2011

See diplomatic cable on p. 475.

CABLES SHOW
DELICATE U.S. DEALINGS
WITH EGYPT'S LEADERS

By MARK LANDLER and ANDREW W. LEHREN

WASHINGTON — It was Hillary Rodham Clinton's first meeting as secretary of state with President Hosni Mubarak, in March 2009, and the Egyptians had an odd request: Mrs. Clinton should not thank Mr. Mubarak for releasing an opposition leader from prison because he was ill.

In fact, a confidential diplomatic cable signed by the American ambassador to Egypt, Margaret Scobey, advised Mrs. Clinton to avoid even mentioning the name of the man, Ayman Nour, even though his imprisonment in 2005 had been condemned worldwide, not least by the Bush administration.

The cable is among a trove of dispatches made public by the antisecrecy group WikiLeaks that paint a vivid picture of the delicate dealings between the United States and Egypt, its staunchest Arab ally. They show in detail how diplomats repeatedly raised concerns with Egyptian officials about jailed dissidents and bloggers, and kept tabs on reports of torture by the police.

But they also reveal that relations with Mr. Mubarak warmed up because President Obama played down the public "name and shame" approach of the Bush administration. A cable prepared for a visit by Gen. David H. Petraeus in 2009 said the United States, while blunt in private, now avoided "the public confrontations that had become routine over the past several years."

This balancing of private pressure with strong public support for Mr. Mubarak has become increasingly tenuous in recent days. Throngs of angry Egyptians have taken to the streets and the White House, worried about being identified with a reviled regime, has challenged the president publicly.

On Thursday, Mr. Obama praised Mr. Mubarak as a partner but said he needed to undertake political and economic reforms. In an interview posted on YouTube, Mr. Obama said neither the police nor the protesters should resort to violence. "It is very important," he added, "that people have mechanisms in order to express legitimate grievances."

It is not known what Mrs. Clinton said to Mr. Mubarak in their first meeting, at the Red Sea resort of Sharm el Sheik. But she set the public tone afterward, when she was asked by an Arab television journalist about a State Department report critical of Egypt's human rights record.

"We hope that it will be taken in the spirit in which it is offered, that we all have room for improvement," Mrs. Clinton said, adding that Mr. Mubarak and his wife, Suzanne, were friends of her family, and that it was up to the Egyptian people to decide the president's future.

The cables, which cover the first year of the Obama presidency, leave little doubt about how valuable an ally Mr. Mubarak has been, detailing how he backed the United States in its confrontation with Iran, played mediator between Israel and the Palestinians and supported Iraq's fledgling government, despite his opposition to the American-led war.

Privately, Ambassador Scobey pressed Egypt's interior minister to free three bloggers, as well as a Coptic priest who performed a wedding for a Christian convert, according to one of her cables to Washington. She also asked that three American pro-democracy groups be granted formal permission to operate in the country, a request the Egyptians rejected.

However effusive the Americans were about Mr. Mubarak in public, the cables offered a less flattering picture of Egypt's first lady, Suzanne Mubarak. During a visit to the Sinai, one reported, she commandeered a bus that had been bought with money from the United States Agency for International Development and that had been meant to carry children to school.

Egyptian state security was concerned enough about American activities in Sinai, according to another cable, that it surreptitiously recorded a meeting between diplomats and members of a local council.

Yet many more of the cables describe collaboration between the United States and Egypt. In her 2009 visit, Mrs. Clinton was trying to revive the moribund peace talks between Israel and the Palestinians. Mr. Mubarak was central to this: the cables detail his efforts to broker a cease-fire between Israelis and the militant group Hamas in Gaza, as well as American pressure on him to curb the smuggling of weapons to Hamas from Egypt through tunnels.

Mrs. Clinton was also laying out Mr. Obama's rationale for engaging Iran—an overture, the cables report, that Mr. Mubarak predicted would fail. A May 2009 cable before Mr. Mubarak's first visit to the Obama White House noted that Egyptian officials told a visiting American diplomat, Dennis B. Ross, that "we should prepare for confrontation through isolation."

Like other Arab leaders, Mr. Mubarak is depicted in the cables as obsessed with Iran, which he told American diplomats was extending its tentacles from "the Gulf to Morocco" through proxies like Hamas and Hezbollah. He views these groups—particularly Hamas, a "brother" of Egypt's banned Muslim Brotherhood—as a direct threat to his own rule.

In a meeting with General Petraeus on June 29, 2009, Mr. Mubarak said the Iranian government wanted to establish "pockets" of influence inside Egypt, according to a cable. General Petraeus told him the United States was responding to similar fears among Persian Gulf states by deploying more Patriot missiles and upgrading its F-16 fighter jets stationed in the region.

Despite obvious American sympathy for Mr. Mubarak's security concerns, there is little evidence that the diplomats believed the president, now 82, was at risk of losing his grip on power. The May 2009 cable noted that riots over bread prices had broken out in Egypt in 2008 for the first time since 1977. And it said the growing influence of the Muslim Brotherhood had prompted the government to resort to "heavy-handed tactics against individuals and groups."

But the cable, again signed by Ambassador Scobey, portrayed Mr. Mubarak as the ultimate survivor, a "tried and true realist" who would rather "let a few individuals suffer than risk chaos for society as a whole."

"During his 28-year rule," the cable said, "he survived at least three assassination attempts, maintained peace with Israel, weathered two wars in Iraq and post-2003 regional instability, intermittent economic downturns, and a manageable but chronic internal terrorist threat."

Another cable, dated March 2009, offered a pessimistic analysis of the prospects for the "April 6 Movement," a Facebook-based group of mostly young Egyptians that has received wide attention for its lively political debate and helped mobilize the protests that have swept Egypt in the last two days. Leaders of the group had been jailed and tortured by the police. There were also signs of internal divisions between secular and Islamist factions, it said.

The United States has defended bloggers with little success. When Ambassador Scobey raised several arrests with the interior minister, he replied that Egypt did not infringe on freedom of the press, but that it must respond when "people are offended by blogs." An aide to the minister told the ambassador that The New York Times, which has reported on the treatment of bloggers in Egypt, was "exaggerating the blogger issue," according to the cable.

American diplomats also cast a wide net to gather information on police brutality, the cables show. Through contacts with human rights lawyers, the embassy follows numerous cases, and raised some with the Interior Ministry. Among the most harrowing, according to a cable, was the treatment of several members of a Hezbollah cell detained by the police in late 2008.

Lawyers representing the men said they were subjected to electric shocks and sleep deprivation, which reduced them to a "zombie state." They said the torture was more severe than what they normally witnessed.

To the extent that Mr. Mubarak has been willing to tolerate reforms, the cable said, it has been in areas not related to public security or stability. For example, he has given his wife latitude to campaign for women's rights and against practices like female genital mutilation and child labor, which are sanctioned by some conservative Islamic groups.

Still, Mr. Mubarak generally views broader reforms as an invitation to extremism. "We have heard him lament the results of earlier U.S. efforts to encourage reform in the Islamic world," said a cable, noting that he often invoked the shah of Iran—a secular leader who came under pressure from Washington, only to be replaced by an even more repressive, hostile government.

Even the private encounters with Mr. Mubarak have layers of sensitivity. While Mrs. Clinton was advised to steer clear of mentioning Ayman Nour, the cable signed by Ambassador Scobey suggested she might broach the topic of Saad Eddin Ibrahim, an Egyptian-American author and critic of Mr. Mubarak who fled Egypt after being found guilty of defaming the country.

"If you have any one-on-one opportunity with President Mubarak," the ambassador wrote, "you may wish to suggest that annulling these cases and allowing him to return to Egypt would also be well received by the new administration."

It is not clear whether Mrs. Clinton did so.

—This article was originally published on January 27, 2011

CABLES DEPICT
AFGHAN GRAFT,
STARTING AT TOP

By SCOTT SHANE, MARK MAZZETTI and DEXTER FILKINS

WASHINGTON—From hundreds of diplomatic cables, Afghanistan emerges as a looking-glass land where bribery, extortion and embezzlement are the norm and the honest official is a distinct outlier.

Describing the likely lineup of Afghanistan's new cabinet last January, the American Embassy noted that the agriculture minister, Asif Rahimi, "appears to be the only minister that was confirmed about whom no allegations of bribery exist."

One Afghan official helpfully explained to diplomats the "four stages" at which his colleagues skimmed money from American development projects: "When contractors bid on a project, at application for building permits, during construction, and at the ribbon-cutting ceremony." In a seeming victory against corruption, Abdul Ahad Sahibi, the mayor of Kabul, received a four-year prison sentence last year for "massive embezzlement." But a cable from the embassy told a very different story: Mr. Sahibi was a victim of "kangaroo court justice," it said, in what appeared to be retribution for his attempt to halt a corrupt land-distribution scheme.

It is hardly news that predatory corruption, fueled by a booming illicit narcotics industry, is rampant at every level of Afghan society. Transparency International, an advocacy organization that tracks government corruption around the globe, ranks Afghanistan as the world's third most corrupt country, behind Somalia and Myanmar.

But the collection of confidential diplomatic cables obtained by WikiLeaks and made available to a number of publications, offers a fresh sense of its pervasive nature, its overwhelming scale, and the dispiriting challenge it poses to American officials who have made shoring up support for the Afghan government a cornerstone of America's counterinsurgency strategy in Afghanistan.

The cables make it clear that American officials see the problem as beginning at the top. An August 2009 report from Kabul complains that President Hamid Karzai and his attorney general "allowed dangerous individuals to go free or re-enter the battlefield without ever facing an Afghan court." The embassy was particularly concerned that Mr. Karzai pardoned five border police officers caught with 124 kilograms (about 273 pounds) of heroin and intervened in a drug case involving the son of a wealthy supporter.

The American dilemma is perhaps best summed up in an October 2009 cable sent by Ambassador Karl W. Eikenberry, written after he met with Ahmed Wali Karzai, the president's half brother, the most powerful man in Kandahar and someone many American officials believe prospers from the drug trade. (Mr. Karzai denies any involvement with narcotics trafficking.)

"The meeting with AWK highlights one of our major challenges in Afghanistan: how to fight corruption and connect the people to their government, when the key government officials are themselves corrupt," Ambassador Eikenberry wrote.

American officials seem to search in vain for an honest partner. A November 2009 cable described the acting governor of Khost Province, Tahir Khan Sabari, as "a refreshing change," an effective and trustworthy leader. But Mr. Sabari told his American admirers that he did not have "the $200,000-300,000 for a bribe" necessary to secure the job permanently.

Ahmed Zia Massoud held the post of first vice president from 2004 to 2009; the brother of the Northern Alliance leader Ahmed Shah Massoud, he was discussed as a future president. Last year, a cable reported, Mr. Massoud was caught by customs officials carrying $52 million in unexplained cash into the United Arab Emirates.

A diplomatic cable is not a criminal indictment, of course, and in an interview Mr. Massoud denied taking any money out of Afghanistan. "It's not true," he said. "Fifty-two million dollars is a pile of money as big as this room." Yet while his official salary was a few hundred dollars a month, he lives in a waterfront house on Palm Jumeirah, a luxury Dubai community that is also home to other Afghan officials. When a reporter visited the dwelling this year, a Rolls-Royce was parked out front.

The cables describe a country where everything is for sale. The Transportation Ministry collects $200 million a year in trucking fees, but only

$30 million is turned over to the government, according to a 2009 account to diplomats by Wahidullah Shahrani, then the commerce minister. As a result, "individuals pay up to $250,000 for the post heading the office in Herat, for example, and end up owning beautiful mansions as well as making lucrative political donations," said Mr. Shahrani, who also identified 14 of Afghanistan's governors as "bad performers and/or corrupt."

Then again, another cable reports "rumors" that Mr. Shahrani himself "was involved in a corrupt oil import deal." He denied the rumors, saying that they were inventions by two rivals who were "among the most corrupt in Afghanistan," the cable said.

Pity the diplomat who must sort out whose version of reality to believe. One cable reported the American ambassador's attempt to size up Mr. Shahrani, who later became the minister of mines. "Ambassador Eikenberry noted Shahrani's extravagant home, suggesting that the Afghans knew best who is corrupt," the cable said.

The cables lay out allegations of bribes and profit-skimming in the organization of travel to Saudi Arabia for the hajj, or pilgrimage; in a scheme to transfer money via cellphones; in the purchase of wheat seed; in the compilation of an official list of war criminals; and in the voting in Parliament.

Dr. Sayed Fatimie, the minister of health, told diplomats in January that members of Parliament wanted cash to confirm his appointment. "Expressing shock at the blatancy of these extortion attempts, Fatimie said MPs had offered their own votes and the votes of others they could purportedly deliver for $1,000 apiece," a cable said.

The case of the Kabul mayor, Mr. Sahibi, shows how complicated it can be to sort out corruption charges. A Jan. 7 cable signed by Ambassador Eikenberry gave an account sharply at odds with media reports, which treated the prosecution as a landmark in the campaign for honest government.

The cable, referring to embassy interviews with Mr. Sahibi, said the charges against him were based on a decision to lease a piece of city property to shopkeepers. Three months after the lease was signed, another bidder offered $16,000 more. The "loss" of the potential additional revenue became the "massive embezzlement" described by prosecutors, the cable said.

Mr. Sahibi told the Americans he had been summoned to appear in court on Dec. 7 to be assigned a hearing date. Instead, he said, he was given a four-year sentence and a $16,000 fine.

As for the motive behind his prosecution, Mr. Sahibi said that in less than two years as mayor "he had found files for approximately 32,000 applicants who paid for nonexistent plots of land in Kabul." He said he halted the program and "invalidated the illegal claims of some important people," who took their revenge with the bogus criminal case.

The embassy cable largely supported Mr. Sahibi's version of events, saying that the mayor's "official decision may have antagonized powerful people who then sought the power of the state to discredit him." Far from being a blow against corruption, the cable suggested, the case was a travesty of justice.

The widespread corruption is made possible in part by a largely unregulated banking infrastructure and the ancient hawala money transfer network that is the method of choice for politicians, insurgents and drug traffickers to move cash around the Muslim world.

Last year, a cable signed by Ambassador Eikenberry said that the hawala favored by the Afghan elite, New Ansari, "is facilitating bribes and other wide-scale illicit cash transfers for corrupt Afghan officials" and providing financial services to narco-traffickers through front companies in Afghanistan and the United Arab Emirates. He asked Washington to send more investigators and wiretap analysts to assist nascent Afghan task forces that were examining New Ansari.

The anticorruption task forces already faced significant obstacles. For instance, Afghanistan's interior minister asked that the American government "take a low profile on the New Ansari case" to avoid the perception that investigations were being carried out "at the behest of the United States."

Months later, when the New Ansari investigators carried out a predawn raid on the house of a top aide to President Karzai whom investigators heard soliciting a bribe on a wiretap, Mr. Karzai intervened to release the man from jail and threatened to take control of the anticorruption investigations. In November, the Afghan government dropped all charges against the aide.

The resulting standoff between Kabul and Washington forced the Obama administration to take stock of its strategy: was trying to root out corruption, at the risk of further alienating Mr. Karzai, really worth it? And with American troops set to begin leaving Afghanistan next summer, and the American public having long ago lost the appetite for nation-building, was trying to root out corruption a Sisyphean task?

In September, President Obama acknowledged the dilemma. "Are there going to be occasions where we look and see that some of our folks on the ground have made compromises with people who are known to have engaged in corruption?" he asked. "There may be occasions where that happens."

A February cable described exactly such a compromise, reporting on a police chief at a border crossing in southern Afghanistan, Col. Abdul Razziq, who was reputed to be corrupt—and good at his job.

Western officials, it said, "walk a thin tightrope when working with this allegedly corrupt official who is also a major security stabilizing force."

Scott Shane and Mark Mazzetti reported from Washington, and Dexter Filkins from Kabul, Afghanistan. Andrew W. Lehren contributed reporting from New York.

—This article was originally published on December 2, 2010

CABLES OFFER SHIFTING PORTRAIT OF KARZAI

By HELENE COOPER and CARLOTTA GALL

WASHINGTON—Oman's foreign minister says that he is "losing confidence" in him. A British diplomat says Britain feels "deep frustration" with him, while an Australian official complains that he "ignores reality." A diplomat from the United Arab Emirates says Afghanistan would be better off without him. NATO's secretary general speculates that he has a split personality.

The portrait of President Hamid Karzai of Afghanistan that emerges from a cache of confidential American diplomatic cables obtained by WikiLeaks and made available to a number of news organizations reflects his trajectory from the eager leader anointed by the West to an embattled politician who often baffles, disappoints or infuriates his official allies.

American and foreign diplomats have tried to keep their complaints about Mr. Karzai private. But now, thanks to the cables, there is a more official chronicling—brutally candid views of Mr. Karzai recorded by State Department officials after high-level meetings, detailing the steady deterioration in his reputation in the nine years since he took office.

For the Obama administration, the disclosure of the cables—dating from 2004 to 2009—could exacerbate an already fraught relationship, one that began as lukewarm, turned frigid and is back to lukewarm, mostly because the administration sees no alternative to working with Mr. Karzai.

Lt. Gen. Karl W. Eikenberry, the retired Army officer who became the American ambassador to Afghanistan in April 2009, was blunt about his criticisms in a July 2009 cable. "It remains to be seen whether Karzai can or will refrain from this 'blame America' tactic he uses to deflect criticism of his administration," he wrote. "Indeed, his inability to grasp the most rudimentary principles of state-building and his deep seated insecurity as a leader combine to make any admission of fault unlikely, in turn confounding our best efforts to find in Karzai a responsible partner."

Mr. Karzai's plunge in global opinion, as documented in the cables, almost directly mirrors the fortunes of the United States and its NATO allies in Afghanistan. The leader described early on is an optimistic, proactive figure, filled with helpful suggestions and gratitude for the Western alliance that liberated his country from the Taliban.

"Karzai was upbeat," said one cable from the American Embassy in Kabul in February 2006. "Karzai repeated several times that he was much more confident about the current security situation than he was at this time last year, and characterized himself as a 'relatively happy man.'" Mr. Karzai, the cable continued, emphasized that NATO needed to "complete the win" that is "ours for the taking this year."

He also knew how to schmooze. In early cables, Mr. Karzai comes off as dashing, smooth and cosmopolitan, ready to flatter American officials with bon mots about country music and Starbucks coffee.

A Nov. 24, 2005, cable, in which Mr. Karzai is described as offering a rosy assessment of the war, also recounts how he chatted with visiting members of Congress from Washington.

"President Karzai was gracious and made frequent reference to his fondness for the U.S.," the cable said. "Karzai recounted how much he had enjoyed partaking of turkey and celebrating Thanksgiving." The message continued, "The Congressmen and President Karzai closed the meeting with some banter about exporting pomegranates to the U.S. and making them part of the traditional Thanksgiving feast."

Even General Eikenberry, who in 2007 was leaving his post as the commander in Afghanistan, had glowing things to say about the early Karzai. "President Karzai is a more confident commander in chief and chief executive," he is described as telling Pervez Musharraf, then Pakistan's leader, who is known to have loathed Mr. Karzai, in a January 2007 cable from the American Embassy in Islamabad. General Eikenberry said Mr. Karzai had replaced "corrupt poor-performing officials."

"Reconstruction assistance is taking root in districts throughout the country," he added.

But a different man emerges in the later cables. To be certain, Mr. Karzai was presiding over a country riven by tribal tensions, a growing insurgency, warring politicians and a populace increasingly suspicious of the American troops on their soil. Still, his American and NATO critics perhaps were reflecting both disappointment in the progress of the war against the Taliban and indignation that the man they put in charge was no longer toeing the line.

One British diplomat said as much, as reported in an October 2008 cable from the American Embassy in London, which gave a readout of meetings between Pentagon officials and their British counterparts. According to the cable, John Day, then the policy director of the British Defense Ministry, told Eric Edelman, a Pentagon official, that his government felt "deep frustration" with Mr. Karzai, adding that "I remind people that we—the international community—selected him."

By 2009, General Eikenberry, the newly appointed American ambassador to Afghanistan, also had clearly soured on the Afghan leader. In a cable in July of that year, he said Mr. Karzai was "often agitated, accusing the U.S. of working against him." The American diplomat matter-of-factly portrayed his weekly visits with Mr. Karzai as tiresome battles to keep the Afghan leader from going off on wild tangents.

"When Karzai drifted towards a reiteration of his anti-U.S. conspiracy theories on several occasions, I was able to refocus the conversation on how the U.S. and Afghanistan governments can work together in the near and medium term to achieve combined success," General Eikenberry wrote at one point. (A few months later, he wrote his now famous leaked confidential cable complaining that Mr. Karzai was not an "adequate strategic partner" for the United States in Afghanistan.)

Meanwhile, James B. Steinberg, Mr. Obama's deputy secretary of state, characterized Mr. Karzai as "indecisive and unprepared" during a meeting with the British ambassador to Washington, according to a February 2009 cable. And Mr. Edelman, a top Pentagon policy official in the Bush administration, told a group of NATO officials in 2008 that Mr. Karzai was "eager to divert attention to Pakistan as a source of all of Afghanistan's problems."

Mr. Karzai first burst onto the international stage in the style of Che Guevara, slipping over the Afghan border from Pakistan in 2001 as United States forces pounded the Taliban, before being installed by the West. President George W. Bush invited him to his first State of the Union speech after Sept. 11, 2001, where Mr. Karzai sat in the audience as a symbol of heroes who emerged from the terrorist attacks.

But just a few years later, the Bush administration and NATO countries in Afghanistan were grappling with the problems of Mr. Karzai that are now widely known—his personal insecurity and lack of trust in the United States, his falling popularity at home, his failure to combat the booming narcotics trade and corruption, and his seeming inability to run an effective government.

His relationship with the United States, the cables show, has been one of constant support and reassurance from the United States that it would remain in Afghanistan even after its troops withdrew, but also relentless pressure on President Karzai to follow an American agenda, whether on relations with Pakistan, counternarcotics or corruption. The friction points include his half brother, Ahmed Wali Karzai, whom, the cables show, Western officials suspect of benefiting from drug trafficking, charges Ahmed Wali Karzai denies.

There are no cables available from 2010, as Mr. Karzai's relationship with the West has become even more strained: in a speech this spring, he threatened to join the Taliban.

To the diplomats who deal with him, Mr. Karzai is a querulous ally at best, the cables make clear. In one June 2008 cable, American Embassy staff members in Brussels dutifully recorded—and sent back to Washington—musings from Jaap de Hoop Scheffer, then NATO's secretary general, about whether there were two Mr. Karzais.

"SecGen wondered aloud which Karzai would show up for the Afghan Donors Conference in Paris—the erratic Pashtun politician or the rational national leader," the cable said.

Helene Cooper reported from Washington, and Carlotta Gall from Kabul, Afghanistan. Andrew W. Lehren contributed reporting from New York.

—This article was originally published on December 2, 2010
See diplomatic cable on p. 419.

NUCLEAR FUEL MEMOS EXPOSE WARY DANCE WITH PAKISTAN

By JANE PERLEZ, DAVID E. SANGER and ERIC SCHMITT

ISLAMABAD, Pakistan—Less than a month after President Obama testily assured reporters in 2009 that Pakistan's nuclear materials "will remain out of militant hands," his ambassador here sent a secret message to Washington suggesting that she remained deeply worried.

The ambassador's concern was a stockpile of highly enriched uranium, sitting for years near an aging research nuclear reactor in Pakistan. There was enough to build several "dirty bombs" or, in skilled hands, possibly enough for an actual nuclear bomb.

In the cable, dated May 27, 2009, the ambassador, Anne W. Patterson, reported that the Pakistani government was yet again dragging its feet on an agreement reached two years earlier to have the United States remove the material.

She wrote to senior American officials that the Pakistani government had concluded that "the 'sensational' international and local media coverage of Pakistan's nuclear weapons made it impossible to proceed at this time." A senior Pakistani official, she said, warned that if word leaked out that Americans were helping remove the fuel, the local press would certainly "portray it as the United States taking Pakistan's nuclear weapons."

The fuel is still there.

It may be the most unnerving evidence of the complex relationship—sometimes cooperative, often confrontational, always wary—between America and Pakistan nearly 10 years into the American-led war in Afghanistan. The cables, obtained by WikiLeaks and made available to a number of news organizations, make it clear that underneath public reassurances lie deep clashes over strategic goals on issues like Pakistan's support for the Afghan

Taliban and tolerance of Al Qaeda, and Washington's warmer relations with India, Pakistan's archenemy.

Written from the American Embassy in Islamabad, the cables reveal American maneuvering as diplomats try to support an unpopular elected government that is more sympathetic to American aims than is the real power in Pakistan, the army and intelligence agency so crucial to the fight against militants. The cables show just how weak the civilian government is: President Asif Ali Zardari told Vice President Joseph R. Biden Jr. that he worried that the military might "take me out."

Frustration at American inability to persuade the Pakistani Army and intelligence agency to stop supporting the Afghan Taliban and other militants runs through the reports of meetings between American and Pakistani officials.

That frustration preoccupied the Bush administration and became an issue for the incoming Obama administration, the cables document, during a trip in January 2009 that Mr. Biden made to Pakistan 11 days before he was sworn in. In a meeting with Gen. Ashfaq Parvez Kayani, the army chief of staff, Mr. Biden asked several times whether Pakistan and the United States "had the same enemy as we move forward."

"The United States needs to be able to make an objective assessment of Pakistan's part of the bargain," Mr. Biden said, according to a Feb. 6, 2009, cable.

General Kayani tried to reassure him, saying, "We are on the same page in Afghanistan, but there might be different tactics." Mr. Biden replied that "results" would test that.

The cables reveal at least one example of increased cooperation, previously undisclosed, under the Obama administration. Last fall, the Pakistani Army secretly allowed 12 American Special Operations soldiers to deploy with Pakistani troops in the violent tribal areas near the Afghan border.

The Americans were forbidden to conduct combat missions. Even though their numbers were small, their presence at army headquarters in Bajaur, South Waziristan and North Waziristan was a "sea change in thinking," the embassy reported.

The embassy added its usual caution: The deployments must be kept secret or the "Pakistani military will likely stop making requests for such assistance."

Within the past year, however, Pakistan and the United States have gingerly started to publicly acknowledge the role of American field advisers. Lt. Col. Michael Shavers, an American military spokesman in Islamabad, said in a statement that "at the request of the Pakistanis," small teams of Special Operations forces "move to various locations with their Pakistani military counterparts throughout Pakistan."

Moreover, last week in a report to Congress on operations in Afghanistan, the Pentagon said that the Pakistani Army had also accepted American and coalition advisers in Quetta.

The cables do not deal with the sharp increase under Mr. Obama in drone attacks against Al Qaeda and the Taliban in the tribal areas with Pakistan's tacit approval. That is because the cables are not classified at the highest levels.

A Deep Skepticism

Over all, though, the cables portray deep skepticism that Pakistan will ever cooperate fully in fighting the full panoply of extremist groups. This is partly because Pakistan sees some of the strongest militant groups as insurance for the inevitable day that the United States military withdraws from Afghanistan—and Pakistan wants to exert maximum influence inside Afghanistan and against Indian intervention.

Indeed, the consul general in Peshawar wrote in 2008 that she believed that some members of the Haqqani network—one of the most lethal groups attacking American and Afghan soldiers—had left North Waziristan to escape drone strikes. Some family members, she wrote, relocated south of Peshawar; others lived in Rawalpindi, where senior Pakistani military officials also live.

In one cable, Ms. Patterson, a veteran diplomat who left Islamabad in October after a three-year stint as ambassador, said more money and military assistance would not be persuasive. "There is no chance that Pakistan will view enhanced assistance levels in any field as sufficient compensation for abandoning support for these groups, which it sees as an important part of its national security apparatus against India."

In a rare tone of dissent with Washington, she said Pakistan would only dig in deeper if America continued to improve ties with India, which she said "feeds Pakistani establishment paranoia and pushes them closer to both Afghan and Kashmir focused terrorist groups."

The groups Ms. Patterson referred to were almost certainly the Haqqani network of the Afghan Taliban and Lashkar-e-Taiba, a group financed by Pakistan in the 1 990s to fight India in Kashmir that is accused of the 2008 terrorist attacks in Mumbai, India.

The highly enriched uranium that Ms. Patterson wanted removed from the research reactor came from the United States in the mid-1960s. In those days, under the Atoms for Peace program, little thought was given to proliferation, and Pakistan seemed too poor and backward to join the nuclear race.

But by May 2009, all that had changed, and her terse cable to the State and Defense Departments, among others, touched every nerve in the fraught relationship: mutual mistrust, the safety of the world's fastest-growing nuclear arsenal, broken promises and a pervasive fear that any talk about Pakistan's vulnerability would end whatever cooperation existed.

The reactor had been converted to use low-enriched uranium, well below bomb grade, in 1990, according to the International Atomic Energy Agency, or I.A.E.A. But the bomb-grade uranium had never been returned to the United States and remains in storage nearby. Ms. Patterson's cable noted that Pakistan had "agreed in principle to the fuel removal in 2007."

But time and again the Pakistanis balked, and she reported that an interagency group within the Pakistani government had decided to cancel a visit by American technical experts to get the fuel out of the country. She concluded that "it is clear that the negative media attention has begun to hamper U.S. efforts to improve Pakistan's nuclear security and nonprolif-eration practices."

Any progress, she suggested, would have to await a "more conducive" political climate.

On Monday, Pakistan's Foreign Affairs Ministry issued a statement confirming that "the US suggestion to have the fuel transferred was plainly refused by Pakistan." It said that the United States had provided the fuel but did not mention that, under the terms of such transfers, the United States retained the right to have the spent fuel returned.

The ambassador's comments help explain why Mr. Obama and his aides have expressed confidence in Pakistan's nuclear security when asked in public. But at the beginning of the administration's review of its Afghani-stan and Pakistan strategy, a highly classified intelligence report delivered to Mr. Obama said that while Pakistan's weapons were well secured, there was deep, continuing concern about "insider access," meaning elements in the military or intelligence services.

In fact, Ms. Patterson, in a Feb. 4, 2009, cable, wrote that "our major concern is not having an Islamic militant steal an entire weapon but rather the chance someone working in GOP [government of Pakistan] facilities could gradually smuggle enough material out to eventually make a weapon."

Mr. Obama's review concluded by determining that there were two "vital" American interests in the region. One was defeating Al Qaeda. The second, not previously reported, was making sure terrorists could never gain access to Pakistan's nuclear program. That goal was classified, to keep from angering Islamabad.

Asked about the status of the fuel at the research reactor, Damien LaVera, a spokesman for the National Nuclear Security Administration of the Energy Department, said, "The United States supplied Pakistan with fuel for a research reactor decades ago for the purpose of producing medical isotopes and scientific research." Implicitly acknowledging that the material remains there, Mr. LaVera said "the fuel is under I.A.E.A. safeguards and has not been part of Pakistan's nuclear weapons program."

One secret cable offers another glimpse into another element of the nuclear gamesmanship between the United States and its Pakistani allies: Even while American officials were trying to persuade Pakistani officials to give up nuclear material, they were quietly seeking to block Pakistan from trying to buy material that would help it produce tritium, the crucial ingredient needed to increase the power of nuclear weapons.

After providing specific details of the proposed sale, a Dec. 12, 2008, secret cable to the American Embassy in Singapore, seeking help to stop a transaction that was about to take place, concluded, "We would have great concern over Pakistan's potential use of tritium to advance its nuclear weapons program."

Reports of Army Abuses

The cables also reveal that the American Embassy had received credible reports of extrajudicial killings of prisoners by the Pakistani Army more than a year before the Obama administration publicly acknowledged the problem and before a video that is said to show such killings surfaced on the Internet.

The killings are another source of tension, complicated by American pressure on Pakistan to be more aggressive in confronting militants on its own soil.

In a Sept. 10, 2009, cable labeled "secret/noforn," meaning that it was too delicate to be shared with foreign governments, the embassy confronted allegations of human rights abuses in the Swat Valley and the tribal areas since the Pakistani Army had begun fighting the Taliban a few months earlier.

While carefully worded, the cable left little doubt about what was going on. It spoke of a "growing body of evidence" that gave credence to the allegations.

"The crux of the problem appears to center on the treatment of terrorists detained in battlefield operations and have focused on the extrajudicial killing of some detainees," the cable said. "The detainees involved were in the custody of Frontier Corps or Pakistan army units." The Frontier Corps is a paramilitary force partly financed by the United States to fight the insurgents.

The Pakistani Army was holding as many as 5,000 "terrorist detainees," the cable said, about twice as many as the army had acknowledged.

Concerned that the United States should not offend the Pakistani Army, the cable stressed that any talk of the killings must be kept out of the press.

"Post advises that we avoid comment on these incidents to the extent possible and that efforts remain focused on dialogue and the assistance strategy," the ambassador wrote. This September, however, the issue exploded into public view when a video emerged showing Pakistani soldiers executing six unarmed young men in civilian clothes. In October, the Obama administration suspended financing to half a dozen Pakistani Army units believed to have killed civilians or unarmed prisoners.

The cables verge on gossipy, as diplomats strained to understand the personalities behind the fractious Pakistani government, and particularly two men: General Kayani and President Zardari.

Often, the United States finds that Mr. Zardari, the accidental leader after the assassination of his wife, Benazir Bhutto, is sympathetic to American goals—stiff sanctions on terrorist financing, the closing down of terrorist training camps—but lacks the power to fulfill his promises against resistance from the military and intelligence agencies.

Mr. Zardari's chief antagonist, General Kayani, emerges as a stubborn guarantor of what he sees as Pakistan's national interest, an army chief who meddles in civilian politics but stops short of overturning the elected order.

Early in the Obama administration, General Kayani made clear a condition for improved relations. As the director general of the Directorate for Inter-Services Intelligence, or ISI, from 2004 to 2007, he did not want a "reckoning with the past," said a cable in 2009 introducing him to the new administration.

"Kayani will want to hear that the United States has turned the page on past ISI operations," it said. General Kayani was probably referring to the peace accords with the Taliban from 2004 to 2007 that resulted in the strengthening of the militants.

If the general seems confidently in charge, the cables portray Mr. Zardari as a man not fully aware of his weakness.

At one point he said he would not object if Abdul Qadeer Khan, revered in Pakistan as the father of its nuclear weapons program, were interviewed by the International Atomic Energy Agency but tacitly acknowledged that he was powerless to make that happen.

Mr. Zardari, who spent 11 years in prison on ultimately unproved corruption charges, feared for his position and possibly—the wording is ambiguous—his life: the cables reveal that Vice President Biden told Prime Minister Gordon Brown of Britain in March 2009 that Mr. Zardari had told him that the "ISI director and Kayani will take me out."

His suspicions were not groundless. In March 2009, a period of political turmoil, General Kayani told the ambassador that he "might, however reluctantly," pressure Mr. Zardari to resign and, the cable added, presumably leave Pakistan. He mentioned the leader of a third political party, Asfandyar Wali Khan, as a possible replacement.

"Kayani made it clear regardless how much he disliked Zardari he distrusted Nawaz even more," the ambassador wrote, a reference to Nawaz Sharif, a former prime minister.

By 2010, after many sessions with Mr. Zardari, Ms. Patterson had revised the guarded optimism that characterized her early cables about Mr. Zardari.

"Pakistan's civilian government remains weak, ineffectual and corrupt," she wrote on Feb. 22, 2010, the eve of a visit by the F.B.I. director,

Robert S. Mueller III. "Domestic politics is dominated by uncertainty about the fate of President Zardari."

That assessment holds more than eight months later, even as Mr. Obama in October extended an invitation to Mr. Zardari to visit the White House next year, as the leader of a nation that holds a key to peace in Afghanistan but appears too divided and mistrustful to turn it for the Americans.

Jane Perlez reported from Islamabad, and David E. Sanger and Eric Schmitt from Washington. William J. Broad and Andrew W. Lehren contributed reporting from New York.

—This article was originally published on November 30, 2010

U.S. OPPOSED RELEASE
OF NUCLEAR DEALER

By DAVID E. SANGER

WASHINGTON—In early 2008, when rumors floated that Pakistan was about to release from house arrest Abdul Qadeer Khan, the man who created the world's largest black market in nuclear technology, the Bush administration stayed silent.

Struggling to get Pakistan's help in the war against Al Qaeda, it could not risk reminding the world of a case Pakistani officials kept saying was closed.

In private, it was a different story.

Richard A. Boucher, the top State Department official for South Asia, wrote on April 10, 2008, that the embassy in Islamabad should "express Washington's strong opposition to the release of Dr. Khan and urge the Government of Pakistan to continue holding him under house arrest." Releasing him, he wrote, would "undermine" what Pakistan had done to fight proliferation.

"The damage done to international security by Dr. Khan and his associates is not a closed book," he wrote, noting that the United States and others were still dealing with the Khan network's sale of technology to Iran and North Korea "and possible other states."

The world, he said, was dealing "with the reality that the uranium enrichment technology and nuclear weapons designs that were sold to Libya are now available to other states and non-state actors."

Dr. Khan was released 10 months later. Pakistan has barred him from being interviewed by international inspectors or the United States, including about his allegation that others in the Pakistani government knew of his work.

—This article was originally published on November 30, 2010

VAST HACKING BY A CHINA FEARFUL OF THE WEB

By JAMES GLANZ and JOHN MARKOFF

As China ratcheted up the pressure on Google to censor its Internet searches last year, the American Embassy sent a secret cable to Washington detailing one reason top Chinese leaders had become so obsessed with the Internet search company: they were Googling themselves.

The May 18, 2009, cable, titled "Google China Paying Price for Resisting Censorship," quoted a well-placed source as saying that Li Changchun, a member of China's top ruling body, the Politburo Standing Committee, and the country's senior propaganda official, was taken aback to discover that he could conduct Chinese-language searches on Google's main international Web site. When Mr. Li typed his name into the search engine at google.com, he found "results critical of him."

That cable from American diplomats was one of many made public by WikiLeaks that portray China's leadership as nearly obsessed with the threat posed by the Internet to their grip on power—and, the reverse, by the opportunities it offered them, through hacking, to obtain secrets stored in computers of its rivals, especially the United States.

Extensive hacking operations suspected of originating in China, including one leveled at Google, are a central theme in the cables. The operations began earlier and were aimed at a wider array of American government and military data than generally known, including on the computers of United States diplomats involved in climate change talks with China.

One cable, dated early this year, quoted a Chinese person with family connections to the elite as saying that Mr. Li himself directed an attack on Google's servers in the United States, though that claim has been called into question. In an interview with The New York Times, the person cited in the cable said that Mr. Li personally oversaw a campaign against Google's operations in China but the person did not know who directed the hacking attack.

The cables catalog the heavy pressure that was placed on Google to comply with local censorship laws, as well as Google's willingness to comply —up to a point. That coercion began building years before the company finally decided to pull its search engine out of China last spring in the wake of the successful hacking attack on its home servers, which yielded Chinese dissidents' e-mail accounts as well as Google's proprietary source code.

The demands on Google went well beyond removing material on subjects like the Dalai Lama or the 1989 Tiananmen Square massacre. Chinese officials also put pressure on the United States government to censor the Google Earth satellite imaging service by lowering the resolution of images of Chinese government facilities, warning that Washington could be held responsible if terrorists used that information to attack government or military facilities, the cables show. An American diplomat replied that Google was a private company and that he would report the request to Washington but that he had no sense about how the government would act.

Yet despite the hints of paranoia that appear in some cables, there are also clear signs that Chinese leaders do not consider the Internet an unstoppable force for openness and democracy, as some Americans believe.

In fact, this spring, around the time of the Google pullout, China's State Council Information Office delivered a triumphant report to the leadership on its work to regulate traffic online, according to a crucial Chinese contact cited by the State Department in a cable in early 2010, when contacted directly by The Times.

The message delivered by the office, the person said, was that "in the past, a lot of officials worried that the Web could not be controlled."

"But through the Google incident and other increased controls and surveillance, like real-name registration, they reached a conclusion: the Web is fundamentally controllable," the person said.

That confidence may also reflect what the cables show are repeated and often successful hacking attacks from China on the United States government, private enterprises and Western allies that began by 2002, several years before such intrusions were widely reported in the United States.

At least one previously unreported attack in 2008, code-named Byzantine Candor by American investigators, yielded more than 50 megabytes of e-mails and a complete list of user names and passwords from an American government agency, a Nov. 3, 2008, cable revealed for the first time.

Precisely how these hacking attacks are coordinated is not clear. Many appear to rely on Chinese freelancers and an irregular army of "patriotic hackers" who operate with the support of civilian or military authorities, but not directly under their day-to-day control, the cables and interviews suggest.

But the cables also appear to contain some suppositions by Chinese and Americans passed along by diplomats. For example, the cable dated earlier this year referring to the hacking attack on Google said: "A well-placed contact claims that the Chinese government coordinated the recent intrusions of Google systems. According to our contact, the closely held operations were directed at the Politburo Standing Committee level."

The cable goes on to quote this person as saying that the hacking of Google "had been coordinated out of the State Council Information Office with the oversight" of Mr. Li and another Politburo member, Zhou Yongkang." Mr. Zhou is China's top security official.

But the person cited in the cable gave a divergent account. He detailed a campaign to press Google coordinated by the Propaganda Department's director, Liu Yunshan. Mr. Li and Mr. Zhou issued approvals in several instances, he said, but he had no direct knowledge linking them to the hacking attack aimed at securing commercial secrets or dissidents' e-mail accounts—considered the purview of security officials.

Still, the cables provide a patchwork of detail about cyberattacks that American officials believe originated in China with either the assistance or knowledge of the Chinese military.

For example, in 2008 Chinese intruders based in Shanghai and linked to the People's Liberation Army used a computer document labeled "salary increase—survey and forecast" as bait as part of the sophisticated intrusion scheme that yielded more than 50 megabytes of e-mails and a complete list of user names and passwords from a United States government agency that was not identified.

The cables indicate that the American government has been fighting a pitched battle with intruders who have been clearly identified as using Chinese-language keyboards and physically located in China. In most cases the intruders took great pains to conceal their identities, but occasionally they let their guard down. In one case described in the documents, investigators tracked one of the intruders who was surfing the Web in Taiwan "for personal use."

In June 2009 during climate change talks between the United States and China, the secretary of state's office sent a secret cable warning about e-mail "spear phishing" attacks directed at five State Department employees in the Division of Ocean Affairs of the Office of the Special Envoy for Climate Change.

The messages, which purport to come from a National Journal columnist, had the subject line "China and Climate Change." The e-mail contained a PDF file that was intended to install a malicious software program known as Poison Ivy, which was meant to give an intruder complete control of the victim's computer. That attack failed.

The cables also reveal that a surveillance system dubbed Ghostnet that stole information from the computers used by the exiled Tibetan spiritual leader, the Dalai Lama, and South Asian governments and was uncovered in 2009 was linked to a second broad series of break-ins into American government computers code-named Byzantine Hades. Government investigators were able to make a "tenuous connection" between those break-ins and the People's Liberation Army.

The documents also reveal that in 2008 German intelligence briefed American officials on similar attacks beginning in 2006 against the German government, including military, economic, science and technology, commercial, diplomatic, and research and development targets. The Germans described the attacks as preceding events like the German government's meetings with the Chinese government.

Even as such attacks were occurring, Google made a corporate decision in 2006, controversial even within the company, to establish a domestic Chinese version of its search engine, called google.cn. In doing so, it agreed to comply with China's censorship laws.

But despite that concession, Chinese officials were never comfortable with Google, the cables and interviews show.

The Chinese claimed that Google Earth, the company's satellite mapping software, offered detailed "images of China's military, nuclear, space, energy and other sensitive government agency installations" that would be an asset to terrorists. A cable sent on Nov. 7, 2006, reported that Liu Jieyi, an assistant minister of foreign affairs, warned the American Embassy in Beijing that there would be "grave consequences" if terrorists exploited the imagery.

A year later, another cable pointed out that Google searches for politically delicate terms would sometimes be automatically redirected to Baidu, the Chinese company that was Google's main competitor in China. Baidu is known for scrubbing its own search engine of results that might be unwelcome to government censors.

Google conducted numerous negotiations with officials in the State Council Information Office and other departments involved in censorship, propaganda and media licensing, the cables show. The May 18, 2009, cable that revealed pressure on the company by Mr. Li, the propaganda chief, said Google had taken some measures "to try and placate the government." The cable also noted that Google had asked the American government to intervene with China on its behalf.

But Chinese officials became alarmed that Google still did less than its Chinese rivals to remove material Chinese officials considered offensive. Such material included information about Chinese dissidents and human rights issues, but also about central and provincial Chinese leaders and their children—considered an especially taboo topic, interviews with people quoted in the cables reveal.

Mr. Li, after apparently searching for information online on himself and his children, was reported to have stepped up pressure on Google. He also took steps to punish Google commercially, according to the May 18 cable.

The propaganda chief ordered three big state-owned Chinese telecommunications companies to stop doing business with Google. Mr. Li also demanded that Google executives remove any link between its sanitized Chinese Web site and its main international one, which he deemed "an illegal site," the cable said.

Google ultimately stopped complying with repeated censorship requests. It stopped offering a censored version of its search engine in China earlier this year, citing both the hacking attacks and its unwillingness to continue obeying censorship orders.

James Glanz reported from New York, and John Markof from San Francisco. Andrew W. Lehren contributed reporting from New York.

—This article was originally published on December 4, 2010
See diplomatic cable on p. 446.

CHINA RESISTED
U.S. PRESSURE ON RIGHTS
OF NOBEL WINNER

By MICHAEL WINES

BEIJING—It was just before Christmas 2009, and Ding Xiaowen was not happy.

The United States ambassador had just written China's foreign minister expressing concern for Liu Xiaobo, the Beijing intellectual imprisoned a year earlier for drafting a pro-democracy manifesto. Now Mr. Ding, a deputy in the ministry's American section, was reading the riot act to an American attaché.

Mr. Ding said he would try to avoid "becoming emotional," according to a readout on the meeting that was among thousands of leaked State Department cables released this month. Then he said that a "strongly dissatisfied" China firmly opposed the views of the American ambassador, Jon Huntsman, and that Washington must "cease using human rights as an excuse to 'meddle' in China's internal affairs."

On Friday, exactly one year after Mr. Huntsman wrote his protest, Mr. Liu, now serving an 11-year prison sentence for subversion, will receive the Nobel Peace Prize in a ceremony that he is unable to attend. And if anything is clear, it is that China no longer resists becoming emotional.

In the two months since the Nobel committee honored Mr. Liu, China has waged an extraordinary and unprecedented campaign, domestically and internationally, to discredit the award and to dissuade other governments from endorsing it.

It sent diplomats to capitals worldwide, sometimes to two and three offices, to warn that attendance at the awards ceremony in Oslo would be a black mark on relations with China. It staged a briefing for its neighbors, the 10 members of the Association of Southeast Asian Nations, to make clear its unhappiness with the award. It has punished Norway, the site of the ceremony, by suspending trade negotiations.

On the Chinese island of Hainan last month, State Councilor Dai Bingguo, China's most powerful foreign policy figure, bluntly told Secretary of State Hillary Rodham Clinton that his government regarded the Nobel award as an American conspiracy to embarrass Beijing.

Perhaps most strikingly, China's media and spokespeople have trained a stream of vitriol on the award and its sponsors. The prize is "an anti-China farce" and its sponsors are "clowns," a Foreign Ministry spokeswoman, Jiang Yu, said this week at a briefing. Honoring Mr. Liu is "a crazy act," "a political tool" and "a trick that a few radical people use to entertain themselves," the Communist Party tabloid Global Times reported Wednesday.

On Oct. 15, after the award was announced, the state-run news service Xinhua called the Nobel decision "a desecration of the rule of law" and Mr. Liu an opportunist who had "tried his best to maintain the Western hegemony of his Western masters and make China a vassal of the West."

And on Tuesday, a somewhat murky Beijing group announced a counter-Nobel, the Confucius Peace Prize, apparently in response to a Global Times commentary last month that called for an Eastern alternative to prizes based on values it said were Western.

At least 19 governments, most of them staunch China allies like Myanmar, North Korea and Russia, have decided to boycott the Nobel ceremony on Friday. But the list also includes the Philippines, whose president, Benigno S. Aquino III, has been an advocate of human rights in places like Myanmar, where China holds great influence.

Philippine press reports quoted diplomats on Wednesday as saying that Manila opted out of the ceremony because it did not want to annoy China, already angered over a bungled hostage rescue in August that left eight Hong Kong residents dead.

But a senior adviser to Mr. Aquino, who spoke on condition of anonymity because he was not authorized to speak on the matter, said that Foreign Secretary Alberto G. Romulo "did it without telling us." The adviser called the move "a clumsy attempt to balance the administration's more distant stance on China."

"This administration will be a voice for human rights in this part of the world," the official said, "and now, this."

Why China's leaders have made Mr. Liu's award a foreign policy red line is far from clear. Political analysts and scholars variously suggested that Mr. Liu's manifesto, Charter 08, was too radical and represented a threat, that China's newfound global prominence had given it an oversize impression of its influence and that party leaders were toeing a hard nationalist position as jockeying began for a new leadership in 2012.

Dozens of leaked State Department cables made it apparent that American diplomats closely followed the travails of Mr. Liu and other activists and regularly pressed Chinese officials to honor international norms for basic freedoms, even as Washington muted its public position on Chinese behavior.

Embassy officials also met frequently with Mr. Liu's wife, Liu Xia, and friends to monitor his case and the increase in repression of political dissidents.

As early as two weeks after Mr. Liu was first detained, President George W. Bush's ambassador, Clark T. Randt Jr., "urged the Chinese government to release him and stop harassing peaceful dissidents," a Dec. 29, 2008, cable stated.

The next June, as the Chinese government announced Mr. Liu's formal arrest on subversion charges, embassy officials expressed "grave concern" and again called for his release. On Dec. 9, 2009, shortly before Mr. Liu was convicted, Mr. Huntsman met with five Chinese human rights lawyers; he sent a letter to the foreign minister the next day calling on the government "to respect those rights it had itself guaranteed in the PRC constitution and to protect internationally recognized freedoms for all Chinese citizens."

That letter led to Mr. Ding's dressing-down of the attaché 11 days later. According to the cable, Mr. Ding said then that Mr. Huntsman's letter contained "inappropriate comments" on Mr. Liu's case and that "certain 'so-called' human rights lawyers and dissidents had sought to advance their 'selfish interests' " by attacking the Beijing government.

"In a lengthy and disjointed digression," the cable added, Mr. Ding said that regardless of rights to speak and assemble freely, the most fundamental human rights were to food and shelter. And "in this area it was 'a basic fact' that the PRC had made huge progress."

The American attaché's response, the cable stated, was that "U.S. concerns over abuses of internationally recognized human rights norms remained."

Carlos H. Conde contributed reporting from Manila, and Seth Mydans from Bangkok. Li Bibo contributed research from Beijing.

—This article was originally printed on December 8, 2010

NORTH KOREA KEEPS
THE WORLD GUESSING

By DAVID E. SANGER

WASHINGTON—With North Korea reeling from economic and succession crises, American and South Korean officials early this year secretly began gaming out what would happen if the North, led by one of the world's most brutal family dynasties, collapsed.

Over an official lunch in late February, a top South Korean diplomat confidently told the American ambassador, Kathleen Stephens, that the fall would come "two to three years" after the death of Kim Jong-il, the country's ailing leader, Ms. Stephens later cabled Washington. A new, younger generation of Chinese leaders "would be comfortable with a reunited Korea controlled by Seoul and anchored to the United States in a benign alliance," the diplomat, Chun Yung-woo, predicted.

But if Seoul was destined to control the entire Korean Peninsula for the first time since the end of World War II, China—the powerful ally that keeps the North alive with food and fuel—would have to be placated. So South Korea was already planning to assure Chinese companies that they would have ample commercial opportunities in the mineral-rich northern part of the peninsula.

As for the United States, the cable said, "China would clearly 'not welcome' any U.S. military presence north of the DMZ," the heavily mined demarcation line that now divides the two Koreas.

This trove of cables ends in February, just before North Korea began a series of military actions that has thrown some of Asia's most prosperous countries into crisis. A month after the lunch, the North is believed to have launched a torpedo attack on the Cheonan, a South Korean warship, that killed 46 sailors.

Three weeks ago it revealed the existence of a uranium enrichment plant, potentially giving it a new pathway to make nuclear bomb material.

And last week it shelled a South Korean island, killing two civilians and two marines and injuring many more.

None of that was predicted in the dozens of State Department cables about North Korea obtained by WikiLeaks, and in fact even China, the North's closest ally, has often been startlingly wrong, the cables show. But the documents help explain why some South Korean and American officials suspect that the military outbursts may be the last snarls of a dying dictatorship.

They also show that talk of the North's collapse may be rooted more in hope than in any real strategy: similar predictions were made in 1994 when the country's founder, Kim Il-sung, suddenly died, leaving his son to run the most isolated country in Asia. And a Chinese expert warned, according to an American diplomat, that Washington was deceiving itself once again if it believed that "North Korea would implode after Kim Jongil's death."

The cables about North Korea—some emanating from Seoul, some from Beijing, many based on interviews with government officials, and others with scholars, defectors and other experts—are long on educated guesses and short on facts, illustrating why their subject is known as the Black Hole of Asia. Because they are State Department documents, not intelligence reports, they do not include the most secret American assessments, or the American military's plans in case North Korea disintegrates or lashes out.

They contain loose talk and confident predictions of the end of the dynasty that has ruled North Korea for 65 years. Those discussions were fueled by a rash of previously undisclosed defections of ranking North Korean diplomats, who secretly sought refuge in the South.

But they were also influenced by a remarkable period of turmoil inside North Korea, including an economic crisis set off by the government's failed effort to revalue the currency and sketchy intelligence suggesting that the North's military might not abide the rise of Mr. Kim's son Kim Jong-un, who was recently made a four-star general despite having no military experience.

The cables reveal that in private, the Chinese, long seen as North Korea's last protectors against the West, occasionally provide the Obama administration with colorful assessments of the state of play in North Korea. Chinese officials themselves sometimes even laugh about the frustrations of dealing with North Korean paranoia. In April 2009, just before a North Korean nuclear test, He Yafei, the Chinese vice foreign minister, told American officials at a lunch that the country wanted direct talks with the United States and to get them was acting like a "spoiled child" to get the attention of the "adult."

When James B. Steinberg, the deputy secretary of state, sat down in September 2009 with one of China's most powerful officials, Dai Bingguo, state councilor for foreign affairs, Mr. Dai joked that in a recent visit to North Korea he "did not dare" to be too candid with the ailing and mercurial North Korean leader. But the Chinese official reported that although Kim Jong-il had apparently suffered a stroke and had obviously lost weight, he still had a "sharp mind" and retained his reputation among Chinese officials as "quite a good drinker." (Mr. Kim apparently assured Mr. Dai during a two-hour conversation in Pyongyang, the capital, that his infirmities had not forced him to give up alcohol.)

But reliable intelligence about Mr. Kim's drinking habits, it turns out, does not extend to his nuclear program, about which even the Chinese seem to be in the dark.

On May 13, 2009, as American satellites showed unusual activity at North Korea's nuclear test site, officials in Beijing said they were "unsure" that North Korean "threats of another nuclear test were serious." As it turns out, the North Koreans detonated a test bomb just days later.

Soon after, Chinese officials predicted that negotiations intended to pressure the North to disarm would be "shelved for a few months." They have never resumed.

The cables also show that almost as soon as the Obama administration came to office, it started raising alarms that the North was buying up components to enrich uranium, opening a second route for it to build nuclear weapons. (Until now, the North's arsenal has been based on its production of plutonium, but its production capacity has been halted.)

In June 2009, at a lunch in Beijing shortly after the North Korean nuclear test, two senior Chinese Foreign Ministry officials reported that China's experts believed "the enrichment was only in its initial phases." In fact, based on what the North Koreans revealed this month, an industrial-scale enrichment plant was already under construction. It was apparently missed by both American and Chinese intelligence services.

The cables make it clear that the South Koreans believe that internal tensions in the North have reached a boiling point. In January of this year, South Korea's foreign minister, who later resigned, reported to a visiting

American official that the South Koreans saw an "increasingly chaotic" situation in the North.

In confidence, he told the American official, Robert R. King, the administration's special envoy for North Korean human rights issues, that a number of "high-ranking North Korean officials working overseas" had recently defected to the South. Those defections were being kept secret, presumably to give American and South Korean intelligence agencies time to harvest the defectors' knowledge.

But the cables also reveal that the South Koreans see their strategic interests in direct conflict with China's, creating potentially huge diplomatic tensions over the future of the Korean Peninsula.

The South Koreans complain bitterly that China is content with the status quo of a nuclear North Korea, because they fear that a collapse would unleash a flood of North Korean refugees over the Chinese border and lead to the loss of a "buffer zone" between China and the American forces in South Korea.

At one point, Ambassador Stephens reported to Washington, a senior South Korean official told her that "unless China pushed North Korea to the 'brink of collapse,'" the North would refuse to take meaningful steps to give up its nuclear program.

Mr. Chun, now the South Korean national security adviser, complained to Ambassador Stephens during their lunch that China had little commitment to the multination talks intended to force North Korea to dismantle its nuclear arsenal. The Chinese, he said, had chosen Wu Dawei to represent Beijing at the talks. According to the cable, Mr. Chun called Mr. Wu the country's "'most incompetent official,' an arrogant, Marx-spouting former Red Guard who 'knows nothing about North Korea, nothing about non-proliferation.'"

But the cables show that when it comes to the critical issue of succession, even the Chinese know little of the man who would be North Korea's next ruler: Kim Jong-un.

As recently as February 2009, the American Consulate in Shanghai—a significant collection point for intelligence about North Korea—sent cables reporting that the Chinese who knew North Korea best disbelieved the rumors that Kim Jong-un was being groomed to run the country. Several Chinese scholars with good contacts in the North said they thought it was likely that "a group of high-level military officials" would take over, and that "at least for the moment none of KJI's three sons is likely to be tapped to succeed him." The oldest son was dismissed as "too much of a playboy," the middle son as "more interested in video games" than governing. Kim Jong-un, they said, was too young and inexperienced.

But within months, a senior Chinese diplomat, Wu Jianghao, was telling his American counterparts that Kim Jong-il was using nuclear tests and missile launchings as part of an effort to put his third son in place to succeed him, despite his youth.

"Wu opined that the rapid pace of provocative actions in North Korea was due to Kim Jong-il's declining health and might be part of a gambit under which Kim Jong-il would escalate tensions with the United States so that his successor, presumably Kim Jong-un, could then step in and ease those tensions," the embassy reported back to Washington in June 2009.

But carrying out plans for an easy ascension may be more difficult than expected, some are quoted as saying. In February of this year the American Consulate in Shenyang reported rumors that Kim Jong-un "had a hand" in the decision to revalue the North's currency, which wiped out the scarce savings of most North Koreans and created such an outcry that one official was executed for his role in the sudden financial shift. The cables also describe secondhand reports of palace intrigue in the North, with other members of the Kim family preparing to serve as regents to Kim Jong-un—or to unseat him after Kim Jong-il's death.

Andrew W. Lehren contributed reporting from New York.

—This article was originally printed on November 29, 2010

BELOW SURFACE,
U.S. HAS DIM VIEW
OF PUTIN AND RUSSIA

By C. J. CHIVERS

Early in 2009, as recession rippled around the world, the United States Embassy in Moscow sent to Washington a cable summarizing whispers within Russia's political class. Prime Minister Vladimir V. Putin, the rumors said, often did not show up at his office.

The embassy titled the cable "Questioning Putin's Work Ethic."

"There are consistent reports that Putin resents or resists the workload he carries," it said, citing Mr. Putin's "fatigue," "hands-off behavior" and "isolation" to the point that he was "working from home."

The cable, approved by the American ambassador, John R. Beyrle, assessed the Kremlin rumors not as indicators of Mr. Putin's weakness, but of the limits of his position in a period of falling commodity prices and tightening credit. Russia's most powerful man sat atop Russia's spoils. The recession left him with less to dole out, eroding "some of his Teflon persona."

"His disengagement reflects," the cable concluded, "his recognition that a sharp reduction in resources limits his ability to find workable compromises among the Kremlin elite."

Officially, the United States has sought since last year what President Obama and his Russian counterpart, Dmitri A. Medvedev, have called a "reset" in relations.

But scores of secret American cables from recent years, obtained by WikiLeaks and made available to several news organizations, show that beneath the public efforts at warmer ties, the United States harbors a dim view of the post-Soviet Kremlin and its leadership, and little hope that Russia will become more democratic or reliable.

The cables portray Mr. Putin as enjoying supremacy over all other Russian public figures, yet undermined by the very nature of the post-Soviet country he helped build.

Even a man with his formidable will and intellect is shown beholden to intractable larger forces, including an inefficient economy and an unmanageable bureaucracy that often ignores his edicts.

In language candid and bald, the cables reveal an assessment of Mr. Putin's Russia as highly centralized, occasionally brutal and all but irretrievably cynical and corrupt. The Kremlin, by this description, lies at the center of a constellation of official and quasi-official rackets.

Throughout the internal correspondence between the American Embassy and Washington, the American diplomats in Moscow painted a Russia in which public stewardship was barely tended to and history was distorted. The Kremlin displays scant ability or inclination to reform what one cable characterized as a "modern brand of authoritarianism" accepted with resignation by the ruled.

Moreover, the cables reveal the limits of American influence within Russia and an evident dearth of diplomatic sources. The internal correspondence repeatedly reflected the analyses of an embassy whose staff was narrowly contained and had almost no access to Mr. Putin's inner circle.

In reporting to Washington, diplomats often summarized impressions from meetings not with Russian officials, but with Western colleagues or business executives. The impressions of a largely well-known cadre of Russian journalists, opposition politicians and research institute regulars rounded out many cables, with insights resembling what was published in liberal Russian newspapers and on Web sites.

The cables sketched life almost 20 years after the Soviet Union's disintegration, a period, as the cables noted, when Mr. Medvedev, the prime minister's understudy, is the lesser part of a strange "tandemocracy" and "plays Robin to Putin's Batman." All the while, another cable noted, "Stalin's ghost haunts the Metro."

Government Corruption

In the secret American description, official malfeasance and corruption infect all elements of Russian public life—from rigging elections, to persecuting rivals or citizens who pose a threat, to extorting businesses.

The corruption was described as a drag on the nation of sufficient significance to merit the attention of Mr. Medvedev and Mr. Putin, who, paradoxically, benefited from cronies who orchestrate graft but support the Kremlin.

A cable describing the government and style of Yuri M. Luzhkov, then the mayor of Moscow, presented the puzzle.

Since 2008, Mr. Medvedev has been the face and cheerleader for the nation's supposed anti-corruption campaign. Yet a veritable kaleidoscope of corruption thrived in Moscow, much of it under the protection of a mayor who served at the president's pleasure.

The embassy wrote of a "three-tiered structure" in Moscow's criminal world, with the mayor at the top, the police and intelligence officials at the second tier and those regarded as a municipality's predators—"ordinary criminals and corrupt inspectors"—at the bottom.

In this world the government effectively was the mafia. Extortion was so widespread, the cable noted, that it had become the business of the Interior Ministry and the federal intelligence service, known by their initials in Russian, the M.V.D. and the F.S.B.

"Moscow business owners understand that it is best to get protection from the MVD and FSB (rather than organized crime groups) since they not only have more guns, resources and power than criminal groups, but they are also protected by the law," the cable noted, citing a Russian source. "For this reason, protection from criminal gangs is no longer so high in demand."

The cable further described a delicate balance.

On one hand, the prime minister and the president benefited from votes Mr. Luzhkov delivered to the country's ruling party, and perhaps from corruption that one embassy source said was so profligate that witnesses saw suitcases, presumably full of cash, being carried into the Kremlin under armed guard.

On the other, the corruption and a flagrantly rigged election in 2009 for the city's legislature had raised the question of whether Mr. Luzhkov was worth the trouble.

The cable ended on a prescient note. "Ultimately, the tandem will put Luzhkov out to pasture," it said. Eight months after this cable was written, Mr. Medvedev dismissed Mr. Luzhkov.

The embassy's consistent assessments left little hope that removing one person would be enough. Russian corruption, the cables said, was structural.

One foreign citizen, whom the embassy described as having "made a fortune in Russia's casino business," said in 2009 "that the 'levels of corruption in business were worse than we could imagine' and that after working here for over 15 years and witnessing first-hand the behavior of GOR [government of Russia] officials at all levels, he could not imagine the system changing."

The same cable noted that even if the government wanted to change it might not be able to, given that "in 2006—at the height of Putin's control in a booming economy—it was rumored within the Presidential Administration that as many as 60 percent of his orders were not being followed."

Secretive Business Deals

In Russia, the separation between the most important businesses and government officials runs from blurry to nonexistent. The cables rendered darkly how Russian companies—often relying on what one cable called "secretive deals involving intermediary companies with unknown owners and beneficiaries"—conducted their affairs.

The cables also detailed two separate but related concerns about Russia's oil and gas sectors: a lack of modern management and capital-improvement programs, and a tendency in Mr. Putin's circle to see energy resources as political levers.

One prominent Western oil executive told Ambassador Beyrle that the inefficiencies "are so huge" that "a well that would take ten days to drill in Canada would take 20" in Russia.

"Multiply that by hundreds or thousands and you can start to imagine the costs to the economy," the cable quoted the executive as saying.

The embassy's 2009 assessment of state-owned Gazprom, Russia's largest company, was similar. "Gazprom, it said, "must act in the interests of its political masters, even at the expense of sound economic decision-making."

The cables also showed how bureaucratic, national and economic power often all converged in the Kremlin, and how the state's suitors grasped that access often equaled results.

The summary of a meeting between an Italian and American diplomats in Moscow documented the Italian diplomat's exasperation with Mr. Putin and Silvio Berlusconi, Italy's prime minister, who had gained Russia's ear.

The diplomat said that the pair enjoyed such a close relationship that they shared a "direct line," and that the Italian Foreign Ministry and Embassy "only learn of conversations" between the premiers "after the fact, and with little detail or background."

The diplomat then "explained that while the close relationship is not ideal from the bureaucracy's perspective and more detrimental than beneficial, it can be useful at times.

"He cited," the cable added, "the case of the sale to Gazprom by Italian energy giant ENI of its 20 percent share in Gazprom's oil subsidiary Gazpromneft. He said Gazprom had insisted on paying far below the market price, but that it ultimately paid the market price after Berlusconi weighed in with Putin."

Other cables described how Western businesses sometimes managed to pursue their interests by personally engaging senior Russian officials, including President Medvedev, rather than getting lost in bureaucratic channels.

The experience in late 2009 of the Intel Corporation, which hoped to import 1,000 encrypted computers for its Russia offices, offered insights into the benefits of courting the top.

"Several high-level Intel officers, including CEO Craig Barrett, and other officials, such as American Chamber of Commerce President Andrew Somers, highlighted to the GOR interlocutors, including President Medvedev, the role Intel plays in employing over 1,000 Russian engineers," a cable said.

"This high-level lobbying secured Intel a meeting with key FSB officials to explain its needs," it continued. "Intel was able to demonstrate the reasonableness of its request and, as a result, by-passed the current extensive licensing requirement."

Chuck Mulloy, an Intel spokesman, said that the meetings were not about one shipment of computers; they created an expedited process for importing such equipment, not only for Intel but for their customers and distributors. "We didn't get this as a one-time thing," he said.

The cables further revealed how the nexus of business and state interests among Russia's ruling elite had fueled suspicions in Washington that Mr. Putin, in spite of his vigorous denials, had quietly amassed a personal fortune.

A confidential cable pointedly mentioned the Swiss oil-trading company Gunvor, as being "of particular note."

The company, the cable said, is "rumored to be one of Putin's sources of undisclosed wealth" and is owned by Gennadi N. Timchenko, who is "rumored to be a former K.G.B. colleague of Putin's." One estimate said the company might control half of Russian oil exports, potentially bringing its owners billions of dollars in profit.

Gunvor's profits were especially high, the cable claimed, because in one of the few deals in which details were known, a source said that the firm included a surcharge of $1 per barrel of oil. More competitive traders, the source said, might mark up a barrel by only a nickel.

The cables provide no evidence to support the allegations about Gunvor and Mr. Luzhkov, the former Moscow mayor; neither has been charged with any crimes.

Patience Unrewarded

If two words were to summarize the secret American assessment of its relations with the Kremlin, it would be these: suspicion and frustration.

A cornerstone of Washington's approach to the relationship has been patience. Privately, American diplomats have described the hope that by moderating public criticism of Russia and encouraging market principles, Russia's government and important companies might with time evolve.

The cables underscore how frustrating the patience has been.

A summary in November 2009 of the security dialogue between the United States and Russia coolly stated that in spite of warm words between Mr. Medvedev and Mr. Obama and the establishment of a new military-to-military working group, there remained "challenges in effecting real, substantive and ongoing" dialogue.

The Defense Ministry, the cable said "has not changed its modus operandi for information exchange nor routine dialoguing since the end of the Cold War."

Russian attendees at meetings, the cable said, "are closely monitored by their Military Intelligence (GRU) handlers," and are reluctant "to engage in any dialogues outside of tightly controlled statements recited from prepared texts."

When diplomats did meet Russian officials who chose to be candid, the message they heard was sometimes blunt.

In June 2009 a delegation of Washington analysts who were accompanied by diplomats met with Aleksandr Y. Skobeltsyn of Russia's Department for Military-Technical Cooperation to discuss American concerns about sales of anti-tank guided missiles and shoulder-launched antiaircraft missiles.

The latter are a special worry in the West, where security officials fear terrorists could fire them at passenger jets.

Mr. Skobeltsyn said that Russia "shared U.S. concerns about re-transfer vulnerabilities, noting that Latin America and Middle East were especially sensitive areas."

"But, he argued, if Russia did not provide these weapons to certain countries, then 'someone else' would."

Outright distrustful relations between the Kremlin and the Soviet Union's former vassals were also evident in the records. At an appearance in Washington in 2009, Foreign Minister Radoslaw Sikorski of Poland said that American forces would be welcome in Poland "to protect against Russian aggression."

The comment, unwelcomed by Russia and the United States alike, ignited a minor flare-up. In a cable after Mr. Sikorski's appearance, the American Embassy said that Poland had established a Bureau of European Security, which "Polish diplomats jokingly refer to as the 'Office of Threats from the East.'"

The back-channel quip eventually provided insight into the diplomatic climate in Moscow. A Polish official, formerly posted to Moscow, noted that Russia's Foreign Ministry "threw this moniker back at him during a meeting."

He told his American colleagues that the "only way" that Russia's Foreign Ministry could have known of the nickname "was to have been listening in on his phone conversations with Warsaw"—a clear suggestion that his office in Russia had been bugged.

Andrew W. Lehren contributed reporting.

—This article was originally published on December 1, 2010
See diplomatic cable on p. 495.

EMBRACING GEORGIA, U.S. MISREAD SIGNS OF RIFTS

By C. J. CHIVERS

Throughout the cold war and often in the years since, Western diplomats covering the Kremlin routinely relied on indirect and secondhand or third-hand sources. Their cables were frequently laden with skepticism, reflecting the authors' understanding of the limits of their knowledge and suspicion of official Russian statements.

A 2008 batch of American cables from another country once in the cold war's grip—Georgia—showed a much different sort of access. In Tbilisi, Georgia's capital, American officials had all but constant contact and an open door to President Mikheil Saakashvili and his young and militarily inexperienced advisers, who hoped the United States would help Georgia shake off its Soviet past and stand up to Russia's regional influence.

The Tbilisi cables, part of more than a quarter-million cables made available to news organizations by WikiLeaks, display some of the perils of a close relationship.

The cables show that for several years, as Georgia entered an esca-lating contest with the Kremlin for the future of Abkhazia and South Ossetia, two breakaway enclaves out of Georgian control that received Russian support, Washington relied heavily on the Saakashvili govern-ment's accounts of its own behavior. In neighboring countries, American diplomats often maintained their professional distance, and privately detailed their misgivings of their host governments. In Georgia, diplo-mats appeared to set aside skepticism and embrace Georgian versions of important and disputed events.

By 2008, as the region slipped toward war, sources outside the Geor-gian government were played down or not included in important cables. Official Georgian versions of events were passed to Washington largely unchallenged.

The last cables before the eruption of the brief Russian-Georgian war showed an embassy relaying statements that would with time be proved wrong.

"Deputy Minister of Defense Batu Kutelia told Ambassador at midday August 7 that Georgian military troops are on higher alert, but will not be deploying," one cable noted, as Georgian heavy military equipment was en route to the conflict zone.

Mr. Kutelia's assurance did not stand, even in real time. In one of the few signs of the embassy's having staff in the field, the cable noted that "embassy observers on the highway" saw about 30 government buses "carrying uniformed men heading north."

Still the embassy misread the signs, telling Washington that while there were "numerous reports that the Georgians are moving military equipment and forces," the embassy's "initial impressions" were that the Georgians "were in a heightened state of alertness to show their resolve."

In fact, Georgia would launch a heavy artillery-and-rocket attack on Tskhinvali, the South Ossetian capital, at 11:35 p.m. on Aug. 7, ending a cease-fire it had declared less than five hours before.

The bombardment plunged Georgia into war, pitting the West against Russia in a standoff over both Russian military actions and the behavior of a small nation that the United States had helped arm and train.

A confidential cable the next morning noted that Georgia's Foreign Ministry had briefed the diplomatic corps, claiming that "Georgia now controlled most of South Ossetia, including the capital." The cable further relayed that "Saakashvili has said that Georgia had no intention of getting into this fight, but was provoked by the South Ossetians and had to respond to protect Georgian citizens and territory."

Rather than emphasize the uncertainties, it added, "All the evidence available to the country team supports Saakashvili's statement that this fight was not Georgia's original intention." Then it continued: "Only when the South Ossetians opened up with artillery on Georgian villages" did the offensive begin.

This exceptionally bold claim would be publicly echoed throughout the Bush administration, which strongly backed Georgia on the world's stage. To support it, the American Embassy appeared to have no staff members in the field beyond "eyes on the ground at the Ministry of Interior command post" on Aug. 8. The cable did not provide supporting sources outside of the Georgian government. Instead, as justification for the Georgian attack the previous night, a Georgian government source, Temuri Yakobashvili, was cited as telling the American ambassador that "South Ossetians continued to shoot at the Georgian villages despite the announcement of the cease-fire."

The cable contained no evidence that the Ossetian attacks after the cease-fire had actually occurred and played down the only independent account, which came from military observers in Tskhinvali from the Organization for Security and Cooperation in Europe.

The observers, in the heart of the conflict zone, did not report hearing or seeing any Ossetian artillery attacks in the hours before Georgia bombarded Tskhinvali. Rather, they reported to an American political officer that "the Georgian attack on Tskhinvali began at 2335 on Aug. 7 despite the cease-fire."

Nonetheless, the American cable, relying on Georgian government sources, offered as "one plausible explanation for all this" that South Ossetia's leader, Eduard Kokoity, had "decided to roll the dice and stimulate a conflict with the Georgians in hopes of bringing in the Russians and thereby saving himself."

It was not Mr. Kokoity who would require saving. On Aug. 9, as Russian forces flowed into Georgia, a cable noted that "President Saakashvili told the Ambassador in a late morning phone call that the Russians are out to take over Georgia and install a new regime."

Still the reliance on one-sided information continued—including Georgian exaggerations of casualties and Mr. Saakashvili's characterization of Russian military actions.

The Saakashvili government was publicly insisting that its bombardments of Tskhinvali were justified and precise. But an American cable noted that when Russian ordnance landed on the Georgian city of Gori, Mr. Saakashvili took a different view of the meaning of heavy weapons attacks in civilian areas. He called the Russian attacks "pure terror."

By then the West and Russia were mostly talking past each other, and Georgia's American-trained military had been humiliated in the field and was fleeing the fight.

A few weeks later, after a more stable cease-fire had been negotiated and at a time when the American economy was sliding into a recession, President George W. Bush announced a $1 billion aid package to help Georgia rebuild.

Andrew W. Lehren contributed reporting.

—This article was originally published on December 1, 2010

CABLES SHED LIGHT ON EX-K.G.B. OFFICER'S DEATH

By ALAN COWELL

LONDON—Shortly after the radiation poisoning in London of a former K.G.B. officer, Alexander V. Litvinenko, a senior Russian official asserted that Moscow had been tailing his killers before he died but had been waved off by Britain's security services, according to a cable in the trove of secret American documents released by WikiLeaks.

The Russian assertion, denied by British officials, seemed to revive a theory that the British intelligence services played a murky role in the killing—a notion voiced at the time by some in Moscow to deflect allegations of the Kremlin's involvement in the murder.

The cable, dated Dec. 26, 2006, and marked "secret," was one of several in the WikiLeaks trove that tried to examine the still unanswered question of who exactly ordered the use of a rare radioactive isotope, polonium 210, to poison Mr. Litvinenko, leading to his death on Nov. 23, 2006. Russia produces polonium commercially, but the process is closely guarded and British investigators have concluded that the isotope could not have been easily diverted without high-level intervention.

In a telephone interview, Marina Litvinenko, the widow of the former K.G.B. officer, called the Russian assertion "disinformation."

"When they prepared this, they never expected polonium would be known as a murder weapon," she said. "But after Nov. 23, they needed some kind of disinformation."

She said that "polonium could not be used without very high level" involvement of the security services.

A separate cable from Paris suggested that at least one senior American official, Daniel Fried, seemed skeptical of statements by Vladimir V. Putin—then Russia's president and now prime minister—that he was unaware of the events leading to the killing, which Britain has blamed on another former K.G.B. officer, Andrei K. Lugovoi.

Mr. Lugovoi, now a member of the Russian Parliament, has denied British charges that he murdered Mr. Litvinenko by slipping polonium into a teapot at a British hotel where the two men met on Nov. 1, 2006. Russia has refused a British request for Mr. Lugovoi's extradition and the relationship between two countries has not fully recovered from deep strains after Mr. Litvinenko's death.

Among several cables mentioning the affair, perhaps the most sensitive covers a meeting in Paris on Dec. 7, 2006, between an American ambassador at large, Henry Crumpton, and Anatoly Safonov, at the time a special representative of Mr. Putin.

That encounter had a whiff of an espionage film script. The two met over a dinner described as "amicable." Both men were veterans of their countries' intelligence services, and were now assigned by their governments to cooperate in counterterrorism.

Mr. Crumpton had led the C.I.A.'s operation in Afghanistan after the Sept. 11, 2001, attacks. Mr. Safonov was a former K.G.B. colonel-general who had risen to high office as deputy director in its successor organization, the F.S.B., in the 1990s, according to Andrei Soldatov, a Russian journalist who has just published a study of that organization called "The New Nobility."

One of Mr. Safonov's subsequent assignments in the 2000s was to head a joint British-Russian counterterrorism group, which was dissolved in the diplomatic freeze provoked by Mr. Litvinenko's death, Mr. Soldatov said in a telephone interview.

According to the leaked cable, "Safonov claimed that Russian authorities in London had known about and followed individuals moving radioactive substances into the city, but were told by the British that they were under control before the poisoning took place."

The cable did not identify the people carrying the material. Mr. Safonov's comments reflected allegations by Mr. Lugovoi who, at the time, accused Mr. Litvinenko of being in the pay of British intelligence. But Mr. Safonov's remarks seemed likely to be taken by British officials as an accusation of incompetence, with the poisoning happening under their eyes. If confirmed, they would also raise the question of how Britain reacted to the idea of Russian spies tailing their citizens on British soil.

The question of who ordered the killing surfaced in a separate leaked cable, also marked "secret," about a meeting in Paris—on the same day as the former spies' dinner—between a French presidential adviser, Maurice

Gourdault-Montagne and Mr. Fried, then the assistant secretary of state for European and Eurasian affairs in the Bush administration. Mr. Fried is now the Guantánamo special envoy, appointed by President Obama and charged with persuading other countries to take detainees held at the prison in Cuba.

The French official, the cable said, ascribed the killing to "rogue elements" in the Russian security services. But Mr. Fried "commented that the short-term trend inside Russia was negative, noting increasing indications that the U.K. investigation into the murder of Litvinenko could well point to some sort of Russian involvement."

Later, it said: "Fried, noting Putin's attention to detail, questioned whether rogue security elements could operate, in the U.K. no less, without Putin's knowledge. Describing the current atmosphere as strange, he described the Russians as increasingly self-confident, to the point of arrogance."

Mr. Fried's reported remark was the first time that such a suggestion by a serving American officer was made public.

That remark reflected some suspicions about high-level Kremlin involvement in the period after Mr. Litvinenko's death, when conspiracy theories blossomed relating to Mr. Litvinenko's activities as a visceral public enemy of Mr. Putin and as a whistle-blower on Russian organized crime. Mr. Litvinenko fled Russia in 2000 and sought asylum in Britain, where he acquired British citizenship shortly before his death.

Mr. Fried declined to comment publicly on the content of the cable.

Another cable, from the American Embassy in Madrid, marked "confidential" and dated Aug. 31, 2009, cited an article in the newspaper El País. The article said that Mr. Litvinenko had tipped off Spanish security officials about Russian organized crime figures in Spain and had provided information about four suspected gangsters at a previously unrecorded meeting with Spanish officials in May 2006.

That report added one more layer to the debate about the motives of his killers—could the killing have been done in revenge for his disclosures about the mob?

Perhaps the most tantalizing item in the cables was related to Dmitri Kovtun, a business associate of Mr. Lugovoi, who passed through Hamburg on his way to London on Nov. 1 and was, by his own account, present when Mr. Lugovoi met Mr. Litvinenko at the Millennium Hotel in the Mayfair district of London on Nov. 1, 2006.

According to a confidential cable from the American consulate in Hamburg, dated Dec. 19, 2006—about a month after Mr. Litvinenko's death—a senior German counterterrorism official, Gerhard Schindler, "said Kovtun left polonium traces on everything he touched" in Hamburg. That much had been publicly reported.

But, the cable said, "German investigators concluded Kovtun did not have polonium traces on his skin or clothes; Schindler said the polonium was coming out of his body, for example through his pores."

That suggested that the exposure took place during an earlier visit to London by Mr. Lugovoi and Mr. Kovtun in October 2006, during which they had met Mr. Litvinenko; they claimed later that they themselves had been victims of a poisoning attempt. Mr. Litvinenko's supporters and British investigators, however, have long described the earlier visit as a part of the conspiracy against Mr. Litvinenko.

The cable from Hamburg said no traces of polonium were found on the Germanwings plane Mr. Kovtun took to London, and German authorities had been preparing to ground the Aeroflot plane that took him to Hamburg from Moscow to test it for traces of the isotope. "Schindler said Russian authorities must have found out about German plans because 'at the last minute' Aeroflot swapped planes," the cable said. "Schindler said he did not expect Aeroflot to fly the other plane to Germany any time soon."

Andrew W. Lehren contributed reporting from New York, Cliford J. Levy from Moscow and Scott Shane from Washington.

—This article was originally published on December 20, 2010

NATO BALANCED BALTIC AND RUSSIAN ANXIETIES

By SCOTT SHANE

WASHINGTON—When fighting broke out between Russia and Georgia in August 2008, a shudder passed through the former Soviet Baltic republics.

Estonia, Latvia and Lithuania had painful memories of Soviet occupation and feared that a resurgent Russia might come after them next. They began lobbying NATO, which they had joined in 2004, for a formal defense plan.

But the request was a delicate one for NATO, an alliance obligated by treaty to respond to an attack on one member as an attack on all. NATO leaders had repeatedly declared that post-Soviet Russia was not a threat, and the incoming Obama administration wanted to pursue what it called a "reset" of relations with Russia.

Cables obtained by WikiLeaks and provided to several news organizations chronicle the secret diplomacy that followed, culminating in a NATO decision in January to expand a defense plan for Poland to cover the three Baltic states. That expanded plan, called Eagle Guardian, is now in place, American officials say.

The Russia-Georgia clash, with television images of Russian armor on the move and tough talk from Moscow, terrified the Baltic republics, which had been occupied by the Soviet Army in 1940 and achieved independence a half-century later.

"Events in Georgia have dominated the news and discussion here like few other events in recent memory," a cable from the American Embassy in Riga, Latvia, reported as the fighting raged in Georgia. Latvians, at least ethnic Latvians, it said, "look at Georgia and think that this could easily be them."

The cable added that "so far, the U.S. willingness to take a tough line in opposition to Russian actions and in support of Georgia has been well received here, but some key figures are asking if the west is fully prepared to deal with a resurgent Russia."

The embassy reported that Latvians were gathering for candlelight vigils outside the Georgian Embassy, Georgian flags were on display around Riga, and sales of Georgian wine and mineral water were up.

With significant ethnic Russian minorities, all three Baltic states were alarmed by Russia's public explanation that it had gone into Georgia to protect the rights of Russian citizens there. Some Latvian leaders said they needed to do more to integrate ethnic Russians into the local culture. Wealthy Latvian businessmen, worried about endangering lucrative deals with Russia, appealed for moderation in the criticism of their giant neighbor.

By October 2009, a cable reported that "leaders in Estonia, Latvia, and Lithuania are pressing hard for NATO Article 5 contingency planning for the Baltic states," referring to the mutual defense provision of the NATO treaty. The cable noted that President Obama had expressed support for such planning.

But the cable, signed by the American ambassador to NATO, Ivo H. Daalder, noted the awkwardness of squaring Baltic worries with closer NATO-Russia ties.

"The Baltic states clearly believe that the Russian Federation represents a future security risk and desire a contingency plan to address that risk. And therein lies the problem," the cable said. "Post-Cold War NATO has consistently said that it no longer views Russia as a threat."

Indeed, during the Bush administration, NATO had accepted the former Soviet republics as members but had avoided including them in defense planning, which might have provoked Russia.

Now, Germany proposed expanding the Poland defense plan to the Baltic states, and NATO planners began their work. The Latvians expressed "profound happiness" at the decision, and an Estonian official called it an "early Christmas present," according to two cables. But American officials urged Baltic officials to keep such talk secret.

"A public discussion of contingency planning would also likely lead to an unnecessary increase in NATO-Russia tensions, something we should try to avoid as we work to improve practical cooperation in areas of common NATO-Russia interest," a December cable told NATO member states.

In January, with the plan approved, a cable signed by Secretary of State Hillary Rodham Clinton advised NATO members to stonewall press inquiries about the details of Baltic defense. (Baltic news organizations have reported on the defense plans in recent months.)

But the cable did suggest a talking point to reassure Russia. "NATO planning is an internal process designed to make the Alliance as prepared as possible for future contingencies," the cable said. "It is not 'aimed' at any other country."

—This article was originally published on December 6, 2010

CABLES PRAISE FRENCH FRIEND WITH 'MERCURIAL' SIDE

By KATRIN BENNHOLD

PARIS—President Nicolas Sarkozy is an unusually solid French friend of America. He is also a "mercurial" man operating in "a zone of monarch-like impunity" surrounded by advisers often too fearful to give honest counsel, according to leaked cables from the United States Embassy in Paris.

Last December, the American ambassador shared an anecdote with Secretary of State Hillary Rodham Clinton: when the mayor of Paris had the Eiffel Tower lighted in Turkey's national colors for a visit by Prime Minister Recep Tayyip Erdogan in April 2009, aides to Mr. Sarkozy, a staunch opponent of Turkey's entry to the European Union, rerouted the presidential plane so he would not see it.

"Élysée contacts have reported to us the great lengths they will go to avoid disagreeing" with Mr. Sarkozy "or provoking his displeasure," said the cable, signed by Ambassador Charles H. Rivkin. It was part of a trove of documents obtained by WikiLeaks and made available to several news organizations.

Five years of correspondence between Paris and Washington chronicle a spectacular post-Iraq turnabout between one of the West's most complicated diplomatic couples. Mr. Sarkozy, who took office in May 2007, was described even last year as "the most pro-American French president since World War II" and a "force multiplier" for American foreign policy interests.

But the cables also convey a nuanced assessment of the French leader as a somewhat erratic figure with authoritarian tendencies and a penchant for deciding policy on the fly. By January 2010, American diplomats wrote of a high-maintenance ally sometimes too impatient to consult with crucial partners before carrying out initiatives, one who favors summit meetings and direct contacts over traditional diplomacy.

Writing to Mrs. Clinton on Dec. 4, 2009, Mr. Rivkin spoke of the need to channel Mr. Sarkozy's "impulsive proposals into constructive directions." Concessions on thorny issues like Afghanistan would be best won by President Obama himself, he suggested.

"In my opinion, it will necessitate periodic presidential intervention to reassure Sarkozy of our commitment as an ally and partner and, in many cases, to close the deal," he wrote.

The French president's office declined to comment, though on Tuesday Mr. Sarkozy told cabinet ministers that the release of the documents was "the height of irresponsibility."

Paul Patin, an American Embassy spokesman, said Tuesday: "President Sarkozy has proved, time and time again, that he is a true friend of the U.S. France is one of our closest allies, and our partnership has only gotten stronger during his presidency."

In general, few foreign policy disagreements surface between France and the United States under Mr. Sarkozy. A major difference, however, concerns Turkey, with Washington a fervent supporter of Turkey's ambition to join the European Union and fretful that Mr. Sarkozy's opposition threatens to "antagonize a strategic ally."

The delight among American diplomats at the arrival of a self-professed pro-American candidate after years of difficult relations with Jacques Chirac was evident in correspondence well before Mr. Sarkozy's election.

In 2005, Mr. Sarkozy, then the interior minister, told Craig R. Stapleton, then the American ambassador, that although he would have advised against the Iraq invasion he still felt it "personally when American soldiers die in combat." Mr. Sarkozy said he took it as a personal responsibility that "no U.S. Embassy or Consulate was so much as touched" in anti-American protests.

"Very much unlike nearly all other French political figures, Sarkozy is viscerally pro-American," said a cable signed by Mr. Stapleton. "For most of his peers, the U.S. is a sometimes reviled or admired, but decidedly foreign, other. Sarkozy identifies with America; he sees his own rise in the world as reflecting an American-like saga."

If Mr. Sarkozy's Atlanticist outlook was never doubted—even in the most recent leaked cable from Jan. 25 this year, French-American relations are called "one of the best"—concerns about a "thin-skinned, authoritarian" streak surfaced by October 2007, as he divorced his second wife, Cécilia. Two months later, diplomats spoke of Mr. Sarkozy's "unprecedented" concentration of power over foreign affairs and "increasing willingness to downgrade human rights considerations in his dealings with foreign leaders."

Praised for leadership during the 2008 Russia-Georgia war and the global financial crisis, Mr. Sarkozy was criticized by European diplomats referred to in a cable for an "increasingly erratic" last half of his 2008 European Union presidency.

A year later, when two scandals sank Mr. Sarkozy's approval ratings, American diplomats started telling Washington that the president lacked advisers willing to question him. One scandal involved a cabinet member and the other the promotion of the president's son, Jean, then 23, to lead France's most prestigious business district. "Combined, these stories have bolstered the impression that Sarkozy is operating in a zone of monarch-like impunity," said an Oct. 21, 2009, cable.

In December 2009, Mr. Rivkin told Mrs. Clinton: "Sarkozy's own advisers likewise demonstrate little independence and appear to have little effect on curbing the hyperactive president, even when he is at his most mercurial." He added: "After two years in office, many seasoned key Élysée staff are leaving for prestigious onward assignments as a reward for their hard work, raising questions as to whether new faces will be any more willing to point out when the emperor is less than fully dressed."

This snapshot is broadly corroborated in interviews with French officials who had dealings with Mr. Sarkozy in recent years. Describing the president's entourage as loyal but intimidated underlings guarding access to their boss, one senior official, insisting on anonymity, said that Mr. Sarkozy's management style heightened the risks of the centralized French presidential system.

Another official said that fear of Mr. Sarkozy's ire was artificially inflated in his entourage and questioned whether, for example, Mr. Sarkozy would have actually thrown a tantrum on seeing the Eiffel Tower in Turkish colors.

Bernard Kouchner, who until recently was Mr. Sarkozy's foreign minister, was more diplomatic. But he essentially agreed that under the French system, too much power was vested in one man and two dozen advisers vis-à-vis the 12,000 career diplomats. "We need a more collaborative approach and more efficient decision-making," he said.

—This article was originally published on November 30, 2010
See diplomatic cable on p. 490.

FRANCE, TURNING TO A NEW PARTNER, DISMAYS AN OLD ONE OVER A SHIP

By MICHAEL R. GORDON

WASHINGTON—Sometimes, friends disagree.

After France, one of America's closest allies, announced in February that it hoped to sell a Mistral—a ship that carries helicopters and can conduct amphibious assaults—to Russia, with the option to sell several more, American officials soon raised objections.

The proposed transaction would be the largest sale by a Western country to Russia since the end of World War II. The commander of the Russian Navy has said that if his Black Sea fleet had had such a ship during the 2008 war with Georgia, it would have been able to carry out its operations in 40 minutes instead of 26 hours.

Some Eastern European NATO members, including Lithuania and Estonia, protested the deal, according to a cable by Ivo H. Daalder, the United States ambassador to NATO. The United States opposed it as well. In a November 2009 cable titled "Mistral Sale Could Destabilize Black Sea," John R. Bass, the American ambassador to Georgia, recommended that the Obama administration discourage the sale or at least seek a stipulation that the Russians should not deploy the vessel in the Black Sea.

"This sale would render the already difficult task of getting Russia to comply with its ceasefire commitments nearly impossible, and it would potentially increase the militarization of, and instability in, the Black Sea region," Ambassador Bass's cable noted.

Hervé Morin, France's defense minister at the time, defended the sale in a February meeting with Defense Secretary Robert M. Gates, arguing that that a single ship would not change the military balance and that the sale was a "way to send a message of partnership to Russia at a critical time."

But Mr. Gates argued that the sale would send the wrong message to Russia given France's role in brokering a cease-fire in Georgia, "which Russia was not fully honoring." The Russians say that they intend to decide shortly between the French proposal and several other offers. A French shipbuilder said that if France won the contract, the first ship would be built in 2013.

—This article was originally published on December 6, 2010

OFFICIALS PRESSED GERMANS ON KIDNAPPING BY C.I.A.

By MICHAEL SLACKMAN

BERLIN—American officials exerted sustained pressure on Germany not to enforce arrest warrants against Central Intelligence Agency officers involved in the 2003 kidnapping of a German citizen mistakenly believed to be a terrorist, diplomatic cables made public by WikiLeaks show.

John M. Koenig, the American deputy chief of mission in Berlin, issued a pointed warning in February 2007 urging that Germany "weigh carefully at every step of the way the implications for relations with the U.S." in the case of Khaled el-Masri, a German of Lebanese descent. Mr. Masri said he was held in a secret United States prison in Afghanistan and tortured before his captors acknowledged their mistake and let him go.

The United States' concern over the Masri case was detailed in cables sent from the United States Embassies in Germany, Spain and Macedonia in 2006 and 2007.

The cables indicated what was long suspected by German opposition leaders who led a parliamentary inquiry into the case: intense political pressure from Washington was the reason that Germany never pressed for the arrest and extradition of 13 operatives believed to be from the C.I.A. who were ultimately charged in indictments issued in Spain and in Munich.

"I am not surprised by this," said Hans-Christian Ströbele, a member of the Green bloc in Parliament who then sat on the legislative investigative committee. "It was confirmed once again that the U.S. government kept the German government" from seeking the arrest of the agents.

In one cable, written before Mr. Koenig's warning to Germany's deputy national security adviser, the embassy in Berlin reported that diplomatic officials had "continued to stress with German counterparts the potential negative implications for our bilateral relationship, and in particular for our

counter-terrorism cooperation, if further steps are taken to seek the arrest
or extradition of U.S. citizens/officials."

In 2006 and 2007, the Masri case was one of the most difficult issues
between Washington and Berlin, exposing to public scrutiny secret tactics
used in the Bush administration's antiterrorism efforts that were sharply
criticized both in the United States and in Europe. At the time, political
pressure was mounting in Germany to investigate and expose the practice
of extraordinary rendition, which involved capturing suspects and sending
them to third-party countries for questioning in secret prisons.

Mr. Masri was seized on Dec. 31, 2003, as he entered Macedonia
while on vacation; border security guards confused him with an operative
of Al Qaeda with a similar name. He says he was turned over to the C.I.A.,
which flew him to Afghanistan, where he says he was tortured, sodomized
and injected with drugs. After five months, he was dropped on a roadside
in Albania. No charges were brought against him.

The case drew widespread attention in Europe. The cables show that
the United States was especially concerned about cooperation between
Spanish and German prosecutors. The Spanish courts became involved
because they concluded that the plane that transported Mr. Masri had traveled through Spanish territory.

"This coordination among independent investigators will complicate
our efforts to manage this case at a discreet government-to-government
level," read a cable sent from the embassy in Madrid in January 2007.

The cables' release has created a stir in Germany mostly because the
documents contain American diplomats' caustic comments about German
officials and because they show that the embassy had informants in one of the
governing parties. The Masri case, however, has already been so thoroughly
discussed in public, and the degree of Washington's pressure on Berlin is
so well known, that it has not gained much attention.

The one cable that has caught the attention of some in the German
press was written on Feb. 6, 2007, by Mr. Koenig, the second-highest-
ranking diplomat in the embassy, under the title "CHANCELLERY AWARE OF
USG CONCERNS."

Rolf Nikel, Germany's deputy national security adviser, told Mr. Koenig that the two governments had differences over Washington's antiterrorism methods, including German opposition to the prison at Guantánamo
Bay, Cuba, and to rendition. Mr. Nikel said, according to the cable, "the

Chancellery is well aware of the bilateral political implications of the case, but added that this case 'will not be easy,' because of the intense pressure from the parliament and the German media."

Mr. Koenig said that while Washington "recognized the independence of the German judiciary," he added that "to issue international arrest warrants or extradition requests would require the concurrence of the German Federal Government."

His point was that the case could be stopped.

The prosecutor's office in Munich issued warrants for the arrest of the C.I.A. operatives, but Germany's government did not press for arrests or extraditions.

"We already dealt with this, including in the Bundestag, about why the German federal government did not take further action to carry out the arrest warrant," said Mr. Ströbele. "How one deals with the fact that he was taken into custody and tortured—whether more will be revealed on that—what was done in order to keep it a secret: that is what interests me."

Diana Aurisch contributed reporting.

—This article was originally published on December 8, 2010
See diplomatic cable on p. 460.

EUROPE WARY
OF U.S. BANK MONITORS

By ERIC LICHTBLAU

WASHINGTON—When the European Parliament ordered a halt in February to an American government program to monitor international banking transactions for terrorist activity, the Obama administration was blindsided by the rebuke.

"Paranoia runs deep especially about US intelligence agencies," a secret cable from the American Embassy in Berlin said. "We were astonished to learn how quickly rumors about alleged U.S. economic espionage" had taken root among German politicians who opposed the program, it said.

The memo was among dozens of State Department cables that revealed the deep distrust of some traditional European allies toward what they considered American intrusion into their citizens' affairs without stringent oversight.

The program, created in secrecy by the Bush administration after the Sept. 11, 2001, attacks, has allowed American counterterrorism officials to examine banking transactions routed through a vast database run by a Brussels consortium known as Swift. When the program was disclosed in 2006 by The New York Times, just months after the newspaper reported the existence of the National Security Agency's warrantless wiretapping program, it set off protests in Europe and forced the United States to accept new restrictions.

But by 2010, new leaders at the European Parliament had what one State Department memo called "a fixation" on privacy issues. On Feb. 10, the Europeans voted 378 to 196 to halt the Swift program.

Obama administration officials valued it because it allowed them to trace the transactions of suspected terrorist financiers while including "robust" privacy protections, according to the cables.

But many Europeans were skeptical. Some allies not only were concerned that program might be used to steal secrets from European companies, but also considered it of "dubious" value.

In Austria, for example, "the Nazi legacy and familiarity with communist regimes" have fueled "a widespread presumption against government data collection and in favor of stringent privacy protections," officials at the embassy wrote.

Many Germans, meanwhile, remember "how the Stasi," the former East German secret police, "abused information to destroy people's lives," according to a dispatch from the American Embassy in Berlin.

Opposition in Germany was particularly damaging because the country was among a handful of allies that, according to a 2006 cable, organized a "coalition of the constructive" to ensure that the Swift operation was not "ruined by privacy experts."

After German representatives voted against the program, a German official reported to American diplomats that Chancellor Angela Merkel—a strong supporter of the program—was "angrier than he had ever seen her."

After mobilizing top officials, including Secretary of State Hillary Rodham Clinton, Treasury Secretary Timothy F. Geithner and Attorney General Eric H. Holder Jr., the administration was able to reverse course. The European Parliament voted 484 to 109 in July to restart the program after the United States made modest concessions that promised greater European oversight.

—This article was originally published on December 5, 2010

BLACKWATER AIMED
TO HUNT PIRATES

By MARK MAZZETTI

WASHINGTON—Besieged by criminal inquiries and Congressional investigators, how could the world's most controversial private security company
drum up new business? By battling pirates on the high seas, of course.

In late 2008, Blackwater Worldwide, already under fire because of
accusations of abuses by its security guards in Iraq and Afghanistan, reconfig-
ured a 183-foot oceanographic research vessel into a pirate-hunting ship for
hire and then began looking for business from shipping companies seeking
protection from Somali pirates. The company's chief executive officer, Erik
Prince, was planning a trip to Djibouti for a promotional event in March
2009, and Blackwater was hoping that the American Embassy there would
help out, according to a secret State Department cable.

But with the Obama administration just weeks old, American diplomats in Djibouti faced a problem. They are supposed to be advocates for
American businesses, but this was Blackwater, a company that Secretary of
State Hillary Rodham Clinton had proposed banning from war zones when
she was a presidential candidate.

The embassy "would appreciate Department's guidance on the appropriate level of engagement with Blackwater," wrote James C. Swan, the
American ambassador in Djibouti, in a cable sent on Feb. 12, 2009. Blackwater's plans to enter the anti-piracy business have been previously reported,
but not the American government's concern about the endeavor.

According to that cable, Blackwater had outfitted its United
States-flagged ship with .50-caliber machine guns and a small, unarmed
drone aircraft. The ship, named the McArthur, would carry a crew of 33
to patrol the Gulf of Aden for 30 days before returning to Djibouti to
resupply.

And the company had already determined its rules of engagement. "Blackwater does not intend to take any pirates into custody, but will use lethal force against pirates if necessary," the cable said.

At the time, the company was still awaiting approvals from Blackwater lawyers for its planned operations, since Blackwater had informed the embassy there was "no precedent for a paramilitary operation in a purely commercial environment."

Lawsuits filed later by crew members on the McArthur made life on the ship sound little improved from the days of Blackbeard.

One former crew member said, according to legal documents, that the ship's captain, who had been drinking during a port call in Jordan, ordered him "placed in irons" (handcuffed to a towel rack) after he was accused of giving an unauthorized interview to his hometown newspaper in Minnesota. The captain, according to the lawsuit, also threatened to place the sailor in a straitjacket. Another crew member, who is black, claimed in court documents that he was repeatedly subjected to racial epithets.

In the end, Blackwater Maritime Security Services found no treasure in the pirate-chasing business, never attracting any clients. And the Obama administration chose not to sever the American government's relationship with the North Carolina-based firm, which has collected more than $1 billion in security contracts in Iraq and Afghanistan since 2001. Blackwater renamed itself Xe Services, and earlier this year the company won a $100 million contract from the Central Intelligence Agency to protect the spy agency's bases in Afghanistan.

—This article was originally published on November 30, 2010

PIRATES' CATCH EXPOSED
ROUTE OF ARMS IN SUDAN

By JEFFREY GETTLEMAN and MICHAEL R. GORDON

KHARTOUM, Sudan—It was September 2008 and a band of Somali pirates made a startling discovery.

The Ukrainian freighter they had just commandeered in the Gulf of Aden was packed with weapons, including 32 Soviet-era battle tanks, and the entire arsenal was headed for the regional government in southern Sudan. The Ukrainian and Kenyan governments vigorously denied that, insisting that the tanks were intended for the Kenyan military.

"This is a big loss for us," said Alfred Mutua, a spokesman for the Kenyan government, at the time.

But it turns out the pirates were telling the truth—and the Kenyans and Ukrainians were not, at least publicly. According to several secret State Department cables made public by WikiLeaks, the tanks not only were headed to southern Sudan, but they were the latest installment of several underground arms shipments. By the time the freighter was seized, 67 T-72 tanks had already been delivered to bolster southern Sudan's armed forces against the government in Khartoum, an international pariah for its human rights abuses in Darfur.

Bush administration officials knew of the earlier weapons transactions and chose not to shut them down, an official from southern Sudan asserted in an interview, and the cables acknowledge the Kenyan officials' assertions that they had kept American officials informed about the deal. But once the pirates exposed the arms pipeline through Kenya, the Obama administration protested to the Ukrainian and Kenyan governments, even threatening sanctions, the cables show.

Vann H. Van Diepen, a senior State Department official, presented the Ukrainians with a sales contract that showed southern Sudan as the recipient, according to a November 2009 cable from the American Embassy in Kiev. When they dismissed it as a forgery, Mr. Van Diepen "showed the Ukrainians cleared satellite imagery of T-72 tanks unloaded in Kenya, transferred to railyards for onward shipment, and finally in South Sudan," the cable said, referring to the early deliveries of the weapons. "This led to a commotion on the Ukrainian side."

The United States' shifting stance, on policy and legal grounds, on arms for southern Sudan is illuminated in the State Department cables, which were made available to The New York Times and several other news organizations.

The revelations about the tanks—the ones taken by the pirates are now sitting in Kenya, their fate unclear—come at one of the most delicate times in Sudan's history, with the nation, Africa's largest, on the verge of splitting into two. On Jan. 9, southern Sudanese are scheduled to vote in a referendum for their independence from northern Sudan, representing the end of a 50-year war. Huge quantities of weapons have been flowing to both sides, mainly to the north, turning the country into one of the most combustible on the continent. Secretary of State Hillary Rodham Clinton recently called it "a ticking time bomb."

While Kenyan newspapers and other publications have written about the arms shipment since the pirate episode, confirmation that the government of southern Sudan was the recipient has raised concerns among diplomats that the news could further inflame tensions.

Ghazi Salah al-Din al-Atabani, a top adviser to President Omar Hassan al-Bashir of Sudan, chuckled when told of the cables. "We knew it, yeah, we knew it," he said in an interview. He expressed no surprise that the United States appeared to condone some of the shipments, saying: "Officially, we are enemies." Still, he said, the shipments could become "a very hot political issue."

Southern Sudan, mostly Christian and animist, fought even before Sudan's independence in 1956 to split with the Arab government in Khartoum. More than two million people were killed and government-sponsored militias, similar to those that raped and pillaged in Darfur, swept across the region, razing villages and massacring civilians. In 2005, the two sides signed a peace agreement, which granted the south autonomy and the right to vote on secession next year.

The agreement also allows southern Sudan to buy arms to transform its guerrilla army into a defense force, and the United States has also publicly said that it has provided communications and other "nonlethal" equipment and training to the southern army, called the Sudan People's Liberation Army, or S.P.L.A. The cables suggest that effort has gone further than the United States has publicized.

"Over the past two years," says a December 2009 cable, from the embassy in Nairobi, Kenyan officials "have shared full details of their engagement with the SPLA as we have shared details of our training program for the SPLA, including combat arms soldier training."

Several years ago, the southern Sudan government contracted to buy 100 tanks from Ukraine using its own funds. The first shipment of Ukrainian tanks took place in 2007 with little fanfare, and the second shipment was delivered a year later.

In September 2008, however, the Faina, a Ukrainian freighter, was seized by Somali pirates. It was carrying 32 T-72 Soviet-era tanks, 150 grenade launchers, 6 antiaircraft guns and ammunition. Initially, American officials were worried the pirates might offload the weapons in Somalia.

After months of haggling, a $3.2 million ransom was paid, the Somali pirates finally released the ship, and the arms were unloaded in Kenya.

When Ukrainian officials were approached by American officials about the arms shipments in July 2008, they insisted that the weapons were intended for Kenya's military. Even so, some American diplomats understood otherwise and did not appear very concerned. In a cable from Oct. 19, 2008, Alberto M. Fernandez, who served as the chargé d'affaires in Khartoum, reports that he told officials from southern Sudan that while the United States would prefer not to see an arms buildup in the region, it understood that the government there "feels compelled to do the same" as the north. He also cautioned the officials to take care, if there were future shipments, to avoid a repeat hijacking by pirates and "the attention it has drawn."

After the Obama administration took office, a new special envoy for Sudan was appointed and the United States offered incentives for Khartoum to cooperate with the coming referendum. Taking a stricter position than the Bush administration on the tanks, the State Department also insisted that the shipments were illegal, since Sudan was on the United States' list of state sponsors of terrorism.

In a blunt exchange with the Ukrainians in November 2009, Mr. Van Diepen warned that the United States might impose sanctions unless the Ukrainian government acknowledged its role in the past transactions. According to the cable, he cautioned pointedly, "there was nothing for Ukraine to gain from lying and a lot to lose."

In similar conversations with Kenyan officials, the Obama administration again raised the threat of "sweeping sanctions," which it said might be waived if the officials cooperated in investigating the third shipment.

In a Nov. 27, 2009, cable outlining talking points for American diplomats in Nairobi to present to the Kenyans, the State Department acknowledged "the apparent disconnect" between provisions of the peace agreement that allowed southern Sudan to develop its defensive capability and the Americans' legal argument that arms should not be sent there because of the Khartoum government's place on the terrorism list.

"We also recognize that some members of your government informed some members of the USG that this deal was being prepared," the cable, which was sent by Secretary Clinton, added. But the cable argued that southern Sudan did not need the tanks, they would be difficult to maintain and they would "increase the chance of an arms race with Khartoum."

That did not appear to mollify the Kenyans. A cable on Dec. 16, 2009, recounted that the head of Kenya's general staff told American officials that he was "very confused" by the United States position "since the past transfers had been undertaken in consultation with the United States." According to the cable, the Kenyans asked whether the Obama administration was reconsidering whether to move forward with a referendum under the peace accord and whether it was "shifting its support to Khartoum."

In recent months, the Obama administration quietly exempted Ukraine and Kenya from sanctions for the 2007 and 2008 shipments, according to government officials.

It is not clear, however, whether the administration has asked Kenya to hold off sending the tanks that were aboard the seized ship to southern Sudan, at least until after the referendum. A State Department spokesman declined to respond to those questions.

The Kenyans have told southern Sudan officials that the Americans are still asking them not to ship the tanks, according to Gen. Oyay Deng Ajak, the former chief of staff of the southern Sudan military, who asserted that the Americans had been aware of the transaction from the start.

Representative Donald M. Payne, the New Jersey Democrat who heads the House Foreign Affairs subcommittee on Africa, has urged that the tanks be shipped. "Our government knew those tanks were being purchased," he said in an interview. "The fact is the pirates' seizure of the tanks is what made them change their policy. I don't think the Obama administration has a clear policy on Sudan."

Jeffrey Gettleman reported from Khartoum, and Michael R. Gordon from Washington.

—This article was originally published on December 8, 2010

See diplomatic cable on p. 433.

U.S. AIDED
MEXICAN DRUG WAR,
WITH FRUSTRATION

By ELISABETH MALKIN

MEXICO CITY—More than a year ago—before drug cartels killed a gubernatorial candidate and began murdering mayors, before shootings and kidnappings in Mexico's industrial capital, Monterrey, surged to the point that the State Department ordered children of American diplomats there to leave the country—a Mexican official admitted that the government feared it could lose control of parts of the nation.

At a dinner held by Mexico's acting attorney general for a visiting delegation from the Department of Justice in October 2009, the comments by Gerónimo Gutiérrez, then a deputy secretary in the ministry in charge of domestic security, suggested that even then a sense of anxiety about the drug war had begun to take hold in many parts of the Mexican government.

In the account of the meeting, which was included in the American diplomatic cables made public by WikiLeaks and posted on Mexican news Web sites, Mr. Gutiérrez was quoted as saying: "We have 18 months and if we do not produce a tangible success that is recognizable to the Mexican people, it will be difficult to sustain the confrontation into the next administration."

The summary of Mr. Gutiérrez's comments, written by the United States ambassador to Mexico, Carlos Pascual, continued: "He expressed a real concern with 'losing' certain regions. It is damaging Mexico's international reputation, hurting foreign investment, and leading to a sense of government impotence, Gutiérrez said."

The documents released by WikiLeaks capture a moment at the end of 2009 and the beginning of 2010 when Mexican officials were forced to acknowledge—despite their public claims of progress—that their military strategy was not producing the results they had hoped for in the drug war.

The diplomatic cables also show just how entwined the United States has become in Mexico's drug war. The United States government provides Mexico with intelligence to pinpoint where top drug lords are hiding out, trains elite troops, and American officials discuss strategy to try to quell the violence in Ciudad Juárez, which has become ground zero in the drug war.

But the cables suggest frustration that the military, the police and prosecutors are not up to the task. In a blunt assessment, John Feeley, the deputy chief of mission at the American Embassy in Mexico City, concluded in January that military officials "share the parochial, risk-averse habits that often plague their civilian counterparts in Mexican law enforcement agencies."

A year later, there have been some notable successes in capturing or killing cartel leaders and their violent lieutenants. Police intelligence appears to have become more effective. But the military continues to play the top role in the drug war, and the violence that so worried Mexican officials at the end of last year has spread, becoming more entrenched than ever.

The diplomatic cables present a picture of such intense rivalry among Mexico's civilian law enforcement agencies and its military that little gets done.

In his account, Mr. Feeley said that "Mexican security institutions are often locked in a zero-sum competition in which one agency's success is viewed as another's failure, information is closely guarded, and joint operations are all but unheard of."

Mr. Feely continued: "Prosecution rates for organized crime-related offenses are dismal; 2 percent of those detained are brought to trial. Only 2 percent of those arrested in Ciudad Juárez have even been charged with a crime."

The documents also show how anxious the Mexican government was to contain the bloodshed in Juárez, which has intensified this year.

At the October 2009 meeting with the delegation from the Justice Department, Mr. Gutiérrez and Jorge Tello Peón, who was then President Felipe Calderón's top intelligence official for the drug war, said that the government "must succeed in Juárez because Calderón has staked so much of his reputation there, with a major show of force that, to date, has not panned out," according to Mr. Pascual's account.

The content of the documents elicited angry responses from Mexican officials. Late Thursday, the Foreign Relations Ministry said the reports "reflect some deplorable practices from the point of view of respect that should prevail between nations that collaborate for common objectives."

Mr. Pascual hastened to assure Mexicans that relations were still strong. Calling the cables "impressionistic snapshots of a moment in time," he wrote in El Universal newspaper that "like some snapshots, they can be out of focus or unflattering."

Much of what is in the diplomatic cables are similar to what American diplomats say about the need for Mexican law enforcement agencies to do their jobs more effectively. Indeed, much of it is not all that different from the vigorous debate going on inside Mexico.

The army faces charges of human rights abuses, and efforts to reform the police have failed to generate much confidence among ordinary Mexicans.

But the unguarded criticisms in the diplomatic cables have roused prickly nationalist sensibilities in Mexico, especially candid assessments like one from the United States Embassy that stated: "Official corruption is widespread, leading to a compartmentalized siege mentality among 'clean' law enforcement leaders and their lieutenants."

Another sensitive topic is criticism of the military. A cable from Ambassador Pascual last December offered an inside look at how the Mexican Army failed to move to capture one top drug lord, Arturo Beltrán Leyva, last December.

The United States Embassy initially told the army where Mr. Beltrán Leyva was hiding out, but the army did not act. The embassy then told the navy, and an elite American-trained unit moved into action. Mr. Beltrán Leyva escaped the first navy raid, but the embassy several days later located him in a apartment complex in Cuernavaca, about 50 miles south of Mexico City. The navy unit moved in and killed him when he refused to surrender.

Mr. Pascual concluded that the navy's success put the army "in the difficult position of explaining why it has been reluctant to act on good intelligence and conduct operations against high-level targets."

—This article was originally published on December 3, 2010

U.S. DIPLOMATS NOTED CANADIAN MISTRUST

By CHARLIE SAVAGE

WASHINGTON—In early 2008, American diplomats stationed in Ottawa turned on their television sets and were aghast: there was an "onslaught" of Canadian shows depicting "nefarious American officials carrying out equally nefarious deeds in Canada," from planning to bomb Quebec to stealing Canadian water supplies.

In a confidential diplomatic cable sent back to the State Department, the American Embassy warned of increasing mistrust of the United States by its northern neighbor, with which it shares some $500 billion in annual trade, the world's longest unsecured border and a joint military mission in Afghanistan.

"The degree of comfort with which Canadian broadcast entities, including those financed by Canadian tax dollars, twist current events to feed longstanding negative images of the U.S.—and the extent to which the Canadian public seems willing to indulge in the feast—is noteworthy as an indication of the kind of insidious negative popular stereotyping we are increasingly up against in Canada," the cable said.

A trove of diplomatic cables, obtained by WikiLeaks and made available to a number of publications, disclose a perception by American diplomats that Canadians "always carry a chip on their shoulder" in part because of a feeling that their country "is condemned to always play 'Robin' to the U.S. 'Batman.'"

But at the same time, some Canadian officials privately tried to make it clear to their American counterparts that they did not share their society's persistent undercurrent of anti-Americanism.

In July 2008, Canada's intelligence service director, James Judd, discussed a video showing a crying Omar Khadr, then a teenager and a Canadian detainee at the prison at Guantánamo Bay, Cuba. Mr. Judd "observed that the images would no doubt trigger 'knee-jerk anti-Americanism' and 'paroxysms of moral outrage, a Canadian specialty.'"

A cable that briefed President George W. Bush before a visit to Ottawa in late 2004 shed further light on the asymmetrical relationship with Canada —a country, the embassy wrote, that was engaged in "soul-searching" about its "decline from 'middle power' status to that of an 'active observer' of global affairs, a trend which some Canadians believe should be reversed."

It also noted that Canadian officials worried that they were being excluded from a club of English-speaking countries as a result of their refusal to take part in the 2003 invasion of Iraq. The United States had created a channel for sharing intelligence related to Iraq operations with Britain and Australia, but Canada was not invited to join.

The Canadian government "has expressed concern at multiple levels that their exclusion from a traditional 'four-eyes' construct is 'punishment' for Canada's nonparticipation in Iraq and they fear that the Iraq-related channel may evolve into a more permanent 'three-eyes' only structure," the cable said.

Four years later, after President Obama's election, the embassy reported that Canadian officials had a different potential irritant: Mr. Obama was far more popular in Canada than they were.

The embassy also said Mr. Obama's decision to make Ottawa his first foreign trip as president would "do much to diminish—temporarily, at least—Canada's habitual inferiority complex vis-à-vis the U.S. and its chronic but accurate complaint that the U.S. pays far less attention to Canada than Canada does to us."

Still, just a few months earlier, during a national election in Canada, the embassy had marveled that "despite the overwhelming importance of the U.S. to Canada for its economy and security," parliamentary candidates were rarely mentioning anything about relations with their southern neighbor.

"Ultimately, the U.S. is like the proverbial 900-pound gorilla in the midst of the Canadian federal election: overwhelming but too potentially menacing to acknowledge," the cable said.

Andrew W. Lehren contributed reporting from New York.

—This article was originally published on December 1, 2010
See diplomatic cable on p. 437.

CABLE SHOWS NATIONS GOING EASY ON CUBA

By MARK LANDLER

WASHINGTON—Cuba is getting a free pass on its human rights abuses from many of the world's leading democracies, with visitors from Canada, Australia and Switzerland failing to criticize the Castro regime or meet with dissidents while on the island, according to a confidential diplomatic cable sent to the State Department from Havana.

The cable, transmitted in November 2009 and signed by Jonathan D. Farrar, the top American diplomat in Cuba, hinted that there were economic motives behind the accommodating approach. But if so, the cable concluded, these countries were not getting much of a payoff.

The rewards for acquiescing to Cuban sensitivities, it said, were "risible: pomp-full dinners and meetings, and for the most pliant, a photo-op with one of the Castro brothers."

The cable added, "In terms of substance or economic benefits they fare little better than those who stand up to" the government.

And yet, in a cable sent six months earlier, the United States Interests Section in Havana also lamented that the Cuban dissidents supported by Washington for decades were old, out of touch and so split by internecine squabbles that the United States should look elsewhere for future leaders.

While that cable, also signed by Mr. Farrar, said dissidents deserved continued American support, it said that some groups had been infiltrated by Cuban intelligence. "We see very little evidence that the mainline dissident organizations have much resonance among Cubans," it said.

A trove of cables made public by WikiLeaks attests to the strained nature of the Cuban-American relationship, at a time when Cuba's revolutionary leader, Fidel Castro, is in failing health and his ideological feud with Washington has little relevance for other countries eager to build bridges. The United States, by contrast, clings to a trade embargo and a policy of isolating Cuba.

"On the one hand, the U.S. is saying the dissidents are hopeless and aging," said Julia Sweig, a senior fellow and expert on Cuba at the Council on Foreign Relations. "On the other hand, the same interests section is saying that the Canada and E.U. engagement is not helping progress on human rights."

Pointing to Cuba's release of political prisoners and the economic reforms being championed by Fidel Castro's brother Raúl, Ms. Sweig said the engagement of the European Union and other countries appeared to be more fruitful than the implacable cold shoulder from Washington.

The United States operates an interests section, rather than an embassy, in Havana because the two countries have not had diplomatic relations for five decades. The office sends a steady stream of analysis to Washington, with vivid dispatches on Fidel Castro's health problems and sober speculation about how Cuba might change after he finally leaves the scene.

There is also evidence that Raúl Castro, the president, has reached out to the United States. In a cable dated December 2009, Mr. Farrar reported that Mr. Castro sought a "political channel" to the White House. The Cuban president raised the issue with the Spanish foreign minister, Miguel Ángel Moratinos, who passed it on to Mr. Farrar via Spain's ambassador to Cuba, Manuel Cacho.

On Thursday, the State Department spokesman, Philip J. Crowley, ruled out high-level contacts without major political changes. "We have not seen anything approaching fundamental change in Cuba at this point," he said. The administration has held only technical talks about Cuban migration.

A senior State Department official said the United States was encouraged by the release of political prisoners, but noted that most of those people were immediately exiled from the country.

In the cable about how other countries deal with Cuba on official visits, American officials classified those approaches on a scale from kowtowing to confrontational: "best-friends-forever," "keep-it-private," "we-respectfully-disagree" and, in rare cases, "take-your-visit-and-shoveit."

A large majority of countries with diplomatic posts in Havana, it said, do not raise human rights issues with the Cuban government in public or private. A handful of countries—including Britain, Germany and the Czech

Republic—have refused to send senior officials to Cuba, rather than accept the government's restrictions on who they can meet while there.

Other countries fall somewhere in between, agreeing to restrictions but broaching the topic of human rights, mostly behind closed doors. A senior Canadian minister, Peter Kent, broached the issue of political prisoners with officials, but left Havana without voicing public criticism.

Another offender, the cable said, was the European Union, which takes a softer line toward Cuba than many of its member states. Officials at the European mission, it said, told American diplomats they looked forward to Spain's assuming the rotating presidency of the union because it was more moderate than the "radical" Swedes and Czechs.

The cable singles out the Vatican for praise, noting that one of its representatives, Archbishop Claudio Celli, called for "greater information and Internet access for all Cubans." He even praised Cuban bloggers, angering his hosts, though he later softened his comments back in Rome.

It is not exactly clear what quid pro quo countries hope to get for their friendly behavior, but analysts said Europeans were eager to forge commercial ties with Cuba, in part because they feared that if relations between Havana and Washington thawed, Americans would have an edge.

In addition to human rights issues, cables from Havana kept a close eye on Fidel Castro's deteriorating health. A March 2007 cable, signed by Mr. Farrar's predecessor, Michael E. Parmly, sought to debunk official claims of a "Castro comeback" after his long absence from the public stage.

Based on a report from an opposition figure, it said Mr. Castro became critically ill with a perforated intestine while on a plane in July 2006. His condition was complicated because he refused to have a colostomy. A Cuban doctor familiar with the case said that Mr. Castro could not be cured, and that he would "progressively lose his faculties and become ever more debilitated until he dies."

Nearly two years later, another cable reported the latest rumors of Mr. Castro's death. It concluded that his death would have little immediate effect. "We do not believe the announcement of Fidel's death would spark either violent demonstrations or a quick surge in migration," it said.

Andrew W. Lehren contributed reporting from New York, and Scott Shane from Washington.

—This article was originally published on December 17, 2010
See diplomatic cable on p. 443.

U.S. EXPANDS ROLE
OF DIPLOMATS IN SPYING

By MARK MAZZETTI

WASHINGTON—The United States has expanded the role of American diplomats in collecting intelligence overseas and at the United Nations, ordering State Department personnel to gather the credit card and frequent-flier numbers, work schedules and other personal information of foreign dignitaries.

Revealed in classified State Department cables, the directives, going back to 2008, appear to blur the traditional boundaries between statesmen and spies.

The cables give a laundry list of instructions for how State Department employees can fulfill the demands of a "National Humint Collection Directive." ("Humint" is spy-world jargon for human intelligence collection.) One cable asks officers overseas to gather information about "office and organizational titles; names, position titles and other information on business cards; numbers of telephones, cellphones, pagers and faxes," as well as "internet and intranet 'handles', internet e-mail addresses, web site identification-URLs; credit card account numbers; frequent-flier account numbers; work schedules, and other relevant biographical information."

Philip J. Crowley, a State Department spokesman, on Sunday disputed that American diplomats had assumed a new role overseas.

"Our diplomats are just that, diplomats," he said. "They represent our country around the world and engage openly and transparently with representatives of foreign governments and civil society. Through this process, they collect information that shapes our policies and actions. This is what diplomats, from our country and other countries, have done for hundreds of years."

The cables, sent to embassies in the Middle East, Eastern Europe, Latin America and the United States mission to the United Nations, provide no evidence that American diplomats are actively trying to steal the secrets of foreign countries, work that is traditionally the preserve of spy agencies. While the State Department has long provided information about foreign officials' duties to the Central Intelligence Agency to help build biographical profiles, the more intrusive personal information diplomats are now being asked to gather could be used by the National Security Agency for data mining and surveillance operations. A frequent-flier number, for example, could be used to track the travel plans of foreign officials.

Several of the cables also asked diplomats for details about the telecommunications networks supporting foreign militaries and intelligence agencies.

The United States regularly puts undercover intelligence officers in countries posing as diplomats, but a vast majority of diplomats are not spies. Several retired ambassadors, told about the information-gathering assignments disclosed in the cables, expressed concern that State Department employees abroad could routinely come under suspicion of spying and find it difficult to do their work or even risk expulsion.

Ronald E. Neumann, a former American ambassador to Afghanistan, Algeria and Bahrain, said that Washington was constantly sending requests for voluminous information about foreign countries. But he said he was puzzled about why Foreign Service officers—who are not trained in clandestine collection methods—would be asked to gather information like credit card numbers.

"My concerns would be, first of all, whether the person could do this responsibly without getting us into trouble," he said. "And, secondly, how much effort a person put into this at the expense of his or her regular duties."

The requests have come at a time when the nation's spy agencies are struggling to meet the demands of two wars and a global hunt for militants. The Pentagon has also sharply expanded its intelligence work outside of war zones, sending Special Operations troops to embassies to gather information about militant networks.

Unlike the thousands of cables, originally obtained by WikiLeaks, that were sent from embassies to the State Department, the roughly half-dozen cables from 2008 and 2009 detailing the more aggressive intelligence collection were sent from Washington and signed by Secretaries of State Condoleezza Rice and Hillary Rodham Clinton.

One of the cables, signed by Mrs. Clinton, lists information-gathering priorities to the American staff at the United Nations in New York, including "biographic and biometric information on ranking North Korean diplomats."

While several treaties prohibit spying at the United Nations, it is an open secret that countries try nevertheless. In one 2004 episode, a British official revealed that the United States and Britain eavesdropped on Secretary General Kofi Annan in the weeks before the invasion of Iraq in 2003.

The requests for more personal data about foreign officials were included in several cables requesting all manner of information from posts overseas, information that would seem to be the typical business of diplomats.

State Department officials in Asunción, Paraguay, were asked in March 2008 about the presence of Al Qaeda, Hezbollah and Hamas in the lawless "Tri-Border" area of Paraguay, Brazil and Argentina. Diplomats in Rwanda and the Democratic Republic of Congo were asked in April 2009 about crop yields, H.I.V. rates and China's quest for copper, cobalt and oil in Africa.

In a cable sent to the American Embassy in Bulgaria in June 2009, the State Department requested information about Bulgaria's efforts to crack down on money laundering and drug trafficking and for "details about personal relations between Bulgarian leaders and Russian officials or businessmen."

And a cable sent on Oct. 31, 2008, to the embassies in Israel, Jordan, Egypt and elsewhere asked for information on "Palestinian issues," including "Palestinian plans, intentions and efforts to influence US positions on the Palestinian-Israeli negotiations." To get both sides, officials also sought information on "Israeli leadership intentions and strategy toward managing the US relationship."

Andrew W. Lehren contributed reporting from New York.

—This article was originally published on November 28, 2010

CABLES DEPICT U.S. HAGGLING TO CLEAR GUANTÁNAMO

By CHARLIE SAVAGE and ANDREW W. LEHREN

WASHINGTON—Last year, King Abdullah of Saudi Arabia proposed an unorthodox way to return Guantánamo Bay prisoners to a chaotic country like Yemen without fear that they would disappear and join a terrorist group.

The king told a top White House aide, John O. Brennan, that the United States should implant an electronic chip in each detainee to track his movements, as is sometimes done with horses and falcons.

"Horses don't have good lawyers," Mr. Brennan replied.

That unusual discussion in March 2009 was one of hundreds recounted in a cache of secret State Department cables obtained by WikiLeaks and made available to a number of news organizations that reveal the painstaking efforts by the United States to safely reduce the population of the Guantánamo Bay prison in Cuba so that it could eventually be closed.

American diplomats went looking for countries that were not only willing to take in former prisoners but also could be trusted to keep them under close watch. In a global bazaar of sorts, the American officials sweet-talked and haggled with their foreign counterparts in an effort to resettle the detainees who had been cleared for release but could not be repatriated for fear of mistreatment, the cables show.

Slovenia, seeking a meeting with President Obama, was encouraged to "do more" on detainee resettlement if it wanted to "attract higher-level attention from Washington"; its prime minister later "linked acceptance of detainees to 'a 20-minute meeting'" with the president, but the session—and the prisoner transfer—never happened. The Maldives tied acceptance of prisoners to American help in obtaining International Monetary Fund assistance, while the Bush administration offered the Pacific nation of Kiribati "an incentive package" of $3 million to take 17 Chinese Muslim detainees, the cables show. In discussions about creating a rehabilitation program for its own citizens, the president of Yemen repeatedly asked Mr. Brennan, "How many dollars will the U.S. bring?"

Mr. Obama won praise from around the world when, shortly after taking office in 2009, he ordered the Guantánamo Bay prison closed within a year, saying it was contrary to American values and a symbol for terrorist propaganda.

By then, the Bush administration already had transferred more than 500 of the detainees it had sent to Guantánamo, and the Obama administration has since winnowed the population to 174 from 240, with help from Ireland, Spain, Portugal, Belgium and other countries. But Mr. Obama missed his deadline, and the goal has faded as a priority, with domestic opposition to moving some detainees to a prison inside the United States and with other countries that condemned the Guantánamo prison reluctant to take in detainees.

While Mr. Obama went to Norway to collect a Nobel Peace Prize, for example, the Norwegians called resettling Guantánamo detainees "purely a U.S. responsibility." Germany and several other European countries that had criticized the prison eventually accepted a few detainees but balked at taking as many as the United States had hoped.

In the fall of 2009, Lithuania's newly elected president backed out of her country's previous agreement to resettle a prisoner amid an uproar over reports that the Central Intelligence Agency had run a secret jail in Lithuania. The chairman of the Lithuanian Parliament's national security committee privately apologized and suggested using mutual allies to pressure her to reconsider, the cables show.

Other dispatches illuminated the difficulties of resettling Uighurs, Chinese Muslim prisoners who had been ordered freed by a federal judge. China was deemed likely to abuse them, but Beijing demanded their return.

At an October 2009 meeting in Beijing, a Chinese official linked the Uighurs to American hopes to secure supply routes through China for the Afghan war, saying, "More 'prudent' actions by the U.S. on the Guantánamo Uighurs would help remove 'some of the obstacles' on the Chinese side to helping with the shipments."

And an aide to Finland's prime minister confided in August 2009 "that Chinese diplomats in Helsinki have repeatedly warned them about the damage to bilateral relations should Finland accept any Uighurs," a cable said.

Still, a few allies were eager to help. After accepting five Chinese Muslims in 2006, Albania's prime minister in 2009 offered to resettle three to six detainees not from China. American diplomats portrayed his offer as "gracious, but probably extravagant."

"As always, the Albanians are willing to go the extra mile to assist with one of our key foreign policy priorities," a cable said.

The United States repatriated other detainees for prosecution at home. Afghanistan, however, granted pretrial releases to 29 out of 41 such former detainees from Guantánamo, allowing "dangerous individuals to go free or re-enter the battlefield without ever facing an Afghan court," diplomats in Kabul complained in a July 2009 cable.

Perhaps the greatest obstacle to closing the prison has been figuring out what to do with detainees from Yemen, who constitute about half of the remaining prisoners at Guantánamo. In a September 2009 meeting with Mr. Brennan, Mr. Obama's top counterterrorism adviser, Yemen's president, Ali Abdullah Saleh, proposed transferring them all into his prisons. But, a cable later said, "Saleh would, in our judgment, be unable to hold returning detainees in jail for any more than a matter of weeks before public pressure —or the courts—forced their release."

Mr. Saleh's erratic approach compounded the situation. In that same conversation, for example, he "signaled that rehabilitation is not his concern, but rather 'the U.S.'s problem' because he is ready and willing to accept all Yemeni detainees into the Yemen prison system." But moments later, he assured Mr. Brennan that he was committed to "freeing the innocent people after a complete and total rehabilitation."

Neither Mr. Saleh nor the Saudis were enthusiastic about an American proposal to send Yemeni detainees to a Saudi deradicalization program, cables show. But when Mr. Saleh proposed a Yemeni version, the United States showed interest—but also caution.

In March 2009, Mr. Saleh demanded $11 million to build such a program in Aden, but Mr. Brennan replied that "such a program takes time to develop and that Saleh had his hands full dealing with al-Qaeda in Yemen." When the two met again six months later, Mr. Saleh "repeatedly," according to a cable, asked how much money he could expect. When Mr. Brennan "offered $500,000 as an initial investment currently available for the crafting of a rehabilitation program, Saleh dismissed the offer as insufficient," the cable said.

Several cables shed light on the Saudis' rehabilitation program. A March 2009 dispatch estimated that the program had processed 1,500 extremists, including 119 former detainees. That cable put the "recidivism rate" at 8 to 10 percent, arguing that "the real story of the Saudi rehabilitation program is one of success: at least 90 percent of its graduates appear to have given up jihad and reintegrated into Saudi society."

Over time, however, the numbers apparently slipped. In March 2010, Daniel Fried, the State Department's special envoy for closing the Guantánamo prison, told European Union officials that the Saudi program was "serious but not perfect," citing a failure rate of 10 to 20 percent. Another cable noted that of 85 militants on a "most wanted" list published by Saudi authorities in early 2009, 11 were former Guantánamo detainees. But the cables offer details on only a few individual cases—like a Saudi who became a leader of Al Qaeda's Yemen branch and a Kuwaiti who committed a suicide bombing in Iraq in 2008, both of which have been previously reported.

The suicide bomber proved deeply embarrassing for the Kuwaiti government. Months later, in February 2009, Kuwait's interior minister proposed a solution for other detainees who seemed too extremist for reintegration into society: let them die in combat.

"You know better than I that we cannot deal with these people," the minister, Sheik Jaber al-Khaled al-Sabah, told the ambassador, a cable reported. "If they are rotten, they are rotten and the best thing to do is get rid of them. You picked them up in Afghanistan; you should drop them off in Afghanistan, in the middle of the war zone."

Mr. Sabah's private comments contrasted with the public stance of his government. Under domestic pressure to urge the United States to send home all Kuwaitis from Guantánamo, Kuwait has strongly suggested that it is doing so.

The United States often has required countries to impose travel bans—among other restrictions, including continuing surveillance—on freed prisoners, sometimes with mixed success.

In February 2009, for example, a diplomat in Qatar urged Attorney General Eric H. Holder Jr. not to meet with his Qatari counterpart, citing reports that a Qatari former detainee traveled "despite explicit assurances that he would not be permitted to do so." The freed prisoner, Jarallah al-Marri, had traveled to Britain to join a speaking tour with another former prisoner, Moazzam Begg, a British-Pakistani citizen.

Another American diplomat later praised Mr. Begg's activities, saying he had pressed Luxembourg's foreign minister to take in detainees, and—displaying "minimal ill will toward his captors"—reiterated that request at an Amnesty International event.

"Mr. Begg is doing our work for us, and his articulate, reasoned presentation makes for a convincing argument," a January 2010 cable said. "It is ironic that after four years of imprisonment and alleged torture, Moazzam Begg is delivering the same 'message' as we are: please consider accepting GTMO detainees for resettlement."

Charlie Savage reported from Washington, and Andrew W. Lehren from New York.

—This article was originally published on November 29, 2010

U.S. STRAINS
TO STOP ARMS FLOW

By MICHAEL R. GORDON and ANDREW W. LEHREN

WASHINGTON—Just a week after President Bashar al-Assad of Syria assured a top State Department official that his government was not sending sophisticated weapons to Hezbollah, the Obama administration lodged a confidential protest accusing Syria of doing precisely what it had denied doing.

"In our meetings last week it was stated that Syria is not transferring any 'new' missiles to Lebanese Hizballah," noted a cable sent by Secretary of State Hillary Rodham Clinton in February, using an alternative spelling for the militant group. "We are aware, however, of current Syrian efforts to supply Hizballah with ballistic missiles. I must stress that this activity is of deep concern to my government, and we strongly caution you against such a serious escalation."

A senior Syrian Foreign Ministry official, a cable from the American Embassy in Damascus reported, flatly denied the allegation. But nine months later, administration officials assert, the flow of arms had continued to Hezbollah. According to a Pentagon official, Hezbollah's arsenal now includes up to 50,000 rockets and missiles, including some 40 to 50 Fateh-110 missiles capable of reaching Tel Aviv and most of Israel, and 10 Scud-D missiles. The newly fortified Hezbollah has raised fears that any future conflict with Israel could erupt into a full-scale regional war.

The Syrian episode offers a glimpse of the United States' efforts to prevent buildups of arms—including Scud missiles, Soviet-era tanks and antiaircraft weapons—in some of the world's tensest regions. Wielding surveillance photos and sales contracts, American diplomats have confronted foreign governments about shadowy front companies, secretive banks and shippers around the globe, according to secret State Department cables obtained by WikiLeaks and made available to several news organizations.

American officials have tried to block a Serbian black marketer from selling sniper rifles to Yemen. They have sought to disrupt the sale of Chinese missile technology to Pakistan, the cables show, and questioned Indian officials about chemical industry exports that could be used to make poison gas.

But while American officials can claim some successes—Russia appears to have deferred delivery of the S-300 air defense system to Iran—the diplomats' dispatches underscore how often their efforts have been frustrated in trying to choke off trade by Syria and others, including Iran and North Korea.

The United States is the world's largest arms supplier, and with Russia, dominates trade in the developing world. Its role as a purveyor of weapons to certain allies—including Israel, Saudi Arabia and other Persian Gulf states—has drawn criticism that it has fueled an arms race. But it has also taken on a leading role as traffic cop in trying to halt deliveries of advanced weapons and other arms to militants and adversaries.

According to the cables, American diplomats have repeatedly expressed concern that huge cargo planes operated by Badr Airlines of Sudan were flying weapons from Tehran to Khartoum, Sudan, where they were shipped to Hamas, the militant group in Gaza.

Sudan insisted that the cargo was farm equipment, but the United States asked countries in the region to deny overflight rights to the airlines. Jordan and several other countries agreed, but Yemen declined, a February 2009 cable reported.

Egyptian officials, who view Iran with deep wariness, privately issued a threat. Omar Suleiman, the chief of Egypt's intelligence service, told Adm. Mike Mullen, the chairman of the Joint Chiefs of Staff, that Iran not only was providing $25 million a month to support Hamas but also was linked to a Hezbollah cell trying to smuggle arms from Gaza into Egypt, according to an April 2009 cable.

"Egypt had sent a clear message to Iran that if they interfere in Egypt, Egypt will interfere in Iran," noted the cable, adding that the Egyptian official said his country had trained agents for that purpose.

North Korea has abetted the arms race in the Middle East by providing missile technology to Iran and Syria, which then backed Hamas and Hezbollah, according to American intelligence officials and a cable from Mrs. Clinton. The cables tell something of an international detective story: how North Korea's arms industry has conducted many of its transactions through the Korea Mining and Development Corporation, relied on suppliers of machinery and steel from countries including Switzerland, Japan, China and Taiwan, passed money through Chinese and Hong Kong banks and sold weapons to other countries.

To disrupt the transactions, American officials have prodded and protested. Diplomats raised questions in the spring of 2009, for example, about planned purchases from North Korea of rocket launchers by Sri Lanka and Scud missile launchers by Yemen.

In July 2009, Stuart A. Levey, a senior United States Treasury official, warned a top official of the People's Bank of China that "Chinese banks have been targeted by North Korea as the main access point into the international financial system," according to one cable. And in meetings in Hong Kong that month, Mr. Levey complained that a local businessman was helping procure luxury goods for the North Korean leadership. (The Hong Kong banks later suggested that they had shut down the man's accounts.)

It is the arms transactions involving Syria and Hezbollah, however, that appear to be among the Obama administration's gravest concerns. President Obama came into office pledging to engage with Syria, arguing that the Bush administration's efforts to isolate Syria had done nothing to wean it from Iran or encourage Middle East peace efforts.

Even before American diplomats began talks with the Assad government, Senator John Kerry, the Massachusetts Democrat who is the chairman of the Senate Foreign Relations Committee, prodded Mr. Assad in a February 2009 meeting in Damascus to make a gesture that he could take back to the Obama administration as "an indicator of Assad's good will." Mr. Kerry told Mr. Assad that Mr. Obama intended to withdraw American troops from Iraq "as soon as possible" and also hinted to a senior Syrian official that the Obama administration intended to take a firm line against the establishment of new Israeli settlements on the West Bank.

"It is not our goal for the United States to be humiliated," Mr. Assad said, referring to Iraq, according to a cable.

In March 2009, a delegation of State Department and National Security Council officials traveled to Damascus for the first discussions, and in the next several months, each side made some modest gestures.

The United States provided information "regarding a potential threat to a Syrian official" through Syria's Washington ambassador and allowed a senior aide to George J. Mitchell, the American Middle East negotiator, to attend a Syrian holiday event at the Syrian Embassy, a cable reported. Syria, for its part, allowed the Americans to reopen an English-language school and hosted a team of American military officials to discuss how to better regulate the Syria-Iraq border.

Each side, however, wanted the other to take the first major initiative. Syria kept pressing for the lifting of economic sanctions, which had crippled its aviation industry, and the Americans urged Syria to curtail its support for Hezbollah and Hamas.

"The U.S. had publicly recognized its mistakes, e.g. use of torture methods, and would continue to take steps," Daniel B. Shapiro, a senior official on the National Security Council told the Syrians in the meeting, according to a May 2009 cable. "But others needed to reciprocate to ensure that the opportunity did not pass."

By the fall, however, officials at the American Embassy in Damascus appeared concerned that military developments were outpacing the incremental diplomacy.

"Syria's determined support of Hizballah's military build-up, particularly the steady supply of longer-range rockets and the introduction of guided missiles could change the military balance and produce a scenario significantly more destructive than the July-August 2006 war," said a November 2009 cable from the American chargé d'affaires in Damascus.

According to cables, Syrian leaders appeared to believe that the weapons shipments increased their political leverage with the Israelis. But they made Lebanon even more of a tinderbox and increased the prospect that a future conflict might include Syria.

A major worry was that Syria or Iran had provided Hezbollah with Fateh-110 missiles, with the range to strike Tel Aviv. (A United States government official said last week that the 40 to 50 missiles were viewed as especially threatening because they are highly accurate.) Israeli officials told American officials in November 2009 that if war broke out, they assumed that Hezbollah would try to launch 400 to 600 rockets at day and sustain the attacks for at least two months, the cables note.

In February, the White House announced that a new American ambassador would be sent to Syria after a five-year hiatus. The next day, William J. Burns, a State Department under secretary, met with the Syrian leader.

During the session, Mr. Burns repeated American concerns about weapons smuggling to Hezbollah, one dispatch noted. Mr. Assad replied that while he could not be Israel's policeman, no "new" weapons were being sent to Hezbollah.

Soon after the meeting, though, a cable noted that the Americans received intelligence reports that the Syrians were about to provide Hezbollah with Scud-D missiles, which are based on North Korean technology. (Some recent intelligence reports conclude that the group has about 10 such missiles stored in a Syrian warehouse that Hezbollah uses, according to American officials. The Defense Intelligence Agency believes that two have probably been moved to Lebanon, according to the officials, speaking on the condition of anonymity.) The United States officials also worried about Hezbollah's vow to avenge the death of Imad Mughniyah, a senior fighter killed in a 2008 car bombing the militant group said was the work of the Israelis.

In a classified cable in February, Mrs. Clinton directed the embassy to deliver a warning to Faisal al-Miqdad, the deputy foreign minister. "I know you are a strategic thinker, which is why I want to underscore for you that, from our perspective, your operational support for Hizballah is a strategic miscalculation that is damaging your long-term national interests."

The Syrian official's response was dismissive, according to an American cable. He denied that any weapons had been sent, argued that Hezbollah would not take military action if not provoked and expressed surprise at the stern American protest. The complaint, he said, "shows the U.S. has not come to a mature position (that would enable it) to differentiate between its own interests and Israel's."

Michael R. Gordon reported from Washington, and Andrew W. Lehren from New York.

—This article was originally published on December 6, 2010

CABLES PORTRAY EXPANDED REACH OF DRUG AGENCY

By GINGER THOMPSON and SCOTT SHANE

WASHINGTON—The Drug Enforcement Administration has been transformed into a global intelligence organization with a reach that extends far beyond narcotics, and an eavesdropping operation so expansive it has to fend off foreign politicians who want to use it against their political enemies, according to secret diplomatic cables.

In far greater detail than previously seen, the cables, from the cache obtained by WikiLeaks and made available to some news organizations, offer glimpses of drug agents balancing diplomacy and law enforcement in places where it can be hard to tell the politicians from the traffickers, and where drug rings are themselves mini-states whose wealth and violence permit them to run roughshod over struggling governments.

Diplomats recorded unforgettable vignettes from the largely unseen war on drugs:

• In Panama, an urgent BlackBerry message from the president to the American ambassador demanded that the D.E.A. go after his political enemies: "I need help with tapping phones."

• In Sierra Leone, a major cocaine-trafficking prosecution was almost upended by the attorney general's attempt to solicit $2.5 million in bribes.

• In Guinea, the country's biggest narcotics kingpin turned out to be the president's son, and diplomats discovered that before the police destroyed a huge narcotics seizure, the drugs had been replaced by flour.

• Leaders of Mexico's beleaguered military issued private pleas for closer collaboration with the drug agency, confessing that they had little faith in their own country's police forces.

• Cables from Myanmar, the target of strict United States sanctions, describe the drug agency informants' reporting both on how the military junta enriches itself with drug money and on the political activities of the junta's opponents.

Officials of the D.E.A. and the State Department declined to discuss what they said was information that should never have been made public.

Like many of the cables made public in recent weeks, those describing the drug war do not offer large disclosures. Rather, it is the details that add up to a clearer picture of the corrupting influence of big traffickers, the tricky game of figuring out which foreign officials are actually controlled by drug lords, and the story of how an entrepreneurial agency operating in the shadows of the F.B.I. has become something more than a drug agency. The D.E.A. now has 87 offices in 63 countries and close partnerships with governments that keep the Central Intelligence Agency at arm's length.

Because of the ubiquity of the drug scourge, today's D.E.A. has access to foreign governments, including those, like Nicaragua's and Venezuela's, that have strained diplomatic relations with the United States. Many are eager to take advantage of the agency's drug detection and wiretapping technologies.

In some countries, the collaboration appears to work well, with the drug agency providing intelligence that has helped bring down traffickers, and even entire cartels. But the victories can come at a high price, according to the cables, which describe scores of D.E.A. informants and a handful of agents who have been killed in Mexico and Afghanistan.

In Venezuela, the local intelligence service turned the tables on the D.E.A., infiltrating its operations, sabotaging equipment and hiring a computer hacker to intercept American Embassy e-mails, the cables report.

And as the drug agency has expanded its eavesdropping operations to keep up with cartels, it has faced repeated pressure to redirect its counternarcotics surveillance to local concerns, provoking tensions with some of Washington's closest allies.

Sticky Situations

Cables written in February by American diplomats in Paraguay, for example, described the D.E.A.'s pushing back against requests from that country's government to help spy on an insurgent group, known as the Paraguayan

People's Army, or the EPP, the initials of its name in Spanish. The leftist group, suspected of having ties to the Colombian rebel group FARC, had conducted several high-profile kidnappings and was making a small fortune in ransoms.

When American diplomats refused to give Paraguay access to the drug agency's wiretapping system, Interior Minister Rafael Filizzola threatened to shut it down, saying: "Counternarcotics are important, but won't topple our government. The EPP could."

The D.E.A. faced even more intense pressure last year from Panama, whose right-leaning president, Ricardo Martinelli, demanded that the agency allow him to use its wiretapping program—known as Matador—to spy on leftist political enemies he believed were plotting to kill him.

The United States, according to the cables, worried that Mr. Martinelli, a supermarket magnate, "made no distinction between legitimate security targets and political enemies," refused, igniting tensions that went on for months.

Mr. Martinelli, who the cables said possessed a "penchant for bullying and blackmail," retaliated by proposing a law that would have ended the D.E.A.'s work with specially vetted police units. Then he tried to subvert the drug agency's control over the program by assigning nonvetted officers to the counternarcotics unit.

And when the United States pushed back against those attempts—moving the Matador system into the offices of the politically independent attorney general—Mr. Martinelli threatened to expel the drug agency from the country altogether, saying other countries, like Israel, would be happy to comply with his intelligence requests.

Eventually, according to the cables, American diplomats began wondering about Mr. Martinelli's motivations. Did he really want the D.E.A. to disrupt plots by his adversaries, or was he trying to keep the agency from learning about corruption among his relatives and friends?

One cable asserted that Mr. Martinelli's cousin helped smuggle tens of millions of dollars in drug proceeds through Panama's main airport every month. Another noted, "There is no reason to believe there will be fewer acts of corruption in this government than in any past government."

As the standoff continued, the cables indicate that the United States proposed suspending the Matador program, rather than submitting to Mr. Martinelli's demands. (American officials say the program was suspended, but the British took over the wiretapping program and have shared the intelligence with the United States.)

In a statement on Saturday, the government of Panama said that it regretted "the bad interpretation by United States authorities of a request for help made to directly confront crime and drug trafficking." It said that Panama would continue its efforts to stop organized crime and emphasized that Panama continued to have "excellent relations with the United States."

Meanwhile in Paraguay, according to the cables, the United States acquiesced, agreeing to allow the authorities there to use D.E.A. wiretaps for antikidnapping investigations, as long as they were approved by Paraguay's Supreme Court.

"We have carefully navigated this very sensitive and politically sticky situation," one cable said. "It appears that we have no other viable choice."

A Larger Mandate

Created in 1973, the D.E.A. has steadily built its international turf, an expansion primarily driven by the multinational nature of the drug trade, but also by forces within the agency seeking a larger mandate. Since the 2001 terrorist attacks, the agency's leaders have cited what they describe as an expanding nexus between drugs and terrorism in further building its overseas presence.

In Afghanistan, for example, "DEA officials have become convinced that 'no daylight' exists between drug traffickers at the highest level and Taliban insurgents," Karen Tandy, then the agency's administrator, told European Union officials in a 2007 briefing, according to a cable from Brussels.

Ms. Tandy described an agency informant's recording of a meeting in Nangarhar Province between 9 Taliban members and 11 drug traffickers to coordinate their financial support for the insurgency, and she said the agency was trying to put a "security belt" around Afghanistan to block the import of chemicals for heroin processing. The agency was embedding its officers in military units around Afghanistan, she said. In 2007 alone, the D.E.A. opened new bureaus in Tajikistan, Kyrgyzstan and Dubai, United Arab Emirates, as well as in three Mexican cities.

Cables describe lengthy negotiations over the extradition to the United States of the two notorious arms dealers wanted by the D.E.A. as it reached beyond pure counternarcotics cases: Monzer al-Kassar, a Syrian arrested in Spain, and Viktor Bout, a Russian arrested in Thailand. Both men were charged with agreeing to illegal arms sales to informants posing as weapons buyers for Colombian rebels. Notably, neither man was charged with violating narcotics laws.

Late last year in a D.E.A. case, three men from Mali accused of plotting to transport tons of cocaine across northwest Africa were charged under a narco-terrorism statute added to the law in 2006, and they were linked to both Al Qaeda and its North African affiliate, called Al Qaeda in the Islamic Maghreb.

The men themselves had claimed the terrorism link, according to the D.E.A., though officials told The New York Times that they had no independent corroboration of the Qaeda connections. Experts on the desert regions of North Africa, long a route for smuggling between Africa and Europe, are divided about whether Al Qaeda operatives play a significant role in the drug trade, and some skeptics note that adding "terrorism" to any case can draw additional investigative resources and impress a jury.

New Routes for Graft

Most times, however, the agency's expansion seems driven more by external forces than internal ones, with traffickers opening new routes to accommodate new markets. As Mexican cartels take control of drug shipments from South America to the United States, Colombian cartels have begun moving cocaine through West Africa to Europe.

The cables offer a portrait of the staggering effect on Mali, whose deserts have been littered with abandoned airplanes—including at least one Boeing 727—and Ghana, where traffickers easily smuggle drugs through an airport's "VVIP (Very Very Important Person) lounge."

Top-to-bottom corruption in many West African countries made it hard for diplomats to know whom to trust. In one 2008 case in Sierra Leone, President Ernest Bai Koroma moved to prosecute and extradite three South American traffickers seized with about 1,500 pounds of cocaine, while his attorney general was accused of offering to release them for $2.5 million in bribes.

In Nigeria, the D.E.A. reported a couple of years earlier that diplomats at the Liberian Embassy were using official vehicles to transport drugs across the border because they were not getting paid by their war-torn government and "had to fend for themselves."

A May 2008 cable from Guinea described a kind of heart-to-heart conversation about the drug trade between the American ambassador, Phillip Carter III, and Guinea's prime minister, Lansana Kouyaté. At one point, the cable said, Mr. Kouyaté "visibly slumped in his chair" and acknowledged that Guinea's most powerful drug trafficker was Ousmane Conté, the son of Lansana Conté, then the president. (After the death of his father, Mr. Conté went to prison.)

A few days later, diplomats reported evidence that the corruption ran much deeper inside the Guinean government than the president's son. In a colorfully written cable—with chapters titled "Excuses, Excuses, Excuses" and "Theatrical Production"—diplomats described attending what was billed as a drug bonfire that had been staged by the Guinean government to demonstrate its commitment to combating the drug trade.

Senior Guinean officials, including the country's drug czar, the chief of police and the justice minister, watched as officers set fire to what the government claimed was about 350 pounds of marijuana and 860 pounds of cocaine, valued at $6.5 million.

In reality, American diplomats wrote, the whole incineration was a sham. Informants had previously told the embassy that Guinean authorities replaced the cocaine with manioc flour, proving, the diplomats wrote, "that narco-corruption has contaminated" the government of Guinea "at the highest levels."

And it did not take the D.E.A.'s sophisticated intelligence techniques to figure out the truth. The cable reported that even the ambassador's driver sniffed out a hoax.

"I know the smell of burning marijuana," the driver said. "And I didn't smell anything."

Andrew W. Lehren contributed reporting.

—This article was originally published on December 25, 2010
See diplomatic cable on p. 426.

PRIVATE LINKS IN LAWMAKER'S TRIP ABROAD

By ERIC LIPTON

WASHINGTON—When Representative Dana Rohrabacher, Republican of California, visited Honduras early this year to congratulate the newly elected president, the congressman showed up with an unusual delegation.

There at his side was not just the typical collection of Washington foreign policy aides, but also a group of California real estate investors and businessmen, including a dealer in rare coins, and top executives from a fledgling San Diego biofuels company run by a friend of the congressman's wife.

Using his status as a senior Republican on the House Foreign Affairs Committee, Mr. Rohrabacher cheered his hosts in Honduras by openly challenging the Obama administration's foreign policy agenda there, then arranged a series of meetings with top Honduran officials, including the president, during which the congressman "enthusiastically promoted" the biofuel company's plans to perhaps set up operations in Honduras, says a State Department summary of the meetings included in the files obtained by WikiLeaks.

The country was eager to accommodate the congressman—who said in an interview that his actions were entirely appropriate and reflected his activist approach to foreign policy—given that the previous Honduran president had been forced out of office and into exile, and the new government was angling for United States support.

Mr. Rohrabacher's three-day trip to Tegucigalpa and his advocacy for SG Biofuels, a small company run by a family friend, stood out from the dozens of written reports detailing summaries of official visits by members of Congress to foreign nations that were included in the vast trove of State Department documents obtained by the WikiLeaks group and reviewed by The New York Times.

These memos—written by State Department officials who often sit in on lawmakers' meetings with foreign leaders—show that Congressional trips are often much more than simply fact-finding missions. Members of Congress at times push their own foreign policy agendas, even if they conflict with those of the administration in office.

Lawmakers also use their access to top foreign leaders to advocate for homegrown economic interests.

Senator Russ Feingold, Democrat of Wisconsin, used his 2008 trip to India as an opportunity to repeatedly push top officials there to cut import taxes imposed on Harley-Davidson motorcycles—whose maker is based in his home state—as well as discuss more traditional foreign policy matters like border disputes with Pakistan and combating terrorism, a State Department memo on the visit said.

Senator Maria Cantwell, Democrat of Washington, pressed top government officials in China last year to allow SSA Marine—a Seattle-based maritime company—to open a port terminal in China, a State Department cable shows.

Senator Richard G. Lugar, Republican of Indiana and one of the Senate's most influential voices on foreign affairs, has repeatedly pushed leaders in Central Asia to consider working with international oil companies, like Chevron, to expand production capacity. He and his staff have also intervened with nations including Turkey and Norway to defend Eli Lilly & Company, an Indiana-based pharmaceutical company whose employees are major contributors to Mr. Lugar's own political campaigns, against plans to introduce generic versions of some of its most profitable drugs, the documents show.

But Mr. Rohrabacher's trip last February was different because he pushed for small, specific companies with which he had personal and political ties. The coin dealer, John R. Saunders, is a big contributor to Mr. Rohrabacher's campaigns, dating back at least a decade. The president of SG Biofuels, Kirk Haney, is a friend of Mr. Rohrabacher's wife and a former intern in the congressman's office, Mr. Rohrabacher said, as well as a contributor.

Honduras had grabbed international headlines starting in June 2009, when its president at the time, Manuel Zelaya, was detained and then sent into exile, based on a fear by other elected officials there that he was scheming to remain in office despite a one-term limit in Honduras's Constitution.

Mr. Rohrabacher, challenging the stand taken by some Obama administration officials, ridiculed suggestions that Mr. Zelaya's removal was a coup d'état, and used his visit to Honduras to praise government leaders there who played roles in removing Mr. Zelaya, including members of the Supreme Court and the president of the Honduran Congress, Juan Orlando Hernández.

Mr. Rohrabacher, who was a speechwriter for President Ronald Reagan in the 1980s as the United States financed "freedom fighters" in Central America to challenge a perceived communist threat, has long cast himself as a defender of democratic causes in the region. The turn of events in Honduras offered him a chance to return to that role.

"He warned at the danger of allowing 'caudillos' or strongmen, like Cuban President Fidel Castro and Venezuelan President Hugo Chavez, to assume control," the State Department summary of his visit said, recalling his remarks to the new leaders in Honduras.

Just days before Mr. Rohrabacher's arrival, the Obama administration had pressed Honduras's new president, Porfirio Lobo, to name a "truth commission" to investigate Mr. Zelaya's removal, and implied that United States financial assistance to the poor Central American nation might hinge on such a move.

By tradition, members of Congress are not supposed to freelance foreign policy that goes against the sitting administration. But Mr. Rohrabacher, in meetings with members of the Honduran Supreme Court, told them that a truth commission was unnecessary and a waste of time.

Mr. Rohrabacher, in an interview, said that he had long taken an activist approach to foreign policy, and that he was never shy, when he met with foreign leaders, about advocating "things I think are the direction to go," even if they are sometimes not entirely consistent with the views of the sitting administration.

According to the State Department cable, he said in Honduras that his views carried weight. He told the country's top elected officials that "he was an emissary of Honduras' friends in Congress, in particular member of Congress Ileana Ros-Lehtinen," referring to a congresswoman from Florida who is the ranking Republican on the House Foreign Affairs Committee and is now set to become its chairwoman.

But the visit soon shifted to a pitch by Mr. Rohrabacher's companions for possible business deals.

Mr. Saunders, a California real estate executive, antique coin dealer and frequent campaign contributor to Mr. Rohrabacher, said he used the access he had to top Honduras officials, including the head of the country's central bank, to discuss the possibility of buying or at least helping arrange the sale of rare antique American coins from Honduras's gold reserves—a deal he said, at least so far, had not worked out.

Separately, Mr. Rohrabacher, in a meeting with the top science adviser to President Lobo, introduced two executives from SG Biofuels, who then described their plan to set up contracts with farmers in Central America to grow a flowering plant known as jatropha, whose seeds contain oil that can be harvested as diesel fuel.

Mr. Haney, the president of the company, with Mr. Rohrabacher present, also made a presentation to the United States ambassador, who then referred them to other embassy staff members to discuss possible United States foreign aid funds available for the project, the State Department memo says.

Mr. Rohrabacher, in an interview, said he had known Mr. Haney for more than a decade and he invited Mr. Haney—who paid his own costs—not so much to help out his company as to encourage a possible economic opportunity for Honduras.

"I don't do any special favors," Mr. Rohrabacher said. "But if some company is doing something and produces a great new technology that is going to help people, I will help them out."

The senior Honduran official told Mr. Rohrabacher and Mr. Haney that he was reasonably impressed, and that "the jatropha project was an excellent opportunity," the State Department memo says. He assured them that President Lobo wanted to put a priority on building a biofuel industry in Honduras.

SG Biofuels' vice president for marketing, Brian Brokowski, said that while the meetings arranged by Mr. Rohrabacher with the officials in Honduras were helpful, the company was still not committed to setting up a farming operation there like the one it had in neighboring Guatemala.

"We are exploring the potential," he said. "But for now, it is very preliminary."

Ron Nixon and Barclay Walsh contributed research.

—This article was originally published on December 19, 2010

DIPLOMATS HELP PUSH SALES OF JETLINERS ON THE GLOBAL MARKET

By ERIC LIPTON, NICOLA CLARK and ANDREW W. LEHREN

WASHINGTON—The king of Saudi Arabia wanted the United States to outfit his personal jet with the same high-tech devices as Air Force One. The president of Turkey wanted the Obama administration to let a Turkish astronaut sit in on a NASA space flight. And in Bangladesh, the prime minister pressed the State Department to re-establish landing rights at Kennedy International Airport in New York.

Each of these government leaders had one thing in common: they were trying to decide whether to buy billions of dollars' worth of commercial jets from Boeing or its European competitor, Airbus. And United States diplomats were acting like marketing agents, offering deals to heads of state and airline executives whose decisions could be influenced by price, performance and, as with all finicky customers with plenty to spend, perks.

This is the high-stakes, international bazaar for large commercial jets, where tens of billions of dollars are on the line, along with hundreds of thousands of high-paying jobs. At its heart, it is a wrestling match fought daily by executives at two giant companies, Boeing and Airbus, in which each controls about half of the global market for such planes.

To a greater degree than previously known, diplomats are a big part of the sales force, according to hundreds of cables released by WikiLeaks, which describe politicking and cajoling at the highest levels.

It is not surprising that the United States helps American companies doing business abroad, given that each sale is worth thousands of jobs and that their foreign competitors do the same. But like the other WikiLeaks cables, these offer a remarkably detailed look at what had previously been only glimpsed—in this case, the sales war between American diplomats and their European counterparts.

The cables describe letters from presidents, state visits as bargaining chips and a number of leaders making big purchases based, at least in part, on how much the companies will dress up private planes.

The documents also suggest that demands for bribes, or at least payment to suspicious intermediaries who offer to serve as "agents," still take place. Boeing says it is committed to avoiding any such corrupt practices.

State Department and Boeing officials, in interviews last month, acknowledged the important role the United States government plays in helping them sell commercial airplanes, despite a trade agreement signed by the United States and European leaders three decades ago intended to remove international politics from the process.

The United States economy, said Robert D. Hormats, under secretary for economic affairs at the State Department, increasingly relies upon exports to the fast-growing developing world—nations like China and India, as well as those in Latin America and the Middle East.

So pushing sales of big-ticket items like commercial jets, earth-moving equipment or power plants (or stepping in to object if an American company is not being given a fair chance to bid) is central to the Obama administration's strategy to help the nation recover from the recession.

Boeing earns about 70 percent of its commercial plane sales from foreign buyers, and is the single biggest exporter of manufactured goods in the United States. Every $1 billion in sales—and some of these deals carry a price tag of as high as $10 billion—translates into an estimated 11,000 American jobs, according to the State Department.

The Equalizers

"That is the reality of the 21st century; governments are playing a greater role in supporting their companies, and we need to do the same thing," Mr. Hormats, a former top executive at Goldman Sachs, said in an interview.

Said Tim Neale, a Boeing spokesman, "The way I look at it, it levels the playing field."

But Charles A. Hamilton, a former Defense Department official who is a consultant to Airbus, said the government's advocacy undermined arguments by Boeing and the United States that Airbus had an unfair advantage because of its subsidies from European governments.

"The bottom line is anything goes to get the business," said Mr. Hamilton, adding that he was speaking for himself, and not for Airbus. "If they feel like they are losing, they will do just about anything to save a deal."

Airbus executives would not discuss details of their own sales campaigns —and the WikiLeaks documents are mostly focused on American efforts. But one Airbus official, who was not authorized to speak on the record, conceded that, international agreements aside, "commercial jet sales are not totally decoupled from political relationship building."

One example of the horse-trading involved Saudi Arabia, which in November announced a deal with Boeing to buy 12 777-300ER airliners, with options for 10 more, a transaction worth more than $3.3 billion at list prices.

That announcement was preceded by years of intense lobbying by American officials.

One pitch came from the highest levels, the cables show. In late 2006, Israel Hernandez, a senior Commerce Department official, hand-delivered a personal letter from President George W. Bush to the Jeddah office of King Abdullah, urging the king to buy as many as 43 Boeing jets to modernize Saudi Arabian Airlines and 13 jets for the Saudi royal fleet, which serves the extended royal family.

The king read the letter from Mr. Bush, the State Department cable says, and announced that Boeing jets were his favorites. He said he had just turned down two new Airbus jets, opting instead for a slightly used Boeing 747.

But before he would commit to a mostly Boeing fleet, the king had a request.

"I am instructing you," he told Mr. Hernandez politely, according to the State Department cable, "to speak to the president and all concerned authorities," as the king "wanted to have all the technology that his friend, President Bush, had on Air Force One." Once he had his own high-tech plane, with the world's most advanced telecommunications and defense equipment—the king told Mr. Hernandez that "'God willing,' he will make a decision that will 'please you very much.'"

A State Department spokesman confirmed last week that the United States had authorized an "upgrade" to King Abdullah's plane, adding "for security reasons, we won't discuss specifics."

Bangladesh's prime minister, Sheik Hasina Wazed, was equally direct in making a connection for the landing rights at Kennedy Airport, as a condition of the airplane deal, which was then at risk of collapsing.

"If there is no New York route, what is the point of buying Boeing?" a November 2009 cable quotes Ms. Hasina as saying as she pressed American officials. The deal with Boeing went through. So far, flights by the country's national carrier, Biman Bangladesh Airlines, to New York have not been restored.

The request from Turkey for a slot on a future NASA flight came early last year, as Turkish Airlines was considering buying as many as 20 Boeing jets.

The government there owns slightly less than half of the airline, but Turkey's minister of transportation, Binali Yildirim, in a January 2010 meeting with the United States ambassador to Turkey, made clear that the country's president wanted help with its fledgling space program and perhaps assistance from the Federal Aviation Administration to improve its aviation safety.

Requests for Favors

"Cooperation in this area will create the right environment for commercial deals," Mr. Yildirim told the United States ambassador, the cable says.

In a cable back to Washington, James F. Jeffrey, then the United States ambassador to Turkey, called the effort by Turkish authorities to link the Boeing deal to political requests an "unwelcome, but unsurprising degree of political influence in this transaction." But he went on to say that authorizing the F.A.A. to help Turkey improve its aviation safety and space exploration programs could benefit both nations.

"We probably cannot put a Turkish astronaut in orbit, but there are programs we could undertake to strengthen Turkey's capacity in this area that would meet our own goals for improved aviation safety," he wrote. "In any case, we must show some response to the minister's vague request if we want to maximize chances for the sale."

The deal was announced a month later, as Turkish Airlines ordered 20 Boeing planes.

Some sales come to Boeing in part because foreign political leaders want to show friendship to the United States.

King Abdullah II of Jordan, a longtime ally and recipient of billions of dollars in United States aid, told the ambassador in 2004 that "even though the latest Airbus offer was better than Boeing's he intended to make a 'political' decision to have Royal Jordanian buy Boeing aircraft," a State Department cable said, although the United States still had to help Boeing secure the deal.

The cables show that the United States is willing to pull out all the political stops if Boeing is in danger of losing a big deal to Airbus. In late 2007, the board of Gulf Air, the national airline of the oil-rich kingdom of Bahrain, picked Airbus for a huge sale.

Boeing told the American government, which responded that there was still a way to turn the deal around, even though Airbus had offered the planes for about $400 million less than Boeing.

'Far From Over'

"The contest remained far from over," said the cable. "Gulf Air's selection still needed to be endorsed by the government."

The American ambassador at the time, Adam Ereli, and his chief economic officer, went into action, "lobbying Gulf Air management, board members, government officials and representatives of parliament," and appealing directly to the crown prince of Bahrain, in an effort to line up a deal for Boeing that could be final in time for a coming visit by President Bush, the first visit by a sitting United States president.

Within two weeks, the embassy alerted Boeing officials that the crown prince and king of Bahrain had rejected Airbus's offer and directed Gulf Air's chairman to make a deal with Boeing that could be signed while Mr. Bush was in the country.

Seeing that Airbus had been outmaneuvered, France's president, Nicolas Sarkozy, made a last-minute bid to save the deal, the State Department cable says. He offered to visit Bahrain after Mr. Bush had left, but that stop-over was canceled when the Boeing agreement was signed in January 2008. None of the last-minute diplomacy was disclosed.

The cables make clear that both Boeing and the government set limits on their efforts, turning away requests in Turkey and Tanzania to hire "agents" who charge steep commissions—or as some called them, bribes—to gain access to top officials.

Mr. Neale, the company spokesman, says that for Boeing, "it is not just a matter of abiding by U.S. law and laws internationally but a general sense of business ethics." When such requests surfaced, Boeing often reported them to the State Department.

"'Agents' and steep 'commissions' have been at the heart of several corruption scandals here," says a 2007 State Department cable recounting a demand that Boeing hire a mysterious hotel executive in Tanzania to serve as a "go-between" with government officials. Payments like that, the cable said, typically were bribes that "ended up in Swiss bank accounts."

Eric Lipton reported from Washington, Nicola Clark from Paris and Andrew W. Lehren from New York.

—This article was originally published on January 2, 2011
See diplomatic cable on p. 499.

STATE DEPT. DAILY IS WINDOW ON A JITTERY PLANET

By SCOTT SHANE

WASHINGTON—In Tunisia, a man was spotted sitting in a cafe, watching the road to the American ambassador's residence, before driving away in a gray Volkswagen. In Nigeria, extremists, possibly including a "well-trained" operative just arrived from Chad, were believed to be "planning a massive terrorist attack." And Persian-language computer hacking sites had posted dangerous "Trojan horse" programs, suggesting how Iranian agents might attack the United States.

Those were just three of dozens of threats reported in a single issue of a publication with a limited subscriber list: The Diplomatic Security Daily, a classified roundup of potential horrors facing American diplomats or citizens anywhere in the world. A look at one issue, from June 29, 2009, gives a feeling for the nerve-racking atmosphere in which State Department officers routinely operate.

The Diplomatic Security Daily is classified "secret/noforn," a label that prohibits sharing it even with foreign allies, and it goes to American embassies and other outposts to alert them of possible threats. Some 14 issues of The Daily were included in a quarter-million diplomatic cables obtained by The New York Times.

The June 29, 2009, issue is a window on the government's round-the-clock struggle to assess rumors, often vague, about terrorists, assassins, kidnappers, hackers and others who might single out Americans. Few of the threats materialize, but the State Department's Bureau of Diplomatic Security sorts and shares the steady flow of reports.

One case involves intelligence reports that "militants attached to Pakistan's Mumtaz Group" were scheming to kidnap Americans and Britons in Pakistan, conceivably in Peshawar's University Town neighborhood. But was the danger real?

The Mumtaz Group, the report says, may be linked to a dead operative of Al Qaeda who used that nom de guerre. (In fact, The Daily reports in a rare touch of black humor, the alias Mumtaz is "arguably inauspicious," since at least three Qaeda members who used it are now dead.)

The threatened kidnappings might be linked to another militant known as Imran, an Uzbek connected to a fatal attack on an American contractor in 2008. Someone named Imran had reportedly just been captured by Pakistani intelligence—but American intelligence could not be certain it was the same man, The Daily said in its frustratingly inconclusive report.

One striking aspect of the security warnings sent to embassies is how many involve cyber threats. The June 29, 2009, issue, in addition to mentioning the Persian hacker sites, discussed at length Chinese companies and government agencies specializing in computer security, implying that they might pose a hazard.

Such companies had "recruited Chinese hackers," including Lin Yong, known as Lion, to support research projects on attacking computer networks, The Daily reported. There is a strong possibility that China "is harvesting the talents of its private sector in order to bolster offensive and defensive" cyberoperations, the report said.

—This article was originally published on December 6, 2010

IRAN CALLS LEAKED
DOCUMENTS A U.S. PLOT

By WILLIAM YONG and ALAN COWELL

TEHRAN—In Iran's first official reaction to leaked State Department cables quoting Arab leaders as urging the United States to bomb Tehran's nuclear facilities, President Mahmoud Ahmadinejad dismissed the documents as American psychological warfare that would not affect his country's relations with other nations, news reports said.

The documents seemed to show several Arab nations, notably Saudi Arabia, Iran's rival for influence in the Persian Gulf, displaying such hostility that King Abdullah repeatedly implored Washington to "cut off the head of the snake" while there was still time.

Nonetheless, Mr. Ahmadinejad said at a news conference on Monday that Iran's relations with its neighbors would not be damaged by the reports.

"Regional countries are all friends with each other. Such mischief will have no impact on the relations of countries," he said, according to Reuters.

"Some part of the American government produced these documents," he said. "We don't think this information was leaked. We think it was organized to be released on a regular basis and they are pursuing political goals."

News reports quoted Mr. Ahmadinejad as calling the documents "worthless" and without "legal value."

Mr. Ahmadinejad's news conference was scheduled before the leaked cables were published on Sunday and had been expected to focus on such issues as Iran's scheduled negotiations on Dec. 5 with world powers over its nuclear program and plans at home to drastically reduce energy and food subsidies. Mr. Ahmadinejad said on Monday that while Iran and the world powers had agreed on a date, the site of the talks was still under discussion.

Iran says its nuclear program is for peaceful purposes but many Western powers say it is designed to build nuclear weapons. That issue was one of the overarching themes of the first batch of leaked documents published Sunday in The New York Times and four European newspapers.

With steadily increasing sanctions, outside powers have been seeking to persuade Iran to curb its uranium enrichment, a process that can lead to the production of weapons-grade nuclear fuel.

Mr. Ahmadinejad reiterated that Tehran's enrichment program was legal and "nonnegotiable," Reuters said.

"The complete enrichment cycle and the production of fuel are basic rights" of member states of the International Atomic Energy Agency, the United Nations' nuclear watchdog, and "are nonnegotiable," Mr. Ahmadinejad was quoted as saying.

William Yong reported from Tehran, and Alan Cowell from Paris.

—This article was originally published on November 29, 2010

CAUSTIC U.S. VIEWS OF BERLUSCONI CHURN ITALY'S POLITICS

By RACHEL DONADIO and CELESTINE BOHLEN

ROME—In his dealings with American diplomats, Prime Minister Silvio Berlusconi of Italy has often said that he wants his country to be "the best friend of the United States." In cables to Washington, American diplomats added a few caveats.

Preparing President Obama for a meeting with Mr. Berlusconi in June 2009, Elizabeth Dibble, the deputy chief of mission at the United States Embassy in Rome, warned that some in the American government regarded the Italian leader as "feckless, vain and ineffective as a modern European leader." Dealing with him, she said, "requires a careful balance of close consideration."

Such caustic characterizations—revealed in a cache of leaked diplomatic cables obtained by WikiLeaks and released to various news organizations—caused a firestorm in Italy this week. They could further weaken the prime minister ahead of a Dec. 14 parliamentary showdown that could decide the fate of his government. Critics of Mr. Berlusconi are using the revelations to support their calls for his resignation. Experts say that he may yet win the vote but that his infighting government is not expected to last long, certainly not through its full term, which ends in 2013.

While experts said the revelations seemed unlikely to damage the close relations between Italy and the United States, they nevertheless could have a profound impact on Mr. Berlusconi's image and reputation—long the core of his political strength.

"Now he can no longer claim that he is well respected and supported by the U.S. and that he vouches for the trans-Atlantic alliance," said Sergio Fabbrini, director of the Luiss School of Government in Rome. "Now he can no longer use that in domestic politics."

Yet in a country with a wide divergence between what people say in public and in private and where saving face is a national art, some Italian commentators argued—privately—that the leaks reflected far worse on the United States for allowing a security breach that essentially hung their confidential sources out to dry.

Some American diplomats in Italy acknowledged that their sources were already more reluctant to speak candidly with them.

In an effort at damage control, Secretary of State Hillary Rodham Clinton had a one-on-one meeting with Mr. Berlusconi on Wednesday on the margins of a summit meeting in Kazakhstan, telling him Italy was the "best friend" of the United States.

In the cables, American diplomats describe Mr. Berlusconi, 74, as both a canny survivor of Italian politics, his own gaffes and steamy scandals, and a sometimes erratic partner on the international scene, ready to commit Italian soldiers to Afghanistan, but wobbly on critical issues like trade with Iran and relations with Russia.

"Our relationship with Berlusconi is complex," Ms. Dibble wrote. "He is vocally pro-American and has helped address our interest on many levels in a manner and to a degree that the previous government was unwilling or unable to do." Yet, the diplomat noted, there are other areas where Mr. Berlusconi "seems determined to be best friends with Russia, sometimes in direct opposition to American, and even European Union, policy."

It was noted that Mr. Berlusconi had criticized the American missile defense project, eastward expansion of NATO and support for Kosovo's independence as "provocations of Russia." Virtually alone among European leaders, he defended Russia's military push into Georgia during the August 2008 war and has backed joint energy projects between Gazprom in Russia and the Italian energy company ENI, at a time when the European Union is pushing for less dependence on Russian gas.

Mr. Berlusconi's ties with Russia and Vladimir V. Putin, its former president and current prime minister, are clearly a subject of American concern. Mrs. Clinton's office sent off questions to the American Embassies in Rome and Moscow, asking for anything that might cast light on the relationship. "What personal investments, if any, do they have that might drive their foreign and economic policies?" the cable asked.

Italy's cooperation on American-led sanctions against Iran has also fallen short of public promises, diplomats reported. "The Italians want to have it both ways: they want to be seen as playing a leadership role in the international effort to ratchet up sanctions on Iran, while also wanting to leave the door open to future business deals for Italian companies," said a cable sent by the embassy on Feb. 10 this year.

Diplomats in recent encounters have found the Italian leader tired and weakened by a spate of scandals and a souring political atmosphere: in one meeting with the ambassador, he fell asleep. Writing about a lunch with Mr. Berlusconi in Milan last Dec. 30, soon after the Italian leader had been hit in the face with a model of the Milan cathedral, the ambassador said Gianni Letta, Mr. Berlusconi's top adviser and a longstanding confidant of American diplomats, was clearly assuming the "position as co-regent."

Mr. Letta offers a frank assessment of the Berlusconi government. In a cable from October 2009, he is said to describe Mr. Berlusconi as "physically and politically weak," a statement that in the current unstable political climate comes across as particularly damning to Mr. Berlusconi, who places a profound value on personal loyalty.

Rachel Donadio reported from Rome, and Celestine Bohlen from Paris. Gaia Pianigiani contributed reporting from Rome.

—This article was originally published on December 2, 2010

BLUNT AND BLUSTERY, PUTIN RESPONDS TO STATE DEPARTMENT CABLES ON RUSSIA

By ELLEN BARRY

MOSCOW—Prime Minister Vladimir V. Putin responded Wednesday to criticism of Russia revealed in United States diplomatic cables published by the Web site WikiLeaks, warning Washington not to interfere in Russian domestic affairs.

His comments, made in an interview broadcast Wednesday night on CNN's "Larry King Live," referred to a cable that said "Russian democracy has disappeared" and that described the government as "an oligarchy run by the security services," a statement attributed to the American defense secretary, Robert M. Gates.

Mr. Putin said in the interview that Mr. Gates had been "deeply misled." Asked about a cable that described President Dmitri A. Medvedev as "playing Robin to Putin's Batman," he said the author had "aimed to slander one of us."

Mr. King, whose program is carried on CNN's channels around the world, has long had a reputation for softball questions. So Mr. Putin's decision to appear on the program allowed his voice to be heard both in the United States and abroad while avoiding being challenged on contentious topics like his own grip on power and the limits on human rights and free speech in Russia.

In the interview, Mr. Putin also warned that Russia would develop and deploy new nuclear weapons if the United States did not accept its proposals on integrating Russian and European missile defense forces—amplifying a comment made by Mr. Medvedev in his annual state of the nation address on Tuesday.

"We've just put forward a proposal showing how jointly working, tackling the shared problem of security, could share responsibility between ourselves," he said. "But if our proposals will be met with only negative answers, and if on top of that additional threats are built near our borders as this, Russia will have to ensure her own security through different means," including "new nuclear missile technologies."

Mr. Putin said Moscow would like to avoid this situation.

"This is no threat on our part," he said. "We are simply saying this is what we expect to happen if we don't agree on a joint effort there." Last month, during a NATO-Russia summit meeting in Lisbon, the delegations discussed President Obama's invitation for Russia to take some role in the future missile shield, perhaps through linkage between Russian facilities and the European shield.

At that meeting, Mr. Medvedev proposed "sectoral missile defense," which would divide the missile defense shield into "zones of responsibility," and involve deep coordination between the European and Russian sectors, said Dmitri V. Trenin, a military analyst and director of the Carnegie Moscow Center. According to this plan, Russia would shoot down missiles flying over its territory toward Europe, and NATO would shoot down missiles flying over European territory toward Russia, he said.

NATO's proposals for cooperation are less ambitious, and some members remain deeply mistrustful of Russian involvement, he said.

Mr. Putin appeared relaxed in the hourlong interview with Mr. King, who first interviewed him in 2000. He said he was "thankful" for President Obama's softening of rhetoric toward Russia and for his revision of a planned missile defense shield in Europe.

Asked about the arrest this summer of 11 people accused of spying for Russia, Mr. Putin said the agents were not active, but would have "become pertinent in crisis periods, like when diplomatic relations were suspended or cut."

His comment seemed to address one of the central mysteries of the summer spy scandal: why the agents were passing on information that was readily accessible without spying.

In the interview, Mr. Putin broke from the restrained response Russian leaders have so far given to the WikiLeaks cables, which have so far offered few real revelations about sensitive topics like corruption. The comments attributed to Mr. Gates, in a cable dated Feb. 8, 2010, used the harshest language made public so far.

Mr. Putin said that several American presidents had been elected through the electoral college system even though they did not win a majority of the popular vote, but that Russia did not press the point.

"When we are talking with our American friends and tell them there are systemic problems" with the electoral college system, "we hear from them: 'Don't interfere with our affairs. This is our tradition, and it's going to continue like that.' We are not interfering.

"But to our colleagues, I would also like to advise you not to interfere with the sovereign choice of the Russian people," he said.

He played down the impact of the cables' release, and went on to suggest that they might be fakes being circulated for obscure political purposes.

"Some experts believe that somebody is deceiving WikiLeaks, that their reputation is being undermined to use them for their own political purposes later on," he said. "That is one of the possibilities there. That is the opinion of the experts."

Brian Stelter contributed reporting from New York.

—This article was originally published on December 1, 2010

LEAKED CABLES STIR RESENTMENT AND SHRUGS

By ALAN COWELL

PARIS—In the world of diplomacy, known for its ambiguity and opacity, the WikiLeaks organization says its function is to "keep government open." But with the release of some 250,000 American diplomatic cables, the outcome may be more ambiguous, closing doors to United States diplomats, turning candor to reticence and leaving many people leery of baring their souls and secrets to American officials.

There is, so far, no evidence of any deep damage to American diplomacy—with many nations, in public anyway, brushing off the sometimes embarrassing revelations. Their own interest in a relationship with the United States, some suggested, trumps momentary awkwardness.

"Relationships between countries don't get affected on the basis of what one ambassador has allegedly written," said Qamar Zaman Kaira, the information minister in Pakistan, a nation whose contacts with the United States are at once important, fraught and complex.

But there is no shortage of anger either—in Turkey, Russia, Mexico and elsewhere. "I am worried about the Americans spying; they have always been very interfering," said President Felipe Calderón of Mexico.

And in an age when years of diplomatic cables can be stored on a single flash drive, it appeared that WikiLeaks might not be alone: Al Akhbar, a Lebanese newspaper that supports the Shiite militant and political group Hezbollah, has been posting documents from eight Arab countries, including Lebanon, Iraq, Egypt and Libya.

On Friday, evidence mounted of at least the beginning of damage to American allies, with officials from Canada and Germany either leaving their jobs or offering to do so as a result of the revelations.

The first casualty of the leaks was Helmut Metzner, the chief of staff to Foreign Minister Guido Westerwelle of Germany. Mr. Metzner resigned late Thursday after being identified in one document as a "young, up-and-coming party loyalist" who provided American Embassy officials in Berlin with an account of what were supposed to be confidential negotiations last year to form a new German coalition.

In Canada, there was still no official response on Friday to a reported offer by William Crosbie, the Canadian ambassador in Afghanistan, to resign in advance of publication of a leaked cable recording his views on President Hamid Karzai and his family.

In Germany, leaked cables told a different story, describing events in Berlin that might once have inspired a cold war spy thriller if not for the fact that both players involved—the United States and Germany—are allies in NATO and in many other ways.

According to the cables, negotiations were under way last year to form a coalition between the Christian Democrats, led by Chancellor Angela Merkel, and Mr. Westerwelle's Free Democrats.

One cable, quoted in the British newspaper The Guardian, reported how American diplomats relied on "a fly on the wall, a young, up-and-coming party loyalist who was taking notes during the marathon talks" to provide documents and information about the negotiations.

When word of the mole's existence emerged this week, Mr. Westerwelle reacted dismissively. On Friday, Wulf Oehme, a spokesman for the Free Democrats, said Mr. Metzner had been suspended from his job, though not expelled from the party.

Secretary of State Hillary Rodham Clinton, on a trip to Central Asia and the Middle East, continued to smooth over any tensions with foreign leaders. She traveled on Friday to Bahrain, whose king was quoted in the leaked cables as urging Washington to stop Iran from getting nuclear weapons by any means necessary.

Bahrain's foreign minister, while declining to confirm the remarks attributed to King Hamad bin Isa al-Khalifa, said the Persian Gulf kingdom had repeatedly told Iran that it should not pursue a military nuclear program. None of the comments attributed to the king, he said, contradicted Bahrain's position.

"Every country in the Middle East has the right for nuclear power for peaceful use," the foreign minister, Sheik Khalid bin Ahmed al-Khalifa, said after meeting with Mrs. Clinton.

But, he added: "When it comes to taking that power and developing it into a cycle for weapons grade, this is something that we can never accept and we can never live with in this region. We've said it to Iran."

Samples of opinion, from Asia to Europe to Latin America, showed the global reaction to the WikiLeaks cables.

Bernard Kouchner, who until recently was the foreign minister in France, predicted: "We will all terribly mistrust each other. That is the risk."

A Chinese intellectual, who spoke on the condition of anonymity because he feared exposure, said the disclosures had left some Chinese who had had contact with United States diplomats "nervous" about the possibility of persecution by the authorities, who had blocked access in China to the WikiLeaks Web site.

Turkey, the subject of many of the cables, has become increasingly critical of Washington's handling of the secret material, calling the disclosures the latest blow in the deterioration of the United States' image as the world's leading power and questioning how the documents could have been so easily leaked.

Analysts in Britain, which once prided itself on its so-called special relationship with Washington, seemed to acknowledge that the cables reflected the nation's eroded status in their criticism of British leaders and the British military. Over the past decade, said Prof. Malcolm Chalmers of the Royal United Services Institute, "We all have fewer illusions about just how important the U.K. is anyway."

The diplomatic revelations also reached into delicate relationships that Washington is seeking to nurture, like in Moscow, where the leaked cables made disparaging references to President Dmitri A. Medvedev and Prime Minister Vladimir V. Putin.

"We are not paranoiacs, and we do not link Russian-American relations to any leaks," Mr. Medvedev said on Friday. "However, these leaks are revealing. They show the full measure of cynicism behind the assessments and judgments which prevail in the foreign policy of various nations, in this case the United States."

Oddly, though, in two places where the leaked cables seemed to have raised some of the most unsettling questions, the response has been muted.

In the Arab world, much of the press is owned by members of the Saudi royal family and tends to avoid topics that could embarrass the kingdom. The cables quoted King Abdullah of Saudi Arabia and Persian Gulf leaders as urging the United States to bomb Iran's nuclear facilities, but the response, in the words of Osama Nogali, a spokesman for the Saudi Foreign

Ministry, has been to say that the cables "do not concern" the kingdom since they reflect American analysis.

In Kabul, Afghanistan, some business leaders worried that the disclosures could have a more roundabout effect, further undermining American commitment to support the government.

"Afghan corruption is not just an Afghan domestic issue, it is also a U.S. domestic issue because it's your money," said Saad Mohseni, the chairman of Moby Group, the largest media company in Afghanistan. "Your tolerance of corruption in our country will raise questions back home in the United States public, the media and even Congress."

Conversely, some places, notably Israel, saw the WikiLeaks disclosures as helpful, since they seemed to show Arab leaders quietly saying what had long been publicly argued by Israeli leaders—that the region's main threat was Iran.

"At least on the Iranian issue—and apparently on more than a few other matters—the leaders of the world, including the Arab world, think as we do, but are ashamed to admit it," said Sever Plocker, a columnist for the newspaper Yediot Aharonot.

Reporting was contributed by Ellen Barry from Moscow; Katrin Bennhold and Scott Sayare from Paris; Michael Slackman and Stefan Pauly from Berlin; Mark Landler from Manama, Bahrain; Edward Wong and Jonathan Ansfield from Beijing; Elisabeth Malkin from Mexico City; Salman Masood from Islamabad, Pakistan; Alissa J. Rubin from Kabul, Afghanistan; Jack Healy from Baghdad; Celia W. Dugger from Johannesburg; Jeffrey Gettleman from Nairobi, Kenya; Robert F. Worth from Sana, Yemen; Sebnem Arsu from Istanbul; Ravi Somaiya from London; and Ethan Bronner from Jerusalem.

—This article was originally published on December 3, 2010

FROM WIKILEMONS,
CLINTON TRIES
TO MAKE LEMONADE

By MARK LANDLER

MANAMA, Bahrain—When American diplomats get together these days, there is lots of dark talk about the fallout from the sensational disclosure of secret diplomatic cables. Will angry foreign governments kick out ambassadors? Will spooked locals stop talking to their embassy contacts?

Behind all the public hand-wringing, however, there is another, more muted reaction: pride.

The WikiLeaks affair has turned an unaccustomed spotlight on the diplomatic corps—pinstriped authors who pour their hearts and minds into cables, which are filed to the State Department and, until now, were often barely read by desk officers, let alone senior diplomats.

Whatever damage the leaks may do, and nobody doubts it could be substantial, they have showcased the many roles of the Foreign Service officer in the field: part intelligence analyst, part schmoozer, part spy—and to judge by these often artful cables, part foreign correspondent.

The pride of authorship is shared by their boss, Secretary of State Hillary Rodham Clinton, who found a silver lining in the disclosures, even after she spent last week trying to smooth the feathers of foreign leaders described in the cables as feckless, profligate, vain, corrupt or worse.

"What you see are diplomats doing the work of diplomacy: reporting and analyzing and providing information, solving problems, worrying about big, complex challenges," Mrs. Clinton said to reporters at the end of a four-country trip to Central Asia and the Persian Gulf that wound up being a contrition tour.

"In a way," she said, "it should be reassuring, despite the occasional tidbit that is pulled out and unfortunately blown up."

Not all the tidbits reflect well on the diplomats, of course. Memos from the United States Embassy in Georgia, for example, showed that it relied so heavily on the Georgian government for intelligence that it badly misjudged the country's actions in its war with Russia in 2008.

But the overall quality of the cables—their detail, analysis, and in some cases, laugh-out-loud humor—has won fans in unlikely places. "It's very entertaining reading," said Aigul Solovyeva, a member of Parliament in Kazakhstan who met Mrs. Clinton there this week.

Richard E. Hoagland, the ambassador to Kazakhstan, thinks good cable-writing is so essential that he has written a guide for junior diplomats, "Ambassador's Cable Drafting Tips." Many of the tips would be familiar to any cub reporter trying to get an editor to bite on a story.

"The trick is to catch readers' attention," he advises. "The first three to five words are all they will see in their electronic queue."

His specific recommendations? Avoid flabby writing, citing as a typically egregious example any memo that starts: " 'The ambassador used the opportunity of the meeting to raise the issue of' . . ."

And work on storytelling: "Despite what some in Washington will tell you, there is nothing at all wrong with colorful writing, as long as it communicates something." But he adds a caveat: "Cute writing is never acceptable—cute is for toddlers, not for professional diplomats."

Mr. Hoagland, who accompanied Mrs. Clinton to meetings this week, declined to discuss the substance of the leaked cables. But he was happy to discuss style. As a general rule, he said he instructs staff members to think like journalists. "Not everything we churn out is great writing," he said, "but we try to keep up the standards."

The embassy in Kazakhstan met many of Mr. Hoagland's standards for cable-writing, even before he became ambassador there. Cables about Kazakhstan's high-living leaders are written in a satirical tone worthy of Borat, the fictional (and wild) Kazakh played in the movie by Sacha Baron Cohen.

One described Kazakhstan's defense minister turning up drunk for a meeting with an American official, "slouching back in his chair and slurring all kinds of Russian participles." He explained that he had just been at a cadet graduation reception, "toasting Kazakhstan's newly-commissioned officers."

The memo concluded: "Who was toasted more—the defense minister or the cadets—is a matter of pure speculation."

A 2006 cable from the embassy in Moscow showed that the staff there was also alert to the literary quality of the events on which they reported, and the value of telling details. The memo offered an account of a society wedding in Dagestan in Russia's Caucasus, where guests threw $100 bills at child dancers and took alcohol-sodden water-scooter jaunts on the Caspian Sea. But it also showed how the wedding was a "microcosm of the social and political relations of the North Caucasus."

For Mrs. Clinton, the pride in the diplomats' work is a small compensation for a difficult week in which she has discussed the WikiLeaks case with more than two dozen foreign leaders, working to soothe bruised egos and explain how the security breach happened.

The job of damage control has fallen mainly to her. President Obama has not called any foreign leaders about the disclosures. Defense Secretary Robert M. Gates, meanwhile, has been reserved even though the cables were believed to be purloined from a Department of Defense computer system by an army private, Bradley Manning, who is now in a military jail.

Mrs. Clinton's reaction to shouldering the burden has been every bit as artful as the cables that have landed her in so much trouble.

"It was a DoD system, and a DoD obviously military intel guy," she said. "But we're part of one government, and we're part of one country, and we have to work together, and that's what we're doing."

—This article was originally published on December 4, 2010

WIKILEAKS AND THE PERILS OF OVERSHARING

By NOAM COHEN

THE recent release of internal State Department cables by WikiLeaks, assisted by a coalition of news outlets in the United States and Europe, has been viewed as a national security matter—have confidential sources been compromised? Could relations between the United States and Russia (or Italy or France or Pakistan) be permanently damaged?

But one can take an even longer view of the meaning of the WikiLeaks campaign: by exposing the candid workings of government, the project and its leader, Julian Assange, have transformed the debate over Internet privacy from one about the individual to one about the government.

In the aftermath, many of the sharpest critics of WikiLeaks have belittled what has been learned, saying the material appears meant to humiliate the United States with embarrassing assessments of world leaders rather than inform the public of gross misbehavior. The damage to the government instead relates to the loss of the confidentiality needed to conduct foreign affairs.

The conservative commentator Tunku Varadarajan, writing in The Daily Beast, was among the most direct in making the point: "Diplomacy, to work at all effectively, must draw a line between the 'consultative process' and the 'work product.' This is but part of the human condition: Human beings need to consult, speculate, brainstorm, argue with each other—yes, even to gossip and say dopey things—in order to find their way through the difficult task of coming to an official, or publicly stated position which would then be open (legitimately) to criticism."

So, without a zone of privacy it becomes impossible for a government to sustain complicated, even contradictory, ideas about relationships and about the world—in other words, it becomes impossible to think. And, imagine that: apparently governments need to think.

Were he not talking about geopolitics and accusing Mr. Assange of being a Marxist (skipping right past the Socialist label), Mr. Varadarajan would sound a lot like the commentators who worry about the generation growing up engulfed by modern Internet technologies.

These young people, too, lack the ability to say and do dopey things without it seemingly haunting them forever. They may never have bought a book without being profiled. Or queried a search engine without being sized up for an advertisement. Or proffered, and maybe then withdrawn, friendship, without it being logged.

The author and critic Zadie Smith made these points in an essay titled "Generation Why?" in The New York Review of Books. It included a scathing assessment of what Facebook and other Web technologies have wrought among her college students. She fears that by sharing so much—and having so much shared about themselves—these young people have lost any hope for an inner life.

Whether the formats or the people are to blame is almost beside the point. "I am dreaming of a Web that caters to a kind of person who no longer exists," she writes. "A private person, a person who is a mystery, to the world and—which is more important—to herself."

In the essay's climax, she describes teaching an experimental novel "about a man who decides to pass most of his time in his bathroom," who lacks "interiority." She concludes: "To my students this novel feels perfectly realistic; an accurate portrait of their own denuded selfhood, or, to put it neutrally, a close analogue of the undeniable boredom of urban twenty-first-century existence."

Of course, there are reasons privacy is allocated the way it is—that is, why governments should get it, and individuals less so. The Internet economy thrives on data collection about users—to deliver better advertisements or to allow "friends" to share what they consume. And, naturally, diplomats need to be able to be candid back home, and be sociable at official functions.

In fact, the catty nature of many of the cables—comparing Vladimir V. Putin and Dmitri A. Medvedev to Batman and Robin, for example—reminds one of high school, and the perils of oversharing. You feel for the United States these days: I have home room with Dmitri, how can I look him in the face now?

To an outsider looking in, another teenage expression comes to mind: T.M.I., or too much information.

"The whole thing seems a little Facebooky," said Lisa Lynch, a journalism professor at Concordia University in Montreal, who has written about WikiLeaks. She said she was surprised no one had displayed the information in the cables as Facebook status updates: "You know, Sarkozy is no longer in a relationship with the United States."

Still, there was a larger purpose in the cable releases, she said. And it was not to teach the world the importance of privacy by showing the powerful how it feels to be transparent to the world. WikiLeaks has swept up the obscure and the weak (albeit obnoxious) in its past, as when it named members of the racist British National Party who certainly did not seek to be exposed.

Taking advantage of new technologies, Ms. Lynch said, the project has leveled the playing field, "reversing hierarchies of who gets censored and who gets surveilled."

In the process, WikiLeaks is perhaps trying to render governments as brain-addled as Ms. Smith sees her students.

In an essay attributed to Mr. Assange—posted to his Web site in 2006 shortly before the start of WikiLeaks and given the name "State and Terrorist Conspiracies"—he describes his views on authoritarian governments, the governments that he is trying to bedevil.

He speaks explicitly about trying to prevent oppressive governments from communicating internally: a government "that cannot think is powerless to preserve itself," he writes in the essay.

One scholar, Aaron Bady, last week wrote an analysis of "State and Terrorist Conspiracies" on his blog, saying that Mr. Assange's strategy for combating an authoritarian government was "to degrade its ability to conspire, to hinder its ability to 'think' as a conspiratorial mind. The metaphor of a computing network is mostly implicit, but utterly crucial: he seeks to oppose the power of the state by treating it like a computer and tossing sand in its diodes."

Put differently, governments, like teenagers, need to know when to keep their mouths shut: WikiLeaks is trying hard to make that task impossible.

—This article was originally published on December 5, 2010

KARZAI'S RESPONSE
TO CABLES RELIEVES U.S.

By ELISABETH BUMILLER

KABUL, Afghanistan—Defense Secretary Robert M. Gates called it "extraordinarily embarrassing," which might also describe the sentiments beneath the decorous tableau on Wednesday night in the palace of President Hamid Karzai of Afghanistan.

A little more than a week after the disclosure of a cache of secret American diplomatic cables that quoted Karl W. Eikenberry, the United States ambassador to Afghanistan, describing Mr. Karzai's "inability to grasp the most rudimentary principles of state-building," among other criticisms, Mr. Karzai, Mr. Eikenberry and Mr. Gates shared their first public forum together since the cables were leaked.

Not that anyone would have known that something was amiss. Mr. Eikenberry sat genially in the front row of American spectators, busily taking notes, as Mr. Gates stood alongside Mr. Karzai, smiling broadly. Asked about the cables obtained by WikiLeaks and made available to a number of news organizations, Mr. Gates first acknowledged that they were "extraordinarily embarrassing for the United States." Then he tried to limit the damage.

"At the end of the day, nations and leaders make decisions based on their interests," Mr. Gates said. "And I would say that America's best partners and friends, and I include among them President Karzai, have responded to this in my view in an extraordinarily statesmanlike way."

Mr. Gates shifted to a higher gear: "And I'm deeply grateful, and frankly I think the American government will not forget this statesmanlike response. I think I also could say with great confidence, President Karzai and I have been meeting together privately now for four years. I don't think either of us would be embarrassed to have a single thing we said to each other made public." Mr. Gates was praising Mr. Karzai for his response four days earlier to the disclosures, when in a news conference with the Pakistani prime minister, Yousaf Raza Gilani, he dismissed the cables as beneath his interest.

Mr. Karzai also said, referring to criticism from his own ministers as reported in the cables, that people might say things casually in private that did not reflect their more considered views. His response was a relief to American officials, who embraced him in 2001 as a promising leader but had been alternately exasperated and infuriated over the ensuing years by what they considered his erratic behavior.

As Mr. Eikenberry wrote in a July 2009 cable, Mr. Karzai had a "deep-seated insecurity as a leader." That cable was a forerunner to his assessment in a November 2009 cable that called Mr. Karzai "not a reliable partner" for the United States. The November cable was leaked months before the current trove, souring relations between Mr. Eikenberry and Mr. Karzai before the WikiLeaks disclosures.

Mr. Gates was in Afghanistan to make an assessment of the war for a White House review, to be completed this month. The conclusion of the report—that there has been progress since President Obama sent 30,000 additional American forces but more work needs to be done—has already been described by administration officials.

"As I return to Washington, the United States government will be finishing work on an evaluation of the situation here, and I will go back convinced that our strategy is working," Mr. Gates said at the news conference. There remains deep skepticism about the strategy in parts of official Washington and Afghanistan, even among military officers.

Earlier on Wednesday, Mr. Gates heard largely optimistic reviews in a trip to Helmand and Kandahar Provinces in the south. Maj. Gen. Richard Mills, the commander of 20,000 United States Marines in Helmand Province, said that "the conditions are set in certain parts of the province right now for us to be able to turn over significant responsibility in the realm of security to the Afghans themselves"—a goal of Mr. Obama, who wants to begin the withdrawal of some United States forces next July.

At Forward Operating Base Howz-e-Madad in Kandahar Province, where fighting was fierce this summer and fall, Col. Art Kandarian told reporters traveling with Mr. Gates that "four months ago you would not be able to fly in here without taking some fire at this location." He said his troops were now working to clear insurgents and homemade bombs from Afghanistan's Highway 1.

—This article was originally published on December 8, 2010

PAKISTANI NEWSPAPERS APOLOGIZE FOR FAKE CABLES STORIES

(FROM THE LEDE BLOG)

By ROBERT MACKEY

As the Guardian's Islamabad correspondent Declan Walsh reported, several Pakistani newspapers appeared to fall for a hoax on Thursday, by publishing articles supposedly based on leaked American cables obtained by WikiLeaks that turned out to not exist.

The fake cables described by articles, including one on the front page of The News, were said to contain damning information about India and generally supported the worldview of hawks in Pakistan's military and intelligence services.

The Lede explained on Thursday that both the Guardian and The New York Times, which have copies of all of the leaked cables, performed searches of the full archive and were unable to find any cables even remotely like those described in the Pakistani press.

On Friday, two Pakistani newspapers that published articles based on the fake cables, The News and The Express Tribune, published retractions.

The Express Tribune apologized to readers for its article, "WikiLeaks: What U.S. Officials Think About the Indian Army," explaining: "It now transpires that the story, which was run by a news agency, Online, was not authentic."

The News blamed a local news agency, reporting:

A story filed by a news agency about purported WikiLeaks cables disclosing India's involvement in Balochistan and Waziristan, carried by The News, Daily Jang and many other Pakistani newspapers, has been widely criticised as not being accurate. The prestigious British newspaper The Guardian described the report as "the first case of WikiLeaks being exploited for propaganda purposes."

The report said that US diplomats described senior Indian generals as vain, egotistical and genocidal, and that India's government was secretly allied with Hindu fundamentalists. It also claimed that Indian spies were covertly supporting Islamist militants in the tribal belt and Balochistan.

The story was released by the Islamabad-based Online news agency and was run by The News and Daily Jang with the confidence that it was a genuine report and must have been vetted before release. However, several inquiries suggest that this was not the case.

The News added, "A check on the Internet as well as The Guardian report showed that the story was not based on WikiLeaks cables, and had in fact originated from some local websites such as The Daily Mail and Rupee News known for their close connections with certain intelligence agencies."

Pakistan's Daily Mail, which is an Islamabad news site unrelated to the British newspaper of the same name, has a reputation for reporting unreliable conspiracy theories that serve to deflect blame from Pakistani officials. In September, The Lede pointed to a post headlined, "How To Plant Idiotic Stories," on Cafe Pyala, a blog that looks at the Pakistani media. In that case, Cafe Pyala traced a fake news story suggesting that a Pakistani cricket scandal was actually a nefarious Indian plot back to the local Daily Mail, which it called, "the purveyor of all conspiracy theories headquartered in Islamabad which pretends to be a global paper." Cafe Pyala added, "its focus seems plainly to be crude propaganda about India. No points for guessing who's probably behind it."

In a post about the articles based on the fake cables on Thursday, Cafe Pyala noted that the newspapers reported their source as simply, "agencies," before asking, "How stupid do the "agencies" really think Pakistanis are?"

On Friday though, one Pakistani blogger stuck by the idea that Islamabad's Daily Mail, alone among the world's news organizations, had somehow come into possession of cables obtained by WikiLeaks that no one else has seen. Ahmed Quraishi, a Pakistani journalist, blogger and conspiracy theorist, refused to admit that the Daily Mail story he had made so much of a day earlier was based on cables that do not exist.

In a post headlined, "Ignore Guardian's Claim Of 'Fake' India Wiki-Leaks," Mr. Quraishi, citing no evidence, insisted that the Guardian and The Times must be lying, writing:

> Substantial parts of the story in Pakistani media is correct. It's only that The Guardian and the other newspapers are misleading the world public opinion by a selective focus on the things they want from WikiLeaks cables.

> WikiLeaks did a good job of exposing US bully diplomacy, and here comes NYT, Guardian and 2 or 3 other 'partner' newspapers of WikiLeaks to selectively release the material to suit US policy objectives.

—This article was originally published on December 10, 2010

RON PAUL'S DEFENSE
OF WIKILEAKS

(FROM THE LEDE BLOG)

By ROBERT MACKEY

Thanks to the reader who drew our attention to Ron Paul, the libertarian Texas Congressman, defending WikiLeaks on the House floor on Thursday in Washington.

As The Lede noted last week, Mr. Paul has also defended the publication of the leaked cables on his Twitter feed, writing: "Re: WikiLeaks—In a free society, we are supposed to know the truth. In a society where truth becomes treason, we are in big trouble."

In his speech to the House on Thursday, Mr. Paul compared the publication of the leaked cables by WikiLeaks to the publication of the Pentagon Papers in 1971, which the Supreme Court ruled to be legal at the time. He concluded by asking nine questions he said were raised by the leaks and the outcry against Mr. Assange.

Do the America people deserve know the truth regarding the ongoing war in Iraq, Afghanistan, Pakistan and Yemen?

Could a larger question be, How can an Army private gain access to so much secret information?

Why is the hostility mostly directed at Assange, the publisher, and not our government's failure to protect classified information?

Are we getting our money's worth from the $80 billion dollars per year we spend on intelligence gathering?

Which has resulted in the greatest number of deaths: lying us into war or WikiLeaks revelations or the release of the Pentagon Papers?

If Assange can be convicted of a crime for publishing information that he did not steal, what does this say about the future of the First Amendment and the independence of the Internet?

Could it be that the real reason for the near-universal attacks on WikiLeaks is more about secretly maintaining a seriously flawed foreign policy of empire than it is about national security?

Is there not a huge difference between releasing secret information to help the enemy in a time of declared war, which is treason, and the releasing of information to expose our government lies that promote secret wars, death and corruption?

Was it not once considered patriotic to stand up to our government when it's wrong?

—This article was originally published on December 10, 2010

OBAMA CALLS TURKISH AND MEXICAN LEADERS ON DIPLOMATIC LEAKS

By JACKIE CALMES

WASHINGTON—President Obama for the first time joined in his administration's diplomatic repair work in the wake of the disclosure of numerous American cables by WikiLeaks, calling the leaders of Turkey and Mexico on Saturday in an effort to smooth things over.

Separate White House statements about the phone calls did not characterize Mr. Obama's messages as apologies, nor would administration officials. The statement about Mr. Obama's call to President Felipe Calderón of Mexico began by describing it as congratulatory, to praise Mexico for its work in acting as host to the just-completed Cancún conference on climate change.

But the two presidents also talked about "the deplorable actions by WikiLeaks," the statement said, "and agreed its irresponsible acts should not distract our two countries from our important cooperation."

Mr. Obama also called the Turkish prime minister, Recep Tayyip Erdogan. He "expressed his regrets for the deplorable action by WikiLeaks and the two leaders agreed that it will not influence or disrupt the close cooperation between the United States and Turkey."

Overall the WikiLeaks disclosures of diplomatic reports between Americans in Washington and foreign capitals have been more embarrassing than revelatory or harmful to national security, officials and analysts say. Nonetheless, those dealing with Turkey, an ally straddling the West and the volatile Middle East, and Mexico, a troubled neighbor battling a corrosive drug war, illustrate the diplomatic problems created by exposing even routine communications to international light.

Publicized cables about Turkey, a member of NATO, depicted doubts about how reliable an ally the country was, given its mildly Islamist and anti-Israel government. But Mr. Obama and Mr. Erdogan "discussed the enduring importance of the U.S.-Turkish partnership and affirmed their commitment to work together on a broad range of issues," the White House said.

As for Mexico, American diplomats in the leaked cables quoted officials there admitting pessimism about the nation's war on drug lords even as the government publicly had boasted of progress, while other cables conveyed Americans' criticisms of the Mexican military, police and judiciary and of public corruption in the country generally.

But, according to the White House, Mr. Obama and Mr. Calderon "reaffirmed their shared commitment to work together against transnational criminal organizations, to enhance border cooperation, and to improve the economic well-being of people in both countries."

—This article was originally published on December 11, 2010

WIKILEAKS TAPS POWER OF THE PRESS

By DAVID CARR

Has WikiLeaks changed journalism forever?

Perhaps. Or maybe it was the other way around.

Think back to 2008, when WikiLeaks simply released documents that suggested the government of Kenya had looted its country. The follow-up in the mainstream media was decidedly muted.

Then last spring, WikiLeaks adopted a more journalistic approach—editing and annotating a 2007 video from Baghdad in which an Apache helicopter fired on men who appeared to be unarmed, including two employees of Reuters. The reviews were mixed, with some suggesting that the video had been edited to political ends, but the disclosure received much more attention in the press.

In July, WikiLeaks began what amounted to a partnership with mainstream media organizations, including The New York Times, by giving them an early look at the so-called Afghan War Diary, a strategy that resulted in extensive reporting on the implications of the secret documents.

Then in November, the heretofore classified mother lode of 250,000 United States diplomatic cables that describe tensions across the globe was shared by WikiLeaks with Le Monde, El Pais, The Guardian and Der Spiegel. (The Guardian shared documents with The New York Times.) The result was huge: many articles have come out since, many of them deep dives into the implications of the trove of documents.

Notice that with each successive release, WikiLeaks has become more strategic and has been rewarded with deeper, more extensive coverage of its revelations. It's a long walk from WikiLeaks's origins as a user-edited site held in common to something more akin to a traditional model of publishing, but seems to be in keeping with its manifesto to deliver documents with "maximum possible impact."

Julian Assange, WikiLeaks's founder and guiding spirit, apparently began to understand that scarcity, not ubiquity, drives coverage of events. Instead of just pulling back the blankets for all to see, he began to limit the disclosures to those who would add value through presentation, editing and additional reporting. In a sense, Mr. Assange, a former programmer, leveraged the processing power of the news media to build a story and present it in comprehensible ways. (Of course, as someone who draws a paycheck from a mainstream journalism outfit, it may be no surprise that I continue to see durable value in what we do even amid the journalistic jujitsu WikiLeaks introduces.)

And by publishing only a portion of the documents, rather than spilling information willy-nilly and recklessly endangering lives, WikiLeaks could also strike a posture of responsibility, an approach that seems to run counter to Mr. Assange's own core anarchism.

Although Mr. Assange is now arguing that the site is engaged in what he called a new kind of "scientific journalism," his earlier writings suggest he believes the mission of WikiLeaks is to throw sand in the works of what he considers corrupt, secretive and inherently evil states. He initiated a conspiracy in order to take down what he saw as an even greater conspiracy.

"WikiLeaks is not a news organization, it is a cell of activists that is releasing information designed to embarrass people in power," said George Packer, a writer on international affairs at The New Yorker. "They simply believe that the State Department is an illegitimate organization that needs to be exposed, which is not really journalism."

By shading his radicalism and collaborating with mainstream outlets, Mr. Assange created a comfort zone for his partners in journalism. They could do their jobs and he could do his.

"The notion that this experience has somehow profoundly changed journalism, the way that information gets out or changed the way that diplomacy happens, seems rather exaggerated," said Bill Keller, the executive editor of The New York Times, which used information from the leaks to report a series of large articles.

"It was a big deal, but not an unfamiliar one. Consumers of information became privy to a lot of stuff that had been secret before," Mr. Keller said. "The scale of it was unusual, but was it different in kind from the Pentagon Papers or revelation of Abu Ghraib or government eavesdropping? I think probably not."

In this case, the media companies could also take some comfort in knowing that the current trove did not contain, with a few notable exceptions, any earth-shaking revelations. No thinking citizen was surprised to learn that diplomats don't trust each other and say so behind closed doors. But as it has became increasingly apparent that WikiLeaks was changing the way information is released and consumed, questions were raised about the value of traditional journalistic approaches.

"People from the digital world are always saying we don't need journalists at all because information is everywhere and there in no barrier to entry," said Nicholas Lemann, dean of the Columbia Journalism School. "But these documents provide a good answer to that question. Even though journalists didn't dig them out, there is a great deal of value in their efforts to explain and examine them. Who else would have had the energy or resources to do what these news organization have done?"

WikiLeaks certainly isn't being afforded the same protections we give other media outlets in free countries. It has come under significant attack as PayPal, Amazon and Visa have all tried to bar WikiLeaks from their services, a move that would seem unthinkable had it been made against mainstream newspapers. (Can you imagine the outcry if a credit card company decided to cut off The Washington Post because it didn't like what was on the front page?)

Sen. Joseph Lieberman has said that Mr. Assange should be charged with treason while Sarah Palin has called him "an anti-American operative with blood on his hands." (Indeed, Senator Lieberman has suggested that the Justice Department should examine the role of The New York Times in the leaks.)

Mr. Packer is very much against the prosecution of WikiLeaks on grounds of treason because, he said, "discerning the legal difference between what WikiLeaks did and what news organizations do is difficult and would set a terrible precedent."

But Mr. Assange, who is in jail in Britain in connection with a Swedish extradition request, is a complicated partner. So far, WikiLeaks has been involved in a fruitful collaboration, a new form of hybrid journalism emerging in the space between so-called hacktivists and mainstream media outlets, but the relationship is an unstable one.

WikiLeaks may be willing to play ball with newspapers for now, but the organization does not share the same values or objectives. Mr.

Assange and the site's supporters see transparency as the ultimate objective, believing that sunshine and openness will deprive bad actors of the secrecy they require to be successful. Mainstream media may spend a lot of time trying to ferret information out of official hands, but they largely operate in the belief that the state is legitimate and entitled to at least some of its secrets.

And Mr. Assange has placed a doomsday card on the table: he has said that if WikiLeaks's existence is threatened, the organization would be willing to spill all the documents in its possession out into the public domain, ignoring the potentially mortal consequences. (His lawyers told ABC News that they expect he will be indicted on espionage charges in the United States.) Mr. Packer said such an act "is something no journalistic organization would ever do, or threaten to do."

And what if WikiLeaks was unhappy with how one of its ad hoc media partners had handled the information it provided or became displeased with the coverage of WikiLeaks? The same guns in the info-war that have been aimed at its political and Web opponents could be trained on media outlets.

Steve Coll, president of the New America Foundation and an author and a contributor to The New Yorker who has written extensively about Afghanistan, said that the durability of the WikiLeaks model remained an open question.

"I'm skeptical about whether a release of this size is ever going to take place again," he said, "in part because established interests and the rule of law tend to come down pretty hard on incipient movements. Think of the initial impact of Napster and what subsequently happened to them."

Of course, Napster is no longer around but the insurgency it represented all but tipped the music industry.

"Right now, media outlets are treating this as a transaction with a legitimate journalistic organization," he said. "But at some point, they are going to have to evolve into an organization that has an address and identity or the clock will run out on that level of collaboration."

Emily Bell, the director of the Tow Center for Digital Journalism at Columbia Journalism School, said that WikiLeaks had already changed the rules by creating a situation where competitive news organizations were now cooperating to share a scoop.

"WikiLeaks represents a new kind of advocacy, one that brings to mind the activism of the '60s, one in which people want to get their own hands on information and do their own digging," she said. "What you are seeing is just a crack in the door right now. No one can tell where this is really going."

—This article was originally published on December 12, 2010

AIR FORCE BLOCKS SITES THAT POSTED SECRET CABLES

By ERIC SCHMITT

WASHINGTON—The Air Force is barring its personnel from using work computers to view the Web sites of The New York Times and more than 25 other news organizations and blogs that have posted secret cables obtained by WikiLeaks, Air Force officials said Tuesday.

When Air Force personnel on the service's computer network try to view the Web sites of The Times, the British newspaper The Guardian, the German magazine Der Spiegel, the Spanish newspaper El País and the French newspaper Le Monde, as well as other sites that posted full confidential cables, the screen says "Access Denied: Internet usage is logged and monitored," according to an Air Force official whose access was blocked and who shared the screen warning with The Times. Violators are warned that they face punishment if they try to view classified material from unauthorized Web sites.

Some Air Force officials acknowledged that the steps taken might be in vain since many military personnel could gain access to the documents from home computers, despite admonishments from superiors not to read the cables without proper clearances.

Cyber network specialists within the Air Force Space Command last week followed longstanding procedures to keep classified information off unclassified computer systems. "News media Web sites will be blocked if they post classified documents from the WikiLeaks Web site," said Lt. Col. Brenda Campbell, a spokeswoman for the Air Force Space Command, a unit of which oversees Air Force cyber systems. "This is similar to how we'd block any other Web site that posted classified information."

Colonel Campbell said that only sites posting full classified documents, not just excerpts, would be blocked. "When classified documents appear on a Web site, a judgment will be made whether it will be blocked," she said. "It's an issue we're working through right now."

Spokesmen for the Army, Navy and Marines said they were not blocking the Web sites of news organizations, largely because guidance has already been issued by the Obama administration and the Defense Department directing hundreds of thousands of federal employees and contractors not to read the secret cables and other classified documents published by WikiLeaks unless the workers have the required security clearance or authorization.

"Classified information, whether or not already posted on public web-sites or disclosed to the media, remains classified, and must be treated as such by federal employees and contractors, until it is declassified by an appropriate U.S. Government authority," said a notice sent on Dec. 3 by the Office of Management and Budget, which is part of the White House, to agency and department heads.

A Defense Department spokesman, Col. David Lapan, in an e-mail on Tuesday night sought to distance the department from the Air Force's action to block access to the media Web sites: "This is not DoD-directed or DoD-wide."

The Air Force's action was first reported on The Wall Street Journal's Web site late Tuesday and underscores the wide-ranging impact of the recent release of secret State Department documents by WikiLeaks, and five news organizations, including The Times. It also illustrates the contortions the military and other government agencies appear to be going through to limit the spread of classified information that has become widely available in the public domain.

"It is unfortunate that the U.S. Air Force has chosen not to allow its personnel access to information that virtually everyone else in the world can access," said a spokeswoman for The Times, Danielle Rhoades Ha. A senior administration official said Tuesday that the administration's policy contained some leeway, for instance, to allow certain employees to download information in order for them to be able to verify that classified informa-tion was leaking into the public domain, and to assess damage to national security and potential danger to sources.

Steven Aftergood of the Federation of American Scientists, a secrecy specialist, said dozens of agencies, as well as branches of the military and government contractors, had issued their own policy instructions based on the Office of Management and Budget memo.

"It's a self-defeating policy that will leave government employees less informed than they ought to be," Mr. Aftergood said.

William J. Broad contributed reporting from New York.

—This article was originally published on December 14, 2010

ZIMBABWE: FIRST LADY SUES OVER CABLE

By CELIA W. DUGGER

President Robert Mugabe's wife, Grace, has sued The Standard, an independent weekly, for reporting on a State Department cable obtained by WikiLeaks. The cable quoted a mining executive implicating her and the head of the Reserve Bank, Gideon Gono, in illegally profiting from the sale of diamonds mined in eastern Zimbabwe. Through her lawyer, she called the report false and demanded damages of $15 million, The Herald, a newspaper controlled by Mr. Mugabe, reported Thursday.

—This article was originally published on December 16, 2010

U.S. SENDS WARNING TO PEOPLE NAMED IN CABLE LEAKS

By MARK LANDLER and SCOTT SHANE

WASHINGTON—The State Department is warning hundreds of human rights activists, foreign government officials and businesspeople identified in leaked diplomatic cables of potential threats to their safety and has moved a handful of them to safer locations, administration officials said Thursday.

The operation, which involves a team of 30 in Washington and embassies from Afghanistan to Zimbabwe, reflects the administration's fear that the disclosure of cables obtained by the organization WikiLeaks has damaged American interests by exposing foreigners who supply valuable information to the United States.

Administration officials said they were not aware of anyone who has been attacked or imprisoned as a direct result of information in the 2,700 cables that have been made public to date by WikiLeaks, The New York Times and several other publications, many with some names removed. But they caution that many dissidents are under constant harassment from their governments, so it is difficult to be certain of the cause of actions against them.

The officials declined to discuss details about people contacted by the State Department in recent weeks, saying only that a few were relocated within their home countries and that a few others were moved abroad.

The State Department is mainly concerned about the cables that have yet to be published or posted on Web sites—nearly 99 percent of the archive of 251,287 cables obtained by WikiLeaks. With cables continuing to trickle out, they said, protecting those identified will be a complex, delicate and long-term undertaking. The State Department said it had combed through a majority of the quarter-million cables and distributed many to embassies for review by diplomats there.

"We feel responsible for doing everything possible to protect these people," said Michael H. Posner, the assistant secretary of state for democracy, human rights and labor, who is overseeing the effort. "We're taking it extremely seriously."

Contrary to the administration's initial fears, the fallout from the cables on the diplomatic corps itself has been manageable. The most visible casualty so far could be Gene A. Cretz, the ambassador to Libya, who was recalled from his post last month after his name appeared on a cable describing peculiar personal habits of the Libyan leader, Col. Muammar el-Qaddafi. While no decision has been made on Mr. Cretz's future, officials said he was unlikely to return to Tripoli. In addition, one midlevel diplomat has been moved from his post in an undisclosed country.

But other senior diplomats initially considered at risk—for example, the ambassador to Russia, John R. Beyrle, whose name was on cables critical of Prime Minister Vladimir V. Putin—appeared to have weathered the disclosures.

There is anecdotal evidence that the disclosure of the cables has chilled daily contacts between human rights activists and diplomats. An American diplomat in Central Asia said recently that one Iranian contact, who met him on periodic trips outside Iran, told him he would no longer speak to him. Sarah Holewinski, executive director of the Campaign for Innocent Victims in Conflict, said people in Afghanistan and Pakistan had become more reluctant to speak to human rights investigators for fear that what they said might be made public.

WikiLeaks came under fire from human rights organizations last July, after it released a large number of documents about the war in Afghanistan without removing the names of Afghan citizens who had assisted the American military. When it later released documents about the Iraq war, the group stripped names from the documents.

A Pentagon spokesman, Maj. Chris Perrine, said Thursday that the military was not aware of any confirmed case of harm to anyone as a result of being named in the Afghan war documents. But he noted that the Taliban had said it would study the WikiLeaks documents to punish collaborators with the Americans.

State Department officials believe that a wide range of foreigners who have spoken candidly to American diplomats could be at risk if publicly identified. For example, a businessman who spoke about official corruption, a gay person in a society intolerant of homosexuality or a high-ranking government official who criticized his bosses could face severe reprisals, the officials said.

Human rights advocates share the State Department's concern that many people could be at risk if cables become public without careful redaction. "There are definitely people named in the cables who would be very much endangered," said Tom Malinowski, Washington director for Human Rights Watch.

In one case, Mr. Malinowski said, the State Department asked Human Rights Watch to inform a person in a Middle Eastern country that his exchanges with American diplomats had been reported in a cable.

In addition to The Times, The Guardian, Le Monde, El País and Der Spiegel have had the entire cable database for several months. The Norwegian newspaper Aftenposten said last month that it had obtained the entire collection, and newspapers in several other countries have obtained a selection of cables relating to their regions.

WikiLeaks's founder, Julian Assange, has said the group will continue to release additional cables on its own Web site as well, though to date it has moved cautiously and has reproduced the redactions made by newspapers publishing the cables.

Government officials are also worried that foreign intelligence services may be trying to acquire the cable collection, a development that would heighten concerns about the safety of those named in the documents.

For human rights activists in this country, disclosures by WikiLeaks, which was founded in 2006, have been a decidedly mixed development. Amnesty International gave WikiLeaks an award in 2009 for its role in revealing human rights violations in Kenya. Human Rights Watch wrote to President Obama last month to urge the administration not to pursue a prosecution of WikiLeaks or Mr. Assange.

But they are concerned that the cables could inflict their own kind of collateral damage, either by endangering diplomats' sources or discouraging witnesses and victims of abuses from speaking to foreign supporters.

Sam Zarifi, director of Amnesty International's operations in Asia, said the cables had provided valuable "empirical information" on abuses in several countries. "This is a new way to distribute information," Mr. Zarifi said. "We just want to make sure it has the same safeguards as traditional journalism."

—This article was originally published on January 6, 2011

PART FOUR
THE WAR LOGS

*An archive of classified military documents offers an unvarnished view
of the wars in Afghanistan and Iraq.*

The Afghan opium trade is a source of money
for extremist groups that is hard to stanch.

The detention center at a military base in Baghdad in 2007.

VIEW IS BLEAKER THAN OFFICIAL PORTRAYAL OF WAR IN AFGHANISTAN

A six-year archive of classified military documents made public on Sunday offers an unvarnished, ground-level picture of the war in Afghanistan that is in many respects more grim than the official portrayal.

The secret documents, released on the Internet by an organization called WikiLeaks, are a daily diary of an American-led force often starved for resources and attention as it struggled against an insurgency that grew larger, better coordinated and more deadly each year.

The New York Times, the British newspaper The Guardian and the German magazine Der Spiegel were given access to the voluminous records several weeks ago on the condition that they not report on the material before Sunday.

The documents—some 92,000 reports spanning parts of two administrations from January 2004 through December 2009—illustrate in mosaic detail why, after the United States has spent almost $300 billion on the war in Afghanistan, the Taliban are stronger than at any time since 2001.

As the new American commander in Afghanistan, Gen. David H. Petraeus, tries to reverse the lagging war effort, the documents sketch a war hamstrung by an Afghan government, police force and army of questionable loyalty and competence, and by a Pakistani military that appears at best uncooperative and at worst to work from the shadows as an unspoken ally of the very insurgent forces the American-led coalition is trying to defeat.

The material comes to light as Congress and the public grow increasingly skeptical of the deepening involvement in Afghanistan and its chances for success as next year's deadline to begin withdrawing troops looms.

The archive is a vivid reminder that the Afghan conflict until recently was a second-class war, with money, troops and attention lavished on Iraq while soldiers and Marines lamented that the Afghans they were training were not being paid.

The reports—usually spare summaries but sometimes detailed narratives—shed light on some elements of the war that have been largely hidden from the public eye:

• The Taliban have used portable heat-seeking missiles against allied aircraft, a fact that has not been publicly disclosed by the military. This type of weapon helped the Afghan mujahedeen defeat the Soviet occupation in the 1980s.

• Secret commando units like Task Force 373—a classified group of Army and Navy special operatives—work from a "capture/kill list" of about 70 top insurgent commanders. These missions, which have been stepped up under the Obama administration, claim notable successes, but have sometimes gone wrong, killing civilians and stoking Afghan resentment.

• The military employs more and more drone aircraft to survey the battlefield and strike targets in Afghanistan, although their performance is less impressive than officially portrayed. Some crash or collide, forcing American troops to undertake risky retrieval missions before the Taliban can claim the drone's weaponry.

• The Central Intelligence Agency has expanded paramilitary operations inside Afghanistan. The units launch ambushes, order airstrikes and conduct night raids. From 2001 to 2008, the C.I.A. paid the budget of Afghanistan's spy agency and ran it as a virtual subsidiary.

Over all, the documents do not contradict official accounts of the war. But in some cases the documents show that the American military made misleading public statements—attributing the downing of a helicopter to conventional weapons instead of heat-seeking missiles or giving Afghans credit for missions carried out by Special Operations commandos.

White House officials vigorously denied that the Obama administration had presented a misleading portrait of the war in Afghanistan.

"On Dec. 1, 2009, President Obama announced a new strategy with a substantial increase in resources for Afghanistan, and increased focus on Al Qaeda and Taliban safe-havens in Pakistan, precisely because of the grave situation that had developed over several years," said Gen. James L. Jones, White House national security adviser, in a statement released Sunday.

"We know that serious challenges lie ahead, but if Afghanistan is permitted to slide backwards, we will again face a threat from violent extremist groups like Al Qaeda who will have more space to plot and train," the statement said.

General Jones also decried the decision by WikiLeaks to make the documents public, saying that the United States "strongly condemns the disclosure of classified information by individuals and organizations which could put the lives of Americans and our partners at risk, and threaten our national security."

"WikiLeaks made no effort to contact us about these documents—the United States government learned from news organizations that these documents would be posted," General Jones said.

The archive is clearly an incomplete record of the war. It is missing many references to seminal events and does not include more highly classified information. The documents also do not cover events in 2010, when the influx of more troops into Afghanistan began and a new counterinsurgency strategy took hold.

They suggest that the military's internal assessments of the prospects for winning over the Afghan public, especially in the early days, were often optimistic, even naïve.

There are fleeting—even taunting—reminders of how the war began in the occasional references to the elusive Osama bin Laden. In some reports he is said to be attending meetings in Quetta, Pakistan. His money man is said to be flying from Iran to North Korea to buy weapons. Mr. bin Laden has supposedly ordered a suicide attack against the Afghan president, Hamid Karzai. These reports all seem secondhand at best.

—This article was originally published on July 25, 2010

THE IRAQ ARCHIVE:
THE STRANDS OF A WAR

A huge trove of secret field reports from the battlegrounds of Iraq sheds new light on the war, including such fraught subjects as civilian deaths, detainee abuse and the involvement of Iran.

The secret archive is the second such cache obtained by the independent organization WikiLeaks and made available to several news organizations. Like the first release, some 77,000 reports covering six years of the war in Afghanistan, the Iraq documents provide no earthshaking revelations, but they offer insight, texture and context from the people actually fighting the war.

A close analysis of the 391,832 documents helps illuminate several important aspects of this war:

• The war in Iraq spawned a reliance on private contractors on a scale not well recognized at the time and previously unknown in American wars. The documents describe an outsourcing of combat and other duties once performed by soldiers that grew and spread to Afghanistan to the point that there are more contractors there than soldiers.

• The documents suggest that the so-called surge worked not only because the American military committed to more troops and a new strategy but because Iraqis themselves, exhausted by years of bloody war, were ready for it. The conditions, the documents suggest, may not be repeatable in the still intensifying war in Afghanistan.

• The deaths of Iraqi civilians—at the hands mainly of other Iraqis, but also of the American military—appear to be greater than the numbers made public by the United States during the Bush administration.

• While the abuse of Iraqi prisoners by Americans, particularly at the Abu Ghraib prison, shocked the American public and much of the world, the documents paint an even more lurid picture of abuse by America's Iraqi allies—a brutality from which the Americans at times averted their eyes.

• Iran's military, more than has been generally understood, intervened aggressively in support of Shiite combatants, offering weapons, training and sanctuary and in a few instances directly engaging American troops.

The Iraqi documents were made available to The Times, the British newspaper The Guardian, the French newspaper Le Monde and the German magazine Der Spiegel on the condition that they be embargoed until now. WikiLeaks has never stated where it obtained the information, although an American Army intelligence analyst, Pfc. Bradley Manning, has been arrested and accused of being a source of classified material.

As it did with the Afghan war logs, The Times has redacted or withheld any documents that would put lives in danger or jeopardize continuing military operations. Names of Iraqi informants, for example, have not been disclosed. WikiLeaks said that it has also employed teams of editors to scrub the material for posting on its Web site.

WikiLeaks has been under strong pressure from the United States and the governments of other countries but is also fraying internally, in part because of a decision to post many of the Afghan documents without removing the names of informants, putting their lives in danger. A profile of WikiLeaks's contentious founder, Julian Assange, appears here.

The New York Times told the Pentagon which specific documents it planned to post and showed how they had been redacted. The Pentagon said it would have preferred that The Times not publish any classified materials but did not propose any cuts. Geoff Morrell, the Defense Department press secretary, strongly condemned both WikiLeaks and the release of the Iraq documents.

"We deplore WikiLeaks for inducing individuals to break the law, leak classified documents and then cavalierly share that secret information with the world, including our enemies," he said.

"We know terrorist organizations have been mining the leaked Afghan documents for information to use against us and this Iraq leak is more than four times as large. By disclosing such sensitive information, WikiLeaks continues to put at risk the lives of our troops, their coalition partners and those Iraqis and Afghans working with us."

—This article was originally published on October 22, 2010

PAKISTAN AIDS INSURGENCY IN AFGHANISTAN, REPORTS ASSERT

By MARK MAZZETTI, JANE PERLEZ, ERIC SCHMITT
and ANDREW W. LEHREN

Americans fighting the war in Afghanistan have long harbored strong suspicions that Pakistan's military spy service has guided the Afghan insurgency with a hidden hand, even as Pakistan receives more than $1 billion a year from Washington for its help combating the militants, according to a trove of secret military field reports made public Sunday.

The documents, made available by an organization called WikiLeaks, suggest that Pakistan, an ostensible ally of the United States, allows representatives of its spy service to meet directly with the Taliban in secret strategy sessions to organize networks of militant groups that fight against American soldiers in Afghanistan, and even hatch plots to assassinate Afghan leaders.

Taken together, the reports indicate that American soldiers on the ground are inundated with accounts of a network of Pakistani assets and collaborators that runs from the Pakistani tribal belt along the Afghan border, through southern Afghanistan, and all the way to the capital, Kabul.

Much of the information—raw intelligence and threat assessments gathered from the field in Afghanistan— cannot be verified and likely comes from sources aligned with Afghan intelligence, which considers Pakistan an enemy, and paid informants. Some describe plots for attacks that do not appear to have taken place.

But many of the reports rely on sources that the military rated as reliable.

While current and former American officials interviewed could not corroborate individual reports, they said that the portrait of the spy agency's collaboration with the Afghan insurgency was broadly consistent with other classified intelligence.

Some of the reports describe Pakistani intelligence working alongside Al Qaeda to plan attacks. Experts cautioned that although Pakistan's militant groups and Al Qaeda work together, directly linking the Pakistani spy agency, the Directorate for Inter-Services Intelligence, or ISI, with Al Qaeda is difficult.

The records also contain firsthand accounts of American anger at Pakistan's unwillingness to confront insurgents who launched attacks near Pakistani border posts, moved openly by the truckload across the frontier, and retreated to Pakistani territory for safety.

The behind-the-scenes frustrations of soldiers on the ground and glimpses of what appear to be Pakistani skullduggery contrast sharply with the frequently rosy public pronouncements of Pakistan as an ally by American officials, looking to sustain a drone campaign over parts of Pakistani territory to strike at Qaeda havens. Administration officials also want to keep nuclear-armed Pakistan on their side to safeguard NATO supplies flowing on routes that cross Pakistan to Afghanistan.

This month, Secretary of State Hillary Rodham Clinton, in one of the frequent visits by American officials to Islamabad, announced $500 million in assistance and called the United States and Pakistan "partners joined in common cause."

The reports suggest, however, that the Pakistani military has acted as both ally and enemy, as its spy agency runs what American officials have long suspected is a double game—appeasing certain American demands for cooperation while angling to exert influence in Afghanistan through many of the same insurgent networks that the Americans are fighting to eliminate.

Behind the scenes, both Bush and Obama administration officials as well as top American commanders have confronted top Pakistani military officers with accusations of ISI complicity in attacks in Afghanistan, and even presented top Pakistani officials with lists of ISI and military operatives believed to be working with militants.

Benjamin Rhodes, deputy national security adviser for strategic communications, said that Pakistan had been an important ally in the battle against militant groups, and that Pakistani soldiers and intelligence officials had worked alongside the United States to capture or kill Qaeda and Taliban leaders.

Still, he said that the "status quo is not acceptable," and that the havens for militants in Pakistan "pose an intolerable threat" that Pakistan must do more to address.

"The Pakistani government—and Pakistan's military and intelligence services—must continue their strategic shift against violent extremist groups within their borders," he said. American military support to Pakistan would continue, he said.

Several Congressional officials said that despite repeated requests over the years for information about Pakistani support for militant groups, they usually receive vague and inconclusive briefings from the Pentagon and C.I.A.

Nonetheless, senior lawmakers say they have no doubt that Pakistan is aiding insurgent groups. "The burden of proof is on the government of Pakistan and the ISI to show they don't have ongoing contacts," said Senator Jack Reed, a Rhode Island Democrat on the Armed Services Committee who visited Pakistan this month and said he and Senator Carl Levin of Michigan, the committee chairman, confronted Pakistan's prime minister, Yousaf Raza Gilani, yet again over the allegations.

Such accusations are usually met with angry denials, particularly by the Pakistani military, which insists that the ISI severed its remaining ties to the groups years ago. An ISI spokesman in Islamabad said Sunday that the agency would have no comment until it saw the documents. Pakistan's ambassador to the United States, Husain Haqqani, said, "The documents circulated by WikiLeaks do not reflect the current on-ground realities."

The man the United States has depended on for cooperation in fighting the militants and who holds most power in Pakistan, the head of the army, Gen. Parvez Ashfaq Kayani, ran the ISI from 2004 to 2007, a period from which many of the reports are drawn. American officials have frequently praised General Kayani for what they say are his efforts to purge the military of officers with ties to militants.

American officials have described Pakistan's spy service as a rigidly hierarchical organization that has little tolerance for "rogue" activity. But Pakistani military officials give the spy service's "S Wing"—which runs external operations against the Afghan government and India—broad autonomy, a buffer that allows top military officials deniability.

American officials have rarely uncovered definitive evidence of direct ISI involvement in a major attack. But in July 2008, the C.I.A.'s deputy director,

Stephen R. Kappes, confronted Pakistani officials with evidence that the ISI helped plan the deadly suicide bombing of India's Embassy in Kabul.

From the current trove, one report shows that Polish intelligence warned of a complex attack against the Indian Embassy a week before that bombing, though the attackers and their methods differed. The ISI was not named in the report warning of the attack.

Another, dated August 2008, identifies a colonel in the ISI plotting with a Taliban official to assassinate President Hamid Karzai. The report says there was no information about how or when this would be carried out. The account could not be verified.

General Linked to Militants

Lt. Gen. Hamid Gul ran the ISI from 1987 to 1989, a time when Pakistani spies and the C.I.A. joined forces to run guns and money to Afghan militias who were battling Soviet troops in Afghanistan. After the fighting stopped, he maintained his contacts with the former mujahedeen, who would eventually transform themselves into the Taliban.

And more than two decades later, it appears that General Gul is still at work. The documents indicate that he has worked tirelessly to reactivate his old networks, employing familiar allies like Jaluluddin Haqqani and Gulbuddin Hekmatyar, whose networks of thousands of fighters are responsible for waves of violence in Afghanistan.

General Gul is mentioned so many times in the reports, if they are to be believed, that it seems unlikely that Pakistan's current military and intelligence officials could not know of at least some of his wide-ranging activities.

For example, one intelligence report describes him meeting with a group of militants in Wana, the capital of South Waziristan, in January 2009. There, he met with three senior Afghan insurgent commanders and three "older" Arab men, presumably representatives of Al Qaeda, who the report suggests were important "because they had a large security contingent with them."

The gathering was designed to hatch a plan to avenge the death of "Zamarai," the nom de guerre of Osama al-Kini, who had been killed days earlier by a C.I.A. drone attack. Mr. Kini had directed Qaeda operations in Pakistan and had spearheaded some of the group's most devastating attacks.

The plot hatched in Wana that day, according to the report, involved driving a dark blue Mazda truck rigged with explosives from South Waziristan to Afghanistan's Paktika Province, a route well known to be used by the insurgents to move weapons, suicide bombers and fighters from Pakistan.

In a show of strength, the Taliban leaders approved a plan to send 50 Arab and 50 Waziri fighters to Ghazni Province in Afghanistan, the report said.

General Gul urged the Taliban commanders to focus their operations inside Afghanistan in exchange for Pakistan turning "a blind eye" to their presence in Pakistan's tribal areas. It was unclear whether the attack was ever executed.

The United States has pushed the United Nations to put General Gul on a list of international terrorists, and top American officials said they believed he was an important link between active-duty Pakistani officers and militant groups.

General Gul, who says he is retired and lives on his pension, dismissed the allegations as "absolute nonsense," speaking by telephone from his home in Rawalpindi, where the Pakistani Army keeps its headquarters. "I have had no hand in it." He added, "American intelligence is pulling cotton wool over your eyes."

Senior Pakistani officials consistently deny that General Gul still works at the ISI's behest, though several years ago, after mounting American complaints, Pakistan's president at the time, Pervez Musharraf, was forced publicly to acknowledge the possibility that former ISI officials were assisting the Afghan insurgency. Despite his denials, General Gul keeps close ties to his former employers. When a reporter visited General Gul this spring for an interview at his home, the former spy master canceled the appointment. According to his son, he had to attend meetings at army headquarters.

Suicide Bomber Network

The reports also chronicle efforts by ISI officers to run the networks of suicide bombers that emerged as a sudden, terrible force in Afghanistan in 2006.

The detailed reports indicate that American officials had a relatively clear understanding of how the suicide networks presumably functioned, even if some of the threats did not materialize. It is impossible to know why the attacks never came off—either they were thwarted, the attackers shifted targets, or the reports were deliberately planted as Taliban disinformation.

One report, from Dec. 18, 2006, describes a cyclical process to develop the suicide bombers. First, the suicide attacker is recruited and trained in Pakistan. Then, reconnaissance and operational planning gets under way, including scouting to find a place for "hosting" the suicide bomber near the target before carrying out the attack. The network, it says, receives help from the Afghan police and the Ministry of Interior.

In many cases, the reports are complete with names and ages of bombers, as well as license plate numbers, but the Americans gathering the intelligence struggle to accurately portray many other details, introducing sometimes comical renderings of places and Taliban commanders.

In one case, a report rated by the American military as credible states that a gray Toyota Corolla had been loaded with explosives between the Afghan border and Landik Hotel, in Pakistan, apparently a mangled reference to Landi Kotal, in Pakistan's tribal areas. The target of the plot, however, is a real hotel in downtown Kabul, the Ariana.

"It is likely that ISI may be involved as supporter of this attack," reads a comment in the report.

Several of the reports describe current and former ISI operatives, including General Gul, visiting madrasas near the city of Peshawar, a gateway to the tribal areas, to recruit new fodder for suicide bombings.

One report, labeled a "real threat warning" because of its detail and the reliability of its source, described how commanders of Mr. Hekmatyar's insurgent group, Hezb-i-Islami, ordered the delivery of a suicide bomber from the Hashimiye madrasa, run by Afghans.

The boy was to be used in an attack on American or NATO vehicles in Kabul during the Muslim Festival of Sacrifices that opened Dec. 31, 2006. According to the report, the boy was taken to the Afghan city of Jalalabad to buy a car for the bombing, and was later brought to Kabul. It was unclear whether the attack took place.

The documents indicate that these types of activities continued throughout last year. From July to October 2009, nine threat reports detailed movements by suicide bombers from Pakistan into populated areas of Afghanistan, including Kandahar, Kunduz and Kabul.

Some of the bombers were sent to disrupt Afghanistan's presidential elections, held last August. In other instances, American intelligence learned that the Haqqani network sent bombers at the ISI's behest to strike Indian officials, development workers and engineers in Afghanistan. Other plots were aimed at the Afghan government.

Sometimes the intelligence documents twin seemingly credible detail with plots that seem fantastical or utterly implausible assertions. For instance, one report describes an ISI plan to use a remote-controlled bomb disguised as a golden Koran to assassinate Afghan government officials. Another report documents an alleged plot by the ISI and Taliban to ship poisoned alcoholic beverages to Afghanistan to kill American troops.

But the reports also charge that the ISI directly helped organize Taliban offensives at key junctures of the war. On June 19, 2006, ISI operatives allegedly met with the Taliban leaders in Quetta, the city in southern Pakistan where American and other Western officials have long believed top Taliban leaders have been given refuge by the Pakistani authorities. At the meeting, according to the report, they pressed the Taliban to mount attacks on Maruf, a district of Kandahar that lies along the Pakistani border.

The planned offensive would be carried out primarily by Arabs and Pakistanis, the report said, and a Taliban commander, "Akhtar Mansoor," warned that the men should be prepared for heavy losses. "The foreigners agreed to this operation and have assembled 20 4x4 trucks to carry the fighters into areas in question," it said.

While the specifics about the foreign fighters and the ISI are difficult to verify, the Taliban did indeed mount an offensive to seize control in Maruf in 2006.

Afghan government officials and Taliban fighters have widely acknowledged that the offensive was led by the Taliban commander Mullah Akhtar Muhammad Mansour, who was then the Taliban shadow governor of Kandahar.

Mullah Mansour tried to claw out a base for himself inside Afghanistan, but just as the report quotes him predicting, the Taliban suffered heavy losses and eventually pulled back.

Another report goes on to describe detailed plans for a large-scale assault, timed for September 2007, aimed at the American forward operating base in Managi, in Kunar Province.

"It will be a five-pronged attack consisting of 83-millimeter artillery, rockets, foot soldiers, and multiple suicide bombers," it says.

It is not clear that the attack ever came off, but its planning foreshadowed another, seminal attack that came months later, in July 2008. At that time, about 200 Taliban insurgents nearly overran an American base in Wanat, in Nuristan, killing nine American soldiers. For the Americans, it was one of the highest single-day tolls of the war.

Tensions With Pakistan

The flood of reports of Pakistani complicity in the insurgency has at times led to barely disguised tensions between American and Pakistani officers on the ground.

Meetings at border outposts set up to develop common strategies to seal the frontier and disrupt Taliban movements reveal deep distrust among the Americans of their Pakistani counterparts.

On Feb. 7, 2007, American officers met with Pakistani troops on a dry riverbed to discuss the borderlands surrounding Afghanistan's Khost Province.

According to notes from the meeting, the Pakistanis portrayed their soldiers as conducting around-the-clock patrols. Asked if he expected a violent spring, a man identified in the report as Lt. Col. Bilal, the Pakistani officer in charge, said no. His troops were in firm control.

The Americans were incredulous. Their record noted that there had been a 300 percent increase in militant activity in Khost before the meeting.

"This comment alone shows how disconnected this particular group of leadership is from what is going on in reality," the notes said.

The Pakistanis told the Americans to contact them if they spotted insurgent activity along the border. "I doubt this would do any good," the American author of the report wrote, "because PAKMIL/ISI is likely involved with the border crossings." "PAKMIL" refers to the Pakistani military.

A year earlier, the Americans became so frustrated at the increase in roadside bombs in Afghanistan that they hand-delivered folders with names, locations, aerial photographs and map coordinates to help the Pakistani military hunt down the militants the Americans believed were responsible.

Nothing happened, wrote Col. Barry Shapiro, an American military liaison officer with experience in both Afghanistan and Pakistan, after an Oct. 13, 2006, meeting. "Despite the number of reports and information detailing the concerns," Colonel Shapiro wrote, "we continue to see no change in the cross-border activity and continue to see little to no initiative along the PAK border" by Pakistan troops. The Pakistani Army "will only react when asked to do so by U.S. forces," he concluded.

Carlotta Gall contributed reporting.

—This article was originally published on July 25, 2010

see war log on p. 510.

INSIDE THE FOG OF WAR:
REPORTS FROM THE GROUND
IN AFGHANISTAN

The reports portray a resilient, canny insurgency that has bled American forces through a war of small cuts. The insurgents set the war's pace, usually fighting on ground of their own choosing and then slipping away.

Sabotage and trickery have been weapons every bit as potent as small arms, mortars or suicide bombers. So has Taliban intimidation of Afghan officials and civilians—applied with pinpoint pressure through threats, charm, violence, money, religious fervor and populist appeals.

FEB. 19, 2008 | ZABUL PROVINCE
Intelligence Summary: Officer Threatened
An Afghan National Army brigade commander working in southern Afghanistan received a phone call from a Taliban mullah named Ezat, one brief report said. "Mullah Ezat told the ANA CDR to surrender and offered him $100, 000(US) to quit working for the Afghan Army," the report said. "Ezat also stated that he knows where the ANA CDR is from and knows his family."

MAY 9, 2009 | KUNAR PROVINCE
Intelligence Summary: Taliban Recruiter
A Taliban commander, Mullah Juma Khan, delivered a eulogy at the funeral of a slain insurgent. He played on the crowd's emotions, according to the report: "Juma cried while telling the people an unnamed woman and her baby were killed while the woman was nursing the baby." Finally he made his pitch: "Juma then told the people they needed to be angry at CF [Coalition Force] and ANSF [Afghan National Security Forces] for causing this tragedy" and "invited everyone who wants to fight to join the fighters who traveled with him."

The insurgents use a network of spies, double agents, collaborators and informers—anything to undercut coalition forces and the effort to build a credible and effective Afghan government capable of delivering security and services.

The reports repeatedly describe instances when the insurgents have been seen wearing government uniforms, and other times when they have roamed the country or appeared for battle in the very Ford Ranger pickup trucks that the United States had provided the Afghan Army and police force.

NOV. 20, 2006 | KABUL
Incident Report: Insurgent Subterfuge

After capturing four pickup trucks from the Afghan National Army, the Taliban took them to Kabul to be used in suicide bombings. "They intend to use the pick-up trucks to target ANA compounds, ISAF and GOA convoys, as well as ranking GOA and ISAF oficials," said a report, referring to coalition forces and the government of Afghanistan. "The four trucks were also accompanied by an unknown quantity of ANA uniforms to facilitate carrying out the attacks."

The Taliban's use of heat-seeking missiles has not been publicly disclosed—indeed, the military has issued statements that these internal records contradict.

In the form known as a Stinger, such weapons were provided to a previous generation of Afghan insurgents by the United States, and helped drive out the Soviets. The reports suggest that the Taliban's use of these missiles has been neither common nor especially effective; usually the missiles missed.

MAY 30, 2007 | HELMAND PROVINCE
Incident Report: Downed Helicopter

An American CH-47 transport helicopter was struck by what witnesses described as a portable heat-seeking surface-to-air missile after taking off from a landing zone.

The helicopter, the initial report said, "was engaged and struck with a Missile . . . shortly after crossing over the Helmand River. The missile struck the aircraft in the left engine. The impact of the missile projected the aft end of the aircraft up as it burst into flames followed immediately by a nose dive into the crash site with no survivors."

The crash killed seven soldiers: five Americans, a Briton and a Canadian.

Multiple witnesses saw a smoke trail behind the missile as it rushed toward the helicopter. The smoke trail was an important indicator. Rocket-propelled grenades do not leave them. Heat-seeking missiles do. The crew of other helicopters reported the downing as a surface-to-air missile strike. But that was not what a NATO spokesman told Reuters.

"Clearly, there were enemy fighters in the area," said the spokesman, Maj. John Thomas. "It's not impossible for small-arms fire to bring down a helicopter."

The reports paint a disheartening picture of the Afghan police and soldiers at the center of the American exit strategy.

The Pentagon is spending billions to train the Afghan forces to secure the country. But the police have proved to be an especially risky investment and are often described as distrusted, even loathed, by Afghan civilians. The reports recount episodes of police brutality, corruption petty and large, extortion and kidnapping. Some police officers defect to the Taliban. Others are accused of collaborating with insurgents, arms smugglers and highway bandits. Afghan police officers defect with trucks or weapons, items captured during successful ambushes or raids.

MARCH 10, 2008 | PAKTIA PROVINCE
Investigation Report: Extortion by the Police
This report captured the circular and frustrating efort by an American investigator to stop Afghan police oficers at a checkpoint from extorting payments from motorists. After a line of drivers described how they were pressed to pay bribes, the American investigator and the local police detained the accused checkpoint police oficers.

"While waiting," the investigator wrote, "I asked the seven patrolmen we detained to sit and relax while we sorted through a problem without ever mentioning why they were being detained. Three of the patrolmen responded by saying that they had only taken money from the truck drivers to buy fuel for their generator."

Two days later when the American followed up, he was told by police oficers that the case had been dropped because the witness reports had all been lost.

One report documented the detention of a military base worker trying to leave the base with GPS units hidden under his clothes and taped to his leg. Another described the case of a police chief in Zurmat, in Paktia Province, who was accused of falsely reporting that his officers had been in a firefight so he could receive thousands of rounds of new ammunition, which he sold in a bazaar.

Coalition trainers report that episodes of cruelty by the Afghan police undermine the effort to build a credible security force to take over when the allies leave.

OCT. 11, 2009 | BALKH PROVINCE
Incident Report: Brutal Police Chief

This report began with an account of Afghan soldiers and police officers harassing and beating local civilians for refusing to cooperate in a search. It then related the story of a district police commander who forced himself on a 16-year-old girl. When a civilian complained, the report continued, "The district commander ordered his bodyguard to open fire on the AC [Afghan civilian]. The bodyguard refused, at which time the district commander shot [the bodyguard] in front of the AC."

Rivalries and friction between the largest Afghan security services—the police and the army—are evident in a number of reports. Sometimes the tensions erupted in outright clashes, as was recorded in the following report from last December that was described as an "enemy action." The "enemy" in this case was the Afghan National Security Force.

DEC. 4, 2009 | ORUZGAN PROVINCE
Incident Report: Police and Army Rivalry

A car accident turned deadly when an argument broke out between the police and the Afghan National Army. "The argument escalated and ANA & ANP started to shoot at each other," a report said.

An Afghan soldier and three Afghan police officers were wounded in the shootout. One civilian was killed and six others were wounded by gunfire.

One sign of the weakness of the police is that in places they have been replaced by tribal warlords who are charged—informally but surely—with providing the security the government cannot. Often the warlords operate above the law.

NOV. 22, 2009 | KANDAHAR PROVINCE
Incident Report: Illegal Checkpoint

A private security convoy, ferrying fuel from Kandahar to Oruzgan, was stopped by what was thought to be 100 insurgents armed with assault rifles and PK machine guns, a report said.

It turned out the convoy had been halted by "the local Chief of Police," who was "demanding $2000-$3000 per truck" as a kind of toll. The chief, said the report, *from NATO headquarters in Southern Afghanistan, "states he needs the money to run his operation."*

The chief was not actually a police chief. He was Matiullah Khan, a warlord and an American-backed ally of President Karzai who was arguably Oruzgan's most powerful man. He had a contract, the Ministry of Interior said, to protect the road so NATO's supply convoys could drive on it, but he had apparently decided to extort money from the convoys himself.

Late in the day, Mr. Matiullah, after many interventions, changed his mind. The report said that friendly forces "report that the COMPASS convoy is moving again and did not pay the fee required."

The documents show how the best intentions of Americans to help rebuild Afghanistan through provincial reconstruction teams ran up against a bewildering array of problems—from corruption to cultural misunderstandings —as they tried to win over the public by helping repair dams and bridges, build schools and train local authorities.

A series of reports from 2005 to 2008 chart the frustrations of one of the first such teams, assigned to Gardez, in Paktia Province.

NOV. 28, 2006 | PAKTIA PROVINCE
Civil Affairs Report: Orphanage Opens
An American civil affairs officer could barely contain her enthusiasm as she spoke at a ribbon-cutting ceremony for a new orphanage, built with money from the American military.

The officer said a friend had given her a leather jacket to present to "someone special," the report noted. She chose the orphanage's director. "The commander stated that she could think of no one more deserving then someone who cared for orphans," it said.

The civil affairs team handed out blankets, coats, scarves and toys. The governor even gave money from his own pocket. "All speeches were very positive," the report concluded.

DEC. 20, 2006 | PAKTIA PROVINCE
Civil Affairs Report: Not Many Orphans
The team dropped by to check on the orphanage. "We found very few orphans living there and could not find most of the HA [humanitarian assistance] we had given them," the report noted.

The team raised the issue with the governor of Paktia, who said he was also concerned and suspected that the money he had donated had not reached the children. He visited the orphanage himself. Only 30 children were there; the director had claimed to have 102.

OCT. 16, 2007 | PAKTIA PROVINCE
Civil Affairs Report: An Empty Orphanage

Nearly a year after the opening of the orphanage, the Americans returned for a visit. "There are currently no orphans at the facility due to the Holiday. (Note: orphans are defined as having no father, but may still have mother and a family structure that will have them home for holidays.)"

FEB. 25, 2007 | PAKTIA PROVINCE
District Report: Lack of Resources

As the Taliban insurgency strengthened, the lack of a government presence in the more remote districts—and the government's inability to provide security or resources even to its own oficials—is evident in the reports.

An oficial from Dand Wa Patan, a small sliver of a district along the border with Pakistan, so urgently wanted to talk to the members of the American team that he traveled three and a half hours by taxi—he had no car—to meet them.

"He explained that the enemy had changed their tactics in the area and were no longer fighting from the mountains, no longer sending rockets toward his compound and other areas," the report noted. "He stated that the enemy focus was on direct action and that his family was a primary target."

Ten days earlier the Taliban crept up to the wall of his family compound and blew up one of the security towers, the report said. His son lost his legs in the explosion.

He pleaded for more police oficers, weapons and ammunition. He also wanted a car so he could drive around the district he was supposed to oversee.

But the Americans' situation was not much better. For months the reports show how a third—or even a half—of the team's vehicles were out of service, awaiting spare parts.

NOV. 15, 2006 | PAKTIA PROVINCE
Civil Affairs Report: Local Corruption

For a while the civil afairs team worked closely with the provincial governor, described as "very charismatic." Yet both he and the team are hampered by corrupt, negligent and antagonistic oficials.

The provincial chief of police is described in one report as "the axel of corruption."

"He makes every efort to openly and blatantly take money from the ANP troopers and the oficers," one sympathetic oficer told the Americans.

Other oficers are more clever. One forged rosters, to collect pay for imaginary police oficers. A second set up illegal checkpoints to collects tolls around Gardez. Still another stole food and uniforms, leaving his soldiers underfed and ill equipped for the winter.

The governor, meanwhile, was all but trapped. Such animosity developed between him and a senior security oficial that the governor could not leave his ofice for weeks at a time, fearing for his life. Finally, the corrupt oficials were replaced. But it took months.

SEPT. 24, 2007 | PAKTIA PROVINCE

Civil Affairs Report: The Cost of Corruption

Their meetings with Afghan district oficials gave the American civil afairs oficers unique insights into local opinions. Sometimes, the Afghan oficials were brutally honest in their assessments.

In one case, provincial council oficials visited the Americans at their base in Gardez to report threats—the Taliban had tossed a grenade into their ofice compound and were prowling the hills. Then the oficials began a tirade.

"The people of Afghanistan keep loosing their trust in the government because of the high amount of corrupted government oficials," the report quoted them as saying. "The general view of the Afghans is that the current government is worst than the Taliban."

"The corrupted government oficials are a new concept brought to Afghanistan by the AMERICANS," the oldest member of the group told the civil afairs team.

In conclusion, the civil afairs oficer who wrote the report warned, "The people will support the Anti-Coalition forces and the security condition will degenerate." He recommended a public information program to educate Afghans about democracy.

The reports also evoke the rivalries and tensions that swirl within the presidential palace between President Karzai's circle and the warlords.

OCT. 16, 2006 | KABUL

Intelligence Summary: Political Intrigue

In a short but heated meeting at the presidential palace, the Kabul police chief, Brig. Gen. Mir Amanullah Gozar, angrily refuted accusations made publicly by Jamil Karzai that he was corrupt and lacked professional experience. The report of the meeting identified Jamil Karzai as the president's brother; he is in fact a cousin.

General Gozar "said that if Jamil were not the president's Brother he would kidnap, torture, and kill him," the report said. He added that he was aware of plans by the American-led coalition to remove him from his post.

He threatened the president, saying that if he were replaced he would reveal "allegations about Karzai having been a drug trader and supporter of the Pakistan-led insurgency in Afghanistan," presumably a reference to Mr. Karzai's former links with the Taliban.

Incident by incident, the reports resemble a police blotter of the myriad ways Afghan civilians were killed—not just in airstrikes but in ones and twos—in shootings on the roads or in the villages, in misunderstandings or in a cross-fire, or in chaotic moments when Afghan drivers ventured too close to convoys and checkpoints.

The dead, the reports repeatedly indicate, were not suicide bombers or insurgents, and many of the cases were not reported to the public at the time. The toll of the war—reflected in mounting civilian casualties—left the Americans seeking cooperation and support from an Afghan population that grew steadily more exhausted, resentful, fearful and alienated.

From the war's outset, airstrikes that killed civilians in large numbers seized international attention, including the aerial bombardment of a convoy on its way to attend President Karzai's inauguration in 2001. An airstrike in Azizabad, in western Afghanistan, killed as many as 92 people in August 2008. In May 2009, another strike killed 147 Afghan civilians.

SEPT. 3, 2009 | KUNDUZ PROVINCE
Incident Report: Mistaken Airstrike

This report, filed about the activities of a Joint Terminal Attack Controller team, which is responsible for communication from the ground and guiding pilots during surveillance missions and airstrikes, offers a glimpse into one of the bloodiest mistakes in 2009.

It began with a report from the police command saying that "2X FUEL TRUCKS WERE STOLEN BY UNK NUMBER OF INS" and that the insurgents planned to cross the Kunduz River with their prizes. It was nighttime, and the river crossing was not illuminated. Soon, the report noted, the "JTAC OBSERVED KDZ RIVER AND REPORTED THAT IT DISCOVERED THE TRUCKS AS WELL AS UP TO 70 INS" at "THE FORD ON THE RIVER. THE TRUCKS WERE STUCK IN THE MUD." How the JTAC team was observing the trucks was not clear, but many aircraft have infrared video cameras that can send a live feed to a computer monitor on the ground.

According to the report, a German commander of the provincial reconstruction team "LINKED UP WITH JTAC AND, AFTER ENSURING THAT

NO CIVILIANS WERE IN THE VICINITY," he *"AUTHORIZED AN AIRSTRIKE." An F-15 then dropped two 500-pound guided bombs. The initial report said that "56X INS KIA [insurgents killed in action] (CONFIRMED) AND 14X INS FLEEING IN NE DIRECTION. THE 2X FUEL TRUCKS WERE ALSO DESTROYED."*

The initial report was wrong. The trucks had been abandoned, and a crowd of civilians milled around them, removing fuel. How the commander and the JTAC had ensured "that no civilians were in the area," as the report said, was not explained.

The first sign of the mistake documented in the initial report appeared the next day, when another report said that at "0900 hrs International Media reported that US airstrike had killed 60 civilians in Kunduz. The media are reporting that Taliban did steal the trucks and had invited civilians in the area to take fuel."

The reports show that the smaller incidents were just as insidious and alienating, turning Afghans who had once welcomed Americans as liberators against the war.

MARCH 5, 2007 | GHAZNI PROVINCE
Incident Report: Checkpoint Danger

Afghan police oficers shot a local driver who tried to speed through their checkpoint on a country road in Ghazni Province south of Kabul. The police had set up a temporary checkpoint on the highway just outside the main town in the district of Ab Band.

"A car approached the check point at a high rate of speed," the report said. All the police oficers fled the checkpoint except one. As the car passed the checkpoint it knocked down the lone policeman. He fired at the vehicle, apparently thinking that it was a suicide car bomber.

"The driver of the vehicle was killed," the report said. "No IED [improvised explosive device] was found and vehicle was destroyed."

The police oficer was detained in the provincial capital, Ghazni, and questioned. He was then released. The American mentoring the police concluded in his assessment that the policeman's use of force was appropriate. Rather than acknowledging the public hostility such episodes often engender, the report found a benefit: it suggested that the shooting would make Afghans take greater care at checkpoints in the future.

"Efects on the populace clearly identify the importance of stopping at checkpoints," the report concluded.

MARCH 21, 2007 | PAKTIKA PROVINCE
Incident Report: A Deaf Man Is Shot

Members of a C.I.A. paramilitary unit moved into the village of Malekshay in Paktika Province close to the border with Pakistan when they saw an Afghan running away at the sight of their convoy, one report recounted. Members of the unit shot him in the ankle, and medics treated him at the scene. The unit had followed military procedure—first shouting at the man, then firing warning shots and only after that shooting to wound, the report said.

Yet elders in the village told the unit that the man, Shum Khan, was deaf and mute and that he had fled from the convoy out of nervousness. Mr. Khan was "unable to hear the warnings or warning shots. Ran out of fear and confusion," the report concludes. The unit handed over supplies in compensation.

The reports reveal several instances of allied forces accidentally firing on one another or on Afghan forces in the fog of war, often with tragic consequences.

APRIL 6, 2006 | HELMAND PROVINCE
Incident Report: Friendly Fire

A British Army convoy driving at night in southern Afghanistan suddenly came under small-arms fire. One of the British trucks rolled over. The British troops split into two groups, pulled back from the clash and called in airstrikes from American A-10 attack planes. After several confusing minutes, commanders realized that the Afghan police had attacked the British troops, mistaking them for Taliban fighters. One Afghan police oficer was killed and 12 others were wounded.

The shifting tactics of the Americans can be seen as well in the reports, as the war strategy veered from freely using force to trying to minimize civilian casualties. But as the documents make clear, each approach has its frustrations for the American effort.

Strict new rules of engagement, imposed in 2009, minimized the use of airstrikes after some had killed civilians and turned Afghans against the war. But the rules also prompted anger from American troops and their families. The troops felt that their lives were not sufficiently valued because they had to justify every request for air or artillery support, making it easier for the Taliban to fight.

OCT. 1, 2008 | KUNAR PROVINCE

Incident Report: Barrage

In the days when field commanders had a freer hand, an infantry company commander observed an Afghan with a two-way radio who was monitoring the company's activities. Warning of "IMMINENT THREAT," the commander said he would "destroy" the man and his equipment—in other words, kill him. A short while later, a 155-millimeter artillery piece at a forward operating base in the nearby Pech Valley began firing high-explosive rounds—24 in all.

NOV. 13, 2009 | HELMAND PROVINCE

Incident Report: Escalation of Force

As the rules tightened, the reports picked up a tone that at times seemed lawyerly. Many make reference, even in pitched fights, to troops using weapons in accordance with "ROE Card A"—which guides actions of self-defense rather than attacks or offensive acts. This report described an Apache helicopter firing warning shots after coming under fire. Its reaction was described as "an escalation of force."

The helicopter pilots reported that insurgents "engaged with SAF [surface-to-air fire]" and that "INTEL suggested they were going to be fired upon again during their extraction."

The helicopters "fired 40x 30mm warning shots to deter any further engagement."

The report included the information that now is common to incident reports in which Western forces fire. "The terrain was considered rurally open and there were no CIV PID IVO [civilians positively identified in the vicinity of] the target within reasonable certainty. There was no damage to infrastructure. BDA [battle damage assessment] recording conducted by AH-64 Gun Tape. No follow up required. The next higher command was consulted. The enemy engaged presented, in the opinion of the ground forces, an imminent threat. Engagement is under ROE Card A. Higher HQ have been informed."

The reports show in previously unknown detail the omnipresence of drones in Afghanistan, the Air Force's missile-toting Predators and Reapers that hunt militants. The military's use of drones in Afghanistan has rapidly expanded in the past few years; the United States Air Force now flies about 20 Predator and Reaper aircraft a day—nearly twice as many as a year ago—over vast stretches of hostile Afghan territory. Allies like Britain and Germany fly their own fleets.

The incident reports chronicle the wide variety of missions these aircraft carry out: taking photographs, scooping up electronic transmissions, relaying images of running battles to field headquarters, attacking militants with bombs and missiles. And they also reveal the extent that armed drones are being used to support American Special Operations missions.

Documents in the Afghan archive capture the strange nature of the drone war in Afghanistan: missile-firing robots killing shovel-wielding insurgents, a remote-controlled war against a low-tech but resilient insurgency.

DEC. 9, 2008 | KANDAHAR PROVINCE
Incident Report: Predator Attack

Early one winter evening in southern Afghanistan, an Air Force Predator drone spotted a group of insurgents suspected of planting roadside bombs along a roadway less than two miles from Forward Operating Base Hutal, an American outpost.

Unlike the drones the C.I.A. operated covertly across the border in Pakistan, this aircraft was one of nearly a dozen military drones patrolling vast stretches of hostile Afghan territory on any given day.

Within minutes after identifying the militants, the Predator unleashed a Hellfire missile, all but evaporating one of the figures digging in the dark.

When ground troops reached the crater caused by the missile, costing $60,000, all that was left was a shovel and a crowbar.

SEPT. 13, 2009 | BADAKHSHAN PROVINCE
Incident Report: A Lost Drone

Flying over southern Afghanistan on a combat mission, one of the Air Force's premier armed drones, a Reaper, went rogue.

Equipped with advanced radar and sophisticated cameras, as well as Hellfire missiles and 500-pound bombs, the Reaper had lost its satellite link to a pilot who was remotely steering the drone from a base in the United States.

Again and again, the pilot struggled to regain control of the drone. Again and again, no response. The reports reveal that the military in Afghanistan lost many of the tiny five-pound surveillance drones with names like Raven and Desert Hawk that troops tossed out like model airplanes to peer around the next hill. But they had never before lost one of the Reapers, with its 66-foot wingspan.

As a last resort, commanders ordered an Air Force F-15E Strike Eagle fighter jet to shoot down the $13 million aircraft before it soared unguided into neighboring Tajikistan.

Ground controllers picked an unpopulated area over northern Afghanistan and the
jet fired a Sidewinder missile, destroying the Reaper's turbo-prop engine. Suddenly,
the satellite link was restored, but it was too late to salvage the flight. At 5:30 a.m.,
controllers steered it into a remote mountainside for a final fiery landing.

As the Afghanistan war took priority under the Obama administration,
more Special Operations forces were shifted from Iraq to conduct secret
missions. The C.I.A.'s own paramilitary operations inside Afghanistan grew
in tandem—as did the agency's close collaboration with Afghanistan's own
spy agency.

Usually, such teams conducted night operations aimed at top Taliban
commanders and militants on the "capture/kill" list. While individual commandos have displayed great courage, the missions can end in calamity as
well as success. The expanding special operations have stoked particular
resentment among Afghans—for their lack of coordination with local forces,
the civilian casualties they frequently inflicted and the lack of accountability.

JUNE 17, 2007 | PAKTIKA PROVINCE
INCIDENT REPORT: Botched Night Raid

Shortly after five American rockets destroyed a compound in Paktika Province,
helicopter-borne commandos from Task Force 373—a classified Special Operations
unit of Army Delta Force operatives and members of the Navy Seals—arrived to
finish the job.

The mission was to capture or kill Abu Laith al-Libi, a top commander for Al
Qaeda, who was believed to be hiding at the scene of the strike.

But Mr. Libi was not there. Instead, the Special Operations troops found a group
of men suspected of being militants and their children. Seven of the children had been
killed by the rocket attack.

Some of the men tried to flee the Americans, and six were quickly killed by encircl-
ing helicopters. After the rest were taken as detainees, the commandos found one child
still alive in the rubble, and performed CPR for 20 minutes.

Word of the attack spread a wave of anger across the region, forcing the local governor
to meet with village elders to defuse the situation.

American military oficials drew up a list of "talking points" for the governor,
pointing out that the target had been a senior Qaeda commander, that there had been
no indications that women and children would be present and that a nearby mosque
had not been damaged.

After the meeting, the governor reported that local residents were in shock, but that he had "pressed the Talking Points." He even "added a few of his own that followed in line with our current story."

The attack was caused by the "presence of hoodlums," the governor told the people. It was a tragedy that children had been killed, he said, but "it could have been prevented had the people exposed the presence of insurgents in the area."

He promised that the families would be compensated for their loss.

Mr. Libi was killed the following year by a C.I.A. drone strike.

APRIL 6, 2008 | NUR IS TAN PROVINCE
Incident Report: A Raging Firefight

As they scrambled up the rocks toward a cluster of mud compounds perched high over the remote Shok Valley, a small group of American Green Berets and Afghan troops, known as Task Force Bushmaster, were confronted with a hail of gunfire from inside the insurgent stronghold.

They were there to capture senior members of the Hezb-e-Islami Gulbuddin militant group, part of a mission that the military had dubbed Operation Commando Wrath.

But what they soon discovered on that remote, snowy hilltop was that they were vastly outnumbered by a militant force of hundreds of fighters. Reinforcements were hours away.

A firefight raged for nearly seven hours, with sniper fire pinning down the Green Berets on a 60-foot rock ledge for much of that time.

Casualties mounted. By midmorning, nearly half of the Americans were wounded, but the militants directed their gunfire on the arriving medevac helicopters, preventing them from landing.

"TF Bushmaster reports they are combat inefective and request reinforcement at this time."

For a time, radio contact was lost.

Air Force jets arrived at the scene and began pummeling the compounds with 2,000-pound bombs, but the militants continued to advance down the mountain toward the pinned-down group.

The task force reported that there were "50-100 insurgents moving to reinforce against Bushmaster elements from the SW."

Carrying wounded Americans shot in the pelvis, arm and legs—as well as two dead Afghans—the group made its way down toward the valley floor. Eventually, the helicopters were able to arrive to evacuate the dead and wounded.

Ten members of the Green Berets would receive Silver Stars for their actions during the battle, the highest number given to Special Forces soldiers for a single battle since the Vietnam War. By Army estimates, 150 to 200 militants were killed in the battle.

MARCH 8, 2008 | BAGRAM AIR BASE
Meeting Report: A Plea for Help

Toward the end of a long meeting with top American military commanders, during which he delivered a briefing about the security situation in eastern Afghanistan, corruption in the government and Pakistan's fecklessness in hunting down militants, Afghanistan's top spy laid out his problem.

Amrullah Saleh, then director of the National Directorate of Security, told the Americans that the C.I.A. would no longer be handling his spy service's budget. For years, the C.I.A. had essentially run the N.D.S. as a subsidiary, but by 2009 the Afghan government was preparing to take charge of the agency's budget.

Mr. Saleh estimated that with the C.I.A. no longer bankrolling the Afghan spies, he could be facing a budget cut of 30 percent.

So he made a request. With the budget squeeze coming, Mr. Saleh asked the Americans for any AK-47s and ammunition they could spare.

If they had any spare boots, he would also take those, he said.

This article was written and reported by C. J. CHIVERS, CARLOTTA GALL, ANDREW W. LEHREN, MARK MAZZETTI, JANE PERLEZ, and ERIC SCHMITT, with contributions from JACOB HARRIS and ALAN MCLEAN.

—This article was originally published on July 25, 2010

STRATEGIC PLANS SPAWNED BITTER END FOR A LONELY OUTPOST

By C. J. CHIVERS

Nothing in the documents made public on Sunday offers as vivid a miniature of the Afghan war so far—from hope to heartbreak—as the field reports from one lonely base: Combat Outpost Keating.

The outpost was opened in 2006 in the Kamdesh district of Nuristan Province, an area of mountain escarpments, thick forests and deep canyons with a population suspicious of outsiders. The outpost's troops were charged with finding allies among local residents and connecting them to the central government in Kabul, stopping illegal cross-border movement and deterring the insurgency.

But the outpost's fate, chronicled in unusually detailed glimpses of a base over nearly three years, illustrates many of the frustrations of the allied effort: low troop levels, unreliable Afghan partners and an insurgency that has grown in skill, determination and its ability to menace.

The outpost was small, isolated and exposed to high ground, one compound in a network of tiny firebases the American and Afghan governments built far from Afghanistan's cities. The area, near the border with Pakistan, was suspected of being an insurgent corridor.

Some early reports from the area were upbeat. Although it was obvious from the outset that there were so few troops that the outpost, like others of its kind, could barely defend its bunkers and patrol at the same time, much less disrupt a growing insurgency, the dispatches carried notes of cheerful confidence when they described the campaign for local hearts and minds.

"It was clear our meeting had produced tangible results," the outpost reported in December 2006, after the Americans distributed pencils, notebooks, erasers and pencil sharpeners in a nearby village, along with prayer rugs and winter gloves for children.

Later, after a larger handout of clothing, first-aid kits and school supplies to villagers, the report summarized the pitch to local residents: "Our friendship grows every day." It also noted that the "positive nonlethal effects" of the donations "stimulated a frank discussion on security issues."

The security situation was, in a word, bad. The road to the base was overlooked by high ground; all traffic was vulnerable to ambushes. Most of the movement of supplies and troops was done by helicopters, which were exposed to ground fire.

Transport helicopters were scarce. Attack helicopters, which might provide fire support if the outpost was attacked, were based at Jalalabad— more than a 30-minute flight away.

Before long the optimistic reports about handouts of milk and soccer balls and the good will of the local residents gave way to a realization that insurgents controlled almost everything up to the outpost's gates.

The Afghan forces held little promise: the Americans training them noted that local police chiefs complained that their officers were not being paid and that most of them "will not work, they will walk off the job." The reports describe how the insurgents gradually moved to cut off the outpost, physically and socially.

Feb. 17, 2007: Armed men in Afghan Army uniforms ambushed three Afghan trucks as they left a nearby base after delivering supplies. The drivers were allowed to live. But one had been wounded by shrapnel. The insurgents sliced off the others' ears.

April 29, 2007: Men who identified themselves as "We the Mujahedeen" posted so-called night letters on a mosque. The handwritten letters complained about American infidels and the "sold-out mullahs," contractors, police officers, soldiers and officials who worked with them. It listed the names of Afghans who worked as the outpost's security guards.

"These people are hated by God," the letter said, according to a translation in the intelligence summary. "Soon we will start our operations."

Insurgents Send a Message

The local villagers tore up the letters. The next day, six insurgents stopped a car owned by Fazal Ahad, the leader of a local council, or shura, that cooperated with the Americans on security issues, as he drove with other council members down a canyon road. The insurgents sent a brutal but measured message to the villagers.

"The fighters secured Fazal Ahad and told the others they could leave now and live, or follow them and die," said the military's report of the incident. After the released men fled, villagers reported hearing a gunshot. Fazal Ahad was dead.

The outposts in outer Nuristan Province had become defensive positions kept alive by helicopters that would typically fly only at night. Local residents were caught between sides. Development was idled. The reports compose a portrait in futility: the enemy was strong, the post's ranks were small and counterinsurgency efforts had no traction. The area was more treacherous, and less safe, than when the push into the canyons had begun.

In the summer of 2009, as President Obama explored options for continuing the war, Gen. Stanley A. McChrystal, then his new commander in Kabul, revisited the idea of dividing the limited available forces and distributing them in remote outposts. New thinking took hold: forces were to be concentrated where they could have the greatest effect.

Combat Outpost Keating, along with several other tiny firebases in eastern Afghanistan, was ordered to shut down. By fall, the United States was quietly withdrawing from part of its archipelago of little posts.

But before Combat Outpost Keating could be closed, the insurgents struck.

Early on Oct. 3, they massed for a coordinated attack, pounding the little outpost with mortar shells and rocket-propelled grenades and raking it from above with heavy machine-gun fire.

Groups of gunmen rushed the post's defensive wire. They simultaneously hit a smaller observation post nearby. At least 175 enemy gunmen were involved in the offensive; some accounts described a force twice that size.

The first classified summaries of the attack are a frightening record of a small unit caught at the juncture between old and new ways to fight the war. They depict American troops isolated and overwhelmed on enemy turf. The reports include excerpts of real-time computer messages to headquarters typed by soldiers in the outpost and accounts of pilots who attacked the insurgents from the air.

At first, the outpost reported that Keating and the observation post were "IN HEAVY CONTACT."

Typing in the casual familiarity of Internet chat, on a secure server, a soldier immediately asked that an "Air Tic Be Opened."

That was military jargon for shifting available close-air support to troops taking fire. The sense of urgency was clear; the reason chilling.

"We need it now," another soldier typed. "We have mortars pinned down and fire coming from everywhere."

The battle escalated from there. The outpost relayed details. "We are taking casiltys," the first soldier typed within minutes—the first reports of wounded troops. He added: "GET SOMETHING UP!"

The consequences of decisions made in distant headquarters were now taking shape for young enlisted men. The enemy had the high ground. The outpost had the low ground. The troops were outnumbered, and starting to drop. Fire support was far away.

The arrival of attack helicopters, the outpost was told, would take time. "IT'S A 40 MINUTE FLIGHT."

The outpost asked about jets.

"We are taking fire from inside urmul village," it reported. "Our mortars are still pinned down unable to fire."

Jets were on the way. Soon a soldier was describing where aircraft should drop their ordnance. "Multiple enemies running through" the Afghan National Police station "and fire coming from the mosque," he typed.

He added, "The police station is shooting at us."

A Frantic Call for Help

Forty minutes into the fighting, he reported that the observation post was about to detonate its Claymore mines—a sign that the attackers were almost at its walls. "They are that close to the wire," the soldier typed.

Eight minutes later he reported that the attackers were breaching Keating's last defensive ring. The post was at risk of falling, and having the fighting go hand-to-hand.

"Enemy in the wire at keating," he typed. "ENEMUY IN THE WIRE ENEMY IN THE WIRE!!!"

An entry soon after was a model of understatement: "We need support."

Insurgents entered the outpost. The American attack helicopters began to arrive, joining F-15s and an aircraft with jamming equipment to block the insurgents' two-way radios. One of the pilots' initial reports described, in laconic terms, flying through gantlets of fire, and occasionally finding a shooting gallery of insurgent targets.

Hellfire missiles were fired on the local mosque, from where soldiers on the ground said the insurgents were firing. The mosque was destroyed.

As bombs exploded above and around the base and helicopters made strafing runs, the soldiers consolidated in a building that was not burning and began to counterattack.

As the four-hour mark of the battle approached, a higher command noted that soldiers at the outpost reported that they "have retaken another bldg, can't push any further due to lack of manpower."

Outside the perimeter, the insurgents still fired.

At the nine-hour mark, the higher command summarized word from the ground: "Only one building left that is not on fire. Have consolidated all casualties at that location."

Late in the day, American reinforcements were shuttled by helicopter to nearby terrain. They bounded downhill toward the outpost. The fighting by then had stopped.

The outpost had held on, but barely. Eight soldiers were dead. Almost two dozen others had been wounded. Several Afghan soldiers and guards were killed or wounded, too.

The Americans evacuated their casualties. Over the next days they declared the outpost closed and departed—so quickly that they did not carry out all of their stored ammunition.

The outpost's depot was promptly looted by the insurgents and bombed by American planes in an effort to destroy the lethal munitions left behind.

—This article was originally published on July 25, 2010

MIX OF TRUST AND DESPAIR HELPED TURN TIDE IN IRAQ

By SABRINA TAVERNISE

Christoph Bangert for The New York Times

During the worst days of sectarian violence in Iraq in 2006, bodies were often dumped by a road.

The Iraq war archive, taken as a whole with its details of incidents small and large, offers a cautionary postscript for the current military strategy in Afghanistan.

That same strategy, based on an infusion of additional troops, is often credited with rescuing Iraq. The American military applied it and turned around an increasingly hopeless war, according to one narrative. And while it is true that the additional troops offered better security, the reports in the archive suggest that the approach was also successful because many Iraqis were ready for it.

A unique set of conditions had coalesced on the ground. The warring communities were exhausted from the frenzy of killing. Mixed neighborhoods and cities were largely cleansed. The militias, both Sunni and Shiite, long seen as defenders of their communities, had begun to cannibalize them, making local residents newly receptive to American overtures.

The war that emerges from the documents is a rapidly changing set of circumstances with its own logic and arc, whose fluidity was underestimated by the military, the media and Washington policy makers. The troop increase, devised and led by Gen. David H. Petraeus, who is now the commander in Afghanistan, came around the time that many Iraqis were so fed up with their local militias that they were ready to risk cooperating with the Americans by giving them information. Two years earlier, they were not.

That is not to say that the troop increase, commonly known as the surge, and the accompanying strategic changes, were unimportant. On the contrary, that risky gamble was central in initiating the reduction in violence. Without it, Iraqis would have been stuck.

Taken together, the archives from Iraq and Afghanistan suggest that each war has had its own alchemy. Now General Petraeus is confronting a far different society. It remains to be seen whether Pashtun society is ready to resist the Taliban, as Sunnis were in Iraq, whether tribal leaders in Afghanistan are strong enough to lead that resistance or whether the Taliban and a deeply discredited central government are ready to reconcile. Afghanistan is a poorer, far less literate and centralized country than Iraq; each valley is its own nation, a patchwork that makes it tricky to apply any policy nationwide.

In Iraq, Americans expected to be hailed as liberators, but they were resented as occupiers, and Iraqis eventually turned to the Americans largely out of exhaustion and despair. In Afghanistan, Americans were welcomed at first, but as the war dragged on, Afghans lost faith in the Americans' ability to protect them—and it is unclear whether that faith can be restored. The lesson of Iraq is that without it, no strategy, however well conceived, can be successful.

If Afghanistan is a war of small cuts, Iraq was a gash. In the war's bloodiest months, according to the archive's reports, more than 3,000 Iraqi civilians were dying, more than 10 times the current civilian casualty rate in Afghanistan, a country with a larger population.

The reports read like nightmares. In January 2005, a human head was thrown from an Opel Omega into the Mufrek traffic circle in the city of Baquba. The next month, 47 workers from a brick factory were found murdered north of Baghdad. One report noted that a discovery of six bodies at a sewage treatment plant in Baghdad was the third such episode at the same plant in recent weeks. Later during that month, there were also two more similar discoveries there. All the bodies had gunshot wounds to the head.

The Pentagon was slow to acknowledge what had become abundantly clear on the ground—that Iraq had sunk into sectarian war. The military began to release partial civilian casualty figures in 2005 under pressure from Congress. The word "sect" appears only 12 times in the archive in 2005, the year that systematic cleansing began. Corpses that were surfacing in garbage dumps, rivers and empty lots were blandly categorized as a "criminal event" and seem to have been given about as much importance as traffic accidents.

In a briefing for reporters several days after the bombing of a shrine in Samarra in 2006, the event that unleashed an all-out civil war, Maj. Gen. Rick Lynch, the military spokesman at the time, said: "Over the last three days what we've seen is not widespread sectarian violence. And we believe that there has not been widespread sectarian violence because of a capable Iraqi government."

But the Iraqi government, or at least part of it, was one of the perpetrators. The documents in the archive cite hundreds of cases of prisoner abuse by the Iraqi Army and the police. A jail in the western province of Anbar in June 2006 had "large amounts of blood on the cell floor," an unhinged metal cell door positioned against a back wall and electrical wires with blood at the ends. (The Americans reprimanded the police.)

There were killings. A report from February 2006 described how Iraqis carrying official Ministry of Interior identification cards used false documents to remove 12 prisoners from a police jail in Basra. Their fate? "Prisoners are now dead," the report stated. "All prisoners are of Sunni religion."

Sectarian turf wars burned hotly until mixed neighborhoods were largely cleansed. But exactly when the tide turned remains foggy. According to the existing reports, the single worst month for civilian deaths was

December 2006, two months before the buildup's first brigade arrived. Casualties dropped slightly in January. In February, when the first new brigade arrived, the recorded casualties dropped by a quarter, though it is the shortest month.

Around that time, Moktada al-Sadr, the anti-American cleric, decamped to Iran, perhaps fearing American troops.

What the documents suggest strongly is that Iraqis themselves were looking for an escape from the orgy of sectarian killing made worse by the growth of ordinary, but still violent, crime. Uses of the word "kidnap" in the reports increase sharply in 2007, as do "theft," "loot," and "carjacking." Torments varied according to location. In Sunni areas, the fundamentalist militants of Al Qaeda in Mesopotamia had brutalized and alienated people. As early as September 2006, tribes in Anbar came together to oppose Al Qaeda in Mesopotamia.

General Petraeus was quick to seize that opportunity, turning the tribes' cooperation into a program that he aggressively expanded throughout the country, working with American diplomats to push a reluctant Iraqi prime minister to accept it.

His predecessor, Gen. George W. Casey Jr.—who had been pursuing a policy of drawing down American troops—had seen it more as a local program.

That effort became perhaps the turning point in the war. The appearance in the documents of the initials S.O.I., a reference to the Sons of Iraq, the Sunni groups that banded together against insurgents, spiked in 2008. In Shiite areas, militias like the Mahdi Army, known as JAM (for Jaish al-Mahdi) by the military, once seen as protectors, had turned into parasites, extorting, kidnapping for ransom and demanding protection money, Mafia-style. A February 2007 report noted that the young son of a businessman was kidnapped by Mahdi Army members. The family paid $15,000 for his release, but he was killed anyway.

Iraqis of all stripes began to use the Americans as a bridge, coming forward with information about everything from Al Qaeda hide-outs to gas station extortions. Uses of the word "source" peak in 2007, with five times as many references as in 2004. "Tip" follows the same pattern. A report from May 2007 noted the arrest of a bus driver who was extorting a gas station on behalf of the Mahdi Army. The owner of the gas station provided the tip.

Meanwhile, Americans' understanding of Iraq had become more sophisticated. If at first the sectarian war was played down or ignored, by 2007 the word sect had become part of the military's template for daily violence reports. The often fruitless search operations that were the hallmark of the early years of the war suddenly became effective as Iraqis gave Americans information. The holdouts were many, and the Americans waged hard-fought campaigns, with heavy casualties, to eliminate them.

By 2007, the detainee population had exploded. Among the prisoners was a much feared Shiite militia leader, Abu Dura, captured by the Americans in a raid based on a local tip.

The Iraqi partners were not ideal. The documents in the archive contain references to shady politicians, like the head of security for Fadilah, a Shiite political party, who, according to one report, was believed to have received money from Iran and to "control a secret arm of the Fadilah Party that conducts kidnappings and assassination operations to influence local politics."

Even the Sunni tribal forces that eventually helped turn the tide of the war were prone to raucous shooting episodes, including one in 2008, in which sheiks had to be airlifted to an American hospital after being wounded in a shootout over sheep food.

By 2009, civilian deaths had dropped to the lowest levels recorded in the archive. In interviews in the summer of 2008, Iraqis said they were so deeply frightened by the killings in 2006 that they would do anything to avoid being dragged into that kind of violence again.

But war is always clearest in retrospect, and it remains to be seen whether Afghanistan has reached that point.

Jacob M. Harris contributed reporting from New York.

—This article was originally published on October 23, 2010

A GRIM PORTRAIT OF CIVILIAN DEATHS IN IRAQ

By SABRINA TAVERNISE and ANDREW W. LEHREN

Lynsey Addario for The New York Times

A father wrapped his son's body at a Baghdad morgue
after a bomb killed the young man in 2004.

The reports in the archive disclosed by WikiLeaks offer an incomplete, yet startlingly graphic portrait of one of the most contentious issues in the Iraq war—how many Iraqi civilians have been killed and by whom.

The reports make it clear that most civilians, by far, were killed by other Iraqis. Two of the worst days of the war came on Aug. 31, 2005, when a stampede on a bridge in Baghdad killed more than 950 people after several earlier attacks panicked a huge crowd, and on Aug. 14, 2007, when truck bombs killed more than 500 people in a rural area near the border with Syria.

But it was systematic sectarian cleansing that drove the killing to its most frenzied point, making December 2006 the worst month of the war, according to the reports, with about 3,800 civilians killed, roughly equal to the past seven years of murders in New York City. A total of about 1,300 police officers, insurgents and coalition soldiers were also killed in that month.

The documents also reveal many previously unreported instances in which American soldiers killed civilians—at checkpoints, from helicopters, in operations. Such killings are a central reason Iraqis turned against the American presence in their country, a situation that is now being repeated in Afghanistan.

The archive contains reports on at least four cases of lethal shootings from helicopters. In the bloodiest, on July 16, 2007, as many as 26 Iraqis were killed, about half of them civilians. However, the tally was called in by two different people, and it is possible that the deaths were counted twice.

In another case, in February 2007, an Apache helicopter shot and killed two Iraqi men believed to have been firing mortars, even though they made surrendering motions, because, according to a military lawyer cited in the report, "they cannot surrender to aircraft, and are still valid targets."

The shooting was unusual. In at least three other instances reported in the archive, Iraqis surrendered to helicopter crews without being shot. The Pentagon did not respond to questions from The Times about the rules of engagement for the helicopter strike.

The pace of civilian deaths served as a kind of pulse, whose steady beat told of the success, or failure, of America's war effort. Americans on both sides of the war debate argued bitterly over facts that grew hazier as the war deepened.

The archive does not put that argument to rest by giving a precise count. As a 2008 report to Congress on the topic makes clear, the figures serve as "guideposts," not hard totals. But it does seem to suggest numbers that are roughly in line with those compiled by several sources, including Iraq Body Count, an organization that tracked civilian deaths using press reports, a method the Bush administration repeatedly derided as unreliable and producing inflated numbers. In all, the five-year archive lists more than

100,000 dead from 2004 to 2009, though some deaths are reported more than once, and some reports have inconsistent casualty figures. A 2008 Congressional report warned that record keeping in the war had been so problematic that such statistics should be looked at only as "guideposts."

In a statement on Friday, Iraq Body Count, which did a preliminary analysis of the archive, estimated that it listed 15,000 deaths that had not been previously disclosed anywhere.

The archive tells thousands of individual stories of loss whose consequences are still being felt in Iraqi families today.

Misunderstandings at checkpoints were often lethal. At one Marine checkpoint, sunlight glinting off a windshield of a car that did not slow down led to the shooting death of a mother and the wounding of three of her daughters and her husband. Hand signals flashed to stop vehicles were often not understood, and soldiers and Marines, who without interpreters were unable to speak to the survivors, were left to wonder why.

According to one particularly painful entry from 2006, an Iraqi wearing a tracksuit was killed by an American sniper who later discovered that the victim was the platoon's interpreter.

The archive's data is incomplete. The documents were compiled with an emphasis on speed rather than accuracy; the goal was to spread information as quickly as possible among units. American soldiers did not respond to every incident.

And even when Americans were at the center of the action, as in the western city of Falluja in 2004, none of the Iraqis they killed were categorized as civilians. In the early years of the war, the Pentagon maintained that it did not track Iraqi civilian deaths, but it began releasing rough counts in 2005, after members of Congress demanded a more detailed accounting on the state of the war. In one instance in 2008, the Pentagon used reports similar to the newly released documents to tabulate the war dead.

This month, The Associated Press reported that the Pentagon in July had quietly posted its fullest tally of the death toll of Iraqi civilians and security forces ever, numbers that were first requested in 2005 through the Freedom of Information Act. It was not clear why the total—76,939 Iraqi civilians and members of the security forces killed between January 2004 and August 2008—was significantly less than the sum of the archive's death count.

The archive does not have a category for the main causes of Iraqi deaths inflicted by Americans. Compared with the situation in Afghanistan, in Iraq aerial bombings seemed to be less frequently a cause of civilian deaths, after the initial invasion. The reports were only as good as the soldiers calling them in. One of the most infamous episodes of killings by American soldiers, the shootings of at least 15 Iraqi civilians, including women and children in the western city of Haditha, is misrepresented in the archives. The report stated that the civilians were killed by militants in a bomb attack, the same false version of the episode that was given to the news media.

Civilians have borne the brunt of modern warfare, with 10 civilians dying for every soldier in wars fought since the mid-20th century, compared with 9 soldiers killed for every civilian in World War I, according to a 2001 study by the International Committee of the Red Cross.

—This article was originally published on October 22, 2010

see war log on p. 512.

DETAINEES FARED WORSE IN IRAQI HANDS, LOGS SAY

By SABRINA TAVERNISE and ANDREW W. LEHREN

The public image of detainees in Iraq was defined by the photographs, now infamous, of American abuse at Abu Ghraib, like the hooded prisoner and the snarling attack dog. While the documents disclosed by WikiLeaks offer few glimpses of what was happening inside American detention facilities, they do contain indelible details of abuse carried out by Iraq's army and police.

The six years of reports include references to the deaths of at least six prisoners in Iraqi custody, most of them in recent years. Beatings, burnings and lashings surfaced in hundreds of reports, giving the impression that such treatment was not an exception. In one case, Americans suspected Iraqi Army officers of cutting off a detainee's fingers and burning him with acid. Two other cases produced accounts of the executions of bound detainees.

And while some abuse cases were investigated by the Americans, most noted in the archive seemed to have been ignored, with the equivalent of an institutional shrug: soldiers told their officers and asked the Iraqis to investigate.

A Pentagon spokesman said American policy on detainee abuse "is and has always been consistent with law and customary international practice." Current rules, he said, require forces to immediately report abuse; if it was perpetrated by Iraqis, then Iraqi authorities are responsible for investigating.

That policy was made official in a report dated May 16, 2005, saying that if "if US forces were not involved in the detainee abuse, no further investigation will be conducted until directed by HHQ." In many cases, the order appeared to allow American soldiers to turn a blind eye to abuse of Iraqis on Iraqis.

Even when Americans found abuse and reported it, Iraqis often did not act. One report said a police chief refused to file charges "as long as the abuse produced no marks." Another police chief told military inspectors that his officers engaged in abuse "and supported it as a method of conducting investigations."

It is a frightening portrait of violence by any standards, but particularly disturbing because Iraq's army and police are central to President Obama's plan to draw down American troops in Iraq. Iraqi forces are already the backbone of security in Iraq, now that American combat troops are officially gone, and are also in charge of running its prisons.

The archive contains extensive, often rambling accounts of American abuse from Iraqi prisoners, but few were substantiated. The most serious came during arrests, which were often violent when people resisted. In those cases, investigations were opened. In a case reminiscent of Abu Ghraib, in which guards photographed themselves with Iraqis whom they had posed in humiliating positions, a soldier was censured for writing a mocking slur with a marker on the forehead of a crying detainee.

The United States took steps to improve its detention system after the scandal at the Abu Ghraib prison erupted in 2004, tightening rules governing the treatment of prisoners and separating the hardened radicals of Al Qaeda in Mesopotamia from other prisoners.

But the documents show that Americans did sometimes use the threat of abuse by Iraqi authorities to get information out of prisoners. One report said an American threatened to send a detainee to the notorious Wolf Brigade, a particularly violent Iraqi police unit, if he did not supply information.

Some of the worst examples of Iraqi abuse came later in the war. In August 2009, an Iraqi police commando unit reported that a detainee committed suicide in its custody, but an autopsy conducted in the presence of an American "found bruises and burns on the detainee's body as well as visible injuries to the head, arm, torso, legs, and neck." The report stated that the police "have reportedly begun an investigation."

Then in December, 12 Iraqi soldiers, including an intelligence officer, were caught on video in Tal Afar shooting to death a prisoner whose hands were tied. The document on the episode says that the reporting is preliminary; it is unclear whether there was a follow-up.

Years of abuse under Saddam Hussein produced an exceptionally violent society. Iraqis used cables, metal rods, wooden poles and live electrical wires to hurt prisoners. One report on a detainee cited "bruises in a roughly boot shape from upper to lower back." In another, a detainee is said to have bruises from beatings with a board. Another detainee suffered blurred vision, bleeding in his ears and nose, bruises on his back, arms and legs and hemorrhaging in his eyes. Americans told the local Iraqi Army commander but did not open an inquiry because no American was involved.

American soldiers, however, often intervened. During a visit to a police unit in Ramadi, an American soldier entered a cell after hearing screams and found two badly dehydrated detainees with bruises on their bodies. He had them transferred out of Iraqi custody.

In August 2006, an American sergeant in Ramadi heard whipping noises in a military police station and walked in on an Iraqi lieutenant using an electrical cable to slash the bottom of a detainee's feet. The American stopped him, but later he found the same Iraqi officer whipping a detainee's back.

One beaten detainee said in 2005 that "when the Marines finally took him, he was treated very well, and he was thankful and happy to see them."

Early on, space for detainees was limited, and Iraqis would stuff them into makeshift jails, increasing the chances for abuse. In November 2005, American soldiers found 95 blindfolded detainees with sores and broken bones crammed into a police internment center.

—This article was originally published on October 22, 2010

See war log on p. 513.

LEAKED REPORTS DETAIL IRAN'S AID FOR IRAQI MILITIAS

By MICHAEL R. GORDON and ANDREW W. LEHREN

On Dec. 22, 2006, American military officials in Baghdad issued a secret warning: The Shiite militia commander who had orchestrated the kidnapping of officials from Iraq's Ministry of Higher Education was now hatching plans to take American soldiers hostage.

What made the warning especially worrying were intelligence reports saying that the Iraqi militant, Azhar al-Dulaimi, had been trained by the Middle East's masters of the dark arts of paramilitary operations: the Islamic Revolutionary Guards Corps in Iran and Hezbollah, its Lebanese ally.

"Dulaymi reportedly obtained his training from Hizballah operatives near Qum, Iran, who were under the supervision of Iranian Islamic Revolutionary Guard Corps Quds Force (IRGC-QF) officers in July 2006," the report noted, using alternative spellings of the principals involved.

Five months later, Mr. Dulaimi was tracked down and killed in an American raid in the sprawling Shiite enclave of Sadr City in Baghdad—but not before four American soldiers had been abducted from an Iraqi headquarters in Karbala and executed in an operation that American military officials say literally bore Mr. Dulaimi's fingerprints.

Scores of documents made public by WikiLeaks, which has disclosed classified information about the wars in Iraq and Afghanistan, provide a ground-level look—at least as seen by American units in the field and the United States' military intelligence—at the shadow war between the United States and Iraqi militias backed by Iran's Revolutionary Guards.

During the administration of President George W. Bush, critics charged that the White House had exaggerated Iran's role to deflect criticism of its handling of the war and build support for a tough policy toward Iran, including the possibility of military action.

But the field reports disclosed by WikiLeaks, which were never intended to be made public, underscore the seriousness with which Iran's role has been seen by the American military. The political struggle between the United States and Iran to influence events in Iraq still continues as Prime Minister Nuri Kamal al-Maliki has sought to assemble a coalition—that would include the anti-American cleric Moktada al-Sadr—that will allow him to remain in power. But much of the American's military concern has revolved around Iran's role in arming and assisting Shiite militias.

Citing the testimony of detainees, a captured militant's diary and numerous uncovered weapons caches, among other intelligence, the field reports recount Iran's role in providing Iraqi militia fighters with rockets, magnetic bombs that can be attached to the underside of cars, "explosively formed penetrators," or E.F.P.'s, which are the most lethal type of roadside bomb in Iraq, and other weapons. Those include powerful .50-caliber rifles and the Misagh-1, an Iranian replica of a portable Chinese surface-to-air missile, which, according to the reports, was fired at American helicopters and downed one in east Baghdad in July 2007.

Iraqi militants went to Iran to be trained as snipers and in the use of explosives, the field reports assert, and Iran's Quds Force collaborated with Iraqi extremists to encourage the assassination of Iraqi officials.

The reports make it clear that the lethal contest between Iranian-backed militias and American forces continued after President Obama sought to open a diplomatic dialogue with Iran's leaders and reaffirmed the agreement between the United States and Iraq to withdraw American troops from Iraq by the end of 2011.

A Revolutionary Force

Established by Ayatollah Ruhollah Khomeini after the 1979 Iranian revolution, the Islamic Revolutionary Guards Corps has expanded its influence at home under President Mahmoud Ahmadinejad, a former member of the corps, and it plays an important role in Iran's economy, politics and internal security. The corps's Quds Force, under the command of Brig. Gen. Qassem Soleimani, has responsibility for foreign operations and has often sought to work though surrogates, like Hezbollah.

While the American government has long believed that the Quds Force has been providing lethal assistance and training to Shiite militants in Iraq, the field reports provide new details about Iran's support for Iraqi militias and the American military's operations to counter them.

The reports are written entirely from the perspective of the American-led coalition. No similar Iraqi or Iranian reports have been made available. Nor do the American reports include the more comprehensive assessments that are typically prepared by American intelligence agencies after incidents in the field.

While some of the raw information cannot be verified, it is nonetheless broadly consistent with other classified American intelligence and public accounts by American military officials. As seen by current and former American officials, the Quds Force has two main objectives: to weaken and shape Iraq's nascent government and to diminish the United States' role and influence in Iraq.

For people like General Soleimani, "who went through all eight years of the Iran-Iraq war, this is certainly about poking a stick at us, but it is also about achieving strategic advantage in Iraq," Ryan C. Crocker, the American ambassador in Iraq from 2007 until early 2009, said in an interview.

"I think the Iranians understand that they are not going to dominate Iraq," Mr. Crocker added, " but I think they are going to do their level best to weaken it—to have a weak central government that is constantly off balance, that is going to have to be beseeching Iran to stop doing bad things without having the capability to compel them to stop doing bad things. And that is an Iraq that will never again threaten Iran."

Politics and Militias

According to the reports, Iran's role has been political as well as military. A Nov. 27, 2005, report, issued before Iraq's December 2005 parliamentary elections, cautioned that Iranian-backed militia members in the Iraqi government were gaining power and giving Iran influence over Iraqi politics.

"Iran is gaining control of Iraq at many levels of the Iraqi government," the report warned.

The reports also recount an array of border incidents, including a Sept. 7, 2006, episode in which an Iranian soldier who aimed a rocket-propelled grenade launcher at an American platoon trying to leave the border area was shot and killed by an American soldier with a .50-caliber machine gun. The members of the American platoon, who had gone to the border area with Iraqi troops to look for "infiltration routes" used to smuggle bombs and other weapons into Iraq, were concerned that Iranian border forces were trying to surround and detain them. After this incident, the platoon returned to its base in Iraq under fire from the Iranians even when the American soldiers were "well inside Iraqi territory," a report noted.

But the reports assert that Iran's Quds Force and intelligence service has turned to many violent and shadowy tactics as well.

The reports contain numerous references to Iranian agents, but the documents generally describe a pattern in which the Quds Force has sought to maintain a low profile in Iraq by arranging for fighters from Hezbollah in Lebanon to train Iraqi militants in Iran or by giving guidance to Iraqi militias who do the fighting with Iranian financing and weapons.

The reports suggest that Iranian-sponsored assassinations of Iraqi officials became a serious worry.

A case in point is a report that was issued on March 27, 2007. Iranian intelligence agents within the Badr Corps and Jaish al-Mahdi, two Shiite militias, "have recently been influencing attacks on ministry officials in Iraq," the report said.

According to the March report, officials at the Ministry of Industry were high on the target list. "The desired effect of these attacks is not to simply kill the Ministry of Industry Officials," the report noted, but also "to show the world, and especially the Arab world, that the Baghdad Security Plan has failed to bring stability," referring to the troop increase that Gen. David H. Petraeus was overseeing to reduce violence in Iraq.

News reports in early 2007 indicated that a consultant to the ministry and his daughter were shot and killed on the way to his office. The March report does not mention the attack, but it asserts that one gunman was carrying out a systematic assassination campaign, which included killing three bodyguards and plotting to attack ministry officials while wearing a stolen Iraqi Army uniform.

The provision of Iranian rockets, mortars and bombs to Shiite militants has also been a major concern. A Nov. 22, 2005, report recounted an effort by the Iraqi border police to stop the smuggling of weapons from Iran, which "recovered a quantity of bomb-making equipment, including explosively formed projectiles," which are capable of blasting a metal projectile through the door of an armored Humvee.

A Shiite militant from the Jaish al-Mahdi militia, also known as the Mahdi Army, was planning to carry out a mortar attack on the Green Zone in Baghdad, using rockets and mortar shells shipped by the Quds Force, according to a report on Dec. 1, 2006. On Nov. 28, the report noted, the Mahdi Army commander, Ali al-Sa'idi, "met Iranian officials reported to be IRGC officers at the border to pick up three shipments of rockets."

A Dec. 27, 2008, report noted one instance when American soldiers from the 82nd Airborne Division captured several suspected members of the Jaish al-Mahdi militia and seized a weapons cache, which also included several diaries, including one that explained "why detainee joined JAM and how they traffic materials from Iran."

The attacks continued during Mr. Obama's first year in office, with no indication in the reports that the new administration's policies led the Quds Force to end its support for Iraqi militants. The pending American troop withdrawals, the reports asserted, may even have encouraged some militant attacks.

A June 25, 2009, report about an especially bloody E.F.P. attack that wounded 10 American soldiers noted that the militants used tactics "being employed by trained violent extremist members that have returned from Iran." The purpose of the attack, the report speculated, was to increase American casualties so militants could claim that they had "fought the occupiers and forced them to withdraw."

An intelligence analysis of a Dec. 31, 2009, attack on the Green Zone using 107-millimeter rockets concluded that it was carried out by the Baghdad branch of Kataib Hezbollah, a militant Shiite group that American intelligence has long believed is supported by Iran. According to the December report, a technical expert from Kataib Hezbollah met before the attack with a "weapons facilitator" who "reportedly traveled to Iran, possibility to facilitate the attacks on 31 Dec."

That same month, American Special Operations forces and a specially trained Iraqi police unit mounted a raid that snared an Iraqi militant near Basra who had been trained in Iran. A Dec. 19, 2009, report stated that the detainee was involved in smuggling "sticky bombs"— explosives that are attached magnetically to the underside of vehicles—into Iraq and was "suspected of collecting information on CF [coalition forces] and passing them to Iranian intelligence agents."

A Bold Operation

One of the most striking episodes detailed in the trove of documents made public by WikiLeaks describes a plot to kidnap American soldiers from their Humvees. According to the Dec. 22, 2006, report, a militia commander, Hasan Salim, devised a plan to capture American soldiers in Baghdad and hold them hostage in Sadr City to deter American raids there.

To carry out the plan, Mr. Salim turned to Mr. Dulaimi, a Sunni who converted to the Shiite branch of the faith while studying in the holy Shiite city of Najaf in 1995. Mr. Dulaimi, the report noted, was picked for the operation because he "allegedly trained in Iran on how to conduct precision, military style kidnappings."

Those kidnappings were never carried out. But the next month, militants conducted a raid to kidnap American soldiers working at the Iraqi security headquarters in Karbala, known as the Provincial Joint Coordination Center.

The documents made public by WikiLeaks do not include an intelligence assessment as to who carried out the Karbala operation. But American military officials said after the attack that Mr. Dulaimi was the tactical commander of the operation and that his fingerprints were found on the getaway car. American officials have said he collaborated with Qais and Laith Khazali, two Shiite militant leaders who were captured after the raid along with a Hezbollah operative. The Khazali brothers were released after the raid as part of an effort at political reconciliation and are now believed to be in Iran.

The documents, however, do provide a vivid account of the Karbala attack as it unfolded.

At 7:10 p.m., several sport utility vehicles of the type typically used by the American-led coalition blocked the entrance to the headquarters compound. Twenty minutes later, an "unknown number of personnel, wearing American uniforms and carrying American weapons attacked the PJCC," the report said.

The attackers managed to kidnap four American soldiers, dragging them into an S.U.V., which was pursued by police officers from an Iraqi

SWAT unit. Calculating that they were trapped, the militants shot the handcuffed hostages and fled. Three of the American soldiers who had been abducted died at the scene. The fourth later died of his wounds, the report said, and a fifth American soldier was killed in the initial attack on the compound.

Summing up the episode, the American commander of a police training team noted in the report that that the adversary appeared to be particularly well trained. "PTT leader on ground stated insurgents were professionals and appeared to have a well planned operation," the report said.

—This article was originally published on October 22, 2010

USE OF CONTRACTORS ADDED TO WAR'S CHAOS IN IRAQ

By JAMES GLANZ and ANDREW W. LEHREN

The remains of a car in which two women were killed in 2007
by private guards riding in a convoy.

The first shots sailed past Iraqi police officers at a checkpoint. They took off in three squad cars, their lights flashing.

It was early in the Iraq war, Dec. 22, 2004, and it turned out that the shots came not from insurgents or criminals. They were fired by an American private security company named Custer Battles, according to an incident report in an archive of more than 300,000 classified military documents made public by WikiLeaks.

The company's convoy sped south in Umm Qasr, a grubby port city near the Persian Gulf. It shot out the tire of a civilian car that came close. It fired five shots into a crowded minibus. The shooting stopped only after the Iraqi police, port security and a British military unit finally caught up with the convoy.

Somehow no one had been hurt, and the contractors found a quick way to prevent messy disciplinary action. They handed out cash to Iraqi civilians, and left.

The documents sketch, in vivid detail, a critical change in the way America wages war: the early days of the Iraq war, with all its Wild West chaos, ushered in the era of the private contractor, wearing no uniform but fighting and dying in battle, gathering and disseminating intelligence and killing presumed insurgents.

There have been many abuses, including civilian deaths, to the point that the Afghan government is working to ban many outside contractors entirely.

The use of security contractors is expected to grow as American forces shrink. A July report by the Commission on Wartime Contracting, a panel established by Congress, estimated that the State Department alone would need more than double the number of contractors it had protecting the American Embassy and consulates in Iraq.

Contractors were necessary at the start of the Iraq war because there simply were not enough soldiers to do the job. In 2004, their presence became the symbol for Iraq's descent into chaos, when four contractors were killed in Falluja, their bodies left mangled and charred.

Even now—with many contractors discredited for unjustified shootings and a lack of accountability amply described in the documents—the military cannot do without them. There are more contractors over all than actual members of the military serving in the worsening war in Afghanistan.

The archive, which describes many episodes never made public in such detail, shows the multitude of shortcomings with this new system: how a failure to coordinate among contractors, coalition forces and Iraqi troops, as well as a failure to enforce rules of engagement that bind the military, endangered civilians as well as the contractors themselves. The military was often outright hostile to contractors, for being amateurish, overpaid and, often, trigger-happy.

Contractors often shot with little discrimination—and few if any consequences—at unarmed Iraqi civilians, Iraqi security forces, American troops and even other contractors, stirring public outrage and undermining much of what the coalition forces were sent to accomplish.

The mayhem cropped up around Iraq, notably in one episode reported in March 2005 in which a small battle erupted involving three separate security companies.

At a notoriously dangerous checkpoint on the main road to the Baghdad airport, a cement truck entered a lane reserved for Department of Defense vehicles. A guard from Global, a British company, fired a warning shot, and when a man initially identified as an Iraqi opened the door and tried to flee, guards from a tower started firing, too. The man dropped to the ground. Then members of an Iraqi private security team parked nearby also opened fire, shooting through the chest not the driver but a worker from DynCorp International, an American security company.

When the truck driver was finally questioned, he turned out to be a Filipino named José who worked with yet a third company, KBR, the American logistics and security giant.

The conclusion drawn from this chaos was, "IT IS BELIEVED THE DRIVER ENTERED THE DOD LANE BY ACCIDENT."

For all the contractors' bravado—Iraq was packed with beefy men with beards and flak jackets—and for all the debates about their necessity, it is clear from the documents that the contractors appeared notably ineffective at keeping themselves and the people they were paid to protect from being killed.

In fact, the documents seem to confirm a common observation on the ground during those years in Iraq: far from providing insurance against sudden death, the easily identifiable, surprisingly vulnerable pickup trucks and S.U.V.'s driven by the security companies were magnets for insurgents, militias, disgruntled Iraqis and anyone else in search of a target.

Most of the documents are incident reports and match what is known of the few cases that have been made public, although even this cache is unlikely to be a complete record of incidents involving contractors. During the six years covered by the reports, at least 175 private security contractors were killed. The peak appeared to come in 2006, when 53 died. Insurgents and other malefactors kidnapped at least 70 security contractors, many of whom were later killed.

Aegis, a British security company, had the most workers reported killed, more than 30. Most of those were Iraqi drivers, guards and other employees. Not only the military, but journalists and aid workers as well relied on contractors to help protect them.

The security contractors seemed overmatched, often incinerated or torn apart by explosions their vehicles had no chance of warding off. In August 2004, the corpses of two men who had worked with Custer Battles were found charred and abandoned in a truck that was still burning on the road between Tikrit and Mosul, after it was struck by an improvised explosive device and fired upon from a Volkswagen, one report said.

In July 2007, another report said, two were killed when a gun truck operated by ArmorGroup, a British company, flew like a wobbling discus 54 yards through the air, flipping approximately six times, after a huge I.E.D. exploded beneath it in northern Iraq.

And in May 2009, three Americans, including a senior Navy officer, were killed outside Falluja when an I.E.D. overturned a vehicle escorted by Aegis contractors during a visit to a water treatment plant financed by the United States, according to another report and American government statements at the time.

Death came suddenly, from all sides, in all forms.

In late 2004 in Tikrit, seven men emerged from two Daewoo vehicles and mowed down Iraqi workers for Buckmaster, a company hired to destroy old munitions, as the workers got out of a bus, a report said. The gunmen did not flee until they ran out of ammunition, killing 17 and wounding 20 as two Iraqis saved themselves by hiding under seats in the bus.

There were suicide bombings, desert ambushes, aviation disasters and self-inflicted wounds, as when a Ugandan guard working for EOD Technology, an American company, shot and killed his South African supervisor and then himself in 2008 after being terminated, a report said.

A spokesman for EOD confirmed the incident and said that the investigation had been unable to determine "why this particular guard decided to take the actions that he did."

"I think the only elaboration on this incident is to note that it was a very sad and unfortunate event," said the spokesman, Erik S. Quist.

In another case, in Baghdad in the summer of 2009, a British contractor with ArmorGroup was reported to have shot and killed two co-workers, a Briton and an Australian, then run wild through the heavily fortified Green

Zone in an attempt to escape. Finally, a coalition soldier tackled him, a report said, and another soldier "shot a directed-aimed warning shot into sand bags which immediately stopped resistance from suspect so that he could be brought under control."

The alleged killer, Daniel Fitzsimons, is still being held in Baghdad while awaiting trial under Iraqi law.

The contractors also suffered horrific traffic accidents with multiple fatalities all over Iraq, seemingly as a side effect of driving at high speeds on bad roads where a threat can appear at any moment.

The threats were not limited to insurgents, the documents show: private security contractors repeatedly came under fire from Iraqi and coalition security forces, who often seemed unnerved by unmarked vehicles approaching at high speeds and fired warning shots, or worse. Even as the war dragged on, there seemed no universal method for the military to identify these quasi soldiers on the battlefield.

To cope, the contractors were reduced to waving reproductions of coalition flags from inside their vehicles, the documents show—but even that did not always work. After being shot at by an American military guard tower near Baiji in July 2005, contractors with Aegis first waved a British flag. When the shooting continued, the contractors, who said they were transporting a member of the American military at the time, held up an American flag instead. "THE TOWER KEPT SHOOTING," a report said, although no one was injured in the episode.

But whatever the constellation of reasons—from war-zone jumpiness to outright disregard for civilian lives—the security companies are cited time after time for shootings that the documents plainly label as unjustified. This has blackened their reputation, even if it has not lessened the military's dependence on them. "AFTER THE IED STRIKE A WITNESS REPORTS THE BLACKWATER EMPLOYEES FIRED INDISCRIMINATELY AT THE SCENE," read one report from Aug. 22, 2006, referring to the company, now known as Xe Services, that the following year would become notorious for an apparently unprovoked killing of 17 Iraqis at Nisour Square in Baghdad.

In a written statement last week, Xe said, "While it would be inappropriate to comment on specific cases, we work closely with our government customers and cooperate fully in all investigations."

In December 2004, just a few days after the confrontation with Iraqi security forces, another Custer Battles convoy fired into the windshield of a Humvee driven by American military police soldiers in a patrol that was approaching the convoy from behind on another road near Baghdad. The report noted laconically that the security contractors did not stop their convoy until they reached an American checkpoint, "WHERE THEY ADMITTED TO FIRING ON THE MP PTL," the military police patrol.

Many of the companies apparently felt no sense of accountability. Contractors with a Romanian company called Danubia Global killed three Iraqis in Falluja in 2006, another report said, then refused to answer questions on the episode, citing a company policy not to provide information to investigators.

In 2007, a convoy operated by Unity Resources Group, based in Dubai, shot at an approaching vehicle near the Green Zone in Baghdad, wounded a bodyguard for President Jalal Talabani of Iraq and did not report the shooting until Mr. Talabani's staff contacted the American authorities, one report said.

When asked about the incident last week, a Unity official, Jim LeBlanc, said that "in a time of numerous suicide vehicle attacks, a vehicle had presented itself in a profile that was consistent with the behavior of a suicide attacker." Unity guards fired "carefully aimed warning shots" when the vehicle refused to stop, Mr. LeBlanc said, and the company did not initially believe that anyone had been hurt.

Only when contacted by American investigators did Unity realize that "an Iraqi security force member" had been struck by a ricochet, and from that point on, the company fully cooperated, Mr. LeBlanc said. After the investigation, he said, "all Unity members were cleared to immediately return to work."

And still more recently, in July 2009, local contractors with the 77th Security Company drove into a neighborhood in the northern city of Erbil and began shooting at random, setting off a firefight with an off-duty police officer and wounding three women, another report said.

"It is assessed that this drunken group of individuals were out having a good time and firing their weapons," the incident report concluded.

In many other cases, contractors cited what they considered a justifiable "escalation of force" as an Iraqi vehicle moved toward them and did not respond to "hand signals" and other signs that the driver should stop. At that point, the contractors would fire into the vehicle's engine block or through the windshield.

The Iraqis who were shot at, and who the documents show were nearly always civilians, not surprisingly saw things differently. To judge by the disgust that seeps through even the dry, police-blotter language of some of the incident reports, American military units often had a similar perspective. That appears to be especially true of reports on "escalations of force" by Blackwater in the years leading up to the Nisour Square shooting, the documents show.

On May 14, 2005, an American unit "OBSERVED A BLACKWATER PSD SHOOT UP A CIV VEHICLE," killing a father and wounding his wife and daughter, a report said, referring to a Blackwater protective security detail.

On May 2, 2006, witnesses said that an Iraqi ambulance driver approaching an area struck by a roadside bomb was killed by "uncontrolled small arms firing" by Blackwater guards, another report noted.

On Aug. 16, 2006, after being struck by an I.E.D. in the southbound lane of a highway, Blackwater contractors shot and killed an Iraqi in the back seat of a vehicle traveling in the northbound lane, a report said. At least twice—in Kirkuk and Hilla—civilian killings by Blackwater set off civilian demonstrations, the documents say.

And so it went, up to the Sept. 16, 2007, Nisour Square shooting by Blackwater guards that is again noted as an "escalation of force" in the documents. Little new light is shed on the episode by the documents, although in a twist, the report indicated that the street from which the Blackwater convoy charged into the square went by the military code name Skid Row.

The last reference to Custer Battles, which eventually lost a $10 million whistle-blower case in which it was claimed that the company defrauded the United States on billing invoices for the company's work in Iraq, appears in a report dated March 15, 2005, describing an I.E.D. strike on an exit ramp in western Baghdad. An Iraqi driver for the company received shrapnel wounds in the face from the bomb and was wounded in the chest by gunfire that broke out after the explosion. The driver was taken to a local hospital, ultimate fate unknown.

—This article was originally published on October 23, 2010

TENSIONS HIGH ALONG KURDISH-ARAB LINE

By MICHAEL R. GORDON and ANDREW W. LEHREN

The new trove of documents released by WikiLeaks portrays the long history of tensions between Kurds and Arabs in the north of Iraq and reveals the fears of some American units about what might happen after American troops leave the country by the end of 2011.

"Without strong and fair influence, likely from a third party, these tensions may quickly turn to violence after the U.S. forces withdrawal," warned a Sept. 28, 2009, field report.

Experts have long watched the tensions in the region with worry. Their main fear is not that senior Kurdish officials will seek a confrontation with the Shiite-dominated government in Baghdad. The main interest of the political leadership, many experts say, is making sure the oil-rich region continues to grow economically.

Rather, it is that local Kurdish and Arab politicians and security officials may take matters into their own hands if crucial disputes remain unsettled, particularly after the departure of American forces, which have regularly worked behind the scenes to head off confrontations.

Kurds and Arabs are at odds over power-sharing arrangements in the Kirkuk region, the degree of federalism that should be allowed in the Iraqi state, the terms of a new oil law and territorial disputes. Those disputes have been complicated by the fact that American forces initially welcomed the presence of Kurdish troops, the pesh merga, in some parts of northern Iraq to help fend off insurgents.

Relations have been so fraught that Gen. Ray Odierno, who recently left his post as the senior American commander in Iraq, established a series of checkpoints, maintained by American, Iraqi and Kurdish soldiers, to head off confrontations, either accidental or planned.

Obama administration officials have voiced hopes that the Kurds' participation in a new governing coalition will foster long-deferred compromises and lead to the gradual integration of pesh merga fighters into Iraq's army. But little headway has been made on Kurdish-Arab issues in recent years. The administration is also planning to open embassy branch offices in the cities of Mosul and Kirkuk, which would enable American diplomats to focus on Arab and Kurdish issues even after American forces depart.

The reports disclosed by WikiLeaks document a long history of tensions, which insurgents from Al Qaeda in Mesopotamia, a Sunni Arab extremist group, have sought to exploit.

A Sept. 27, 2008, report showed how violence could erupt even when officials on both sides were trying to keep tensions in check. After Iraqi police officers near Khanaqin, in Diyala Province, arrested and roughed up a member of a Kurdish intelligence organization, a local Kurdish leader went to a police station to obtain his release.

The prisoner was let go, but an "ensuing verbal altercation" led to shots being fired and the death of a pesh merga fighter.

A report two months later described a more calculated assault: The planting of a roadside bomb in another northern area.

"The Arabs of that district hate the IP's there because their police chief is a Kurd," who had links to Kurdish intelligence, noted a Nov. 22, 2008, report, using the military's abbreviation for the Iraqi police.

Insurgents have repeatedly sought to stir up trouble between the two sides. On Dec. 11, 2008, a suicide bomber, wearing a vest filled with explosives, blew himself up in a restaurant near Kirkuk that was patronized by Kurdish and Arab officials.

"This attack was likely intended to intimidate the leaders and to dissuade future meetings of political and religious leaders attempting to unite the province," the field report noted.

The report on a particularly tense episode in May 2009 provides an unusual glimpse at the role American military personnel and civilians have played in trying to avert sectarian violence.

Atheel al-Nujaifi, a Sunni Arab and the newly elected governor of Nineveh Province, was already a polarizing figure for the Kurds, and tensions grew when he proclaimed on May 7 that he planned to visit a hang-gliding festival at Bashiqa. This is a small town northeast of Mosul, in Nineveh Province, but which the Kurds have long claimed.

Two days later, a liaison officer from the Kurdish regional government told Brig. Gen. Robert B. Brown, the deputy American military commander for northern Iraq, that if Mr. Nujaifi "traveled into Kurdish controlled area, there would be a potential incident," the May report noted.

In an effort to head off a confrontation, Alexander M. Laskaris, the head of the State Department's provincial reconstruction team in Mosul, called the governor and warned him against making the trip, which did not appear to sway Mr. Nujaifi.

As the festival approached, American soldiers from the Third Brigade Combat Team, First Cavalry Division went to inspect the road to the event. Officially, the pesh merga fighters and Iraqi soldiers shared the common goal of thwarting attacks by insurgents and terrorists, but now they appeared to have squared off like two opposing armies.

Pesh merga fighters at a checkpoint on the road to Bashiqa said that they had been ordered to shoot the governor if he tried to pass. Iraqi soldiers, who had their own checkpoint nearby, reported that they had been ordered to fire on the pesh merga if they shot at the governor, the report noted.

By this time, the issue had been brought to the attention of Prime Minister Nuri Kamal al-Maliki, who also sought to head off trouble. Mr. Maliki ordered the Iraqi military command in the province not to provide security for the trip, apparently calculating that this would prompt the governor to cancel the visit.

None of that seemed to stop Mr. Nujaifi, who arranged for the local police to protect him.

Finally, a face-saving solution was found: the minister of youth and sports in Baghdad canceled the festival. While that solved the immediate problem, the underlying issues remained. As the May 8 report cautioned: "Recent reporting illustrates increased potential for ethnic tensions."

—This article was originally published on October 23, 2010

LEAKS ADD TO PRESSURE ON WHITE HOUSE OVER STRATEGY

By ERIC SCHMITT and HELENE COOPER

WASHINGTON—The White House sought to reassert control over the public debate on the Afghanistan war on Monday as political reaction to the disclosure of a six-year archive of classified military documents increased pressure on President Obama to defend his war strategy.

On Capitol Hill, a leading Senate Democrat said the documents, with their detailed account of a war faring even more poorly than two administrations had portrayed, would intensify Congressional scrutiny of Mr. Obama's policy.

"Those policies are at a critical stage, and these documents may very well underscore the stakes and make the calibrations needed to get the policy right more urgent," said Senator John Kerry, a Massachusetts Democrat who is the chairman of the Foreign Relations Committee and has been an influential supporter of the war.

The disclosures landed at a crucial moment. Because of difficulties on the ground and mounting casualties in the war, the debate over the American presence in Afghanistan has begun earlier than expected. Inside the administration, more officials are privately questioning the policy.

In Congress, House leaders were rushing to hold a vote on a critical war-financing bill as early as Tuesday, fearing that the disclosures could stoke Democratic opposition to the measure. A Senate panel is also set to hold a hearing on Tuesday on Mr. Obama's choice to head the military's Central Command, Gen. James N. Mattis, who would oversee operations in Afghanistan.

Administration officials acknowledged that the documents, released on the Internet by an organization called WikiLeaks, will make it harder for Mr. Obama as he tries to hang on to public and Congressional support until the end of the year, when he has scheduled a review of the war effort. "We don't know how to react," one frustrated administration official said on Monday. "This obviously puts Congress and the public in a bad mood."

Mr. Obama is facing a tough choice: he must either figure out a way to convince Congress and the American people that his war strategy remains on track and is seeing fruit, or move more quickly to a far more limited American presence.

As the debate over the war begins anew, administration officials have been striking tones similar to the Bush administration's to argue for continuing the current Afghanistan strategy, which calls for a significant troop buildup. Richard C. Holbrooke, Mr. Obama's special representative to Afghanistan and Pakistan, said the Afghan war effort came down to a matter of American national security, in testimony before the Foreign Relations Committee two weeks ago.

The White House press secretary, Robert Gibbs, struck a similar note on Monday in responding to the documents, which WikiLeaks made accessible to The New York Times, the British newspaper The Guardian and the German magazine Der Spiegel.

"We are in this region of the world because of what happened on 9/11," Mr. Gibbs said. "Ensuring that there is not a safe haven in Afghanistan by which attacks against this country and countries around the world can be planned. That's why we're there, and that's why we're going to continue to make progress on this relationship."

Several administration officials privately expressed hope that they might be able to use the leaks, and their description of a sometimes duplicitous Pakistani ally, to pressure the government of Pakistan to cooperate more fully with the United States on counterterrorism. The documents seem to lay out rich new details of connections between the Taliban and other militant groups and Pakistan's main spy agency, the Directorate for Inter-Services Intelligence, or ISI.

Three administration officials separately expressed hope that they might be able to use the documents to gain leverage in efforts to get more help from Pakistan. Two of them raised the possibility of warning the Pakistanis that Congressional anger might threaten American aid.

"This is now out in the open," a senior administration official said. "It's reality now. In some ways, it makes it easier for us to tell the Pakistanis that they have to help us."

But much of the pushback from the White House over the past two days has been to stress that the connection between the ISI and the Taliban was well known.

"I don't think that what is being reported hasn't in many ways been publicly discussed, either by you all or by representatives of the U.S. government, for quite some time," Mr. Gibbs said during a briefing on Monday.

While agreeing that the disclosures were not altogether new, some leading Democrats said that the new details underscored deep suspicions they have harbored toward the ISI. "Some of these documents reinforce a longstanding concern of mine about the supporting role of some Pakistani officials in the Afghan insurgency," said Senator Carl Levin, a Michigan Democrat who heads the Armed Services Committee. During a visit to Pakistan this month, Mr. Levin, who has largely supported the war, said he confronted senior Pakistani leaders about the ISI's continuing ties to the militant groups.

The White House appeared to be focusing some of its ire toward Julian Assange, the founder of WikiLeaks.org, the Web site that provided access to about 92,000 secret military reports.

White House officials e-mailed reporters select transcripts of an interview Mr. Assange conducted with Der Spiegel, underlining the quotations the White House apparently found most offensive. Among them was Mr. Assange's assertion, "I enjoy crushing bastards."

At a news conference in London on Monday, Mr. Assange defended the release of the documents. "I'd like to see this material taken seriously and investigated, and new policies, if not prosecutions, result from it."

The Times and the two other news organizations agreed not to disclose anything that was likely to put lives at risk or jeopardize military or antiterrorist operations, and The Times redacted the names of Afghan informants and other delicate information from the documents it published. WikiLeaks said it withheld posting about 15,000 documents for the same reason.

Pakistan strongly denied suggestions that its military spy service has guided the Afghan insurgency.

A senior ISI official, speaking anonymously under standard practice, sharply condemned the reports as "part of the malicious campaign to malign the spy organization" and said the ISI would "continue to eradicate the menace of terrorism with or without the help of the West."

Farhatullah Babar, the spokesman for President Asif Ali Zardari of Pakistan, dismissed the reports and said that Pakistan remained "a part of a strategic alliance of the United States in the fight against terrorism."

While Pakistani officials protested, a spokesman for the Afghan president, Hamid Karzai, said that Mr. Karzai was not upset by the documents and did not believe the picture they painted was unfair.

Speaking after a news conference in Kabul, Mr. Karzai's spokesman, Waheed Omar, was asked whether there was anything in the leaked documents that angered Mr. Karzai or that he thought unfair. "No, I don't think so," Mr. Omar said.

Reporting was contributed by Adam B. Ellick and Salman Masood from Islamabad, Pakistan; Richard A. Oppel Jr. from Kabul, Afghanistan; and Caroline Crampton from London.

—This article was originally published on July 26, 2010

U.S. MILITARY
SCRUTINIZES LEAKS
FOR RISKS TO AFGHANS

By ERIC SCHMITT and CHARLIE SAVAGE

WASHINGTON—The Pentagon is reviewing tens of thousands of classified battlefield reports made public this week about the war in Afghanistan
to determine whether Afghan informants were identified and could be at
risk of reprisals, American officials said Wednesday.

A Pentagon spokesman, Col. David Lapan, said that a Pentagon assessment team had not yet drawn any conclusions, but that "in general, the
naming of individuals could cause potential problems, both to their physical
safety or willingness to continue support to coalition forces or the Afghan
government."

Speaking in Kabul on Thursday, the Afghan president, Hamid Karzai,
called the disclosure of the names of Afghans who had cooperated with
NATO and American forces "extremely irresponsible and shocking."

"Whether those individuals acted legitimately or illegitimately in
providing information to the NATO forces, their lives will be in danger
now," said Mr. Karzai, who spoke at a press conference just after he said he
discussed the issue with his advisors. "Therefore we consider that extremely
irresponsible and an act that one cannot overlook."

A search by The New York Times through a sampling of the documents released by the organization WikiLeaks found reports that gave
the names or other identifying features of dozens of Afghan informants,
potential defectors and others who were cooperating with American and
NATO troops.

The Times and two other publications given access to the documents—the British newspaper The Guardian and the German magazine
Der Spiegel—posted online only selected examples from documents that

had been redacted to eliminate names and other information that could be used to identify people at risk. The news organizations did this to avoid jeopardizing the lives of informants.

The founder of WikiLeaks, Julian Assange, has said that the organization withheld 15,000 of the approximately 92,000 documents in the archive that was released on Sunday to remove the names of informants in what he called a "harm minimization" process. But the 75,000 documents WikiLeaks put online provide information about possible informants, like their villages and in some cases their fathers' names.

Asked on NBC's "Today" show on Wednesday if the killing of an Afghan as a result of the WikiLeaks disclosure would be considered "collateral damage" in his efforts to make details of the war public, Mr. Assange said, "If we had, in fact, made that mistake, then, of course, that would be something that we would take very seriously."

National security officials, meanwhile, are worried that the attention WikiLeaks has received in the past week has elevated its profile and could be used to entice disgruntled officials to send classified information to its Web site, which solicits "classified, censored or otherwise restricted material of political, diplomatic or ethical significance" and asserts that "submitting confidential material to WikiLeaks is safe, easy and protected by law."

One United States official, speaking on the condition of anonymity because of the continuing investigation, said government lawyers were exploring whether WikiLeaks and Mr. Assange could be charged with a crime. One question, some lawyers say, is whether they could be charged with inducing or serving as co-conspirators in violations of the Espionage Act, a 1917 law that prohibits the unauthorized disclosure of national security information.

Indeed, at a press club in London on Tuesday, Mr. Assange told reporters that before the most recent disclosure of documents, WikiLeaks had been warned by officials in the United States government that there had been "thoughts of whether I could be charged as a co-conspirator to espionage, which is serious."

"That doesn't seem to be the thinking within the United States anymore, however," he added. He did not elaborate.

But on Wednesday, Senator Lindsey Graham, Republican of South Carolina, said on Fox News that WikiLeaks itself should be prosecuted for its role, saying, "As far as I know, there's no immunity for a Web site to be able to pass on documents" that were illegally leaked.

At a Senate Judiciary Committee oversight hearing on Wednesday, Senator Jon Kyl, Republican of Arizona, pressed the director of the Federal Bureau of Investigation, Robert S. Mueller III, to say whether he expected that prosecutors would charge "both the individuals who provided the information and those who might have been involved in the dissemination of the information."

Mr. Mueller demurred, saying that "at this juncture, I can't say as to where that particular investigation will lead."

Attorney General Eric H. Holder Jr. was similarly vague about prosecutorial plans, telling reporters in Egypt, where he is on a trip, that what the leak inquiry "will lead to, whether there will be criminal charges brought, will depend on how the investigation goes."

Still, several legal specialists in matters related to leaks of classified information say that prosecuting Mr. Assange or WikiLeaks on charges that they had violated the Espionage Act would face many hurdles, from the diplomatic difficulty in persuading a country to arrest and extradite Mr. Assange to an array of legal defenses he could mount if the United States managed to detain him. Mr. Assange is an Australian activist who has operated in various European cities.

Susan Buckley, a partner at the law firm Cahill Gordon & Reindel who specializes in communications law, said the Espionage Act had rarely been used and so there were few guides for how such a novel case would play out. For example, it is not clear whether the law applies to foreigners for actions overseas, although she noted that in a 1985 case, a judge ruled that the law did apply abroad.

It would also be highly unusual to use the law to go after the recipient and disseminator of a leak, rather than just the person who provided the information. Several scholars said they were aware of only one previous attempt to bring such a prosecution—the 2005 indictment of two former staff members of the American Israel Public Affairs Committee who were accused of passing on information about American policy toward Iran from a military analyst to Israel.

In 2009, prosecutors dropped the case after several court rulings that they said had sharply diminished the likelihood that they would win a conviction. But the Aipac case was controversial from the start, in part because it was seen as a step toward prosecuting journalists who write about classified matters, and a prosecution of Mr. Assange and WikiLeaks could also raise First Amendment issues.

A military spokesman noted that the Army had legal jurisdiction only over service members, and so any decision to prosecute WikiLeaks would be up to the Justice Department. A spokesman said the Justice Department would "not speculate on where the investigation may or may not lead or various other hypothetical scenarios."

Mr. Assange has not said where he obtained the documents. But a military intelligence analyst, Pfc. Bradley Manning, has been charged with leaking other classified documents and videos that have appeared on the WikiLeaks Web site.

The disclosure of documents containing the names of Afghan informants, which was reported Tuesday in The Times of London, could further complicate the Obama administration's efforts to manage the course of the war in Afghanistan.

A search by The New York Times on Wednesday also turned up several examples.

In one 2007 report, for instance, a military officer discussed meeting with a person who was named in the report, who claimed to have worked with allied forces and wanted to continue doing so. The Times withheld details that could identify the man.

In another 2007 report, American troops met privately with an Afghan official, who was named in the report, who told the Americans about the recent movements of a local militant leader and his heavily armed force. The report also identified several other informants who were part of the official's network.

Richard A. Oppel Jr. contributed reporting from Kabul, and Andrew W. Lehren contributed research from New York.

—This article was originally published on July 28, 2010

LEAKED AFGHAN WAR REPORTS HEIGHTEN EUROPEAN DOUBTS

By JUDY DEMPSEY

BERLIN—The revelations contained in newly released U.S. military documents on the war in Afghanistan have led to parliamentary demands in Berlin and London for expanded inquiries into the war that some analysts say could increase pressure in Europe for accelerated troop withdrawals.

But there were signs on Wednesday that the secret military documents might not have any immediate impact on a war that the major parties appear resigned to pursue, at least in the short term: Lawmakers in Washington vigorously debated the documents on Tuesday but then voted to continue financing the Afghan and Iraq wars.

Still, with European publics largely opposed to the Afghan war, the documents—with their grim and granular picture of the war's ground-level challenges—appear certain to exacerbate deeply held doubts, the analysts said.

"The documents show a disconnect between what is happening between the government debate, the people in the field and the public narrative," said Lisa Aronsson, a trans-Atlantic specialist with the Royal United Services Institute in London. "The leaks could accelerate the process of withdrawal."

"This is not welcome news for the allies," she added.

The documents, provided by the WikiLeaks Web site and reported Monday by The New York Times, The Guardian of London and Der Spiegel of Germany, contain suggestions of at least semiofficial Pakistani support for the Taliban and describe the covert and highly targeted efforts of U.S special forces to eliminate enemy figures.

Stephen Flanagan, senior vice president of the Center for Strategic and International Studies in Washington, said some details of special forces operations would add to European doubts on NATO strategy.

"The Europeans, for example, are queasy about these special operations, as if the troops are involved in a kind of dirty war," he said.

In one early tangible sign that the leaks will heighten scrutiny of the Afghan conflict, a parliamentary panel in London, the House of Commons' defense select committee, decided this week to widen its inquiry of the war.

Britain, with 9,500 soldiers in Afghanistan, has said it will end its combat mission by 2015.

The Guardian quoted Whitehall sources as saying that the widened inquiry was likely to examine whether that timetable was realistic and whether it should begin next year.

In Germany, the opposition Left Party on Wednesday renewed its call for the government to withdraw all its 4,665 troops from Afghanistan. "The documents make clear why we should not have any part in this war," said Wolfgang Gehrcke, the party's foreign affairs spokesman.

Other lawmakers, citing the WikiLeaks disclosures, have demanded a review of the parliamentary mandate for the German troop presence.

"What the documents show is that the German government has never been prepared to tell the truth about Afghanistan, particularly the civilian deaths and the use of special forces to target insurgents," said Hans-Christian Ströbele, a Green Party member who serves on the Parliament's Foreign Affairs Committee. "That was not the mandate for our troops."

The leaked documents suggested that there has been close collaboration between Task Force 373, an elite U.S. combat unit trained to kill Taliban and insurgents who attack allied forces, and Task Force 47, an elite unit of the German Army.

When lawmakers asked the government recently about the two elite forces, it played down the sensitivity of the American unit's role, saying that the "core mission" of Task Force 373 was to "conduct reconnaissance and identify individuals who are part of Al Qaeda or the Taliban leadership."

The role of Task Force 47 is highly sensitive, potentially conflicting with the parliamentary mandate for German troops that speaks vaguely only of providing stability in Afghanistan.

"No one in the government has shown any leadership in explaining the real nature of this war," Mr. Ströbele said. "I hope the leaked documents will change that."

Karl-Theodor zu Guttenberg, the German defense minister, was criticized this week for his reluctance to explain the role of Task Force 47.

German press accounts said the documents disclosed that the Americans' Task Force 373 was stationed in the German-controlled Mazar-i-Sharif camp, which could provoke attacks on the camp and might violate the German mandate.

Some documents' depictions of fierce fighting in areas of German deployment go far beyond the scant detail on the war the German public normally hears.

But reaction in France, another key member of the NATO coalition, has been much more muted, said Justin Vaïsse, director of research for the Center on the United States and Europe at the Brookings Institution in Washington.

"It's nothing in magnitude compared with what happened two years ago, in August '08, when 10 French soldiers were killed in a firefight with the Taliban," Mr. Vaïsse said. That, he said, had "really prompted soul-searching about the French presence in Afghanistan and also prompted debate in the National Assembly. Here we have nothing of the sort."

James Carafano, a foreign policy specialist at the conservative Heritage Foundation in Washington, said the WikiLeaks story had fed into existing views.

"I don't think it's going to be a game-changer in European opinion," he said.

NATO spokesmen declined to comment on Wednesday on the leak of the secret military reports, which were compiled between January 2004 and December 2009.

In Washington, the leak was mentioned repeatedly in a vigorous debate in the House of Representatives on a bill to provide $37 billion for the Afghan and Iraq wars. Democrats revealed deepening anxiety over the course of the Afghan conflict.

Still, the measure passed, by 308 votes to 114, with strong Republican support.

Administration officials said the bill's passage showed that the document leak had not jeopardized congressional support for the war.

Brian Knowlton and Carl Hulse contributed reporting from Washington.

—This article was originally published on July 28, 2010

GATES CITES PERIL IN LEAK OF AFGHAN WAR LOGS BY WIKILEAKS

By ERIC SCHMITT and DAVID E. SANGER

Defense Secretary Robert Gates said the release of classified military documents endangered Afghans who had aided American forces.

WASHINGTON—Secretary of Defense Robert M. Gates said Sunday that an announcement by the Taliban that they were going through classified military dispatches from Afghanistan posted by the Web site WikiLeaks "basically proves the point" that the disclosures put at risk the lives of Afghans who had aided American forces.

"Growing up in the intelligence business, protecting your sources is sacrosanct," said Mr. Gates, a former director of the C.I.A. He said that while it was up to the Justice Department to investigate who supplied the documents to the Web site, run by Julian Assange, an Australian activist who is an outspoken opponent of American and NATO involvement in Afghanistan, he had been "mortified, appalled" at Mr. Assange's willingness to make public documents that listed the names of individual Afghans.

"There's also a moral culpability," he told Christiane Amanpour, in her debut as the host of ABC's "This Week." "And that's where I think the verdict is guilty on WikiLeaks. They have put this out without any regard whatsoever for the consequences."

Senator Carl Levin, a Michigan Democrat who heads the Armed Services Committee, said on CNN's "State of the Union" that the Pentagon was assessing the disclosure's impact on operational security in Afghanistan. "There quite clearly was damage," Mr. Levin said.

The New York Times, The Guardian in London and Der Spiegel in Germany published excerpts of the leaked documents, but excluded those that identified individuals or compromised operations. The Times also agreed to forward a request by the administration urging WikiLeaks not to post any documents that would put informants in jeopardy.

As the authorities continued their investigation into the source of the leaks, a Seattle-based software developer who has volunteered for WikiLeaks said he was detained at Newark Liberty International Airport on Thursday and questioned for three hours. The developer, Jacob Appelbaum, 27, said in an interview that as he was returning from an overseas trip, agents from Immigration and Customs Enforcement and from the Army's criminal investigation division asked him about Mr. Assange.

Mr. Appelbaum, an American citizen, said the agents also seized his laptop computer and three cellphones. The laptop was later returned, but the phones were not, he said. Officials from Immigration and Customs Enforcement, part of the Department of Homeland Security, would not comment.

Two American civilians interviewed in recent weeks by the Army's criminal division said that investigators were focusing in part on a group of friends who know Pfc. Bradley Manning, a leading suspect in the leak. Investigators, the civilians said, apparently believe that the friends, who include students from M.I.T. and Boston University, might have connections to WikiLeaks.

Mr. Appelbaum said Sunday that he was not involved with that group. He also said he never met or communicated with Private Manning, who has been charged in a separate case with disclosing to WikiLeaks a classified video of an American helicopter attack in Iraq.

Mr. Appelbaum said the agents at Newark Airport refused him access to a lawyer and threatened to detain him for similar questioning whenever he re-entered the country after traveling abroad, which he said he did twice a month for a day job as an online software developer.

"They questioned my ability to re-enter the U.S. even though I'm a U.S. citizen," he said in a telephone interview from Las Vegas. "It's very troubling to think that every time I cross the border, I'd get this treatment."

Mr. Appelbaum, who develops software for the Tor Project, a software system that allows people to talk anonymously to each other online, filled in for Mr. Assange at a conference last month, apparently because Mr. Assange did not want to enter the United States. "It seems the only reason they're bothering me is that Julian is beyond their reach," Mr. Appelbaum said.

Mr. Appelbaum said he had been a volunteer for WikiLeaks for several months, but was not involved in reviewing information submitted to it. Investigators, however, appear to be examining whether Mr. Assange was assisted by others in obtaining the documents.

—This article was originally published on August 1, 2010

THE DEFENSE DEPARTMENT'S RESPONSE

Following is the response to the WikiLeaks documents from Geoff Morrell, the Defense Department press secretary:

"We deplore WikiLeaks for inducing individuals to break the law, leak classified documents and then cavalierly share that secret information with the world, including our enemies. We know terrorist organizations have been mining the leaked Afghan documents for information to use against us, and this Iraq leak is more than four times as large. By disclosing such sensitive information, WikiLeaks continues to put at risk the lives of our troops, their coalition partners and those Iraqis and Afghans working with us. The only responsible course of action for WikiLeaks at this point is to return the stolen material and expunge it from their Web sites as soon as possible.

"We strongly condemn the unauthorized disclosure of classified information and will not comment on these leaked documents other than to note that 'significant activities' reports are initial, raw observations by tactical units. They are essentially snapshots of events, both tragic and mundane, and do not tell the whole story. That said, the period covered by these reports has been well chronicled in news stories, books and films, and the release of these field reports does not bring new understanding to Iraq's past.

"However, it does expose secret information that could make our troops even more vulnerable to attack in the future. Just as with the leaked Afghan documents, we know our enemies will mine this information, looking for insights into how we operate, cultivate sources and react in combat situations, even the capability of our equipment. This security breach could very well get our troops and those they are fighting with killed."

—This article was originally published on October 22, 2010

WIKILEAKS FOUNDER GETS SUPPORT IN REBUKING U.S. ON WHISTLE-BLOWERS

By JOHN F. BURNS and RAVI SOMAIYA

LONDON—Julian Assange, the WikiLeaks founder, and Daniel Ellsberg, who leaked the Pentagon Papers, lashed out together on Saturday at the Obama administration's aggressive pursuit of whistle-blowers, including those responsible for the release of secret documents on the Iraq war.

Mr. Assange also said that WikiLeaks, which released the trove of almost 400,000 Iraq war documents on Friday, would shortly be posting an additional 15,000 remaining secret documents on the Afghan war.

Mr. Assange, speaking at a news conference in a London hotel a stone's throw from the headquarters of Britain's foreign intelligence agency, MI6, was joined by Mr. Ellsberg, 79, the former military analyst who leaked a 1,000-page secret history of the Vietnam War in 1971 that became known as the Pentagon Papers.

Mr. Ellsberg, who said he had flown overnight from California to attend, described Mr. Assange admiringly as "the most dangerous man in the world" for challenging governments, particularly the United States. He said the WikiLeaks founder had been "pursued across three continents" by Western intelligence services and compared the Obama administration's threat to prosecute Mr. Assange to his own treatment under President Richard M. Nixon.

Both men hit out at what they described as the Obama administration's aggressive pursuit of whistle-blowers, which Mr. Ellsberg said put the United States on a path to the kind of repressive legal framework that Britain has under its broad Official Secrets Act. He said the criminal investigations under President Obama of three Americans accused of leaking government secrets represented a new low.

The three men he was referring to were Pfc. Bradley Manning, a former military intelligence analyst suspected of providing the documents on Afghanistan and Iraq to WikiLeaks; Thomas Drake, an official with the National Security Agency who was indicted this year; and Shamai Kedem Leibowitz, an F.B.I. linguist who pleaded guilty to leaking five classified documents in late 2009.

Mr. Ellsberg said the Pentagon's demand that Mr. Assange "return" any classified materials in his possession was carefully couched in language similar to that used in the aftermath of the Pentagon Papers release, when he was threatened with criminal prosecution for espionage. "Secrecy," Mr. Ellsberg said, "is essential to empire."

Mr. Assange also dismissed what he described as the Pentagon's deliberately "nonchalant" reaction to his release of the Iraq documents on Friday. He said they "constituted the most comprehensive and detailed account of any war ever to have entered the public record."

The Pentagon spokesman Geoff Morrell condemned the Iraq leak on Friday, saying that these documents, and a previous WikiLeaks release of classified material on the war in Afghanistan, were a gift to "terrorist organizations" and "put at risk the lives of our troops." But he also played down the historical significance of the latest leak, characterizing the reports as "mundane" and saying that much of the material had been well chronicled in past accounts of the war.

Mr. Assange said the response was "not credible," since the comment was issued before the Pentagon could feasibly have read the vast archive posted on the organization's Web site on Friday night. He said the statement had been "an attempt to act in a nonchalant manner" to convey the sense that the documents were "of no consequence."

He said that the documents showed "Iraq was a bloodbath on every corner," and that they chronicled 15,000 previously unknown civilian deaths there. Adding those deaths to 107,000 others that had been recorded by the group Iraq Body Count, WikiLeaks has estimated the civilian toll since 2003 at more than 120,000. That, he said, put the human cost of the Iraq conflict five times higher than that of Afghanistan.

Mr. Ellsberg, who described Iraq as a "hopeless, deadly, stalemated war," said many of the civilian deaths there could be counted as murder.

—This article was originally published on October 23, 2010

LEAKED REPORTS STIR POLITICAL DISPUTES IN IRAQ

By JACK HEALY and JOHN LELAND

BAGHDAD—The release of thousands of classified Iraq war records quickly became part of Iraq's fraught political terrain on Saturday, with Prime Minister Nuri Kamal al-Maliki denouncing the leak as a move to derail his bid for a second term.

Mr. Maliki, who has been mired in a stalemate with his political rivals since parliamentary elections last March, defended his administration against allegations it had permitted the abuse of prisoners and other misuses of power. In a statement, he dismissed the records as a politically timed smear and a series of "media games and bubbles."

"The Iraqi people know who their leaders are," he said.

His opponents called the records an indictment of his administration, and some compared the accounts of whippings and beatings of prisoners by Iraqi guards, often under the gaze of Americans, to the grisly tactics of Saddam Hussein.

Much of the attention focused on a report from October 2006, shortly after Mr. Maliki took office, that describes the arrest of 17 men wearing Iraqi Army uniforms in Baghdad's Mansour neighborhood on suspicion of committing robberies. According to the report published by WikiLeaks, the men said they were Iraqi Special Forces "working for the prime minister's office."

Mr. Maliki's political opponents said the report supported their claims that the prime minister had used state forces for nefarious ends.

"For years we have been talking about the armed groups that are working under the name of the Ministry of Interior and Ministry of Defense that have direct connections with some leaders in the government," said Maysoon al-Damluji, a spokeswoman for Iraqiya, the secular political bloc that finished first in Iraq's March 7 elections, slightly ahead of Mr. Maliki's State of Law bloc.

She also said that the reports of abuses of Iraqi prisoners by Iraqi soldiers and police officers were a powerful indictment of Mr. Maliki's government.

"I do not think that Maliki has any chance for the prime minister's position, now he only has Iran and the Sadrists," she said, referring to the party of the anti-American Shiite cleric Moktada al-Sadr, who endorsed Mr. Maliki's list of candidates this month, giving him an edge.

The reports threatened to further divide Iraq along sectarian lines. For many Sunnis, they confirmed longstanding allegations of abuse at the hands of Mr. Maliki's Shiite-led government.

"We have said, and say again, that Maliki should be sentenced to justice and be held accountable for what he has done to the Iraqi people," said Waleed Aboud al-Mohamadi, a member of Parliament from Anbar Province.

Mr. Maliki and his partisans rejected the allegations, insisting that they had followed the law and denying any abuse of prisoners. They also tried to discredit the leaked documents. "These are all just fakes from the Internet and Photoshop," said Hassan al-Sneid, a leader of Mr. Maliki's governing State of Law coalition. "This is just to be seen in the context of a war against Maliki."

The Pentagon, while deploring the release of the documents, has not challenged their authenticity.

Duraid Adnan contributed reporting from Baghdad, and an Iraqi employee of The New York Times from Anbar Province.

—This article was originally published on October 23, 2010

PART FIVE

AFTERMATH

"Watchdog journalists have always eagerly accepted leaks of classified information, but it has usually arrived in dribs and drabs. Now they have been joined by a new counterculture of information vigilantes who promise disclosures by the terabyte. Today, a bureaucrat can hide a library's worth of documents on a key fob and scatter them over the Internet to a dozen countries during a cigarette break."

—from "Can the Government Keep A Secret?" by Scott Shane

Secretary of State Hillary Rodham Clinton condemned the disclosure
of diplomatic cables but managed to find a silver lining.

HOW OUR DIPLOMATS THINK

By DAVID E. SANGER

When Julian Assange, the founder of WikiLeaks, celebrated the initial disclosure of selections from his vast trove of 251,287 State Department cables he left little doubt as to his motive. "This document release reveals the contradictions between the U.S.'s public persona and what it says behind closed doors," Assange wrote on the group's Web site. The cables, he asserted, showed duplicity and mendacity in action, including "the extent of U.S. spying on its allies and the U.N.; turning a blind eye to corruption and human rights abuse in 'client states'; backroom deals with supposed neutral countries; lobbying for U.S. corporations."

Examples of each of those emerge, of course, in the flood of cable traffic between Washington and its far-flung embassies and consulates. Like hospital operating rooms and hotel kitchens, the engine room of global diplomacy can be stomach-churning at times. Yet when historians mine this trove for a glimpse of America's dealings with the world in the early days of Barack Obama's presidency, the surprise may be that in their everyday work American diplomats largely do what they say they are doing. They seem less cynical than one might expect for people who deal daily with petty dictators, maddening bureaucracies and reluctant allies. They are often eloquent and occasionally entertaining. Consider the riotous account of an over-the-top wedding in Dagestan where the president of Chechnya was a guest (see p. 479) or the description of how Libya's leader, Col. Muammar el-Qaddafi, steers clear of elevators and won't go anywhere without his Ukrainian nurse (see p. 422).

"Broadly, America's diplomats come across as insightful and less gray than in the popular imagining," concluded David Gordon, a senior American intelligence official who ran the State Department's office of policy planning during the period of time covered by many of the WikiLeaks cables. "But mostly," he added, "they appear as problem-solvers"—neither the cunning imperialists portrayed by America's many critics around the world nor the staunch advocates for American values that some would like them to be.

More important, the picture of American foreign policy circa 2010 drawn from these quarter-million cables is one of utter pragmatism—with an almost instinctive disdain for ideology. There are few echoes of George W. Bush's second inaugural address, only five years earlier, which promised to make "the expansion of freedom in all the world" America's next great mission. There is little talk of American exceptionalism. The cables make it easy to understand why even some insiders in the Obama administration, when speaking with the protective cloak of anonymity, concede that two years after the president's inauguration, his administration's world view is still under construction.

Perhaps that sensibility reflects the moment: nine years after the invasion of Afghanistan and seven after the toppling of Saddam Hussein, the diplomats whose prose leaked from the electronic ether seem tired of defending grand American goals. The WikiLeaks cache does not include top secret documents, or cover the doings of officials outside the State Department, but even if it doesn't give a full picture of American foreign policy it gives a clear one. The policy makers readers meet are no longer trying to make the world safe for democracy or plotting regime change, much less the expansion of Pax Americana. More often than not, America's diplomats seem to be writing from a defensive crouch. Meeting by meeting, cable by cable, they are trying to extract the United States from two wars that have sapped American influence; attempting to cajole Pakistani or Afghan politicians without stoking more anti-Americanism on the streets of Islamabad or Kabul; trying to deflect Chinese claims of "exclusive territory" in the Yellow Sea without worsening the inevitable frictions between an established power and a rising one. They are forever trying to put a little spine in the Europeans to help out with more troops or money, cajole the Israelis to become more flexible or convince the Japanese that giving in to domestic pressure to throw American forces off their archipelago might not be in the long-term interest of a country surrounded by hostile powers.

In most of those cases, the analysis of what is going wrong seems sensible, and the diplomacy to set it right ranges from the competent to the highly impressive. "When dysfunctional does not begin to describe our political system and institutions," Prof. Stephen Kotkin of Princeton concluded after reading a sampling of the cables, "something in the government is really working—the State Department—far better than anyone thought."

Still, Assange's accusation was not all wrong. Certainly the cables reveal some element of deception, or at least daily shadings of the truth in the name of protecting American interests. In the Bush years, the cables strongly suggest that American officials tacitly accepted a secret arms pipeline that ran from Ukraine to southern Sudan; America's subsequent demand for a crackdown when the arms trafficking became public now looks rather hypocritical. And long after Obama took office, promising a new era of "transparency," Washington refused to make public its belief that some Pakistani military units were responsible for gross human rights abuses, or its suspicions that high-ranking Chinese officials knew about cyberattacks launched on the United States from Chinese soil. Nor did Obama's State Department countermand the C.I.A.'s insistence that American diplomats at the United Nations provide the intelligence agencies with the credit card data or frequent-flier numbers of some of their foreign counterparts. "It was a boneheaded request," one American diplomat said, adding that when he got it, "I threw it in the trash."

In Europe, many reporters, editors and readers dug into the cables for further examples of official doublespeak, and it was not hard to find. According to Javier Moreno, the editor of El País, the Spanish newspaper, which published its own excerpts from the cables, the documents revealed that "none of the Western powers believes that Afghanistan can become a credible nation in the medium term, and much less become a viable democracy, despite the stated aims of those whose soldiers are fighting and dying there." American officials, he wrote, knew that their allies in Afghanistan and Pakistan were "awash with corruption," but rarely admitted as much in public.

All true. But it didn't exactly take WikiLeaks to expose the fact that official optimism about the West's experiment in Afghanistan has run headlong into the realities of a dysfunctional, corrupt state. Nor is it news that Obama has moved the goal posts for success. Since 2007, there has been a flood of articles and books, and even a few movies, documenting the failures and the frustrations. The cables confirm what was long suspected: government officials largely shared the gloomy assessment. What we didn't know were the details of such assessments, and it is the details that paint such a fascinating picture of the day-to-day grind of American diplomacy at work.

If there's one recurrent theme to the cables, it's the sobering one that American power is limited, and growing more so in an age of austerity. Whether the subject is global warming or containing Iran, isolating North Korea or aiding Darfur, the reality is that no single nation, or even bloc of nations, has the leverage anymore to drive the international agenda. "There's a recognition in these cables that you won't be able to create perfect organizations or perfect outcomes," said William Burns, the undersecretary of state for policy. "But that's what diplomacy is about—defining American interests, but knowing that if you are willing to sing in a chorus, you get more done than when you are singing solo."

That reality drives some politicians to distraction, especially those who preach American exceptionalism. But the themes of limited American influence that spill out of many of the most recent cables clearly reflect the world view of a young new president who is trying to adjust his country to the new realities. He said as much in an address to the nation about Afghanistan at West Point at the end of his first year in office. "I refuse to set goals that go beyond our responsibility, our means, or our interests," Obama told the country then, making the case that the American commitment to Afghanistan could not be "open-ended." The United States, he warned, had forgotten Dwight D. Eisenhower's warning about the need to maintain a "balance" between commitments at home and commitments abroad. "The nation I'm most interested in building is our own," Obama said at the time.

In campaigning for office, Obama also vowed to restore "engagement" to American foreign policy. Too often, he argued, America made demands of others but didn't listen to them. Of course, engagement can take many forms, from friendly to wary, naïve to cunning, and it was never quite clear how the idea could translate from a campaign critique of the Bush style to a practical approach to the world.

The cables drawn from the first 13 months of the Obama presidency provide an answer. Obama's style seems to be: Engage, yes, but wield a club as well—and try to counter the global skepticism that a young, inexperienced president is willing to use force. Diplomatic engagement, Obama-style, is a complicated mixture of openness to negotiation and constantly escalating pressure, combined with a series of deadlines. Some are explicit, and some are vague. But hundreds of cables provide a close look at an administration trying to use all these tools.

In Russia, for example, the policy of engagement yielded early results. The president began immediate negotiations on arms reductions, hoping that the resulting treaty would pave the way for a series of other agreements that could inch the world toward vastly reducing, and eventually eliminating, stockpiles of nuclear weapons. The cables tell a fascinating tale of intelligence-sharing with the Russians on missile threats from Tehran and Pyongyang. And there are hints of horse-trading as the Obama administration sank the Bush-era plans for a missile defense site in Poland, seemingly to win Moscow's support for sanctions on Iran.

But the cables also show that engagement has its limits—especially when dealing with a recalcitrant regional power like Iran. Obama reached out to Iran early, with little response. So, as the cables show, he started upping the pressure on the mullahs. Even as the shadow-dancing about face-to-face negotiations played out, the cables show that Obama's aides were drawing Arab states into an informal regional alliance intended to gradually close off Iran's access to banks and ports.

Yet the cables leave open the critical question: What if persuasion and containment fail? Is Barack Obama, the man who came to office promising to extract America from Iraq, willing to risk a confrontation to keep Iran from getting a nuclear weapon? The cables never answer that question. It may be unanswerable until the day that one of Obama's aides walks into the Oval Office and declares that time has run out, and Iran is finally ready to fabricate a weapon. "If you haven't accomplished your goal, you are left with the unpalatable choice of extending the timeline, diminishing your objective or being forced to take the kind of military action you were attempting to avoid," said David Rothkopf, who wrote a history of the National Security Council.

One could ask a similar question about Afghanistan and Pakistan. Yes, the president promised that America's involvement would be limited in time and scope. He set a July 2011 deadline to begin withdrawing American troops, partly to mollify critics in his own party who argued that he was pursuing an unwinnable conflict, and partly as a whip to get President Hamid Karzai to train Afghan troops, so the United States can leave.

But the warning he gets in the cables is clear: Deadlines might make a president sound tough. They may play to the president's base. But they rarely work. "We should be under no illusion," the American ambassador in Pakistan, Anne Patterson, wrote in a brutally clear-eyed secret analysis, "that this effort will not require a multi-year, multi-agency effort" (see p. 455). She went on to say that "in the final analysis, there is no short-cut to deal with the al-Qaeda problem in Pakistan and Afghanistan." Even the escalating use of Predator drones to attack militants drew her skepticism. "The notion that precision or long-range counter-terrorism efforts can suffice are equally illusory," she said. And no amount of money, she added, "will sever that link" between the Pakistani establishment and Afghanistan's Taliban, as long as the Pakistanis believe that sooner or later, the Americans are going to leave the region. Her message was not that the task was hopeless, but that it might be endless. In short, it was the kind of cable that no new American president—especially one who inherited two wars and desperately wanted to disentangle the United States from both—ever wants to read.

Yet that is the sound of a diplomat describing the world as it is. It has rarely been heard so clearly, or broadcast so widely, as it was in November and December 2010. Yes, the cables were embarrassing. No doubt they will do some damage to American relationships, at least for a while. But they were also a reminder that sometimes, buried under all those layers of secrecy, all those piles of e-mail, one can find some ground truths.

CAN THE GOVERNMENT
KEEP A SECRET?

By SCOTT SHANE

Last January, seven months before WikiLeaks became a staple of the news and a nemesis of the United States government, Secretary of State Hillary Rodham Clinton hailed the Internet as "a new nervous system for our planet." "In many respects, information has never been so free," she said in an address at the Newseum in Washington, criticizing Iran, China and other countries for trying to censor the Internet. "Even in authoritarian countries, information networks are helping people discover new facts and making governments more accountable."

At about the same time, unbeknownst to Clinton, a young American soldier named Bradley Manning was embarking on his own experiment in government accountability. A troubled 22-year-old working as a low-level intelligence analyst, Manning almost echoed Clinton's language in a later online chat, explaining why he had downloaded hundreds of thousands of military and State Department documents to share with the anti-secrecy activists of WikiLeaks. "Information should be free," Manning told the former computer hacker who later turned him in to the authorities, Adrian Lamo, according to chat logs published by Wired magazine. "It belongs in the public domain."

There is surely a moral distinction between using the Internet to speak out against a repressive government and using the same tool to bare the confidential documents of a democratic government. Yet the WikiLeaks affair has demonstrated that even the most open society has secrets whose disclosure can detonate powerfully, dominating the news and rattling international relations. The ground reports from the wars in Iraq and Afghanistan and the assortment of confidential diplomatic cables made public by the year's end—fewer than 1 percent of the 251,287 cables obtained by WikiLeaks—have already become a landmark in the permanent contest between openness and secrecy. And WikiLeaks's clamorous appearance on the media landscape has posed a fundamental question: Has technology decisively now tipped the balance of power away from governments and toward individuals, undermining the very possibility of official secrecy?

Watchdog journalists have always eagerly accepted leaks of classified information, but it has usually arrived in dribs and drabs. Now they have been joined by a new counterculture of information vigilantes who promise disclosures by the terabyte. Today, a bureaucrat can hide a library's worth of documents on a key fob and scatter them over the Internet to a dozen countries during a cigarette break. An activist can capture a political protest or an act of police brutality and post it to the world with no publishing infrastructure beyond a video-equipped smart phone.

"What is unique about this case, relative to other leaks in the past, is its size and breadth," said Philip J. Crowley, the State Department spokesman, referring to the cable leaks. "In the past, somebody might have smuggled out a folder with a couple of pieces of classified material and passed them to a single reporter. There was one story, some residual fallout, and then it was over. This is fundamentally different in that it touches every part of the world and every national interest. The marriage of the data, the technology and the media yields impact that is global, not local."

Steven Aftergood, who runs the Project on Government Secrecy at the Federation of American Scientists, said: "I do think it's true that the large contours of national and international policy are much harder to keep secret today. It would not be possible to conduct a secret war in Cambodia, as took place in the Nixon administration." Indeed, within hours of American missile strikes in Yemen against sites suspected of containing Al Qaeda camps last December, amateur video of the destruction was on YouTube. The videos labeled the strikes "American." (The strikes have never been publicly acknowledged by the Defense Department.) Or consider the speed at which news travels. During the Iran-contra affair, American arms sales to Iran were first reported by a Lebanese weekly, Al Shiraa, in November 1986; it was a few days before the American press picked it up. "Now it would take a few minutes," Aftergood said.

Yet there are compelling reasons to believe that the large-scale disclosures by WikiLeaks are not the harbinger of a new era of rampant and highly consequential leaking. WikiLeaks was founded in 2006 and had published thousands of documents before those Manning is accused of providing the organization. Only the unprecedented scale and classified content of the material first brought WikiLeaks to broad public notice. And if technology enabled those disclosures, technology can also make computers more leakproof. Chastened bureaucrats already have made fixes to prevent the hemorrhage of more documents.

In a sense, the WikiLeaks affair is an unintended consequence of the 2001 terrorist attacks. Several official reviews of the 9/11 attacks concluded that the hoarding of intelligence about Al Qaeda by various federal agencies prevented them from piecing together the plot. It was because of the subsequent push to share information more widely that a low-level Iraq war analyst—one of a half-million people with access to the Defense Department's classified Siprnet system—could read State Department cables discussing topics that had nothing to do with his duties: Afghan government corruption, Chinese computer hacking, covert missile strikes in Yemen.

"This was a badly engineered answer to a problem we all knew we needed to fix," said John J. Hamre, president of the Center for Strategic and International Studies and a former deputy secretary of defense. The goal, he said, should be to redesign security measures to give individuals access only to the intelligence they need for their work. But that is a daunting technical challenge, and it may be difficult to achieve without crippling the information-sharing that many experts believe has made the government far more capable of detecting terrorist plots.

In addition to allowing haphazard access to the cables, the military did little to safeguard its computers against the kind of extensive downloading of data of which Manning is accused. "In terms of information security, I'd have to give them a failing grade," said Chris Knotts, vice president for technology at the information-technology consulting firm Force 3 and a security expert. Both in private companies and in government agencies where data is protected, it is common to block USB ports and disable the recording capacity of CD and DVD drives to prevent the large-scale diversion of data. Such alterations, which might well have kept the cables secure, are now being belatedly made on many more computers across the Defense Department. The United States Central Command, for instance, which oversees military operations in the Middle East, has installed software to disable read-write drives on all classified computers; any exception requires the approval of a senior commander, said Pentagon officials.

In addition, the Pentagon is installing software to detect unusual down-loads of data and requiring that two people sign on to move information from a classified to an unclassified computer system. "I don't think you can get to 100 percent," Knotts said, because a determined insider with a high-level clearance will probably find ways to defeat even sophisticated security measures. But such steps will make large-scale leaks far less likely, he concluded.

There are reasons beyond such technical fixes to believe that disclosures on the scale of the recent WikiLeaks case may not be repeated soon. One is Manning's fate. He is among five government employees to be charged by the Obama administration with illegally revealing classified information to the media. That's a record: no previous president has overseen more than a single such prosecution.

WikiLeaks set out with "a 'Field of Dreams' philosophy for inviting leaks—'If we build it, they will come,'" said Thomas S. Blanton, director of the National Security Archive at George Washington University, which obtains and publishes declassified government documents. "They tried to create a safe place for disclosures. But with Bradley Manning behind bars, who's going to rush to follow his example?"

Members of Congress have pressed the Obama administration to find a way to prosecute WikiLeaks's outspoken founder, Julian Assange, as well. The ferocious criticism of the group and of Assange, its cocky provocateur in chief, has been bipartisan. Representative Peter King, a New York Republican, asked the State Department to consider designating WikiLeaks a terrorist group; Senator Dianne Feinstein, the California Democrat who leads the Select Committee on Intelligence, called for espionage charges against Assange. Senator Joseph Lieberman, a Connecticut independent, called for an investigation of The New York Times because it published some of the material obtained by WikiLeaks.

But no recipient of leaked classified information—as opposed to the government leaker himself—has ever been successfully prosecuted, and such a case would face major legal and constitutional obstacles. Jack L. Goldsmith, a Harvard law professor who was a Justice Department official under President George W. Bush, has warned that prosecuting Assange would endanger press freedom. Writing on the Lawfare blog about calls for a WikiLeaks prosecution, Goldsmith said that such an effort would be likely to fail. But a successful prosecution might be worse, he wrote: "Succeeding will harm First Amendment press protections, make a martyr of Assange, and invite further chaotic Internet attacks. The best thing to do—I realize that this is politically impossible—would be to ignore Assange and fix the secrecy system so this does not happen again."

Yet even as the government seeks to rein in WikiLeaks and to plug security holes, WikiLeaks has quietly reined in itself. Its disclosures have been far more restrained than the group's proclaimed dedication to total transparency might suggest. Sharply criticized in July by both government officials and human rights activists for endangering some informants of the American military in Afghanistan, WikiLeaks appears to have taken the lesson to heart. It used a computer program to strip out names from Iraq war documents it posted on the Web, greatly limiting both their value to researchers and the chance that they might put Iraqis at risk.

On the cables, too, contrary to the public statements of many critics, the group has proceeded cautiously. Had it chosen to do so, of course, WikiLeaks could have posted on the Web all of the quarter-million diplomatic cables some six months ago, when it obtained them. Instead, it shared the cables with traditional news organizations and has coordinated the cables' release with them. By the end of 2010, it had published on its Web site fewer than 2,000 of the total cables in its possession, coordinating the initial releases with four European publications and The New York Times. "They've actually embraced the MSM," or mainstream media, "which they used to treat as a cussword," Blanton, the director of the security archive at George Washington University, said in mid-December. "I'm watching WikiLeaks grow up. What they're doing with these diplomatic documents so far is very responsible."

When the newspapers have redacted cables to protect diplomats' sources, WikiLeaks has generally been careful to follow suit. The group's volunteers appear to accept that not all government secrets are illegitimate; they have no interest in revealing the identities of Chinese dissidents, Russian journalists or Iranian activists who talked to American diplomats and whose exposure might subject them to prison or worse. Still, as more and more cables are published, the accidental exposure of vulnerable sources becomes steadily more likely. Moreover, given the varying political allegiances of WikiLeaks volunteers and foreign journalists, some publishers of the cables may not be inclined to redact the names of political adversaries, say, or American contractors, even if they could be put at risk.

In a December essay for the newspaper The Australian, Assange, a 39-year-old Australian citizen, portrayed himself as a journalist and declared his devotion to some core Western press values. "Democratic societies need a strong media and WikiLeaks is part of that media," he wrote. "The media helps keep government honest."

But WikiLeaks has not quite joined the ranks of traditional publishing, and it may yet cast all restraint aside. Reaching back to his hacker roots, Assange created what he calls an "insurance" plan for his own future and that of WikiLeaks. The group has put on the Web, for downloading, encrypted files containing a huge trove of documents that have not yet been released. Thousands of people have downloaded the files. If the United States moves to prosecute, Assange has said, the group will release the encryption key, in effect making public tens of thousands of unredacted cables—and who knows what other dangerous secrets.

It is a 21st-century threat, and a serious one, according to Knotts, the security expert, who said he knows of no way the government could prevent such a release. It is one more challenge for the Obama administration as it negotiates the legal and political minefield that WikiLeaks has created.

PART SIX

OPINIONS

"I can confirm that the situation in Afghanistan is complex,
and defies any attempt to graft it onto easy-to-discern lessons or policy conclusions.
Yet the release of the documents has led to a stampede of commentators
and politicians doing exactly that."

— from "Getting Lost in the Fog of War" by Andrew Exum

INTRODUCTION

By ANDREW ROSENTHAL
Andrew Rosenthal is the editorial page editor of The New York Times.

In the world of opinion journalism, the WikiLeaks documents landed like a brick in still water. Iraq, Afghanistan and other national security issues had dimmed as public issues, but the leaked documents brought them right back to center stage. Some of the reactions were predictable: There were those on the left for whom the documents proved that George W. Bush and Dick Cheney had committed war crimes, and revived hopes that they would some day be called to account. On the right, there were the expected calls for Julian Assange's head, and the heads of the editors who printed articles about the documents. There was talk of treason and espionage prosecutions.

In fact, both positions were extreme and unjustified. The papers were remarkable, on the one hand, for their lack of shocking revelations. No bribery, no assassination plots, no skullduggery, at least in these documents. And it's relatively obvious to anyone who takes a calm look at the papers that there was no treason or espionage involved in their publication and analysis by American news organizations. In the political mainstream, the arguments were more subtle and textured—focusing on what was actually learned in these documents and not just on their release.

For the New York Times Editorial Page, the release of the documents provided a chance to look at Iraq and Afghanistan directly through the eyes of the American government officials who are engaged in those two wars—and to assess what we found. What alarmed us most was the mountain of evidence showing that Pakistan was not just an unreliable and unsteady ally of the United States in Afghanistan, but something even more troubling. The documents confirmed what had often been reported anecdotally by journalists: Pakistan was actually and actively working to undermine United States interests in Afghanistan, harboring elements of Al Qaeda and the Taliban and working with those groups to maintain their political power and oppose the multi-national force in Afghanistan. The documents also supported a claim that officials had made privately to journalists, but was routinely denied by its subjects—some of America's supposed stalwart allies in the Islamic world, including Saudi Arabia, Kuwait and Qatar, had become money laundering hubs for Al Qaeda and other terrorist organizations.

But it was not all bad news. While many people fretted about the effect of the package of leaked diplomatic cables on American interests, we found that they showed an administration that had generally been doing a good job in pursuing its interests in the Middle East and the broader world. Its efforts to contain Iran's nuclear ambitions, for instance, stood out.

On the Times Op-Ed page, there was a steady stream of commentary on the WikiLeaks documents. Maureen Dowd wrote on July 27 about how the leaks on Afghanistan confirmed "the awful truth: We're not in control." The more this country does "for our foreign protectorates," she wrote, "the more angry they get about what we try to do." Frank Rich wrote on July 31 that the public reaction to the Afghan papers "has largely been a shrug," and suggested that was because Americans had already given up on that war. David Brooks wrote a penetrating column on Nov. 29 about the Julian Assange phenomenon, concluding that it may have been easy for Assange to reveal all of these documents because he is an "old-fashioned anarchist," but in fact, the question is far more complicated than that. "For him, it's easy, but for everyone else, it's hard," Brooks wrote.

Our outside Op-Ed contributions on WikiLeaks represented the broad range of opinion on the subject. Mitchell LaFortune, a former Army intelligence analyst, found that "there may be a benefit from the scrutiny the military is likely to face post-WikiLeaks." But Paul Schroeder, a historian, was alarmed by the document dumps and compared the leaking of the diplomatic cables to "the work of irresponsible amateurs using dynamite to expand a tunnel that also contains, say, a city's electrical lines."

The argument over Assange's motives and the value of the individual documents will go on. What is clear is that Assange's use of the internet to accomplish these leaks changed the landscape of investigative journalism, perhaps permanently. They reinforced what government officials should have already known (despite their expressions of shock at the leaks), which is that what can be known will be known. The internet makes the knowing faster and broader and at least a bit more stunning.

PAKISTAN'S DOUBLE GAME

There is a lot to be disturbed by in the battlefield reports from Afghanistan released Sunday by WikiLeaks. The close-up details of war are always unsettling, even more so with this war, which was so badly neglected and bungled by President George W. Bush.

But the most alarming of the reports were the ones that described the cynical collusion between Pakistan's military intelligence service and the Taliban. Despite the billions of dollars the United States has sent in aid to Pakistan since Sept. 11, they offer powerful new evidence that crucial elements of Islamabad's power structure have been actively helping to direct and support the forces attacking the American-led military coalition.

The time line of the documents from WikiLeaks, an organization devoted to exposing secrets, stops before President Obama put his own military and political strategy into effect last December. Administration officials say they have made progress with Pakistan since, but it is hard to see much evidence of that so far.

Most of the WikiLeaks documents, which were the subject of in-depth coverage in The Times on Monday, cannot be verified. However, they confirm a picture of Pakistani double-dealing that has been building for years.

On a trip to Pakistan last October, Secretary of State Hillary Rodham Clinton suggested that officials in the Pakistani government knew where Al Qaeda leaders were hiding. Gen. David Petraeus, the new top military commander in Afghanistan, recently acknowledged longstanding ties between Pakistan's Directorate for Inter-Services Intelligence, known as the ISI, and the "bad guys."

The Times's report of the new documents suggests the collusion goes even deeper, that representatives of the ISI have worked with the Taliban to organize networks of militants to fight American soldiers in Afghanistan and hatch plots to assassinate Afghan leaders.

The article painted a chilling picture of the activities of Lt. Gen. Hamid Gul of Pakistan, who ran the ISI from 1987 to 1989, when the agency and the C.I.A. were together arming the Afghan militias fighting Soviet troops. General Gul kept working with those forces, which eventually formed the Taliban.

Pakistan's ambassador to the United States said the reports were unsubstantiated and "do not reflect the current on-ground realities." But at this point, denials about links with the militants are simply not credible.

Why would Pakistan play this dangerous game? The ISI has long seen the Afghan Taliban as a proxy force, a way to ensure its influence on the other side of the border and keep India's influence at bay.

Pakistani officials also privately insist that they have little choice but to hedge their bets given their suspicions that Washington will once again lose interest as it did after the Soviets were ousted from Afghanistan in 1989. And until last year, when the Pakistani Taliban came within 60 miles of Islamabad, the country's military and intelligence establishment continued to believe it could control the extremists when it needed to.

In recent months, the Obama administration has said and done many of the right things toward building a long-term relationship with Pakistan. It has committed to long-term economic aid. It is encouraging better relations between Afghanistan and Pakistan. It is constantly reminding Pakistani leaders that the extremists, on both sides of the border, pose a mortal threat to Pakistan's fragile democracy—and their own survival. We don't know if they're getting through. We know they have to.

It has been only seven months since Mr. Obama announced his new strategy for Afghanistan, and a few weeks since General Petraeus took command. But Americans are increasingly weary of this costly war. If Mr. Obama cannot persuade Islamabad to cut its ties to, and then aggressively fight, the extremists in Pakistan, there is no hope of defeating the Taliban in Afghanistan.

—This editorial was originally published on July 26, 2010

WIKILEAKS AND
THE DIPLOMATS

The business of diplomacy is often messy and when private communications become public, it can also be highly embarrassing.

But what struck us, and reassured us, about the latest trove of classified documents released by WikiLeaks was the absence of any real skullduggery. After years of revelations about the Bush administration's abuses—including the use of torture and kidnappings—much of the Obama administration's diplomatic wheeling and dealing is appropriate and, at times, downright skillful.

The best example of that is its handling of Iran. As the cables show, the administration has been under pressure from both Israel and Arab states to attack Tehran's nuclear program pre-emptively. It has wisely resisted, while pressing for increasingly tough sanctions on Iran.

The Times and other news media have already reported much of this. What the cables add is sizzle: Defense Minister Ehud Barak of Israel warning that the world has just 6 to 18 months to stop Iran from building a nuclear weapon; King Abdullah of Saudi Arabia imploring Washington to "cut off the head of the snake"; Bahrain's king warning that letting Iran's program proceed was "greater than the danger of stopping it."

The Israelis publicly raise the alarm all the time. Most Arab leaders never do. If they believe Iran poses a major threat, they need to tell their own people and work a lot harder to pressure Iran to abandon its program.

The cables also add insight into how the Obama administration has built the case for sanctions against Iran. To win China's support, it got Saudi Arabia to promise Beijing a steady supply of oil. To win over Russia, it replaced a Bush-era missile defense plan with one that is just as effective that Moscow finds less threatening.

The administration may well be uncomfortable about disclosures of its wheeling and dealing to try to get governments to accept prisoners from Guantánamo Bay, Cuba. Slovenia was told that taking a prisoner was the price for a meeting with President Obama. We wish that the White House had been as energetic and inventive in its attempts to get Congress to shut down the prison.

We were reassured to learn that Washington has been trying to persuade Pakistan to remove nuclear fuel from a reactor so it cannot be diverted for use in a terrorist's weapon. And that the United States and South Korea are prudently discussing how to handle the potential collapse of North Korea. Disconcertingly, there is no sign that Washington or Seoul knew about the North's recently disclosed uranium enrichment plant.

The Obama administration should definitely be embarrassed by its decision to continue a Bush administration policy directing American diplomats to collect the personal data—including credit card numbers and frequent flier numbers—of foreign officials. That dangerously blurs the distinction between diplomats and spies and is best left to the spies.

There are legitimate reasons for keeping many diplomatic conversations secret. The latest WikiLeaks revelations will cause awkward moments not least because they contain blunt assessments of world leaders. The claim by Secretary of State Hillary Rodham Clinton that the leaks threaten national security seems exaggerated. The documents are valuable because they illuminate American policy in a way that Americans and others deserve to see.

—This editorial was originally published on November 29, 2010

FOLLOW THE MONEY

Nine years after the attacks of Sept. 11, 2001, there is still a seemingly limitless stream of cash flowing to terrorist groups from private charities and contributors in Saudi Arabia, Kuwait and Qatar. According to classified State Department cables recently released by WikiLeaks, governments in all three countries—all close American allies—are not doing enough to shut down that flow of money.

In a December 2009 cable to American diplomats in the region, Secretary of State Hillary Rodham Clinton warns that "donors in Saudi Arabia constitute the most significant source of funding to Sunni terrorist groups worldwide" and says that persuading Saudi leaders to treat this as a priority is "an ongoing challenge."

The cable also said that while the Saudi government has taken important steps to criminalize terror financing and restrict the movement of money overseas, it still looks the other way when it comes to certain favored organizations. Fund-raising at pilgrimages to Mecca is believed to produce millions of dollars annually for extremists. The cable suggests an even more serious problem in Kuwait, where Islamic charities are largely unregulated. The three gulf states are also not doing enough to disrupt crimes, including drug trafficking and kidnappings for ransom, that produce revenue for terrorists.

After Sept. 11, Saudi Arabia turned a blind eye to the terrorist threat even though Osama bin Laden and 15 of the 19 hijackers were Saudi-born. Al Qaeda's attempts in recent years to assassinate members of the Saudi royal family has had an impact. The Saudis increasingly share intelligence with Washington and in October provided the information that helped the United States find bombs being shipped to the United States on planes. Still, the kingdom needs to do more, including reforming an educational and political system where extremism is too often encouraged in mosques and schools.

Working with Qatar and Kuwait has apparently been even harder. In the same cable, Mrs. Clinton described Qatar as the "worst in the region" on counterterrorism and Kuwait as a "key transit point" for terrorist money. Kuwait is the only member of the Gulf Cooperation Council without a terrorist financing law. The cable also warns that weak regulatory oversight of the United Arab Emirates' growing financial center makes it vulnerable to abuse by terror financiers.

For years, Arab governments thought they could buy off the extremists to keep them from attacking their countries—and experts say that may still be happening in some cases. As the attacks in Saudi Arabia make clear, there is no immunity. Al Qaeda and its allies are as determined to bring down moderate Muslim governments as they are to destroy the West.

None of these governments are known for political courage. Washington needs to keep reminding them that this is an issue of their own survival, while pressing them and others to share information, adopt tougher controls on money flows, and improve law enforcement.

Another problem is that terrorism can be done on the cheap. Al Qaeda's branch in the Arabian Peninsula recently claimed on a Web site that the October parcel bomb operation cost just $4,200.

—This editorial was originally published on December 8, 2010

BANKS AND WIKILEAKS

The whistle-blowing Web site WikiLeaks has not been convicted of a crime. The Justice Department has not even pressed charges over its disclosure of confidential State Department communications. Nonetheless, the financial industry is trying to shut it down.

Visa, MasterCard and PayPal announced in the past few weeks that they would not process any transaction intended for WikiLeaks. Earlier this month, Bank of America decided to join the group, arguing that WikiLeaks may be doing things that are "inconsistent with our internal policies for processing payments."

The Federal Reserve, the banking regulator, allows this. Like other companies, banks can choose whom they do business with. Refusing to open an account for some undesirable entity is seen as reasonable risk management. The government even requires banks to keep an eye out for some shady businesses—like drug dealing and money laundering—and refuse to do business with those who engage in them.

But a bank's ability to block payments to a legal entity raises a troubling prospect. A handful of big banks could potentially bar any organization they disliked from the payments system, essentially cutting them off from the world economy.

The fact of the matter is that banks are not like any other business. They run the payments system. That is one of the main reasons that governments protect them from failure with explicit and implicit guarantees. This makes them look not too unlike other public utilities. A telecommunications company, for example, may not refuse phone or broadband service to an organization it dislikes, arguing that it amounts to risky business.

Our concern is not specifically about payments to WikiLeaks. This isn't the first time a bank shunned a business on similar risk-management grounds. Banks in Colorado, for instance, have refused to open bank accounts for legal dispensaries of medical marijuana.

Still, there are troubling questions. The decisions to bar the organization came after its founder, Julian Assange, said that next year it will release data revealing corruption in the financial industry. In 2009, Mr. Assange said that WikiLeaks had the hard drive of a Bank of America executive.

What would happen if a clutch of big banks decided that a particularly irksome blogger or other organization was "too risky"? What if they decided—one by one—to shut down financial access to a newspaper that was about to reveal irksome truths about their operations? This decision should not be left solely up to business-as-usual among the banks.

—This editorial was originally published on December 25, 2010

GETTING LOST
IN THE FOG OF WAR

By ANDREW EXUM
Andrew Exum is a fellow at the Center for a New American Security.

Washington

Anyone who has spent the past two days reading through the 92,000 military field reports and other documents made public by the whistle-blower site WikiLeaks may be forgiven for wondering what all the fuss is about. I'm a researcher who studies Afghanistan and have no regular access to classified information, yet I have seen nothing in the documents that has either surprised me or told me anything of significance. I suspect that's the case even for someone who reads only a third of the articles on Afghanistan in his local newspaper.

Let us review, though, what have been viewed as the major revelations in the documents (which were published in part by The Times, The Guardian of London and the German magazine Der Spiegel):

First, there are allegations made by American intelligence officers that elements within Pakistan's spy agency, the Directorate for Inter-Services Intelligence, have been conspiring with Taliban factions and other insurgents. Those charges are nothing new. This newspaper and others have been reporting on those accusations—often supported by anonymous sources within the American military and intelligence services—for years.

Second, the site provides documentation of Afghan civilian casualties caused by United States and allied military operations. It is true that civilians inevitably suffer in war. But researchers in Kabul with the Campaign for Innocent Victims in Conflict have been compiling evidence of these casualties, and their effect in Afghanistan, for some time now. Their reports, to which they add background on the context of the events, contributed to the decision by the former top commander in Afghanistan, Gen. Stanley

McChrystal, to put in place controversially stringent new measures intended to reduce such casualties last year.

Third, the site asserts that the Pentagon employs a secret task force of highly trained commandos charged with capturing or killing insurgent leaders. I suspect that in the eyes of most Americans, using special operations teams to kill terrorists is one of the least controversial ways in which the government spends their tax dollars.

The documents do reveal some specific information about United States and NATO tactics, techniques, procedures and equipment that is sensitive, and will cause much consternation within the military. It may even result in some people dying. Thus the White House is right to voice its displeasure with WikiLeaks.

Yet most of the major revelations that have been trumpeted by Wiki-Leaks's founder, Julian Assange, are not revelations at all—they are merely additional examples of what we already knew.

Mr. Assange has said that the publication of these documents is analogous to the publication of the Pentagon Papers, only more significant. This is ridiculous. The Pentagon Papers offered the public a coherent internal narrative of the conflict in Vietnam that was at odds with the one that had been given by the elected and uniformed leadership.

The publication of these documents, by contrast, dumps 92,000 new primary source documents into the laps of the world's public with no context, no explanation as to why some accounts may contradict others, no sense of what is important or unusual as opposed to the normal march of war.

Many experts on the war, both in the military and the press, have long been struggling to come to grips with the conflict's complexity and nuances. What is the public going to make of this haphazard cache of documents, many written during combat by officers with little sense of how their observations fit into the fuller scope of the war?

I myself first went to Afghanistan as a young Army officer in 2002 and returned two years later after having led a small special operations unit—what Mr. Assange calls an "assassination squad." (I also worked briefly as a civilian adviser to General McChrystal last year.) I can confirm that the situation in Afghanistan is complex, and defies any attempt to graft it onto easy-to-discern lessons or policy conclusions. Yet the release of the documents has led to a stampede of commentators and politicians doing exactly that. It's all too easy for them to find field reports to reaffirm their preconceived opinions about the war.

The Guardian editorialized on Sunday that the documents released reveal "a very different landscape . . . from the one with which we have become familiar." But whoever wrote that has not been reading the reports of his own newspaper's reporters in Afghanistan.

The news media have done a good job of showing the public that the Afghan war is a highly complex environment stretching beyond the borders of the fractured country. Often what appears to be a two-way conflict between the government and an insurgency is better described as intertribal rivalry. And often that intertribal rivalry is worsened or overshadowed by the violent trade in drugs.

The Times, The Guardian and Der Spiegel did nothing wrong in looking over the WikiLeaks documents and excerpting them. Despite the occasional protest from the right wing, most of the press in the United States and in allied nations takes care not to publish information that might result in soldiers' deaths.

But WikiLeaks itself is another matter. Mr. Assange says he is a journalist, but he is not. He is an activist, and to what end it is not clear. This week—as when he released a video in April showing American helicopter gunships killing Iraqi civilians in 2007—he has been throwing around the term "war crimes," but offers no context for the events he is judging. It seems that the death of any civilian in war, an unavoidable occurrence, is a "crime."

If his desire is to promote peace, Mr. Assange and his brand of activism are not as helpful as he imagines. By muddying the waters between journalism and activism, and by throwing his organization into the debate on Afghanistan with little apparent regard for the hard moral choices and dearth of good policy options facing decision-makers, he is being as reckless and destructive as the contemptible soldier or soldiers who leaked the documents in the first place.

—This article was originally published on July 26, 2010

LOST IN A MAZE

By MAUREEN DOWD

Washington
The waterfall of leaks on Afghanistan underlines the awful truth: We're not in control.

Not since Theseus fought the Minotaur in his maze has a fight been so confounding.

The more we try to do for our foreign protectorates, the more angry they get about what we try to do. As Congress passed $59 billion in additional war funding on Tuesday, not only are our wards not grateful, they're disdainful.

Washington gave the Wall Street banks billions, and, in return, they stabbed us in the back, handing out a fortune in bonuses to the grifters who almost wrecked our economy.

Washington gave the Pakistanis billions, and, in return, they stabbed us in the back, pledging to fight the militants even as they secretly help the militants.

We keep getting played by people who are playing both sides.

Robert Gibbs recalled that President Obama said last year that "we will not and cannot provide a blank check" to Pakistan.

But only last week, Secretary of State Hillary Clinton arrived in Pakistan to hand over a juicy check: $500 million in aid to the country that's been getting a billion a year for most of this decade and in 2009 was pledged another $7.5 billion for the next five. She vowed to banish the "legacy of suspicion" and show that "there is so much we can accomplish together as partners joined in common cause."

Gibbs argued that the deluge of depressing war documents from the whistle-blower Web site WikiLeaks, reported by The New York Times and others, was old. But it reflected one chilling fact: the Taliban has been getting better and better every year of the insurgency. So why will 30,000 more troops help?

We invaded two countries, and allied with a third—all renowned as masters at double-dealing. And, now lured into their mazes, we still don't have the foggiest idea, shrouded in the fog of wars, how these cultures work. Before we went into Iraq and Afghanistan, both places were famous for warrior cultures. And, indeed, their insurgents are world class.

But whenever America tries to train security forces in Iraq and Afghanistan so that we can leave behind a somewhat stable country, it's positively Sisyphean. It takes eons longer than our officials predict. The forces we train turn against us or go over to the other side or cut and run. If we give them a maximum security prison, as we recently did in Iraq, making a big show of handing over the key, the imprisoned Al Qaeda militants are suddenly allowed to escape.

The British Empire prided itself on discovering warrior races in places it conquered—Gurkhas, Sikhs, Pathans, as the Brits called Pashtuns. But why are they warrior cultures only until we need them to be warriors on our side? Then they're untrainably lame, even when we spend $25 billion on building up the Afghan military and the National Police Force, dubbed "the gang that couldn't shoot straight" by Newsweek.

Maybe we just can't train them to fight against each other. But why can't countries that produce fierce insurgencies produce good standing armies in a reasonable amount of time? Is it just that insurgencies can be more indiscriminate?

Things are so bad that Robert Blackwill, who was on W.'s national security team, wrote in Politico that the Obama administration should just admit failure and turn over the Pashtun South to the Taliban since it will inevitably control it anyway. He said that the administration doesn't appreciate the extent to which this is a Pashtun nationalist uprising.

We keep hearing that the last decade of war, where we pour in gazillions to build up Iraq and Afghanistan even as our own economy sputters, has weakened Al Qaeda.

But at his confirmation hearing on Tuesday before the Senate Armed Services Committee, Gen. James Mattis, who is slated to replace Gen. David Petraus, warned that Al Qaeda and its demon spawn represent a stark danger all over the Middle East and Central Asia.

While we're anchored in Afghanistan, the Al Qaeda network could roil Yemen "to the breaking point," as Mattis put it in written testimony.

Pakistan's tribal areas "remain the greatest danger as these are strategic footholds for Al Qaeda and its senior leaders, including Osama bin Laden and Ayman al-Zawahiri," the blunt four-star general wrote, adding that they "remain key to extremists' efforts to rally Muslim resistance worldwide."

Questioned by John McCain, General Mattis said that we're not leaving Afghanistan; we're starting "a process of transition to the Afghan forces." But that process never seems to get past the starting point.

During the debate over war funds on Tuesday, Representative Jim McGovern, a Massachusetts Democrat, warned that we are in a monstrous maze without the ball of string to find our way out.

"All of the puzzle has been put together, and it is not a pretty picture," he told The Times's Carl Hulse. "Things are really ugly over there."

—This article was originally published on July 27, 2010

KISS THIS WAR GOODBYE

By FRANK RICH

It was on a Sunday morning, June 13, 1971, that The Times published its first installment of the Pentagon Papers. Few readers may have been more excited than a circle of aspiring undergraduate journalists who'd worked at The Harvard Crimson. Though the identity of The Times's source wouldn't eke out for several days, we knew the whistle-blower had to be Daniel Ellsberg, an intense research fellow at M.I.T. and former Robert McNamara acolyte who'd become an antiwar activist around Boston. We recognized the papers' contents, as reported in The Times, because we'd heard the war stories from the loquacious Ellsberg himself.

But if we were titillated that Sunday, it wasn't immediately clear that this internal government history of the war had mass appeal. Tricia Nixon's wedding in the White House Rose Garden on Saturday received equal play with the Pentagon Papers on The Times's front page. On "Face the Nation" the guest was the secretary of defense, Melvin Laird, yet the subject of the papers didn't even come up.

That false calm vanished overnight once Richard Nixon, erupting in characteristic rage and paranoia, directed his attorney general, John Mitchell, to enjoin The Times from publishing any sequels. The high-stakes legal drama riveted the nation for two weeks, culminating in a landmark 6-to-3 Supreme Court decision in favor of The Times and the First Amendment. Ellsberg and The Times were canonized. I sold my first magazine article, an Ellsberg profile, to Esquire, and, for better or worse, cast my lot with journalism. That my various phone conversations with Ellsberg prompted ham-fisted F.B.I. agents to visit me and my parents only added to the allure.

I mention my personal history to try to inject a little reality into the garbling of Vietnam-era history that has accompanied the WikiLeaks release of the Afghanistan war logs. Last week the left and right reached a rare consensus. The war logs are no Pentagon Papers. They are historic documents describing events largely predating the current administration. They contain no news. They will not change the course of the war.

About the only prominent figures who found serious parallels between then and now were Ellsberg and the WikiLeaks impresario, Julian Assange. They are hardly disinterested observers, but they're on the mark—in large part because the impact of the Pentagon Papers on the Vietnam War (as opposed to their impact on the press) was far less momentous than last week's chatter would suggest. No, the logs won't change the course of our very long war in Afghanistan, but neither did the Pentagon Papers alter the course of Vietnam. What Ellsberg's leak did do was ratify the downward trend-line of the war's narrative. The WikiLeaks legacy may echo that. We may look back at the war logs as a herald of the end of America's engagement in Afghanistan just as the Pentagon Papers are now a milestone in our slo-mo exit from Vietnam.

What was often forgotten last week is that the Pentagon Papers had no game-changing news about that war either and also described events predating the then-current president. By June 1971, the Tet offensive and Walter Cronkite's famous on-air editorial were more than three years in the past. The David Halberstam article that inspired "The Best and the Brightest" had already appeared in Harper's. Lt. William Calley had been found guilty in the My Lai massacre exposed by Seymour Hersh in 1969. Just weeks before the Pentagon Papers surfaced, the Vietnam veteran John Kerry electrified the country by asking a Senate committee, "How do you ask a man to be the last man to die for a mistake?" Most Americans had long been telling pollsters the war was a mistake. By the time the Pentagon Papers surfaced, a plurality also disapproved of how Vietnam was handled by Nixon, who had arrived in office promising to end the war.

The papers' punch was in the many inside details they added to the war's chronicle over four previous administrations and, especially, in their shocking and irrefutable evidence that Nixon's immediate predecessor, Lyndon Johnson, had systematically lied to the country about his intentions and the war's progress. Though Nixon was another liar, none of this incriminated him. His anger about the leak would nonetheless drive him to create a clandestine "plumbers" unit whose criminality (including a break-in at the office of Ellsberg's psychiatrist) would lead to Watergate. Had Nixon not so violently overreacted that June—egged on by Henry Kissinger and fueled by his loathing of The Times and the antiwar movement—the story might have ebbed. Yes, the Pentagon Papers were labeled "top secret"—as opposed to the Afghanistan war logs' "secret" status—but, as Richard Reeves writes in his book "President Nixon," some 700,000 people in and out of government had clearance to read "top secret" documents. Compelling as the papers were, they were hardly nuclear code.

The public's reaction to the Afghanistan war logs has largely been a shrug—and not just because they shared their Times front page with an article about Chelsea Clinton's wedding. President Obama is, to put it mildly, no Nixon, and his no-drama reaction to the leaks robbed their publication of the constitutional cliffhanger of their historical antecedent. Another factor in the logs' shortfall as public spectacle is the fractionalization of the news media, to the point where even a stunt packaged as "news" can trump journalistic enterprise. (Witness how the bogus Shirley Sherrod video upstaged The Washington Post's blockbuster investigation of the American intelligence bureaucracy two weeks ago.) The logs also suffer stylistically: they're often impenetrable dispatches from the ground, in contrast to the Pentagon Papers' anonymously and lucidly team-written epic of policy-making on high.

Yet the national yawn that largely greeted the war logs is most of all an indicator of the country's verdict on the Afghan war itself, now that it's nine years on and has reached its highest monthly casualty rate for American troops. Many Americans at home have lost faith and checked out. The war places way down the list of pressing issues in every poll. Nearly two-thirds of those asked recently by CBS News think it's going badly; the latest Post-ABC News survey finds support of Obama's handling of Afghanistan at a low (45 percent), with only 43 percent deeming the war worth fighting.

Perhaps more telling than either these polls or the defection of liberal House Democrats from last week's war appropriations bill are the signs of wobbling conservative support. The gung-ho neocon axis was predictably belligerent in denouncing WikiLeaks. But the G.O.P. chairman Michael Steele's recent "gaffe"—his since-retracted observation that "a land war in Afghanistan" is doomed—is no anomaly in a fractured party where the antiwar Ron Paul may have as much currency as the knee-jerk hawk John McCain. On the night of the logs' release, Fox News even refrained from its patented shtick of shouting "Treason!" at the "mainstream media." Instead, the go-to Times-basher Bernie Goldberg could be found on "The O'Reilly

Factor" telling Laura Ingraham, a guest host, that the war "has not been going well" and is a dubious exercise in "nation-building."

Obama was right to say that the leaked documents "don't reveal any issues that haven't already informed our public debate in Afghanistan," but that doesn't mean the debate was resolved in favor of his policy. Americans know that our counterinsurgency partner, Hamid Karzai, is untrustworthy. They know that the terrorists out to attack us are more likely to be found in Pakistan, Yemen and Somalia than Afghanistan. And they are starting to focus on the morbid reality, highlighted in the logs, of the de facto money-laundering scheme that siphons American taxpayers' money through the Pakistan government to the Taliban, who then disperse it to kill Americans.

Most Americans knew or guessed the crux of the Pentagon Papers, too. A full year earlier the Senate had repealed the 1964 Gulf of Tonkin resolution; no one needed a "top secret" smoking gun by 1971 to know that L.B.J. had lied about the Tonkin incident. The papers didn't change administration war policy because we were already pulling out of Vietnam, however truculently and lethally (the Christmas 1972 bombing campaign, most notoriously). In 1971, the American troop level was some 213,000, down from a peak of 537,000 in 1968. By 1973 we were essentially done.

Unlike Nixon, Obama is still adding troops to his unpopular war. But history is not on his side either in Afghanistan or at home. The latest Gallup poll found that 58 percent of the country favors his announced timeline, with its promise to start withdrawing troops in mid-2011. It's hard to imagine what could change that equation now.

Certainly not Pakistan. As the president conducts his scheduled reappraisal of his war policy this December, a re-examination of 1971 might lead him to question his own certitude of what he is fond of calling "the long view." The Times won a Pulitzer Prize for its 1971 Pentagon Papers coup. But another of the Pulitzers that year went to the columnist Jack Anderson, who also earned Nixon's ire by mining other leaks to expose the White House's tilt to Pakistan in the Indo-Pakistani War. The one thing no one imagined back then was that four decades later it would be South Asia, not Southeast Asia, that would still be beckoning America into a quagmire.

—This article was originally published on July 31, 2010

IN PAKISTAN, ECHOES OF AMERICAN BETRAYAL

By MOHAMMED HANIF

Mohammed Hanif, a correspondent for the BBC Urdu Service, is the author of the novel "A Case of Exploding Mangoes."

Karachi, Pakistan

Pakistan's premier intelligence agency, the Directorate for Inter-Services Intelligence, has been accused of many bad things in its own country. It has been held responsible for rigging elections, sponsoring violent sectarian groups and running torture chambers for political dissidents. More recently, it has been accused of abducting Pakistanis and handing them over to the United States for cash.

But last week—after thousands of classified United States Army documents were released by WikiLeaks, and American and British officials and pundits accused the ISI of double-dealing in Afghanistan—the Pakistani news media were very vocal in their defense of their spies. On talk show after talk show, the ISI's accusers in the West were criticized for shortsightedness and shifting the blame to Pakistan for their doomed campaign in Afghanistan.

Suddenly, the distinction between the state and the state within the state was blurred. It is our ISI that is being accused, we felt. How, we wondered, can the Americans have fallen for raw intelligence provided by paid informants and, in many cases, Afghan intelligence? And why shouldn't Pakistan, asked the pundits, keep its options open for a post-American Afghanistan?

More generally, the WikiLeaks fallout brought back ugly memories, reminding Pakistanis what happens whenever we get involved with the Americans. In fact, one person at the center of the document dump is our primary object lesson for staying away from America's foreign adventures.

Hamid Gul, now a retired general, led the ISI during the end years of the Soviet occupation of Afghanistan and together with his C.I.A. friends unwittingly in the 1990s spurred the mujahedeen to turn Kabul—the city they had set out to liberate—into rubble. According to the newly released documents, Mr. Gul met with Qaeda operatives in Pakistan in 2006 and told them to "make the snow warm in Kabul . . . set Kabul aflame."

This would seem highly sinister except that, today, Hamid Gul is nothing more than a glorified television evangelist and, as the columnist Nadir Hassan noted, "known only for being on half a dozen talk shows simultaneously." He is also, for Pakistanis, a throwback to the lost years of our American-backed military dictatorships, a stark reminder of why we distrust the United States.

The ISI and the C.I.A. have colluded twice in the destruction of Afghanistan. Their complicity has brought war to Pakistan's cities. After every round of cloak-and-dagger games, they behave like a squabbling couple who keep getting back together and telling the world that they are doing it for the children's sake. But whenever these two reunite, a lot of children's lives are wrecked.

In the West, the ISI is often described as ideologically allied to the Taliban. But Pakistan's military-security establishment has only one ideology, and it's not Islamism. It's spelled I-N-D-I-A. It will do anybody's bidding if it's occasionally allowed to show India a bit of muscle.

Gen. Ashfaq Parvez Kayani, the Pakistani Army chief, has just been given an unexpected three-year extension in his office, due in large part, it is said, to American pressure on Islamabad. Yet General Kayani headed the ISI during the period that the WikiLeaks documents cover. Since he became the head of the Pakistan Army—and a frequent host to Adm. Mike Mullen, the chairman of the Joint Chiefs of Staff—the number of drone attacks on Pakistani territory have increased substantially. It seems he has found a way to overcome his ISI past.

While he generally keeps a low profile, General Kayani in February gave an off-the-record presentation to Pakistani journalists. His point was clear: Pakistan's military remains India-centric. His explanation was simple: we go by the enemy's capacity, not its immediate intentions. This came in a year when Pakistan lost more civilians and soldiers than it has in any war with India.

Yet it has become very clear that an overwhelming majority of Pakistani people do not share the army's India obsession or its yearning for "strategic depth"—that is, a continuing deadly muddle—in Afghanistan. They want a peaceful settlement with India over the disputed territory of Kashmir and a safer neighborhood. None of the leading parties in Parliament made a big deal about India, Afghanistan or jihad in their election campaigns. They were elected on promises of justice, transparency and reasonably priced electricity.

Lately, Americans seem to have woken up to the fact that there is something called a Parliament and a civil society in Pakistan. But even so, it seems that Americans are courting the same ruling class—the military elite's civilian cousins—that has thrived on American aid and obviously wants an even closer relationship with Washington. A popular TV presenter who interviewed Secretary of State Hillary Clinton during her visit later jibed, "What kind of close relationship is this? I don't even get invited to Chelsea's wedding?"

Pakistan's military and civil elite should take a good look around before they pitch another marquee and invite their American friends over for tea and war talk. There are a lot of hungry people looking in, and the strung lights are sucking up electricity that could run a small factory, or illuminate a village. Besides, they're not likely to know what WikiLeaks is—they've been too busy cleaning up after their masters' guests.

—This article was originally published on July 31, 2010

LEARNING FROM WIKILEAKS

By MITCHELL LaFORTUNE

*Mitchell LaFortune, a former Army sergeant, was an intelligence analyst
with the 82nd Airborne Division from 2006 to 2010.*

Saco, Me.

Last summer, as the nation's war effort and attention turned from Iraq
to Afghanistan, the new United States commander there, Gen. Stanley
McChrystal, insisted that the struggle was not about killing the enemy or
capturing ground, but instead a "war of perception." Given the general's
recent firing, increasing deaths on the battlefield and the release last week of
thousands of classified documents by WikiLeaks painting a dismal picture
of the war effort, it is clear that we are losing badly in the war of perception.

I spent two deployments in Afghanistan writing strategic intelligence
reports and briefings similar to what WikiLeaks just made public. True, what
was leaked is not pleasant reading. Yet there is no question in my mind that
the majority of analysts and officers who have served there, despite their
political differences, believe not only that we should continue the fight but
that we very much need to win it.

Why, then, have so many Americans come to a different conclusion
recently—including the 114 House members who voted against President
Obama's war-financing bill on Tuesday? I think they fail to understand the
complexity and scale of the war effort, which leads to a flawed analysis.

For example, many have bemoaned the rash of sophisticated attacks
in eastern Afghanistan. But allied attention has been focused on the easier
fight of evicting the Taliban from the agrarian provinces of the south, not
combating the more complex enemy in the east, where insurgent networks
capitalize on political and cultural differences that will require an entirely
different counterinsurgency strategy.

Many people also operate from a faulty assumption about the war's
purpose. No matter what we've told the Afghans, the true goal of the American-led effort should not be to create a stable, honest government in Kabul.

While that would be a great benefit, what's vital is that we keep in place the robust intelligence and quick-strike military structure we have developed in the country and across the Pakistan border.

Without these human intelligence collectors, communications experts and small-scale military operations, we would free the Taliban in Pakistan to focus on overthrowing the government in Islamabad. If they were to accomplish that feat, Al Qaeda would be given all the time it needs to reconstitute its network and undertake more attacks against the United States and its allies.

That said, there may be a benefit from the scrutiny the military is likely to face post-WikiLeaks. There are many problems with the way we are managing this war. Far too often during my deployments—the first in 2007, the second last year—I watched as operations were conducted out of logistical convenience rather than necessity. We often had troops avoid Taliban-controlled districts to limit civilian and military casualties. Because of the threat of homemade bombs, soldiers had to dress like Robocop while trying to interact with, and win the trust of, local leaders. And the rules of engagement are now so restrictive that I'm amazed that any insurgents were killed in the last year.

For years, the Western military's main focus has been to disrupt the supply lines that provide the insurgents with improvised explosives. This emphasis protects our troops but does little for the Afghan population, specifically creating a secure environment that would allow for economic growth in key cities like Khost, Gardez and Kandahar. This is crucial: if we can't revive the cities we will never make progress in the countryside, which is the ultimate battleground against the insurgents.

If we need a model, we should think about what Afghanistan was like in the 1970s. The country functioned relatively well with a weak central government, strong local leadership and a marginalized religious class. The resistance to the Soviet occupation, steeped in radical Islam, overturned that traditional power structure. By the time the Soviets left, the village mullah had a higher social standing than the tribal leader or local political representative. It was not hard to foresee the rise of the Taliban.

American and Afghan forces dislodged the Taliban government from Kabul in a matter of months, but they have done little to alter the power dynamic across the country. It is the religious figure, not the elected official or tribal elder, who is invariably asked to settle land disputes and other arguments. As I waded through reports from the field in Paktika Province last year, it became apparent that the people turned to Talibanbacked clerics and the Haqqani network, a ruthless terrorist movement allied with the Taliban, as the ultimate arbiters.

The key to turning around the war will be to change that dynamic. In fact, we must clamp down on the three things the Taliban do particularly well: manipulating the news media, intimidating the rural population and providing shadow governance.

The Taliban's media machine runs circles around our public information operations in Afghanistan. Using newspapers, radio broadcasts, the Internet and word of mouth, it puts out messages far faster than we can, exaggerating the effectiveness of its attacks, creating the illusion of a unified insurgency and criticizing the (real and imagined) failings of the Kabul government. To undermine support for United States troops, the Taliban insistently remind the people that America has committed to a withdrawal beginning next summer, they jump on any announcement of our Western allies pulling out troops and they publicize polls that show declining domestic American support for the war.

To counter the spin, we need to add the Taliban's top propagandists to the high-value-target list and direct military operations at the insurgents' media nerve centers. A major reason that people in rural areas are so reluctant to help us is that Taliban propaganda and intimidation have created an atmosphere of fear.

A second initiative is to bring back the traditional rural power structure. We have to restore the power of the tribal leader, the khan. Afghans are fond of saying that the thing they do best is politics; we must let them do it. This means moving toward a far weaker concept of central government and encouraging local solutions to local problems. American aid should go directly to rural communities rather than to the Karzai government. And we must identify key tribal leaders and local politicians and give them around-the-clock protection with American troops. It's astonishing how much credibility a village leader can gain simply by not being assassinated.

Last, we must destroy the credibility of the Taliban's religious authority. The insurgents' concept of Islam is objectionable to most Afghans, but there is little alternative, as most clerics who rejected the Taliban have been killed or have fled. While creating a network of more enlightened religious figures to compete with the hard-liners will take time, we could jump-start progress by creating a group of "mobile mullahs"—well-protected clerics who can travel through rural areas and settle land disputes and other issues. These men should come from the general areas in which they will be performing their duties and be approved by community leaders.

We may not win General McChrystal's war of perception, but we cannot afford a military defeat in Afghanistan. A Taliban victory would not only threaten Pakistan's government, it would provide a dangerous precedent for other looming disaster zones like Yemen. The boot must be kept on the throat of extremism. Yet we do not need to maintain 100,000 troops in Afghanistan or create a sparkling democracy. We simply need to maintain the intelligence structure and military capacity that already exists, and put the power to defeat the insurgents in the hands of the locals.

—This article was originally published on July 31, 2010

THE FRAGILE COMMUNITY

By DAVID BROOKS

Julian Assange, the founder of WikiLeaks, had moved 37 times by the time he reached his 14th birthday. His mother didn't enroll him in the local schools because, as Raffi Khatchadourian wrote in a New Yorker profile, she feared "that formal education would inculcate an unhealthy respect for authority."

She needn't have worried. As a young computer hacker, he formed a group called International Subversives. As an adult, he wrote "Conspiracy as Governance," a pseudo-intellectual online diatribe. He talks of vast "patronage networks" that constrain the human spirit.

Far from respecting authority, Assange seems to be an old-fashioned anarchist who believes that all ruling institutions are corrupt and public pronouncements are lies.

For someone with his mind-set, the decision to expose secrets is easy. If the hidden world is suspect, then everything should be revealed. As The New Yorker reported, WikiLeaks has published technical details about an Army device designed to prevent roadside bombs from detonating. It posted soldiers' Social Security numbers. This week, the group celebrated the release of internal State Department documents with a triumphalist statement claiming that the documents expose the corruption, hypocrisy and venality of U.S. diplomats.

For him, it's easy. But for everyone else, it's hard. My colleagues on the news side of this newspaper do not share Assange's mentality. As the various statements from the editors have made abundantly clear, they face a much thornier set of issues.

As journalists, they have a professional obligation to share information that might help people make informed decisions. That means asking questions like: How does the U.S. government lobby allies? What is the real nature of our relationship with Pakistani intelligence? At the same time, as humans and citizens, my colleagues know they have a moral obligation not to endanger lives or national security.

The Times has thus erected a series of filters between the 250,000 raw documents that WikiLeaks obtained and complete public exposure. The paper has released only a tiny percentage of the cables. Information that might endanger informants has been redacted. Specific cables have been put into context with broader reporting.

Yet it might be useful to consider one more filter. Consider it the World Order filter. The fact that we live our lives amid order and not chaos is the great achievement of civilization. This order should not be taken for granted.

This order is tenuously maintained by brave soldiers but also by talkative leaders and diplomats. Every second of every day, leaders and diplomats are engaged in a never-ending conversation. The leaked cables reveal this conversation. They show diplomats seeking information, cajoling each other and engaging in faux-friendships and petty hypocrisies as they seek to avoid global disasters.

Despite the imaginings of people like Assange, the conversation revealed in the cables is not devious and nefarious. The private conversation is similar to the public conversation, except maybe more admirable. Israeli and Arab diplomats can be seen reacting sympathetically and realistically toward one another. The Americans in the cables are generally savvy and honest. Iran's neighbors are properly alarmed and reaching out.

Some people argue that this diplomatic conversation is based on mechanical calculations about national self-interest, and it won't be affected by public exposure. But this conversation, like all conversations, is built on relationships. The quality of the conversation is determined by the level of trust. Its direction is influenced by persuasion and by feelings about friends and enemies.

The quality of the conversation is damaged by exposure, just as our relationships with our neighbors would be damaged if every private assessment were brought to the light of day. We've seen what happens when conversations deteriorate (look at the U.S. Congress), and it's ugly.

The WikiLeaks dump will probably damage the global conversation. Nations will be less likely to share with the United States. Agencies will be tempted to return to the pre-9/11 silos. World leaders will get their back up when they read what is said about them. Cooperation against Iran may be harder to maintain because Arab leaders feel exposed and boxed in. This fragile international conversation is under threat. It's under threat from WikiLeaks. It's under threat from a Gresham's Law effect, in which the level of public exposure is determined by the biggest leaker and the biggest traitor.

It should be possible to erect a filter that protects not only lives and operations but also international relationships. It should be possible to do articles on specific revelations—Is the U.S. using diplomats to spy on the U.N.? What missile technology did North Korea give to Iran?—without unveiling in a wholesale manner the nuts and bolts of the diplomatic enterprise. We depend on those human conversations for the limited order we enjoy every day.

—This article was originally published on November 29, 2010

HAVE WE LEARNED ANYTHING FROM THE LEAKED CABLES?

By DAVID BROOKS and GAIL COLLINS

DAVID BROOKS: Gail, I've begun to worry about what you might call the Caligula Gap. When you look around the world, or at least around the leaked State Department cables, you see world leaders living full, decadent lives. Muammar el-Qaddafi has his voluptuous Ukrainian nurse. Vladimir Putin has his power and his muscles. Silvio Berlusconi has everything. Even aging Saudi princes go around talking about cutting the heads off snakes, like Clint Eastwood movie characters.

GAIL COLLINS: As much as I appreciate how total dysfunction is good for our business, I am not prepared to wish that we had a president like Silvio Berlusconi.

DAVID BROOKS: I'm trying to imagine what other foreign ministries have been cabling about our leaders: George W. Bush liked to go to bed at 9 p.m. President Obama has a perfect family, plays golf and his most raucous activity ends with him getting 12 stitches in the lip—from a guy. I'm afraid we have not been providing foreign diplomats with enough good cable material—at least since Bill Clinton left town.

GAIL COLLINS: Yeah, they'd have to dig pretty deep. I don't know if foreign diplomats would care all that much about the obscure congressman who liked to play "tickle me" with his male aides, or the governor who pretended to be hiking so he could visit his mistress in Argentina. Although someone did tell me about being on a train in Peru, and telling the Peruvians in the adjoining seat that he was from South Carolina. They all nodded and said, "Ah—Appalachian Trail!"

DAVID BROOKS: Do you think it is because we are Puritans or because we keep electing people with insufficient imaginations? They say that power corrupts and that may be true, but in the U.S. it doesn't corrupt in very colorful ways. Even Richard Nixon was corrupt in a dour and bitter manner.

GAIL COLLINS: The worst president we ever had was maybe Warren Harding, who had sex with his mistress in the Oval Office coat closet. You're right, it doesn't really make the grade.

DAVID BROOKS: I guess I'm wondering if you learned anything about the psychology of global leadership from the State Department cables. I wrote a column this week saying that I don't think we should have access to the cables. I fervently believe that and find myself repulsed by the folks at WikiLeaks. They are bad for the world because they destroy trust, which isn't in great supply to start with, and I wish the establishment still had enough self-confidence to marginalize this sort of behavior and protect the social ecology.

GAIL COLLINS: I'm sort of in the camp where if it's out there and it doesn't endanger national security, the public should get to see it. But I'm guessing that's not the crux of the thought you're pursuing.

DAVID BROOKS: I'm trolling for useful insights from all those cables. Mostly I see a lot of frustrated world leaders who don't possess the means to solve intractable problems.

GAIL COLLINS: I actually see a lot of leaders who have a pretty rational and pragmatic view of the world around them. I agree that reading their private confidences doesn't give me any new hope that they'll be able to solve the great problems of the day. But it does give me more faith that they are all united in a desire not to see the planet get blown up on their watch. Which is something.

DAVID BROOKS: Some people say the documents show that the U.S. is in decline. We can't just run the world the way we used to. Frankly, I don't remember this golden age. Did Jimmy Carter snap his fingers and watch the world get in line? Did Ronald Reagan get international support when it was time to place missiles in Europe to confront the Soviets, or when he tried to launch the Strategic Defense Initiative? I covered a lot of summits during the Clinton administration and I certainly don't remember the U.S. running the show. It was a mad scramble, just as it is now.

GAIL COLLINS: I'll wait until the last cable is out there before making a judgment but so far I've been impressed by how the rest of the world still seems to hope that the United States will figure out a way to solve their problems. Not gonna happen, but I appreciate the sentiment.

DAVID BROOKS: Maybe the good news is that there is no news. I've asked a few world leaders if the secret information they have access to gives them a different picture of the world than the one the rest of us get just reading the paper. They generally say no. What we see on the outside is what they see on the inside. They just have more granularity.

GAIL COLLINS: Yes, so far I've been amazed by how few surprises we've gotten. Unless you were under the impression that the other Arab countries didn't hate Iran. Or that China wasn't fully aware that the leadership of North Korea is entirely composed of nutballs.

DAVID BROOKS: These cables—which don't include "top secret" stuff, admittedly—show no hidden conspiracies, at least of any consequence. Maybe the normal work of journalism covers the world as it really is.

GAIL COLLINS: And that's a thought that will make the folks at WikiLeaks very depressed.

—This article was originally published on December 1, 2010

DO YOU WANT
TO KNOW A (TOP) SECRET?

By ERIC ALTERMAN

Eric Alterman is professor of English and journalism at the City University
of New York. His books include "When Presidents Lie: A History of Official
Deception and its Consequences."

From the standpoint of traditional post-Pentagon Papers, post-Watergate journalism, the decision by The New York Times, along with the Guardian, Le Monde, El Pais and Der Spiegel, to publish news stories based on the purloined State Department documents made available by WikiLeaks was really no decision at all.

News organizations are in the business of publishing news. They can exercise their judgment with regard to whether, in exceptional circumstances—usually those regarding potential loss of life—news might be redacted, delayed or, on extremely rare occasions, permanently withheld. But the likely embarrassment to individuals, or inconvenience to U.S. diplomats, does not even begin to approach this bar.

The manner in which the newspapers received the information is really not that special, either. The press is always attacked for publishing leaks, but the attackers almost always pick the leaks of which they happen to disapprove.

The conservatives who criticize the publication of the WikiLeaks material were not heard complaining when President George W. Bush and his national security team provided Bob Woodward and his coauthor, Dan Balz, with notes and minutes of still-secret National Security Council proceedings regarding the most sensitive matters of U.S. war planning and intelligence collection.

Similarly it was liberals, not conservatives, who took the Bush administration officials to task for leaking the identity of C.I.A. agent Valerie Plame in order to discredit the information provided by her husband, Joseph Wilson.

What is different about the WikiLeaks data is the scale of the leak, the motive of the leaker, and the manner in which it was ultimately made available.

The traditional motive for a high official to orchestrate a leak is to attempt to control the media narrative. That's what President Bush and Karl Rove were doing, and what Daniel Ellsberg did decades earlier when he gave the Pentagon Papers to The New York Times.

But in the case of the WikiLeaks material, the trove of information is so enormous and contains so many stories of real import and/or prurient interest that there is no single narrative to control—nor any means to do so. The target is not any U.S. policy or even the U.S. government. It is secrecy itself.

In this respect, the mainstream media institutions are actually playing a far more useful role than they have in many past cases—including, in particular, the run-up to the war in Iraq. The sheer size of the data drop, coupled with the lack of deadline pressure, allowed editors to present what would have been an unmanageable mountain of material in a careful, considered and (partially) contextualized manner.

It also gave the State Department plenty of time to identify which cables were genuinely deserving of continued secrecy. On the basis of State's suggestions, according to Times Executive Editor Bill Keller, the paper "edited out any information that could identify confidential sources—including informants, dissidents, academics and human rights activists—or otherwise compromise national security."

At the same time, the technological advances that make possible the publication of the documents demonstrate the loss of power and influence of these institutions.

One reason that nobody has ever leaked on this scale before is that nobody could have transported, much less published, 250,000 documents containing who knows how many (millions of?) pages.

When Ellsberg provided his copies of the Pentagon Papers—a fraction of the size of this document dump—first to The Times and then the Washington Post, one of his biggest concerns was how to store and copy the documents without being discovered and arrested.

Today, the digitization of information has empowered "citizen journalists" like the folks at WikiLeaks to actually determine the agenda of the mainstream media—and of world governments—to a degree most of us are only beginning to understand.

The fact is that if The Times and the other papers had, for whatever reason, declined to play along with WikiLeaks, the material would still have been published. But then we would all be talking about the growing irrelevance of the mainstream media in an age when guerrilla "journalists" can easily execute an end run around them. This has already happened many times, and it hardly serves the interests of the press once it is revealed.

So while it is understandable for Secretary of State Hillary Clinton and others to fulminate about the potential loss of confidence in U.S. diplomacy and the difficulties the leaked documents will undoubtedly cause, she—and everybody else attempting to keep secrets from the rest of us—need to understand that the game has new rules.

When 250,000 documents can be placed on a zip drive smaller than a popsicle stick, and thousands of citizen journalists are working to make it available to the public, then the guarantee of secrecy for any powerful institution is only a comforting fiction.

So far, in the case of WikiLeaks, those involved in the publication of the papers appear to have operated responsibly, given their respective motives for playing the game. But mainstream editors and reporters may be forgiven for wondering just how long they can remain central in dramas like this one. When the gate's been toppled, how long does the keeper keep a job?

—This article was originally published on December 2, 2010

DANGEROUS LIAISONS

By DAVID KAHN

David Kahn is the author of
"The Codebreakers" and "The Reader of Gentlemen's Mail."

Great Neck, N.Y.

A British ambassador to Venice in the 17th century observed that "a diplomat is an honest man sent abroad to lie for his country." But for centuries, diplomats did more than lie. They bribed, they stole, they intercepted dispatches. Perhaps this will come as some consolation to the many American diplomats whose faces have been reddened by the trove of diplomatic cables released this week by WikiLeaks: whatever they've done cannot compare in underhandedness with what ambassadors did in the past.

In 16th-century London, for instance, a French ambassador paid another diplomat's secretary 60 crowns a month to read the dispatches to which the secretary had access. By the 1700s, a large part of the British Foreign Office's annual expenses of £67,000 was allocated for bribery.

But as a scene of diplomatic misbehavior, London could hardly measure up to Vienna. Prince Wenzel Anton von Kaunitz, an 18th-century Austrian foreign minister, took no monetary bribes, but he accepted expensive presents like horses, paintings and fine wines from people who wanted to influence him. Viennese prostitutes also enjoyed unusual access to the diplomatic corps; one such woman, during the Congress of Vienna in 1815, received a salary from an adjutant of Czar Alexander I, and provided him with information she learned during her visits with other envoys.

These practices had begun in the Middle Ages, when negotiators of treaties would gather information about the host nation. They continued in the Renaissance with the advent of permanent embassies. And the belief that the ambassador was a legalized spy never left the hosts' minds.

Accordingly, governments intercepted the correspondence of diplomats accredited to them. Specialists in curtained, candle-lighted "black chambers" slid hot wires under wax seals to open letters. Those in foreign languages were translated; those in code, decrypted. Their contents were then passed along to kings and ministers.

The black chamber of Vienna was the most efficient. It received the bags of mail going to and from the embassies at 7 a.m.; letters were opened, copied and returned to the post office by 9:30. When the British ambassador complained that he had gotten British letters sealed not with his seal but with that of another country—clear evidence that they had been opened—Kaunitz calmly replied, "How clumsy these people are."

When the French ambassador to Russia, the Marquis de La Chétardie, in 1744 protested an order for him to leave, an official began reading him his intercepted letters, showing his meddling in Russian affairs. "That's enough!" the marquis said—and began packing.

The mores of diplomacy began to change in the 19th century, pushed first by the spread of democracy and republican government. Public opinion came to regard it as wrong and unbecoming to a democracy to do anything illegal—in particular when representing itself abroad. Other factors in that change, according to the British diplomat and writer Harold Nicolson, lay in the emerging sense of the community of nations and of the importance of public opinion. As Lord Palmerston, the mid-19th-century British prime minister, maintained, opinions are stronger than armies.

This shift was exemplified by a growing belief that mail shouldn't be tampered with. In Britain in the 1840s, there was a huge public outcry over the post office's opening of the mail of the Italian revolutionary Giuseppe Mazzini; at the time, the English historian and politician Thomas Babington Macaulay declared that it was as wrong to take his letter from the mail as to take it from his desk. And when the Vienna Convention on Diplomatic Relations was passed in 1961, among its prescriptions was that "the official correspondence of the mission shall be inviolable."

Ambassadors now regard themselves as ladies and gentlemen. They do not lie. They do not steal. But in some ways, diplomacy has not advanced beyond the old ways. And diplomatic cables can always be intercepted or revealed—as WikiLeaks has demonstrated.

—This article was originally published on December 2, 2010

THE SECRET LIVES OF NATIONS

By PAUL W. SCHROEDER

*Paul W. Schroeder, a professor emeritus of history
at the University of Illinois Urbana-Champaign, is the author of
"The Transformation of European Politics, 1763-1848."*

Champaign, Ill.

While it is too soon to offer any meaningful perspective about the impact of the WikiLeaks disclosures on American foreign policy, it is not too early to reflect on what the leaked diplomatic cables say about the public's understanding of how diplomacy works.

WikiLeaks's justification for releasing confidential State Department materials is that the more the public knows about how our government conducts its foreign relations, the better the outcome will be. This is an old idea: Woodrow Wilson advocated "open covenants of peace, openly arrived at." But history also shows that open diplomacy is often fatally flawed.

Secrecy is an essential part of any negotiation: no corporate merger, complicated legal settlement, amicable divorce or serious political compromise could ever be reached without a reliable level of confidentiality.

But secrecy is nowhere more essential than in foreign relations. For example, had the various diplomats negotiating the end of the cold war and the unification of Germany had to deal with public revelations of the disagreements, half-baked proposals and reckless language in their internal communications—like Margaret Thatcher's opposition to German unification versus Helmut Kohl's determination to achieve it—substantive talks would have been impossible.

Secrecy was likewise vital after World War I. After a series of debilitating leaks, the leaders of the four primary victors—Britain, France, Italy and the United States—abandoned their policy of open diplomacy and went into closed sessions. Only then were they able to navigate the difficult details of the Treaty of Versailles and reach a final, if relatively short-lived, peace.

The WikiLeaks disclosures have been praised by many who believe that they will allow the public to hold the government more accountable and thus improve American foreign policy. On the contrary, leaks like this simply make those in power retreat further into the shadows to defend themselves and their positions. Consider how Richard Nixon and Henry Kissinger cut off all but their inner circle of advisers after the Pentagon Papers were published.

To be fair, there can be value in strategically timed leaks. For example, in 1870 Otto von Bismarck, Prussia's minister-president, leaked a confidential dispatch by King Wilhelm I about his meeting with the French ambassador. Bismarck had edited the document to give the impression that France had made unacceptable demands of the king (which was true) and that Wilhelm had rudely shown the ambassador the door (which was not).

Bismarck's move put both countries' honor on the line and aroused nationalist passions on both sides, escalating an existing crisis into a war that ended in a total Prussian victory, one that fulfilled Bismarck's goal of increasing Prussian power in Central Europe.

Whatever one thinks of Bismarck's aims, his calculated, targeted leak served his purposes well. But releasing confidential diplomatic correspondence to influence foreign relations, whether it's done by governments or by unauthorized individuals, is like using dynamite in a construction zone. Carried out by experts after a careful analysis of the risks involved, it may be effective, like blowing off part of a hillside to build a road.

But the WikiLeaks disclosure, on a scale that, to my knowledge, is historically unprecedented, is totally different — more like the work of irresponsible amateurs using dynamite to expand a tunnel that also contains, say, a city's electrical lines. The leaks will probably not cause war or even a serious crisis, but they will badly damage America's diplomatic machinery, processes and reputation.

None of this means that diplomatic correspondence and negotiations should remain secret forever. But except in special instances, confidential communications ought to be released only after passions have settled and scholars can examine the records in fuller context.

Especially in a democracy, the goal of negotiations should be to quietly reach an agreement, followed by ratification or rejection by elected legislators. In other words, open covenants of peace, secretly arrived at.

—This article was originally published on December 2, 2010

WHY IRAN LOVES WIKILEAKS

By CHAS FREEMAN

Chas Freeman was an assistant secretary of defense
from 1993 to 1994 and the United States ambassador to Saudi Arabia
during the Persian Gulf war.

The editor of WikiLeaks, Julian Assange, has much in common with the anarchists of the early 20th century: he aims to disrupt the established order by impairing its alliances and violating its proprieties. With the release of a quarter-million documents written by American diplomats at home and abroad, many of them shockingly candid, he has gone some distance toward accomplishing this. Take the Middle East, for example.

Most striking were the leaks regarding Arab concerns about Iran's aspirations for regional hegemony and its nuclear programs. According to the documents, King Abdullah of Saudi Arabia exhorted the United States to cripple Iran's nuclear programs with air strikes, urging us to "cut off the head of the snake." While some hard-line analysts and pundits are relieved to find the Arabs "on our side" and feel that this disclosure will help us form a stronger alliance against Tehran, it's more likely that the leaks will simply raise Iran's prestige by adding to the persistent overestimation of its influence and abilities.

More troubling, the leaks will reduce the candor of American dialogue in the region and elsewhere. Arab leaders in particular will now think twice before either speaking honestly or telling American visitors or diplomats what Washington wants to hear.

In addition, Arab rulers, despite all the weapons their states have bought from America and elsewhere, again find themselves exposed to their own people as impotent to handle a serious regional problem. They appear totally dependent on the United States, a country that is deeply unpopular among Arabs for its policies in the region, to take care of it for them.

What comes through loud and clear in these cables is a familiar Gulf Arab refrain: "We have a problem we don't know how to deal with. You

Americans must solve it for us. Do what you think best. We'll look the other way if necessary."

Israel, for its part, has been quick to assert that the leaks show that it and the Gulf Arab states have a common outlook regarding Iran. "More and more states, governments and leaders in the Middle East and the wider region and the world believe this is the fundamental threat," Prime Minister Benjamin Netanyahu said when asked about the cables.

"No one will now be able to allege that Israel is acting irresponsibly," wrote Aluf Benn, a columnist for the Israeli daily Haaretz. "When the King of Saudi Arabia and the King of Jordan call for lopping off the head of the Iranian snake, no one will believe them when they denounce an Israeli operation." But there is little to back up such claims. Israel has long wanted the United States to attack Iran's nuclear facilities. It has also strongly implied that if Washington refuses to do so, it will go ahead on its own—in a manner calculated to leave the United States no choice but to join it in war with Iran.

The Gulf Arabs want to forestall Iranian nuclear ambitions, but they are willing to defer to American judgment about how best to achieve that, and they certainly don't want it to result in a war in their own neighborhood. Clearly, this is a very different position from the one held by Mr. Netanyahu.

There are other ways in which the Arabs and Israelis are at odds on Iran policy. The leaks show that Gulf Arab rulers are concerned above all that a nuclear-armed Iran would have greater prestige in the region and ever-greater influence in Iraq, Syria, Lebanon, the West Bank and Gaza. The nuclear weapons themselves, they feel, are primarily a threat to Israel and American forces in the region.

Yes, Israelis fear that Iran might gratuitously attempt another Holocaust by attacking them. But the leaked documents also show that one of the main worries Israel has about Iran's nuclear ambitions is that it could lose its regional monopoly on nuclear weapons, limiting their leverage on a whole range of issues. One doubts the Gulf Arabs share that concern.

In the end, contrary to the hopes and fears of some, the leaks do not make war with Iran more likely or demonstrate a basis for Arab-Israeli solidarity against Tehran. Mr. Assange's grand accomplishment will be nothing more than to make it far harder for American diplomats to get candid answers from their Gulf Arab and Israeli counterparts.

The Middle East is a place where yes means maybe, maybe means no, no is never heard (except in Israel), and a plea for a foreign solution to regional problems is a cop-out, not a serious request for action. It is where hypocrisy first gained a bad name. WikiLeaks has hurt America without changing that.

—This article was originally published on December 4, 2010

THE BIG AMERICAN LEAK

By THOMAS L. FRIEDMAN

O.K. I admit it. I enjoy reading other people's mail as much as the next guy, so going through the WikiLeaks cables has made for some fascinating reading. What's between the lines in those cables, though, is another matter. It is a rather sobering message. America is leaking power.

Let's start, though, with what's in the cables. I think I've figured it out: Saudi Arabia and its Arab neighbors want the U.S. to decapitate the Iranian regime and destroy its nuclear facilities so they can celebrate in private this triumph over the hated Persians, while publicly joining with their people in the streets in burning Uncle Sam in effigy, after we carry out such an attack on Iran—which will make the Arab people furious at us. The reason the Arab people will be furious at us, even though many of them don't like the Persians either, is because they dislike their own unelected leaders even more and protesting against the Americans, who help to keep their leaders in power, is a way of sticking it to both of us.

Are you with me?

While the Saudis are urging us to take out Iran's nuclear capability, we learn from the cables that private Saudi donors today still constitute the most significant source of funding to Sunni terrorist groups worldwide—not to mention the fundamentalist mosques, charities and schools that spawn the Taliban in Pakistan and Afghanistan. So basically our oil payments are cycled through Saudi Arabia and end up funding the very militants whom our soldiers are fighting. But don't think we don't have allies. . . . The cables tell us about Ahmed Zia Massoud, an Afghan vice president from 2004 to 2009, who now owns a palatial home in Dubai, where, according to one cable, he was caught by customs officials carrying $52 million in unexplained cash. It seems from these cables that the U.S. often has to pay leaders in Pakistan and Afghanistan to be two-faced—otherwise they would just be one-faced and against the U.S. in both public and private.

Are you still with me?

Yes, these are our allies—people whose values we do not and never will share. "O.K.," our Saudi, Gulf, Afghan and Pakistani allies tell us, "we may not be perfect, but the guys who would replace us would be much worse. The Taliban and Al Qaeda are one-faced. They say what they mean in public and private: They hate America."

That's true, but if we are stuck supporting bad regimes because only worse would follow, why can't we do anything to make them reform? That brings us to the sobering message in so many of these cables: America lacks leverage. America lacks leverage in the Middle East because we are addicted to oil. We are the addicts and they are the pushers, and addicts never tell the truth to their pushers.

When we import $28 billion a month in oil, we can't say to the Saudis: "We know the guys who would come after you would be much worse, but why do we have to choose between your misrule and corruption and their brutality and intolerance?" We're just stuck supporting a regime that, sure, fights Al Qaeda at home, but uses our money to fund a religious ideology, schools, mosques and books that ensure that Al Qaeda will always have a rich pool of recruits in Saudi Arabia and abroad. We also lack leverage with the Chinese on North Korea, or with regard to the value of China's currency, because we're addicted to their credit.

Geopolitics is all about leverage. We cannot make ourselves safer abroad unless we change our behavior at home. But our politics never connects the two.

Think how different our conversations with Saudi Arabia would be if we were in the process of converting to electric cars powered by nuclear, wind, domestic natural gas and solar power? We could tell them that if we detect one more dollar of Saudi money going to the Taliban then they can protect themselves from Iran.

Think how different our conversations with China would be if we had had a different savings rate the past 30 years and China was not holding $900 billion in U.S. Treasury securities—but was still dependent on the U.S. economy and technology. We would not be begging them to revalue their currency, and maybe our request that China prevent North Korea from shipping ballistic missile parts to Iran via Beijing airport (also in the cables) wouldn't be rebuffed so brusquely.

And think how much more leverage our sanctions would have on Iran if oil were $20 a barrel and not $80—and Iran's mullah-dictators were bankrupt?

Fifty years ago, the world was shaped in a certain way, to promote certain values, because America had the leverage to shape it that way. We have been steadily losing that leverage because of our twin addictions to Middle East oil and Chinese credit—and the WikiLeaks show just what crow we have to eat because of that. I know, some problems—like how we deal with a failing state like Pakistan that also has nukes—are innately hard, and ending our oil and credit addictions alone will not solve them. But it sure would give us more leverage to do so—and more insulation from the sheer madness of the Middle East if we can't.

—This article was originally published on December 4, 2010

IS JULIAN ASSANGE
HELPING THE NEOCONS?

By ROBERT WRIGHT

It turns out our government has been lying to us about whether we have troops in Pakistan engaging in combat operations. The Pentagon has said the mission of American soldiers is confined to "training Pakistani forces so that they can in turn train other Pakistani military," but in fact our forces have been embedded in Pakistani fighting units, giving them electronic data and other support as they kill the enemy.

We know this because of WikiLeaks. It's also thanks to WikiLeaks that we know about America's arrangement with the President of Yemen: we kill Yemen-based terrorists and he claims that Yemen is doing the killing.

In these respects, I think, WikiLeaks is doing God's work. I realize there are tactical rationales for both of these deceptions, but I don't see them trumping the bedrock right of citizens in a democracy to know when their tax dollars are being used to kill people—especially when those people live in countries we're not at war with. So, if we're going to calculate Julian Assange's net karma, I'd put this stuff on the positive side of the ledger.

And calculate we must. Assange will presumably get Time magazine's Person of the Year nod, and Time will no doubt remind us that the award recognizes impact, not virtue; Hitler and Stalin are past winners. It will be left for us to decide whether to file Assange under good or evil. Let's get started.

Assange has an elaborate rationale for his actions. He laid it out in a grandiose online manifesto that ranges from the undeniably plausible ("If total conspiratorial power is zero, there is no conspiracy") to the eccentrically metaphorical ("What does a conspiracy compute? It computes the next action of the conspiracy") to the flat-out opaque. But the gist of his argument is clear. He thinks a basic problem with the world is "authoritarian regimes," a term that he uses—in stark contrast with its American usage—to include America.

An authoritarian regime, he says, oppresses people and keeps its plans secret from the oppressed. Transparency rips the veil off, exposing these plots. And radical transparency—like the WikiLeaks data dump—makes authoritarian regimes guarded in their future internal communications. This in turn impairs the regime's functioning. As "more leaks induce fear and paranoia," we see "system-wide cognitive decline resulting in decreased ability to hold onto power." (In this respect, as the journalist Glenn Greenwald has noted, Assange is like Osama bin Laden: he wants his enemy to react to his provocations self-destructively.)

Assange wrote these things in 2006, and it's hard to imagine that he didn't have the Bush administration in mind. Certainly Bush was big on centralizing power, and wasn't big on civil liberties, and sometimes he kept his infringements on our liberties secret. Assange is in this sense the anti-Bush, challenging secretive, centralized authority with a transparency that is highly decentralized. (His backers have created mirror Web sites to ensure access to the WikiLeaks documents, and Assange says that more than 100,000 people possess the whole archive in encrypted form.)

Yet in one sense Assange is the anti-anti-Bush.

Bush was criticized for unilateralist tendencies, for failing to nurture good relations with other nations—and, in particular, for writing off suspect nations (see "axis of evil") as barely worth talking to at all. Obama came into office vowing "engagement." He would reach out to other nations, emphatically including those with whom relations were most fraught, like Russia and Muslim nations, even including Iran.

Engagement is the search for win-win outcomes to non-zero-sum games. As any game theorist can tell you, a key to reaching those outcomes is communication, and the communication is most fruitful when there is mutual trust. Well, thanks to Assange, many nations will now hesitate to speak candidly with us, fearing that their private utterances might go public.

Communication, and trust, may also be cooled by our recently revealed appraisals of foreign leaders. I'm guessing the Turks won't warm to the cable from Ankara that looked forward to a day when "we will no longer have to deal with the current cast of [Turkish] political leaders, with their special yen for destructive drama and rhetoric." And Vladimir Putin can't be liking our depiction of him as a slacker thug.

Many of our foreign relations will prove resilient. Longstanding European allies will get over the insults, and will eventually accept assurances that we're tightening the security of our missives. But such ready rapprochement is less likely with the Russias and Turkeys of the world—nations that are more culturally remote from us and were less secure in our friendship to begin with. In other words, the relationships that will suffer the deepest damage are the most fragile ones, the ones that Obama entered office hoping to mend with engagement.

These include many of the relationships that the neoconservatives who shaped Bush's foreign policy were most willing to risk. Neocons have often encouraged policies and utterances that threatened relations with Russia and Turkey, as well as China, Iran and so on. Indeed, neoconservatism sometimes seems devoted to exacerbating the world's major geopolitical fault lines. And now WikiLeaks has advanced the exacerbation. Maybe Assange, when he has time for some fresh conspiracy theorizing, can look into the possibility that neocons have implanted electrodes in his brain.

From where I stand—a position of emphatic anti-Bushism—this is a pretty serious charge: aiding and abetting anti-anti-Bushism. But, from this same standpoint, there's a defense of Assange to be made.

The biggest lesson from all of this is a fact that's already dawned on Tiger Woods, Michael Phelps and Mel Gibson: privacy ain't what it used to be. Technology has made secrets hard to keep.

Sure, we can better insulate our channels of communication—for starters by not giving Army privates access to the family jewels. But we don't want to fall into Assange's trap of constricting our internal communications to a dysfunctional extent—and, besides, we can't control what foreign bureaucracies are doing with shared secrets. We have to face the fact that secrets are less keepable in the age of the Internet, when a single malcontent in any organization can share newsworthy information with the whole world.

So incendiary secrets should be avoided. It's best not to lie about what our troops in Pakistan are doing, and not to conspire with Yemen's government to deceive Yemenis. For one thing, such deceptions, when exposed, embitter foreigners toward America. And these days grassroots hatred of America, especially in Muslim countries, is perhaps our biggest enemy— being, as it is, the wellspring of terrorism.

If our government took this guidance, and quit keeping explosive secrets about what it's doing abroad, then what it's doing abroad would change. If our troops' presence in Pakistan was going to be visible, Pakistan might not let them into the country. And the Yemeni government might veto transparently American drone strikes.

This would mean killing fewer terrorists in the short run, but it would probably mean creating way fewer of them in the long run. Certainly (as the journalist John Judis has suggested) it would mean doing less of what fueled bin Laden's anti-American wrath in the first place: having a military presence in Muslim countries, a presence that sometimes entails collaborating with repressive regimes and thus absorbing some of the hatred they inspire.

I don't know if this change of course would make up for the considerable short-term damage wrought by WikiLeaks—the harm done to fragile and crucial relations with other states, the blowback that even now is starting to well up in Yemen, Pakistan and elsewhere. But if it does, then Assange's initially pro-neocon impact could be dwarfed by his longer-term, more benign influence. And his karma, as I calculate it, would move into positive territory.

For that to happen—for the United States to respond wisely to the WikiLeaks fiasco—American policymakers will first have to realize that Assange himself isn't all that important. If he had never been born, they would still eventually have to adapt to the age of transparency, to a world in which expedient lies to cover expedient collaborations with dubious regimes are a long-term threat to our national security. Sooner or later, America was bound to wake up to the implications of modern technology. Julian Assange just made it a particularly rude awakening.

Postscript

First, for the record, I think that for the United States to prosecute Assange would be idiotic, un-American and a threat to the future health of investigative journalism. Second, the New Republic piece by John Judis that I linked to above ["A Defense of WikiLeaks," TNR, Dec. 1, 2010] is well worth reading. Judis emphasizes, as I do, the possible virtues of WikiLeaks exposing secret deals with other countries, but he situates his analysis in a different context: the history of imperialism, and the periodic disruption of imperialist schemes by revelation of the secret deals they involve. In this view, America's alliances with dubious regimes—whether to secure oil, cooperation against terrorism, whatever—are a form of neo-imperialism, and WikiLeaks is anti-imperialist. Judis himself doesn't necessarily embrace the characterization of American foreign policy as neo-imperialist, but I'm pretty sure Assange would, and that leads to one other point:

Offputtingly grandiose as Assange's online manifesto is, it arguably envisions exactly the effect that Judis and I are talking about. Assange's definition of "authoritarian regime" seems fluid enough to simultaneously refer to America and the "neo-imperialist" network America has assembled. And if that's the case, then the fraying of that network would be an example of what his paper gleefully envisions: an "authoritarian regime"—i.e. the network of America and certain allies—finds that transparency has rendered the internal information-processing that sustains it no longer viable, and so collapses. (Assange, by the way, seems to see all authoritarian regimes as consisting of conspiracies among their constituents—and since conspiracies always require secrets, transparency is anti-conspiracy and hence, in Assange's paradigm, anti-authoritarian.)

—This article was originally published on December 7, 2010

OUR ENVOYS, OURSELVES

By DEREK LEEBAERT

*Derek Leebaert, a management consultant, is the author of
"Magic and Mayhem: The Delusions of American Foreign Policy
From Korea to Afghanistan."*

Washington

A global power's diplomatic archives are inevitably full of caustic dispatches. In Britain, a new batch of Foreign Office records is declassified each January under the "30-year rule" (a "50-year rule" before 1968). Historians can peruse elegantly handwritten mockeries of President Eisenhower's name as exotically Eastern European, or files deriding Americans as the planet's "most excitable" people—other than Bangladeshis.

For the most part, such documents provide little more than a snapshot of a moment in history or a window into the mind of a particular diplomat. Over the last two weeks, however, WikiLeaks has opened another perspective. Its quarter-million cables provide a sample broad enough to reflect the culture in which American foreign policy takes shape.

We encounter the mind-set of a freewheeling, democratic superpower, a pattern of thought that shows great excitement over celebrities and moments hailed as irreversibly world-changing. In this, the State Department truly represents our national disposition.

A century ago, a foreign journalist asked the theatrical impresario Charles Frohman why one saw only actors' names on Broadway marquees, whereas in Paris the names in lights were those of playwrights. Frohman explained that in America, the emphasis is always on the doer, not the thing done: "There are stars in every walk of American life. It has always been so in democracies." It remains true today: as the most individualistic of all democracies, America creates, rewards, obsesses over stars of every kind and intensely extols personal success.

WikiLeaks has shown how these enthusiasms play out overseas. The pages of the leaked cables hum with high-level gossip and trenchant cameos.

Chancellor Angela Merkel of Germany "avoids risk and is seldom creative"; a "penchant for partying hard" has left Prime Minister Silvio Berlusconi of Italy "a complete mess"; President Nicolas Sarkozy of France is thin-skinned and has "monarchial tendencies"; Prime Minister Vladimir Putin of Russia is like a Mafia godfather but also "resents or resists the workload he carries."

The danger is that personalization, however accurate, can get in the way of sharper assessments of resources, national aims and public attitudes. Knowing delicious details of le tout Paris, for instance, still left Washington unprepared for France's refusal to join in the invasion of Iraq in 2003.

Similarly, as America sets out to build nations in the undeveloped world, it keeps discovering new heroes who, eventually, turn out to be less than the supermen they were once considered. There is Hamid Karzai, previously the savior of Afghanistan, now revealed by WikiLeaks as (at best) unaware that his brother may be a major figure in the opium trade.

This is an old story. In the 1950s there was Syngman Rhee in South Korea; in Vietnam, there was Ngo Dinh Diem, the "Churchill of Asia"; then the shadowy Ahmed Chalabi was supposed by the Bush administration to be "the George Washington of Iraq." The problem is that Washington too often finds itself with few choices but to keep working with such figures even after they no longer appear indispensable (or, like Diem, have to be dispensed with).

America's thirst to single out great figures is matched by the desire to be on hand at history's great events. Repeatedly, however, we fail to put such moments in context, and thus inflate their significance in the grand sweep of history.

Emerson was right to call us "the country of tomorrow." We live in the future, are first to adopt the Next New Thing. From this outlook springs a casual approach to how the world moves and changes: the sense that destiny shifts easily, suddenly, for obvious reasons. Remember how "everything" was deemed to have been transformed by the 9/11 attacks, or the fall of the Berlin Wall, or the 1972 summit meeting in Beijing that President Richard Nixon described as "the week that changed the world."

So in WikiLeaks we see expectations that one death in North Korea—that of the dictator Kim Jong-il—will transform a system in which thousands of people are brutally invested. (Never mind that it rode right on when Mr. Kim's father, Kim Il-sung, died in 1994.) As for Iran, WikiLeaks shows Washington anticipating yet another "different world," which is what Secretary of Defense Robert Gates told Italy's foreign minister would occur should Tehran get nuclear weapons.

The leaking of secret documents is hardly to be encouraged. Wiki-Leaks may imperil the lives of agents or compromise negotiations, and is certainly arming our enemies with awkward knowledge. But that doesn't mean we can't learn from the cables. Let's hope that the exposure of our diplomatic fixations on personalities and allegedly world-changing events will lead us, in fact, to a less excitable, more informed foreign policy.

—This article was originally published on December 11, 2010

WE'VE ONLY GOT AMERICA A

By THOMAS L. FRIEDMAN

Former President José María Figueres of Costa Rica has a saying I like: "There is no Planet B"—so we'd better make Plan A work to preserve a stable environment. I feel the same way about America these days. There is no America B, so we'd better make this one work a lot better than we've been doing, and not only for our sake. When Britain went into decline as the globe's stabilizing power, America was right there, ready to pick up the role. Even with all our imperfections and mistakes, the world has been a better place for it. If America goes weak, though, and cannot project power the way it has, your kids won't just grow up in a different America. They will grow up in a different world. You will not like who picks up the pieces. Just glance at a few recent headlines.

The world system is currently being challenged by two new forces: a rising superpower, called China, and a rising collection of superempowered individuals, as represented by the WikiLeakers, among others. What globalization, technological integration and the general flattening of the world have done is to superempower individuals to such a degree that they can actually challenge any hierarchy—from a global bank to a nation state—as *individuals*.

China has put on a sound and light show these past few weeks that underscored just how much its rising economic clout can be used to warp the U.S.-led international order when it so chooses. I am talking specifically about the lengths to which China went to not only reject the Nobel Peace Prize given to one of its citizens—Liu Xiaobo, a democracy advocate who is serving an 11-year sentence in China for "subversion of state power"—but to intimidate China's trading partners from even sending representatives to attend the Nobel award ceremony at Oslo's City Hall.

Mr. Liu was represented at Friday's Nobel ceremony by an empty chair because China would not release him from prison—only the fifth time in the 109-year history of the prize that the winner was not in attendance. Under pressure from Beijing, the following countries joined China's boycott of the ceremony: Serbia, Morocco, Pakistan, Venezuela, Afghanistan, Colombia, Ukraine, Algeria, Cuba, Egypt, Iran, Iraq, Kazakhstan, Russia, Saudi Arabia, Sudan, Tunisia, Vietnam and the Philippines. What a pathetic bunch.

"The empty chair in Oslo's Town Hall last Friday was not only that of Liu, but of China itself," observed Rowan Callick, a columnist for The Australian. "The world is still waiting for China to play its proper, full role in international affairs. The perversity of such a successful, civilized nation playing a dominant role as a backer—if sometimes merely by default—of cruel, failed or failing states is intensely frustrating."

It gets worse. The Financial Times reported that "outside Mr. Liu's apartment in Beijing, where his wife Liu Xia has been held under house arrest since the award was announced, large blue screens were erected, preventing television cameras from having a view of the building."

Honestly, I thought China's leaders had more self-confidence than that. Clearly, they are feeling very insecure. Think if China had said instead: "We disagree with this award and we will not be attending. But anytime one of our citizens is honored with a Nobel, it is an honor for all of China—and so we will pass this on to his family." It would have been a one-day story, and China's leaders would have looked so strong.

As for the superempowered individuals—some are constructive, some are destructive. I read many WikiLeaks and learned some useful things. But their release also raises some troubling questions. I don't want to live in a country where they throw whistle-blowers in jail. That's China. But I also don't want to live in a country where any individual feels entitled to just dump out all the internal communications of a government or a bank in a way that undermines the ability to have private, confidential communications that are vital to the functioning of any society. That's anarchy.

But here's the fact: A China that can choke off conversations far beyond its borders, and superempowered individuals who can expose conversations far beyond their borders—or create posses of "cyberhacktivists" who can melt down the computers of people they don't like—are now a reality. They are rising powers. A stable world requires that we learn how to get the best from both and limit the worst; it will require smart legal and technological responses.

For that job, there is no alternative to a strong America. Critics said of the British Labour Party of the 1960s that the Britain they were trying to build was half-Sweden and half-heaven. The alternative today to a world ordered by American power is not some cuddly multipolar system—half-Sweden and half-heaven. It is half-China and halfsuperempowered individuals.

Managing that will never be easy. But it will be a lot easier with a healthy America, committed to its core values, powerful enough to project them and successful enough that others want to follow our lead—voluntarily.

—This article was originally published on December 14, 2010

THE WIKILEAKS DEBATE

By TOBIN HARSHAW

Tobin Harshaw, a staff editor with the Op-Ed page of The Times,
writes the Thread column for nytimes.com.

WikiLeaks is a pure product of the Internet, so it's hardly surprising that so much of the debate over its document drops in 2010 involved dueling bloggers and other online pundits. Across the Web, commentators of every stripe assessed the political, ethical, legal and technological ramifications of the case. For some, the WikiLeaks affair was glorious confirmation of the old saying among technology advocates and futurists that "information wants to be free." After WikiLeaks released U.S. military war logs from Afghanistan in July, the blogger Mistermix wrote at the liberal site Balloon Juice, "What really scares a lot of establishment types is not WikiLeaks itself, but that a group of soldiers or civilians with access to information have started to work against the war from the inside, and that they have a secure conduit to get that information to the outside world."

Others, however, found that such freedoms were not worth having. "Assange is giving us a wonderful lesson in why things are classified during war," wrote Joshua Foust, who runs Registan.net, a blog about Central Asia. "His cavalier attitude toward the safety of the people he exposes to mortal danger, as if a really terrible context like a war provides justification for adding further risk to their lives (and his repeated, and thus far unsupported, accusations that Afghans who help us are criminals), is beyond immaturity and callousness, though—it is monstrous. Julian Assange is the worst sort of moralist, one whose sense of justice is so selective (secrecy is of utmost concern for WikiLeaks' sources and employees, but not the government), and his comprehension of consequences so shortsighted and defined by ideology rather than fact, that he doesn't care who he has to offer up to murderous bastards to satisfy his sense of moral outrage."

And there were a few bloggers who found the whole thing overblown. "Is there anything Julian Assange ever gets right?" asked Rusty Shackleford at the right-wing site Jawa Report. "Seriously, on top of being a pathological liar and a paranoid conspiracy theorist, the WikiLeaks founder also doesn't get that we've all known pretty much all of this for years. The ISI helps the Taliban? Check. Drones are prone to crashing? Check. The drones often miss their intended targets? Check. Yawn."

There was no such sleepiness after the release of the Iraq war logs in October, which contained reports of torture, rape and murder by Iraqi security forces and noted the repeated failure of American officials to do anything about it. Chris Bertram, a British philosophy professor who blogs with other academics at Crooked Timber, thinks that the revelation of human-rights abuses cracked the ice beneath the feet of liberal supporters of the war. "It has become commonplace for self-styled leftist erstwhile advocates of the Iraq War to whine that their critics have been unkind to them," he wrote. "Can't those critics accept, they wheedle, that there were reasons on both sides and that the crimes against humanity of the Saddam regime supported at least a prima facie case for intervention? During an earlier phase of discussion, when those advocates were still unapologetic, but whilst the slaughter was well under way, we were treated to numerous disquisitions on moral responsibility: yes there is slaughter, but we are not responsible, it is Al Qaida/the Sunni 'insurgents'/Al- Sadr/Iran."

"Well," he continued, "the latest WikiLeaks disclosures ought to shut them up for good (it won't, of course). 'Our' side has both committed war crimes directly and has acquiesced, enabled, and covered up for the commission of such crimes by others. The incidents are not isolated episodes: rather we have systematic policy. The U.S. government has a duty to investigate and to bring those of its own officials and military responsible to justice. Of course, this won't happen and the Pentagon will pursue the whistle-blowers instead. So it goes."

The assumption that the logs put American forces in a poor light was not universal. On the site Hot Air, the blogger calling himself Allahpundit wrote that "The Times's write-up of the torture documents notes that coalition troops 'often intervened' to stop abuse when they saw it" and that under American policy, "if Iraqi troops or cops were doing the abusing, it was the Iraqi government's problem to deal with them. Al Jazeera notes that, since Iraq officially became sovereign again on June 30, 2004, there was no legal obligation for occupying forces to police Iraqi security." He also thought the revelations could have a major effect on the ground: "It makes it much harder for Obama to argue that Iraq doesn't need us because it's ready to police itself. According to The Guardian, incidents of abuse are recorded in the documents as recently as last December, so the problem can't be dismissed as some long-solved remnant of Iraq's darkest days in 2006. Two, and more importantly: If this news breaks big in Iraq, god only knows what it's going to do to the political situation there."

Doug Mataconis, a lawyer who writes at Outside the Beltway, a centrist site out of suburban Virginia, said: "Certainly, by regional standards, the American abuses were rather tame. The problem is that Americans are—*and should* be—held to much higher standards than the thug regimes of the Middle East. We started the war and set in motion the chain of events that put the new thugs in power. That means we bear at least some share of responsibility for their actions, especially when we're still there working with them as partners."

While left and right may not have seen eye to eye on the significance of the war logs, there was universal agreement that the State Department's diplomatic cables that began to be released in November 2010 shined a spotlight on the dusky world of global diplomacy. "There have been many comparisons of Barack Obama to Jimmy Carter, focused on the economy," wrote William A. Jacobson, a conservative Cornell law professor who blogs at Legal Insurrection. "But the continuing leak of documents by Wiki-Leaks has become for Obama what the Iranian hostage crisis was to Carter." Jacobson's complaint was with the State Department's decision to send WikiLeaks a letter asking it to stop releasing documents. "This is not about open government policy," he wrote, "as if WikiLeaks went a bit too far on its class project. Julian Assange should have been indicted by now, and if the law did not allow more punitive measures in this circumstance, then the law should have been changed after the first document dump. Assange is an enemy of our country and should be treated as such. Instead, we're writing letters and lecturing on accountable and open government. Stick a fork in Obama, he's Jimmy Carter."

As for the documents themselves, Richard Fernandez, an Australian who founded the foreign-policy blog Belmont Club, found in them alarming evidence that Obama's high-minded foreign policy was faring no better than Carter's. "The magisterial rhetoric, the grand phrases from the jut-jawed deliveries" at the teleprompter, Fernandez wrote, "translate to only one idea: kick the can down the road and please don't hit me, mister. The leaked documents, if accurate, suggest a North Korea and Iran openly testing the administration; China engaging in cyberwar against the West; American Islamic allies supporting terrorism while demanding protection and even aid. It shows a potential Iranian threat so regionally worrisome that Saudi Arabia exhorted him to 'cut off the head of the snake.'"

In the days following the initial release of the cables, as bloggers had time to digest the contents, a consensus formed that the most illuminating dispatches were those pertaining to the Middle East. Alastair Campbell, a spokesman for Tony Blair when Blair was prime minister of Britain, wrote at his eponymous blog that "in policy terms perhaps the most significant part of the leak, relates to the venom and anger with which most countries in the Middle East view Iran." He continued: "Though on one level that is not a surprise, the scale, tone and near uniformity of it did surprise me. Reading that part of the first chapter of this particular industrial dump, I was left with the impression that anyone in the U.S. system pushing for a hardening of the policy position vis-à-vis Iran would be able to build a lot of support for such a move."

Omri Ceren, a doctoral candidate in communications at the University of Southern California who blogs at Mere Rhetoric, felt the dispatches explained the disastrous June 2009 meeting between President Obama and King Abdullah of Saudi Arabia. "King Abdullah," he concluded, "expected to talk about militarily confronting Iran, and he couldn't believe it when Obama kept reciting bromides about the earth-shattering importance of the Israeli/Arab conflict and his enthusiasm for solving it." He went on: "It's not that Arab leaders don't care about the Israeli/Arab conflict or that they wouldn't want to see a Palestinian state, or that they won't pay lip service to linkage. It's just that they really, really care about stopping Iran by any means necessary—something that foreign policy experts who obsess over Israel's ostensibly central regional role can't have be true, lest their insistence that a Palestinian state is a necessary prerequisite to action on Iran seem more like personal fantasy than objective analysis."

The blogger and liberal radio host Taylor Marsh, however, felt that the concerns over a rising Iran were best understood in terms of George W. Bush's foreign policy and its unintended consequences. "The Right is making a lot of ruckus about the Saudi comments while pointing fingers at Arabists utilizing the *See Even Saudi Arabia Wants To Strike Iran*" argument, she wrote. "However, the Shia v. Sunni dynamic has been an amped up challenge ever since Pres. Bush let the neoconservatives run things, which began with the disastrous pre-emptive attack on Iraq that altered the balance of power in the region. With shifts in Lebanon, the Shia state rising has as its most important godfathers George W. Bush and Dick Cheney, intended or not, something that has been forgotten."

What, then, of the long-term effect the leaks might have on American foreign policy? Not everyone felt they gave the diplomatic corps a black eye. "The latest dump provided some embarrassing moments for the State Department in particular," wrote James Joyner at the New Atlanticist. "But they also showed that those handling America's day-to-day foreign policy are quite capable." Joyner added: "That diplomats occasionally use undiplomatic language or that functionaries sometimes say things in private about heads of state that they wouldn't dare say in public should shock no one who's spent any time in the work force. So, yes, our representatives abroad in the main look good in these releases."

Michael Cohen at the conservative site Democracy Arsenal made a strong case that the leaks would only make it harder for diplomats to achieve the sorts of aims WikiLeaks's liberal supporters would be likely to approve of. "Anyone who has worked in international affairs would understand (and this goes for Americans and non-Americans) secrecy is an essential element of diplomatic relations," he wrote. "Diplomacy actually relies on a healthy level of hypocrisy. The simple reality is that effective diplomacy and effective counterterrorism often must work in the dark. To suggest otherwise demonstrates a shocking lack of understanding about how diplomats actually operate."

"All that's happened here," he added, "is that it will now be more difficult for U.S. diplomats to do their job; it will fray relations with a key Middle East ally and ironically it will probably lead to more not less secrecy, because diplomats will be more fearful of putting their thoughts down in cables that can then be leaked to The New York Times."

The anonymous Midwestern blogger at Prairie Weather said: "Diplomacy can and does require deep secrecy. Up to a point." But, he went on, "illegal wars sustained through ten years and counting—and through two administrations—are corrosive to a democracy. Understanding and dismantling the secretive structure that make illegal wars possible is a responsible, not irresponsible, move. That's not to say they won't create huge problems for U.S. diplomacy for years to come."

Mustang Bobby, the pseudonymous liberal who blogs at Bark Bark Woof Woof, tartly observed that "in what we've seen so far from WikiLeaks, there doesn't seem to be much of a plan other than to throw everything they've got against the wall and see what sticks. From what I understand in the shadowy world of leakage journalism, the objective is to release selected information to inform the public rather than overwhelm it. In that respect, the people behind the WikiLeaks have yet to show any reason as to why they're doing it other than that they can. If that's meant to serve a purpose other than just show history in the raw and get a lot of pundits their ten minutes on *Hardball* and Fox, it's not very apparent."

But many liberals felt WikiLeaks did a job the establishment press had given up on. "Our elite media has been sloppy, lazy and corrupt for so long they have apparently forgotten what the purpose of a fourth estate actually is," said Jane Hamsher, the founder of Firedoglake.

Nicole Belle at the left-wing site Crooks and Liars, apparently comparing WikiLeaks's actions to warrantless wiretapping and the Patriot Act, said: "I'm of the belief that if this is the price we must pay to show the government that acting as if no one has a right to privacy is a double-edged sword that can hurt them as well, we might as well pay it now. If the government thinks it will damage their interests to have their corrupt actions known, perhaps they might not want to participate in them."

Paul Rosenberg of Open Left felt the government was crying wolf when it warned that the document release would have dire consequences. "Of course," he wrote, "the U.S. government is freaking out, warning of blood on the streets. News flash: There's *already* blood on the streets. As Daniel Ellsberg has explained countless times, this is what they always say. And it's virtually *always* a false alarm. Besides, blood in the streets, that's pretty much what wars, espionage and such are all about, in'it? We're supposed to worry that this massive leak will impede the ability of the U.S. government to connive in secret behind everyone's back? Well, after the past 10 years in particular, who in the world honestly thinks that would be a bad thing?"

For some on the right, however, it just means other (more capable) people will be doing the conniving. "They have effectively destroyed the credibility of the State Department, the favorite foreign policy agency of the doves," wrote the blogger TigerHawk. "What foreign diplomat would dare speak candidly with our Foreign Service now? That will make the State Department even less effective. To get anything done, the American president, whoever he or she may be, will be more likely to turn to our intelligence agencies and military, the relative influence of which on American policy is bound to increase."

The obvious summation of all this is that WikiLeaks is in the eye of the beholder. To some, it valuably exposes the machinations of American realpolitik; to others, it's a dangerous security breach that paradoxically may aid those devoted to a hawkish foreign policy. But what is it to Julian Assange himself? Aaron Bady, a graduate student at the University of California, Berkeley, who blogs as Zunguzungu, did a close reading of Assange's statements and came up with this answer:

"We all basically know that the U.S. state—like all states—is basically doing a lot of basically shady things basically all the time, simply revealing the specific *ways* they are doing these shady things will not be, in and of itself, a necessarily good thing. In some cases, it may be a bad thing, and in many cases, the provisional good it may do will be limited in scope. The question for an ethical human being—and Assange always emphasizes his ethics—has to be the question of what exposing secrets will actually accomplish, what good it will do, what better state of affairs it will bring about. And whether you buy his argument or not, Assange has a clearly articulated vision for how WikiLeaks' activities will 'carry us through the mire of politically distorted language, and into a position of clarity,' a strategy for how exposing secrets will ultimately impede the production of *future* secrets. The point of WikiLeaks—as Assange argues—is simply to make WikiLeaks unnecessary."

SHARING SECRETS
AT ARM'S LENGTH

By ARTHUR S. BRISBANE

Arthur S. Brisbane is the public editor of The New York Times.

The two stories stood side by side: one said that Julian Assange, the founder of WikiLeaks, was on the run, in fear of Western intelligence agencies and seen by some colleagues as "delusional," "erratic" and "imperious." The other story? A chilling account of war in Iraq, for which Mr. Assange and his organization were the primary source.

In publishing its latest installment of "The War Logs," which appeared in print last Saturday and Sunday, The Times confronted a stark duality. The case for reporting on nearly 400,000 classified documents was compelling, while the character of its primary source appeared increasingly sketchy.

Managing its relationship with Mr. Assange and WikiLeaks was only one of The Times's challenges in this exceptional chapter in journalism history.

As in its coverage of the Pentagon Papers, the Cuban missile crisis, surveillance by the National Security Agency and other stories involving secrecy, The Times had to choose whether to cover, how much to cover and when to publish.

The stakes were high. Just as it did in the Pentagon Papers case, when Justice Department lawyers invoked the Espionage Act to try to quash publication, The Times had to consider the possibility that the government would strike back.

More fundamentally, the newspaper had to conduct a fateful cost-benefit analysis that asked: Does the public interest in having this information outweigh the risks to coalition forces and intelligence-gathering in the war zones?

The choices were set in motion early this summer when Bill Keller, The Times's executive editor, got a call from the editor in chief of The Guardian, a British newspaper. WikiLeaks had offered The Guardian a cache of military field reports and had asked it to invite The Times, and later the German magazine Der Spiegel, to have access as well. Mr. Keller sent Eric Schmitt, an experienced war correspondent, to London to take a look at the giant trove, which included 92,000 individual military field reports from Afghanistan and more than 391,000 reports from Iraq.

Mr. Keller said no conditions were placed on the news organizations' use of the material, except that they were obligated to synchronize publication with WikiLeaks's publication online. The Times mapped out its own coverage.

"We chose the documents that struck us as most interesting," Mr. Keller said in an e-mail message. "We did our own analysis of the material. We decided what to write. We did not discuss any of those matters with WikiLeaks, or give them an advance look at our stories."

He emphasized, in other words, The Times's independence from WikiLeaks. The issue emerged as a definitive one in my conversations with veteran journalists, a legal expert and a retired general.

Some say that what's important is the material itself. Whether or not Julian Assange is a rogue with a political agenda, what matters most is that The Times authenticates the information.

"They did exactly the right thing to establish an arms-length distance," said Paul Steiger, editor-in-chief of the news organization ProPublica. "WikiLeaks is not the A.P."

David Rudenstine, a Cardozo Law School professor and author of "The Day the Presses Stopped: A History of the Pentagon Papers Case," said, "If The Times makes the judgment that this is the real thing, I don't think it matters much" who it is dealing with.

Another view holds that it is impossible to separate the legitimacy of the material from its source. In this situation, the challenge is compounded because The Times's source, WikiLeaks, obtained the material from its own source—a leaker whose identity remains uncertain.

"Did the source select which documents to turn over?" asked Bill Kovach, of the Project for Excellence in Journalism, in an e-mail message to me. "What was the nature of the transaction between WikiLeaks and the source(s)? Did WikiLeaks turn over only some documents and not others?"

Mr. Keller said the documents deserved attention, "whatever you think of WikiLeaks as an organization." He added that Times staffers scrutinized the material to satisfy themselves that it had not been manipulated.

More fundamental than the relationship between The Times and WikiLeaks is the basic question of whether it was right to publish the material at all. Most of those I spoke to echoed the comments of Leonard Downie Jr., former executive editor of The Washington Post, who called WikiLeaks's archive "newsworthy and of public interest." But there is an argument to the contrary.

Thomas E. Ricks, author of "Fiasco: The American Military Adventure in Iraq" and now contributing editor to Foreign Policy magazine, believes The Times put those in the field at great risk, with little public gain.

"What you have here is thousands of, basically, the equivalent of telephone logs, situation reports," he said. "These are not policy statements. These are not Rumsfeld ordered 'X.' It is one officer said this or heard this. It is the lowest form of information. It is crappy information being given a status it doesn't deserve, and it carries great risk."

To address the risk to troops and informants, The Times took pains to remove names and other information from the documents it published. Nevertheless, a retired Army general, who asked for anonymity to avoid bringing controversy to the civilian organization he now serves, said the field reports enable Al Qaeda and the Taliban to learn much about the operational practices and mind-set of the coalition's fighting forces.

"Analysis is not nearly as damaging as reports," he said, drawing a distinction between the Pentagon Papers and the WikiLeaks material. Field reports like these make it possible "to get into the mind of the enemy. Anytime you do that you gain a tremendous advantage."

These are powerful arguments. Ultimately, the case presented circumstances that stubbornly defied decision-making templates of the past. Daniel Ellsberg, who exposed the Pentagon Papers, needed a major news organization to publish his material. WikiLeaks, with or without The Times, could publish its material on the Internet. So The Times's choice was whether to use its resources to organize and filter material that was going public, one way or another.

The Times, in my opinion, did take a reputational risk in doing business with WikiLeaks, though it has inoculated itself somewhat by reporting independently on the organization.

The ultimate risk, of course, is to the fighting forces in the field. And I'm sure that wasn't an easy call for The Times's editors. Perhaps the decision wasn't unlike the one that A.M. Rosenthal, then managing editor of

The Times, made in the Pentagon Papers case. As Professor Rudenstine related it: "He didn't think he should play God and decide what was best for the nation. So he decided the question on its news value."

The Times faced some very tough decisions in this situation and took some risks. I think it did what it had to do.

—This article was originally published on October 30, 2010

WHAT IF THE SECRETS STAYED SECRET?

By ARTHUR S. BRISBANE

Arthur S. Brisbane is the public editor of The New York Times.

I read the Monday New York Times with what can only be described as a sinking feeling.

Here on display, based on yet another WikiLeaks release, was the breathtaking disclosure of American diplomats' highly sensitive internal communications about friends and enemies. The discreet world of confidential embassy cables had seemingly been blown apart.

The Times articles, beginning then and continuing even as I write, lasered in on United States diplomats' reporting about the most explosive situations in the world: Iran's pursuit of nuclear weapons, an out-ofcontrol and increasingly weaponized North Korea, deep instability and unreliability in Pakistan. And much more, most of it unsettling, some of it gossipy (Sarkozy is a spoiled Frenchman?) and some of it lurid enough to belong on the E! channel (cue the Chechen-strongman-gone-wild in Dagestan).

Even as The Times has unveiled these stories through the week, snapping into focus one disturbing crisis after another, it has been impossible to ignore the hand of Julian Assange, the curator of purloined secrets and founder of WikiLeaks. For this go-round, Mr. Assange had adroitly orchestrated a media rollout headed by The Guardian of Britain and joined by a handful of European news organizations, with The Times picking up the material from The Guardian.

The image of Mr. Assange as ringmaster is deeply disturbing, especially since he seems to so relish his worldwide notoriety. The image of great news organizations as performers in the ring, though, is even more alarming to me.

These are what some would view as the journalistic "problems" of this latest chapter in the WikiLeaks story: The exposed secret cables seem to

threaten what little stability there is in the world. Extreme damage control
by the United States is now urgently needed across a broad diplomatic front.
And, to cap it off, many view the episode as an exercise in master manipula-
tion of the news media by someone whose aims are obscure.

As unsettling as these issues are, it is appropriate to take a deep breath
and consider the alternative. What if, instead of publishing what it knew, The
Times had chosen to pass on WikiLeaks's 250,000-plus secret documents?

What if The Times had mulled it all over and determined that the
release of such sensitive information would endanger the government's
efforts to advance American interests in the world, and so concluded reluctantly that the newspaper would have to suppress the story?

Journalistic "problems" notwithstanding, it's simply inconceivable that
The Times would choose this path. The Times, like other serious news
organizations in democracies, exists to ferret out and publish information
—most especially information that government, business and other power
centers prefer to conceal. Arming readers with knowledge is what it's about,
and journalists are motivated to pursue that end.

The impulse to obtain and publish inaccessible information is greatly
strengthened in an age in which, if anything, government secrecy is growing.
As The Washington Post reported earlier this year in its illuminating series
"Top Secret America," the government has expanded secrecy so much that
854,000 people now hold top-secret security clearances.

For editors, the opportunity to arm readers with hard-to-get information takes on great urgency. Once an editor assesses the merits of a subject
like this one, the reporting goes forward and the story is published, albeit
sometimes with redactions to avoid putting individuals in peril. The process,
and the logic, are evident in the answer that Bill Keller, executive editor
of The Times, gave me when I asked whether he had misgivings about
publishing this material.

"No question this exercise has had its challenges," he said. "But from
the time we got a good look at the material, there was no doubt that we
wanted to publish. Of course, we considered potential legal risks and anticipated criticism, whatever we decided to do. The business of sorting and
selecting from such a vast archive was daunting. We spent a great deal of
effort on the labor of redacting potentially damaging material. Coordinating
a publication schedule with other news organizations was complicated. But
none of that ever overcame the excitement of a great story."

So were the secret cables in fact newsworthy? Some have said they broke little ground, but I would assess it differently.

The authority of American diplomats' analyses, often quoted verbatim from the cables, strengthened my understanding of the challenges the United States faces abroad. Perhaps for elite foreign policy experts, the material was less revealing. But I don't think that's the point. The real question should be: Are Times readers and Americans at large better informed on these issues because of the stories?

The answer is unquestionably yes. To cite just a few specifics:

North Korea: The Chinese don't know what's going on with Kim Jong-il's nuclear program, a surprising revelation for anyone who thought the Chinese could, as a last resort, put a lid on little brother.

Pakistan: American diplomats seriously doubt that Pakistan's military, which effectively controls the state, will ever suppress extremist groups that conduct operations against our forces in Afghanistan and threaten India. That knowledge implies continuing futility for further American efforts to combat such groups in Afghanistan.

Iran: United States officials believe that Mahmoud Ahmadinejad's government obtained so-called BM-25 missiles from North Korea, enabling Iran to extend its range enough to strike Western Europe or Moscow. This development largely explains the Obama administration's willingness to shift its missile defense strategy in Europe.

But wait, other news organizations have now weighed in to say The Times's coverage of the BM-25 missiles was misleading, that other authorities have cast strong doubt on whether such missiles even exist. That leads me to the further point: Publication isn't necessarily a short hop to the full truth. It is sometimes only a first step. But it is the essential first step in a process that has to start before the marketplace of news and information can establish the facts.

No question, the journalistic "problems" of this latest WikiLeaks episode put a lot of pressure on the news organizations that got the material. The Times was perhaps blessed this time that it didn't have to deal directly with Mr. Assange. But the path ahead was clear to Times journalists, justifiably, from the moment they saw the documents.

Consider:

What if The New York Times in 1964 had possessed a document showing that L.B.J.'s intent to strike against North Vietnam after the Gulf of

Tonkin incident was based on false information? Should it have published the material?

What if The Times had possessed documentary evidence showing that the Bush administration's claims about Saddam Hussein's weapons of mass destruction were unfounded? Should it have published the material?

These questions, which need only be posed rhetorically, supply an answer to the larger question: Would you as a reader rather have the information yourself or trust someone else to hang on to it for you?

—This article was originally published on December 4, 2010

DIPLOMATIC CABLES

A selection of the documents from a cache of a quarter-million confidential American diplomatic cables acquired by WikiLeaks. A small number of names and passages in some of the cables have been removed (XXXXXXXXXXXX) by The New York Times to protect diplomats' confidential sources, to keep from compromising American intelligence efforts or to protect the privacy of ordinary citizens. The ebook edition of *Open Secrets* includes a larger selection of these original documents.

Karzai Intervenes in Drug Cases

President Karzai and his attorney general have repeatedly intervened in major narcotics cases by ordering the release of suspects, including some with political ties to the president.

DATE 2009-08-06 05:28:00

SOURCE Embassy Kabul

CLASSIFICATION SECRET

S E C R E T KABUL 002246

SIPDIS

DEPARTMENT FOR SRAP, SCA/A, INL, EUR/PRM, INR, OSD FOR FLOURNOY, CENTCOM FOR CG CJTF-82, POLAD, JICENT KABUL FOR COS USFOR-A

E.O. 12958: DECL: 08/01/2019 TAGS: PREL, PGOV, MARR, AF SUBJECT: COMPLAINTS TO GIROA ON PRE-TRIAL RELEASES AND PARDONS OF NARCO-TRAFFICKERS

REF: REFTEL KABUL 02245

Classified By: DEPUTY AMBASSADOR FRANCIS J. RICCIARDONE FOR REASONS 1.4 (B) AND (D)

1. (S) SUMMARY: On numerous occasions we have emphasized with Attorney General Aloko the need to end interventions by him and President Karzai, who both authorize the release of detainees pre-trial and allow dangerous individuals to go free or re-enter the battlefield without ever facing an Afghan court. On July 29th, Legal Adviser Harold Hongju Koh and Deputy Ambassador Frances Ricciardone demarched Attorney General Muhammad Ishaq Aloko about our concern over pre-trial releases and presidential pardons of narco-traffickers (Reftel Kabul 02245) In Spring 2008, Post had previous demarched National Security Advisor Rassoul about our concern over pre-trial releases. Despite our complaints

and expressions of concern to the GIRoA, pre-trial releases continue. END SUMMARY

2. (S) Transfers from Bagram Theatre Internment Facility (BTIF) to the Afghan National Detention Facility (ANDF) began in Spring 2007. During that year, there was only one pre-trial release. In 2008, there were 104 pre-trial releases, almost all of which took place after President Karzai formed the Aloko Detainee Commission in April 2008. From January to March of 2009, there were 12 pre-trial releases; and 23 pre-trial releases between April and June 2009. So far in July 2009, there have been 10 pre-trial releases.

3. (S) An August 2005 exchange of diplomatic notes between the USG and the GIRoA provides the legal basis for the GIRoA,s detention and prosecution of detainees transferred into Afghan custody. Even though a multi-agency GIRoA delegation under the Aloko Detainee Commission screens all BTIF detainees who are transferred to the ANDF and assures the USG that these detainees will be prosecuted in an Afghan court, there have been 150 detainees released from the ANDF without trial since 2007, including 29 former Guantanamo Bay (GTMO) detainees. The total number of transfers to date from BTIF to ANDF is 629 detainees, plus 41 from GTMO.

— — — — — — —

PROTECTION OF NARCOTRAFFICKERS

— — — — — — —

4. (SBU) In April, President Karzai pardoned five border policemen who were caught with 124 kilograms of heroin in their border police vehicle. The policemen, who have come to be known as the Zahir Five,, were tried, convicted and sentenced to terms of 16 to 18 years each at the Central Narcotics Tribunal. But President Karzai pardoned all five of them on the grounds that they were distantly related to two individuals who had been martyred during the civil war.

5. (S) Separately, President Karzai tampered with the narcotics case of Haji Amanullah, whose father is a wealthy businessman and one of his supporters. Without any constitutional authority, Karzai ordered the police to conduct a second investigation

which resulted in the conclusion that the defendant had been framed. XXXXXXXXXXXX told XXXXXXXXXXXX he was ashamed,, of the president for his interference in this case and the case of the Zahir Five.

6. (S) In another case, a CJTF investigation concluded that 26 kilograms of heroin seized from a vehicle search belonged to Col. Jaweed, Chief of the Highway Police for Badakshan Province. Jaweed is the nephew of a powerful member of Parliament. Eventually, he was arrested and is currently serving in Pol-i-Charkhi prison. But, there is credible, but unconfirmed, intelligence indicating that President Karzai has signed a letter pardoning Jaweed that has not yet been delivered to the Supreme Court. Daudzai denied any significant pressure in this case.

7. (S) Unconfirmed intelligence also indicates that President Karzai is planning to release drug trafficker Ismal Safed, who is serving a 19-year sentence in Pol-i-Charkhi. Safed is a priority DEA target who was arrested in 2005 in possession of large quantities of heroin and a cache of weapons. In 2008, DEA conducted an operation in which an undercover officer purchased approximately three kilograms of heroin directly from Safed. Daudzai told the Deputy Ambassador that President Karzai will not pardon Safed, and that Post,s concerns about this case will reaffirm President Karzai,s decision not to interfere. E IKENBERRY

Will Extra Aid Persuade Pakistan to Cut Ties to Extremists?

Ambassador Patterson assesses United States policy toward Afghanistan and Pakistan, noting that offers of additional aid will not persuade Pakistan from cutting ties to extremist anti-India groups.

DATE 2009-09-23 15:09:00

SOURCE Embassy Islamabad

CLASSIFICATION SECRET//NOFORN

S E C R E T ISLAMABAD 002295

NOFORN

E.O. 12958: DECL: 09/23/2034 TAGS: PGOV, PREL, PTER, PINR, MOPS, EAID, PK SUBJECT: REVIEWING OUR AFGHANISTAN - PAKISTAN STRATEGY

Classified By: Ambassador Anne W. Patterson, Reasons 1.4 b and d

1. (S/NF) Summary: In response to queries posed by the National Security Council, Embassy Islamabad believes that it is not/not possible to counter al-Qaeda in Pakistan absent a comprehensive strategy that 1) addresses the interlinked Taliban threat in Afghanistan and Pakistan, 2) brings about stable, civilian government in Afghanistan, and 3) reexamines the broader role of India in the region. As the queries presuppose, the ending of Pakistani establishment support to terrorist and extremist groups, some Afghan-focused and some India-focused, is a key element for success. There is no chance that Pakistan will view enhanced assistance levels in any field as sufficient compensation for abandoning support to these groups, which it sees as an important part of its national security apparatus against India. The only way to achieve a cessation of such support is to change the Pakistan government's own perception of its security requirements. End Summary.

2. (S/NF) Al-Qaeda can operate in Pakistan's Federally Administered Tribal Areas (FATA) largely because the Taliban-related groups in these areas continue to challenge the writ of the Pakistani government. Unilateral targeting of al-Qaeda operatives and assets in these regions is an important component of dealing with the overall threat. It is not/ not, however, sufficient in and of itself to force al-Qaeda out of the FATA, so long as the territory remains largely ungoverned space. Increased unilateral operations in these areas risk destabilizing the Pakistani state, alienating both the civilian government and military leadership, and provoking a broader governance crisis in Pakistan without finally achieving the goal. To be effective, we must extend the writ of the Pakistani state into the FATA in such a way that Taliban groups can no longer offer effective protection to al-Qaeda from Pakistan's own security and law enforcement agencies in these areas. We should be under no illusion, however, that this effort will not require a multi-year, multi-agency effort.

3. (S/NF) Taliban groups in Pakistan and the regional threat posed by al-Qaeda, however, cannot be effectively dealt with absent a broader regional strategy that leads to stability in Afghanistan. Fear that the ISAF mission in Afghanistan will end without the establishment of a non-Taliban, Pakhtoon-led government friendly to Pakistan adds to the Pakistani establishment's determination not to cut its ties irrevocably to the Afghan Taliban. They fear that withdrawals of NATO countries on a date certain from Afghanistan is only the thin edge of a wedge that will be followed by other coalition partners, including the United States. Discussions of deadlines, downsizing of the American military presence, or even a denial of the additional troops reportedly to be requested by Gen. McChrystal are taken as evidence that reinforces this perception. General Kayani has been utterly frank about Pakistan's position on this. In such a scenario, the Pakistan establishment will dramatically increase support for Taliban groups in Pakistan and Afghanistan, which they see either as ultimately likely to take over the Afghan

government or at least an important counter-weight to an Indian-controlled Northern Alliance.

4. (S/NF) Most importantly, it is the perception of India as the primary threat to the Pakistani state that colors its perceptions of the conflict in Afghanistan and Pakistan's security needs. The Pakistani establishment fears a pro-India government in Afghanistan would allow India to operate a proxy war against Pakistan from its territory. Justified or not, increased Indian investment in, trade with, and development support to the Afghan government, which the USG has encouraged, causes Pakistan to embrace Taliban groups all the more closely as anti-India allies. We need to reassess Indian involvement in Afghanistan and our own policies towards India, including the growing military relationship through sizable conventional arms sales, as all of this feeds Pakistani establishment paranoia and pushes them closer to both Afghan and Kashmir-focused terrorist groups while reinforcing doubts about U.S. intentions. Resolving the Kashmir dispute, which lies at the core of Pakistan's support for terrorist groups, would dramatically improve the situation. Enhanced USG efforts in this regard should be considered.

5. (S/NF) Money alone will not/not solve the problem of al-Qaeda or the Taliban operating in Pakistan. A grand bargain that promises development or military assistance in exchange for severing ties will be insufficient to wean Pakistan from policies that reflect accurately its most deep-seated fears. The Pakistani establishment, as we saw in 1998 with the nuclear test, does not view assistance -- even sizable assistance to their own entities -- as a trade-off for national security vis-a-vis India. The lack of faith in USG intentions in Pakistan and in relation to India makes such a bargain untenable in the eyes of the Pakistani establishment. Development assistance in the context of the Pakistani counter-insurgency strategy must be accelerated and refined in order to extend the government writ to the FATA, to stabilize regions at-risk for insurgent activity and recruitment, and to offer incentives for those that desire to leave terrorist groups. It can and should

not/not be viewed as a pay-off for behavior change by the Pakistani establishment.

6. (S/NF) In the final analysis there is no short-cut to dealing with the al-Qaeda problem in Pakistan and Afghanistan. It is inextricably linked to and cannot be divorced from the Taliban problem in both countries. Nor can we hope to develop a strategy for minimizing Taliban influence and thereby al-Qaeda operational space in Pakistan's FATA absent a strategy that brings about stability in Afghanistan; the notion that precision or long-range counter-terrorism efforts can suffice are equally illusory. Afghan instability by definition leads the Pakistani establishment to increase support for the Taliban and thereby, unintentionally, create space for al-Qaeda. No amount of money will sever that link. Rather, we must reassess our regional approach and find ways to reassure the Pakistanis that they can address their long-standing national security objectives most effectively -- both to the east and to the west -- by working closely with the U.S. PATTERSON

SECRET

Faked Incineration of Seized Drugs Alleged in Guinea

After a large cocaine seizure in Guinea, this 2008 cable reports, drug control officials under pressure from the United States staged an incineration of the cocaine, along with marijuana and other drugs. But a tipster told American diplomats that the cocaine had been replaced with flour and the destruction was a "farce."

DATE 2008-03-06 14:33:00

SOURCE Embassy Conakry

CLASSIFICATION SECRET

S E C R E T CONAKRY 000184

SIPDIS

DEA / PARIS FOR R. HOUSTON / B. HALEY / T. HEDRICK DEA / LAGOS FOR S. GAYE

E.O. 12958: DECL: 05/12/2018 TAGS: ASEC, GV, PGOV, DEA, PREL, SNAR SUBJECT: SEIZED DRUGS FINALLY INCINERATED . . . OR WERE THEY?

REF: A. CONAKRY 00148 B. CONAKRY 00155 C. PARIS 00838 D. CONAKRY 00166

Classified By: ARSO Elizabeth Esparza for reasons 1.4 (b) and (d)

1. (S) SUMMARY: On April 11, 2008, Guinean police seized a shipment of cocaine, exact quantity unknown, and detained six suspects believed to be of Latin American origin (Reftel A, B). All USG requests for additional information regarding the details of the seizure or the suspects have gone unanswered (Reftel C). The mission focused its efforts to ensure the destruction of the drugs and the result of these efforts proves that corrupt elements of the government are in full control. Exactly one month after the seizure, Ambassador

and ARSO attended the alleged incineration of 390 kilos of cocaine. The incineration was a farce that fooled no one and highlighted the possible complicity of the Guinean Minister of Interior and Security and high-level police officials. END SUMMARY.

— — — — — —

A LONG-ANTICIPATED EVENT

2. (S) Over a ten-day period, the Mission in collaboration with the British Ambassador made several unsuccessful attempts to discuss the transparent destruction of the drugs. Finally, on May 2, 2008, the US and UK Ambassadors met with the Minister of Interior and Security and were given well-rehearsed assurances of the GOG's commitment to combating drug trafficking and an invitation to view the drugs, destruction (Reftel D) . The incineration initially planned for May 7 and rescheduled for May 9, finally took place on May 10, 2008.

3. (U) GOG officials in attendance included Director of OCAD Thermite Mara, Deputy Director of OCAD Zakaria Cisse, Police Director General Sekou Bangoura, Police Controller General Madifing Diane, President of the National Committee Against Drug Trafficking (CNLD) Gare, Deputy General Secretary of CNLD Aguibou Tall, and approximately three dozen OCAD agents. The Minister of Justice and the Minister of Interior and Security were also present.

— — — — — —

EXCUSES, EXCUSES, EXCUSES

4. (S) After consultations with DEA Paris, Ambassador requested permission to take a random sample of the cocaine for testing purposes. Controller General Diane automatically agreed, causing an immediate backlash from Director General Bangoura and OCAD Director Mara. Director General Bangoura found several excuses, to include concern over Ambassador and ARSO,s health and safety. He also explained that the cocaine had been treated with chemicals, rendering it useless. Director General Bangoura, in his usual arrogant and condescending fashion, refused to address the Ambassador, claiming that

this was not a matter of diplomacy, but police business. OCAD Director Mara's enraged response included direct accusations of infringement upon Guinean sovereignty. This heated exchange took place in a very public setting and was documented by the private press.

5. (S) Controller General Diane reports directly to Minister of Interior and Security Keita. OCAD Director Mara reports to Director General Bangoura, who reports to Controller General Diane. The interaction between these officials demostrates an obvious disregard for rank and seniority, which is especially concerning given that respect for hierarchy is usually the norm in Guinean culture. This begs the questions, "who's in charge?".

— — — — —

THEATRICAL PRODUCTION

— — — — —

6. (U) Upon the arrival of Minister of Interior and Security Keita and Minister of Justice Paulette Kourouma, the Ambassador's request for a random sample of the cocaine was quickly denied. The pile was immediately doused with gasoline and ceremoniously lit on fire by the Minister of Justice. The President of the National Committee Against Drug Trafficking was very dramatic in announcing the destruction of 160 kilos of marijuana, 390 kilos of cocaine and 43 boxes of pharmaceutical products (later explained to be expired ibuprofen). The destroyed narcotics were reportedly valued at 6.5 million dollars.

7. (S) After the incineration, ARSO was permitted to take a sample from a pre-designated package of cocaine. The OCAD Deputy Director, the only individual that was allowed to get near the pile of narcotics, handpicked the package. On May 6, 2008, RSO FSN Investigator received a call from XXXXXXXXXXXX, who in the past weeks has provided RSO with sensitive information on the drug seizure (Reftel B). XXXXXXXXXXXX stated that the GoG planned to burn packages of flour. ARSO is unable to prove that the cocaine was in fact substituted with flour; however, the GoG's lack of cooperation and vehement rejection to a request for random sampling raises troubling questions about

the GoG's interest in transparency. And as the Ambassador's driver very keenly observed, "I know the smell of burning marijuana, and I didn't smell anything." The entire event was a theatrical production.

— —

COMMENT

— —

8. (S) The event was a real eye-opener and a facade. The incineration was a ridiculous attempt by the GoG to prove that a law enforcement campaign against narcotics exists. If anything was proven, it was that the traffickers' influence has reached the highest levels of the government. There is an obvious fracture within the security forces, and only a handful of officials appear to be fighting to carry out legitimate duties. The clear reluctance and open animosity displayed by all the senior Ministry of Interior and Security (MIS) officials and the diffident response of the Ministers to the Ambassador's request suggest complicity at the highest levels of the Ministry. The silver-lining of the event is that the heated debate and ridiculous protestation by MIS to the Ambassador's request for a random sampling were witnessed and recorded by elements of the Guinean media (state-owned and independent).

CARTER

Berlusconi and Bono on African Aid

In 2008, diplomats in Rome advised that Silvio Berlusconi, the Italian prime minister, might maintain aid to Africa in order to avoid a "tongue-lashing" by the rock star and aid advocate Bono.

DATE 2008-07-23 13:14:00

SOURCE Embassy Rome

CLASSIFICATION CONFIDENTIAL

C O N F I D E N T I A L ROME 000905

SIPDIS

AF/EPS CAMILLE JACKSON

EO 12958 DECL: 07/23/2018

TAGS ECON, IT

SUBJECT: ITALY: GOI PROGRESS ON AID TO AFRICA FOR G8

PRESIDENCY

Classified By: Econ Counselor William R. Meara for Reasons 1.4 (b) and (d).

1. (U) Summary: The Director of Italy's Sub-Saharan African Assistance Office said assistance levels are not expected to change with the newly installed Berlusconi government. Italy will continue to focus its funding on Ethiopia and Mozambique, with an emphasis on health and education. Development officials hope assistance issues will continue to be a priority for Italy during its 2009 G-8 presidency. End Summary.

2. (U) On June 19 Econoff met with Fabrizio Nava, Director of the Office of Sub-Saharan Africa Assistance, to discuss GOI assistance to Africa. The 2008 GOI budget allocates 4.1 billion Euros for foreign assistance, or .27 percent of GDP, slightly above the percentage of GDP in 2007. The MFA disperses

roughly 750 million of the 4.1 billion Euros through the foreign aid office; Africa receives around 140 to 200 million for bilateral and multilateral humanitarian assistance. The Ministry of Finance controls the remaining foreign assistance account which covers Italy's contributions to the United Nations, EU, World Bank and Italy's debt-forgiveness program. Despite the recent arrival of the center-right government and budget cuts, Nava believed African assistance levels would be maintained.

3. (U) Italy supplies aid to 36 of the countries in Africa. Of these 36, the GOI gives three countries priority: Ethiopia, Mozambique, and Eritrea. Eritrea is now, however, only given emergency aid due to EU restrictions. Nava said that the GOI recently initiated a pilot program focused on budget support to Mozambique. Should GOI deem the program a success, Nava said similar budget support will be given to other African countries starting with Cape Verde.

4. (U) According to Nava, Sudan, Egypt, and Mauritania are lower priorities, but also receive assistance from the GOI. Nava pointed to a recent memorandum of understanding pledging 12 million Euros over the next three years to Mauritania. The funds have been earmarked for poverty alleviation, the improvement of living conditions, cultural programs and training for judges. (Note: Mauritania is a personal concern of Alain Economides, Head of Minister Frattini's Private Office and former Ambassador to the region. End Note.) In Mauritania and Egypt, Nava noted that most GOI aid focuses on agricultural, medical, and educational development. Nava expects work on gender issues, an initiative started by the previous Foreign Minister, to continue to be a priority as well, although he did not provide specifics.

5. (U) Econoff brought up criticism voiced by NGOs such as Bono's "Debt AIDS Trade Africa" (D.A.T.A.) and Action Aid Italy that Italy's aid apparatus is out-of-date and overly focused on infrastructure projects. Nava explained that donating to NGOs is rather difficult due to the small number of them; there are roughly 300 "recognized" NGOs in Italy. In order to be recognized by the GOI, NGOs must go through a three-year

vetting process. Nava observed that over the past two years, the Foreign Ministry has made improvements in disbursing assistance through NGOs and said he believed the trend would continue. In closing, Nava said he expected African assistance be a focus during Italy's 2009 G-8 presidency.

6. (C) Comment: With its 2009 G8 presidency looming, the GOI may decide to maintain funding levels simply to avoid an embarrassing tongue-lashing from Bono et al. End comment. SPOGLI

A Shipload of Tanks Captured by Pirates

The capture of a shipload of tanks by pirates off the Horn of Africa shines a light on Ukraine's arms deals and Kenya's role in them.

DATE 2008-10-02 15:46:00

SOURCE Embassy Nairobi

CLASSIFICATION SECRET//NOFORN

S E C R E T SECTION 01 OF 02 NAIROBI 002290

NOFORN SIPDIS

E.O. 12958: DECL: 10/02/2018 TAGS: MASS, PTER, PHSA, KE, UP, SO, SU SUBJECT: WHITHER M/V FAINA'S TANKS?

REF: A. USDLO KHARTOUM IIR 6 890 0139 08 201536Z FEB 08 B. USDAO NAIROBI IIR 6 854 0108 08 291553Z JAN 08 C. USDAO NAIROBI IIR 6 854 0026 08 091427Z NOV 07

Classified By: PolOff Rachael Doherty, reasons 1.4 (b,d).

—— ——

Summary

—— ——

1. (S-NF) A shipment of 33 Ukrainian T-72 tanks and other ammunition and equipment aboard the M/V Faina, currently under the control of pirates off the coast of Somalia, has raised questions and controversy in Kenya about their final destination. It is a poorly kept secret that the tanks are bound for the Government of South Sudan -- and that the Government of Kenya has been facilitating shipments from Ukraine to the Government of South Sudan since 2007. Since the world's eyes are now on the M/V Faina, it is unlikely that the tanks, if released, would go immediately to their intended destination. Instead, they are likely to sit in a Kenyan military depot until the world's attention shifts elsewhere. In the meantime, the Kenyan military is in an uncomfortable spot. End Summary.

— — — — — —

Kenya Claims T-72s . . .

— — — — — —

2. (C) The hijacking of the Ukrainian-owned, Belize-flagged merchant vessel (M/V) Faina -- and subsequent confimation by the government of Ukraine that there are 33 T-72 tanks and other ammunition and equipment onboard -- has raised questions about the cargo's ultimate destination. In a move likely aimed at stemming controversy, the Government of Kenya has claimed that the ultimate destination for the shipment is the Kenyan Armed Forces. It is a poorly-kept secret, however, that the shipment was originally bound for South Sudan.

3. (S-NF) The contradictions have already been highlighted in the press. Kenyan Government spokesman Alfred Mutua and Kenyan Defense spokesman Bogita Ongeri have both insisted that the tanks belong to Kenya. East Africa Seafarers' Assistance Program spokesman Andrew Mwangura told a different story: that the shipment ultimately was bound for the Government of South Sudan. (Note: Intelligence reporting (refs A-C) confirms Mwangura's story -- not the official GOK stance. After reporting that he was warned by Kenyan government officials to stop talking about the shipment, Mwangura was arrested on October 1. End Note.)

4. (C) MFA Director of Political Affairs Ambassador Ben Ogutu maintained the party line to PolOff on September 30, but expressed relief that the Ministry of Defense has the lead on the issue. "e are just repeating the information that the Ministry has provided to us," Ogutu said. (Note: Ogutu also expressed great interest in what U.S. officials in Washington would say about the arms' ultimate destination. End Note.)

— — — — — — — —

. . . Although They Were Juba-Bound

— — — — — — — —

5. (S-NF) Since last year, Kenya's Ministry of Defense has indeed played a major role in assisting the Government of South Sudan receive arms shipments from the Government of Ukraine. When the shipments are off-loaded at the port of Mombasa, they are transported via rail to Uganda and then onward to

Southern Sudan (ref C). Military officials have expressed discomfort with this arrangement, however, and have made it clear to us that the orders come "from the top." (i.e., President Kibaki)

6. (S-NF) Given the extensive local and international media attention, it is unlikely that the shipment will go directly to Sudan should the cargo be of floaded in Mombasa as originally planned. A high-level military official has indicated to us that if received, the cargo will be of floaded and delivered to a military depot in Kenya, where it will likely sit for a few months before risking the overland shipment to Sudan.

— — — — — — —

NAIROBI 00002290 002 OF 002
Not the First Time
— — — — — —

7. (S-NF) This is not the first time a T-72 shipment to South Sudan has been publicly diverted. In mid-February, the Government of Kenya was reported as "seizing" a shipment of tanks bound for the Sudan People's Liberation Army as it violated the 2003 Comprehensive Peace Agreement to end Sudan's civil war. The "seizure" occurred when Kenya's own security situation was still precarious given the post-election crisis. The tanks were ultimately released and proceeded to Sudan, and the cargo currently aboard the M/V Faina was meant to complete the tank sale. (Note: Although there is no arms embargo against Southern Sudan, the CPA does say that the parties "agree in principle to proportional downsizing of the forces on both sides" following the cease fire. The CPA permits the resupply of lethal military items on approval by the Joint Defense Board and UN mission. End Note.)

8. (C) Comment: While Kenya does see itself as a guarantor of the 2003 Comprehensive Peace Agreement, which was signed in Nairobi, the highest levels of government have nevertheless allowed previous arms shipments to proceed. Kenya's political leadership has thereby put the Kenyan military in a in an uncomfortable spot. Some Kenyan military officials have been questioning whether Kenya should be facilitating arms deliveries since well before the M/V Faina made headlines.

9. (C) Comment, cont: While no one is talking about why Kenya is in this position, we can think of a few reasons. First, it is possible that Kenya's political leadership wants to support the Government of South Sudan but not in a way that will openly provoke Khartoum or potentially threaten South Sudan's eventual independence. Vice President Musyoka's public opposition to the International Criminal Court's indictment of President Bashir (because it could threaten the CPA) illustrates this point. Second, the government appears genuinely sensitive to charges that major arms shipments would be in violation of the spirit of the CPA. Third, given Kenya's track record on corruption, it is always possible that there is a financial benefit for a senior Kenyan official (or two, or more) in return for facilitating the arms shipments. As such, the question of "Who owns the tanks?" will remain a touchy side issue for Kenya in the piracy of the M/V Faina. RANNEBERGER

Anti-American Canadian TV

In a 2008 cable, the American Embassy in Ottawa analyzed the increase in "anti-American melodrama" on Canadian television and advised more public diplomacy to counter it.

DATE 2008-01-25 23:15:00

SOURCE Embassy Ottawa

CLASSIFICATION UNCLASSIFIED//FOR OFFICIAL USE ONLY

UNCLAS SECTION 01 OF 03 OTTAWA 000136

SIPDIS

SENSITIVE SIPDIS

E.O. 12958: N/A TAGS: PGOV, KPAO, CA SUBJECT: PRIMETIME IMAGES OF US-CANADA BORDER PAINT U.S. IN INCREASINGLY NEGATIVE LIGHT

OTTAWA 00000136 001.2 OF 003

1. (SBU) Summary: The Canadian Broadcasting Corporation (CBC) has long gone to great pains to highlight the distinction between Americans and Canadians in its programming, generally at our expense. However, the level of anti-American melodrama has been given a huge boost in the current television season as a number of programs offer Canadian viewers their fill of nefarious American officials carrying out equally nefarious deeds in Canada while Canadian officials either oppose them or fall trying. CIA rendition flights, schemes to steal Canada's water, "the Guantanamo-Syria express," F-16's flying in for bombing runs in Quebec to eliminate escaped terrorists: in response to the onslaught, one media commentator concluded, somewhat tongue-in-cheek, that "apparently, our immigration department's real enemies aren't terrorists or smugglers --they're Americans." While this situation hardly constitutes a public diplomacy crisis per se, the degree of comfort with which Canadian broadcast entities, including those financed by Canadian tax dollars, twist current events to

feed long-standing negative images of the U.S. -- and the extent to which the Canadian public seems willing to indulge in the feast -- is noteworthy as an indication of the kind of insidious negative popular stereotyping we are increasingly up against in Canada. End Summary.

"THE BORDER" -CANADA'S ANSWER TO 24, W/O THAT SUTHERLAND GUY
— — — — — — — — — — — — — —

2. (SBU) When American TV and movie producers want action, the formula involves Middle Eastern terrorists, a ticking nuclear device, and a (somewhat ironically, Canadian) guy named Sutherland. Canadian producers don't need to look so far -- they can find all the action they need right on the U.S.-Canadian border. This piece of real estate, which most Americans associate with snow blowing back and forth across an imaginary line, has for the past three weeks been for Canadian viewers the site of downed rendition flights, F-16 bombing runs, and terrorist suspects being whisked away to Middle Eastern torture facilities. "The Border," which state-owned CBC premiered on January 7, attracted an impressive 710,000 viewers on its first showing -- not exactly Hockey Night in Canada, but equivalent to an American program drawing about eight million U.S. viewers. The show depicts Canadian immigration and customs officers' efforts to secure the U.S.-Canadian border and the litany of moral dilemmas they face in doing so. The CBC bills the high-budget program as depicting the "new war" on the border and "the few who fight it." While the "war" is supposed to be against criminals and terrorists trying to cross the border, many of the immigration team's battles end up being with U.S. government officials, often in tandem with the CIA-colluding Canadian Security and Intelligence Service (CSIS).

3. (SBU) The clash between the Americans and Canadians got started early in the season and has continued unabated. In episode one a Syrian terrorist with a belt full of gel-based explosives is removed from a plane in Canada while the Canadian-Syrian man sitting next to him is rendered by the CIA/CSIS team to Syria -- a fairly transparent reference to QCIA/CSIS team to Syria -- a fairly transparent reference

to the Maher Arar case. Fortunately for the incarcerated individual, the sympathetic Canadian Immigration and Customs Security official recognizes the mistake and shrewdly causes the government to rescue him from a Syrian jail through organized media pressure. The episode ends with a preview of things to come when one of the Canadian immigration officers notes with disgust, "Homeland Security is sending in some hot shot agent."

4. (SBU) Episode two expands on this theme, featuring the arrival of an arrogant, albeit stunningly attractive female DHS officer, sort of a cross between Salma Hayek and Cruella De Vil. The show portrays the DHS official bossing around her stereotypically more compassionate Canadian colleagues while uttering such classic lines as, "Who do you think provides the muscle to protect your fine ideals?" and "You would have killed him. Let the American justice system do it for you." Her fallback line in most situations is "it's a matter of national security."

5. (SBU) But the one-liners and cross-border stereotypes really take off in episode three, in which an American

OTTAWA 00000136 002.2 OF 003

rendition aircraft with three terrorist suspects on the "Guantanamo to Syria express" crashes in Quebec and the terrorists escape -- however, not before killing a Quebec police officer, whose sympathetic widow appears throughout the show. The DHS officer's answer to everything is American firepower, but in this episode even CSIS gets a chance at redemption as the CSIS officer in charge challenges her. Ms. DHS barks back, "You really want to talk territorial sovereignty, or should we talk about getting the terrorists back?" After being chased through the woods of Quebec by a cross-culturally balanced CSISJTF2 team which kills a 15-year-old terrorist in a shootout, the bad guys are finally cornered on the side of a pristine Canadian lake. Then, after a conversation with Washington in which she asks "can you bypass NSA and State?", our DHS official calls in an air-strike on the terrorists without Canadian concurrence. Canadian planes, another official has explained, are "already deployed to Afghanistan, helping our neighbors fight their war on terror." With only seconds to spare before the bombs are dropped on the Quebec site, the planes are called off when the CSIS-JTF team affirms positive control over the terrorists. Finally, in a last-minute allowance for redemption, the CSIS officer informs his DHS colleague that the captured terrorists will not be turned over to the U.S. but will stand trial for the death of the Quebec police officer. She does get the final word, though, hissing the classic phrase "you people are so nave," before the screen goes blank.

DEA ALSO TAKES SOME HITS

6. (SBU) If that isn't enough, "the Border" is only one of the CBC programs featuring cross-border relations. "Intelligence," which depicts a Canadian intelligence unit collaborating with a local drug lord-turned government informant, is just as stinging in its portrayal of U.S.-Canada law enforcement cooperation. Through its two seasons, the program has followed plot lines including a DEA attempt to frame the Canadian informant for murder, a CIA plot to secretly divert Canadian water to the American southwest, and a rogue DEA team that actually starts selling drugs for a profit. A columnist in conservative Canadian daily newspaper "The National Post" commented, "There's no question that the CSIS heroes on 'Intelligence' consider the Americans our most dangerous enemies."

EVEN THE LITTLE MOSQUE GETS IN TO THE ACT

7. (U) Even "Little Mosque on the Prairie," a popular Canadian sitcom that depicts a Muslim community in a small Saskatchewan town, has joined the trend of featuring U.S.-Canada border relations. This time, however, the State Department is the fall guy. A December 2007 episode portrayed a Muslim economics professor trying to remove his name from the No-Fly-List at a U.S. consulate. The show depicts a rude and eccentric U.S. consular officer stereotypically attempting to find any

excuse to avoid being helpful. Another episode depicted how an innocent trip across the border became a jumble of frayed nerves as Grandpa was scurried into secondary by U.S. border officials because his name matched something on the watch list. Qhis name matched something on the watch list.

GIVE US YOUR WATER; OH WHAT THE HECK WE'LL TAKE YOUR COUNTRY TOO

— — — — — — — — — — — —

8. (U) And it appears that the season is just warming up. After CIA renditions, DEA murder plots, DHS missteps, and unhelpful consular officers, a U.S. takeover of Canada may have been the only theme left for the CBC "H20" mini-series. The series was first broadcast in 2005, when it featured an investigation into an American assassination of the Canadian prime minister and a very broad-based (and wildly implausible) U.S. scheme to steal Canadian water. A two-part sequel, set to be broadcast in March and April 2008, will portray the United States as manipulating innocent, trusting Canadians into voting in favor of Canada's becoming part of the United States. Then, after the United States completely takes over Canada, one brave Canadian unites Canadians and Europeans in an attempt to end America's hegemony. Another

OTTAWA 00000136 003.2 OF 003

program could prove more benign but will certainly include its share of digs against all things American: Global TV reportedly is gearing up for a March 2008 debut of its own border security drama, set to feature Canadian search-and-rescue officers patrolling the U.S.-Canada border.

COMMENT

— —

9. (SBU) EKOS pollster Frank Graves told Poloff he thought that at this point such shows are reflective and not causal in determining attitudes in Canada. They play on the deep-seated caution most Canadians feel toward their large neighbor to the south, a sort of zeitgeist that has been in the background for decades. As one example, a December 2007 Strategic Counsel

poll showed that nine percent of Canadians thought U.S. foreign policy was the greatest threat to the world -- twice as high as those who were concerned about weapons of mass destruction. What Graves does find disturbing -- and here he believes that the causal or reflective question is not important -- is that support for a less porous border is increasing in both Canada and the U.S.: in the U.S. because of generalized fear of terrorism and in Canada because of concern over guns, sovereignty, and the impact that a terrorist attack on the U.S. would have on trade. Graves has detected an increasingly wary attitude over the border that he believes could lead to greater distance between the two countries.

10. (SBU) While there is no single answer to this trend, it does serve to demonstrate the importance of constant creative, and adequately-funded public-diplomacy engagement with Canadians, at all levels and in virtually all parts of the country. We need to do everything we can to make it more difficult for Canadians to fall into the trap of seeing all U.S. policies as the result of nefarious faceless U.S. bureaucrats anxious to squeeze their northern neighbor. While there are those who may rate the need for USG public-diplomacy programs as less vital in Canada than in other nations because our societies are so much alike, we clearly have real challenges here that simply must be adequately addressed.

Visit Canada,s Economy and Environment Forum at http: //www. intelink.gov/communities/state/can ada

WILKINS

What Happens After Fidel Dies?

In this Jan. 15, 2009, cable, the diplomats hazarded a guess at what might happen in Cuba after the hero of the revolution dies. Their answer: not much, at least not immediately. The Cuban government has made elaborate preparations for Fidel Castro's death, and the reaction is likely to be muted. The United States does not expect Cubans to leave in large numbers, in part because people may want to stay in the country to see whether there will be changes.

DATE 2009-01-15 17:22:00

SOURCE US Interests Section Havana

CLASSIFICATION SECRET

S E C R E T HAVANA 000035

SI PDI S

E.O. 12958: DECL: 01/14/2019 TAGS: PINS, PGOV, PINR, SMIG, PREL, CU SUBJECT: THE SPECULATION ON FIDEL'S HEALTH

REF: 08 HAVANA 969

Classified By: COM Jonathan Farrar for reasons 1.4 (b) and (d)

1. (C) SUMMARY: Fidel Castro's extended absence from public view, especially during the celebration of the 50th anniversary of the revolution, combined with the long time since he has written one of his occasional "Reflections" pieces is prompting speculation in the international press that his health has taken a turn for the worse. Comments by Venezuelan President Chavez that Fidel will never be seen again have caused some to speculate that he may already be dead. There is, of course, no mention of this in local Cuban press and the rumor mill on the street is subdued, if not silent, on the issue. Whatever the situation, from our vantage point the likelihood of a substantial short term effect on migration or security in Cuba is small, even if the Comandante's death is announced.

WHAT WE KNOW NOW

2. (C) Fidel has not written a "Reflection" piece since December
15. Especially given the significance of the 50th anniversary of
the revolution on January 1, this is unusual. The celebrations
themselves were surprisingly subdued, confined to a short
ceremony featuring President Raul Castro in Santiago (reftel).
It also appears true that Fidel was not seen by the latest
in a continuing stream of international visitors: Presidents
Torrijos of Panama and Correa of Ecuador. It is particularly
noteworthy that Correa did not see him, as he is considered
an up and comer within the South American left. Fidel was last
photographed with Chinese President Hu Jintao in November.
In the picture he appeared alert, but thin and weak. Were it
not for the 50th anniversary celebration, Fidel's current
absence would not have generated as much speculation in the
international press. He has gone silent for extended periods
on other occasions since he stepped out of public view in July
2006. But each time he reemerged after speculation about his
condition in the foreign press reached a certain crescendo.

3. (C) Perhaps because the Cuban public has grown accustomed
to false alarms over the past two years, while the level
of speculation in the international press has increased,
the local rumor mill is not producing much more than usual.
We remain in regular contact with members of the dissident
movement, and none has detected anything out of the ordinary
in the past few weeks. The ongoing crackdown against their
activities, which went into high gear following the hurricanes
last fall, continues unabated. We have noticed no notable
change in the local security posture in Havana, e.g., no
additional police on the street or obvious military movements.

AND WHAT WILL HAPPEN WHEN HE IS DEAD?

4. (S) At this point, we do not believe the announcement of
Fidel's death would alter the local security situation in
any significant way. GOC officials would most likely manage
the death announcement and subsequent funeral arrangements,
etc., in great detail with a view towards putting the best
face on the situation, both domestically and to the world.

Utmost care will be given to ensuring that the Cuban public understands that Raul and the rest of the GOC remain in firm control. The event will be treated with appropriate solemnity, but also designed to achieve maximum propaganda value. It is probable that no announcement will be made until the GOC feels confident that all preparations have been made in accordance with the preceding.

5. (S) We do not believe the announcement of Fidel's death will spark either violent demonstrations or a quick surge in migration. The security arrangements noted in the previous paragraph and the Cuban people's generally conservative nature after 50 years of repression, combined with still significant admiration for Fidel personally, argue against short term disturbances. Far from generating a surge in migration, the announcement of his death could cause a drop in such activity as Cubans wait to see if Fidel's passing brings any change to the island.

6. (S) USINT has reviewed its procedures for dealing with the death of Fidel and is prepared to deal with potential contingencies. FARRAR

Chinese Government Singles Out Google

A "well-placed contact" told American diplomats in Beijing in January that intrusions into Google's computer systems in China were coordinated by the Chinese government. Another source claimed that a top Chinese leader was working closely with Google's Chinese competitor, Baidu, and there was a perception that Google was working with the United States government.

```
DATE XXXXXXXXXXXX

SOURCE Embassy Beijing

CLASSIFICATION SECRET

XXXXXXXXXXXX

SIPDIS

NSC FOR BADER, MEDEIROS, AND LOI

E.O. 12958: DECL: 01/26/2030 TAGS: ECON, PGOV, PHUM, PREL,
EINV, CH SUBJECT: GOOGLE UPDATE: PRC ROLE IN ATTACKS AND
RESPONSE STRATEGY

RE F: XXXXXXXXXXXX

XXXXXXXXXXXX

Classified By: DCM Robert Goldberg. Reasons 1.4 (b), (d).
```

1. (S) Summary: A well-placed contact claims that the Chinese government coordinated the recent intrusions of Google systems. According to our contact, the closely held operations were directed at the Politburo Standing Committee level.

-- Another contact claimed a top PRC leader was actively working with Google competitor Baidu against Google.

-- Chinese concerns over the recent Google threat to take down the company's Chinese-language search engine google.cn over censorship and hacking allegations were focused on the service's growing popularity among Chinese Internet users and a perception that the USG and Google were working in concert.

-- An appeal to nationalism seems to be the Chinese government's chosen option to counter Google's demand to provide unfiltered web content.

-- Contacts in the technology industry tell us that Chinese interference in the operations of foreign businesses is widespread and often underreported to U.S. parent companies. End Summary.

Attacks Directed at High Level

2. (S)

XXXXXXXXXXXX

PRC Sees USG and Google Working Together

3. (C) XXXXXXXXXXXX told PolOff XXXXXXXXXXXX that Google's recent move presented a major dilemma (maodun) for the Chinese government, not because of the cyber-security aspect but because of Google's direct challenge to China's legal restrictions on Internet content. The immediate strategy, XXXXXXXXXXXX said, seemed to be to appeal to Chinese nationalism by accusing Google and the U.S. government of working together to force China to accept "Western values" and undermine China's rule of law. The problem the censors were facing, however, was that Google's demand to deliver uncensored search results was very difficult to spin as an attack on China, and the entire episode had made Google more interesting and attractive to Chinese Internet users. All of a sudden,

XXXXXXXXXXXX

continued, Baidu looked like a boring state-owned enterprise while Google "seems very attractive, like the forbidden fruit." He said it "seems clear" to the Chinese people that Google and the U.S. government were working together on Internet freedom and to undermine Chinese government controls on the Internet. That made some intellectuals happy, XXXXXXXXXXXX said, but "some others" regarded it as interference in China's internal affairs.

Industry: Interference Common, Paranoia Driving PRC Policy

XXXXXXXXXXXX 002 OF 002

4. (C) XXXXXXXXXXXX (please protect) noted the pronounced disconnect between views of U.S. parent companies and local subsidiaries. PRC-based company officials often downplayed the extent of PRC government interference in their operations for fear of consequences for their local markets. Our contact emphasized that Google and other U.S. companies in China were struggling with the stated Chinese goal of technology transfer for the purpose of excluding foreign competition. This consultant noted the Chinese were exploiting the global economic downturn to enact increasingly draconian product certification and government procurement regulations to force foreign-invested enterprises (FIEs) to transfer intellectual property and to carve away the market share of foreign companies.

Chinese Media: American Hypocrisy and Cultural Hegemony

5. (U) The Secretary's speech continued to dominate headlines January 25-26, with the official People's Daily (circ 2.2 million) alleging collusion between U.S. officials and the business community as evidenced by the propinquity of Google's rethink of its China business and the Secretary's speech. Chinese media again accused the U.S. of "cultural hegemony" for setting the standards for "so-called Internet freedom and of hypocrisy for calling for the free flow of information while using the Internet as a political and military tool. People's Daily-affiliated Global Times English (circ 150,000) called the speech a "milestone" showing that U.S. and Western political interests were "taking over every dimension" of cyberspace.

6. (U) The Party-affiliated Beijing News (circ 530,000) opined that the speech showed "a huge gap between Chinese and American information industries, which may lead to a trade war strategy." In an article headlined "China Intensifies Counterattack on Internet Accusation," Global Times Chinese

(circ 1.3 million) quoted Chinese scholar Niu Xinchun as rejecting the theory that U.S.-China conflict would replace the "G2" cooperation model, noting that U.S. attacks usually ended "poorly" when the U.S. considered its practical interests. Many papers quoted statements from the State Council Information Office and Ministry of Industry and Information Technology calling Chinese Internet controls "legitimate" and saying they should not be subject to "unjustifiable interference." Papers continued to conflate Google's China business strategy with the Secretary's speech.

Blogging Circumscribed

7. (SBU) Anecdotally, censors appear to have cracked down on blogging about the Secretary's speech.

XXXXXXXXXXXX

Secretary Clinton's speech is currently blocked in Chinese on state.gov but remains accessible on the U.S. Embassy website in both English and Chinese. HUNTSMAN

North Korea's Future

A top American diplomat speaks with South Korean experts about the future of North Korea and the prospects for Kim Jong-un to succeed his ailing father, Kim Jong-il.

DATE 2010-02-18 04:57:00

SOURCE Embassy Seoul

CLASSIFICATION CONFI DENT IAL

C O N F I D E N T I A L SEOUL 000248

SIPDIS

E.O. 12958: DECL: 02/18/2035 TAGS: PREL, PHUM, PGOV, SOCI, KN, KS, CH SUBJECT: A/S CAMPBELL DISCUSSES DPRK FUTURE WITH EXPERTS

Classified By: AMB D. Kathleen Stephens. Reasons 1.4 (b/d).

SUMMARY
— —

1. (C) A group of five ROK opinion leaders and experts on North Korea issues told A/S Kurt Campbell on February 3 it was difficult to predict whether Kim Jong-il's youngest son Kim Jong-un would be able to succeed his father without sparking instability in the North. Of the five experts, one thought the younger Kim might succeed and one argued his lack of leadership experience made it unlikely he would win the support of the ruling elites. They agreed that Kim Jong-il's brother-in-law Jang Song-taek would prove a strong rival for the younger Kim and would probably be tempted to challenge him. Kim Jong-il had used draconian controls and international aid to discourage coups after having foiled three such attempts in the late 90s. China's strategic interests were fundamentally at odds with U.S.-ROK interests in North Korea. End Summary. Succession in Progress but Success in Doubt

— — — — — — — — — — —

2. (C) Assistant Secretary Kurt Campbell met on February 3 with Korean opinion leaders with a keen interest in DPRK issues to hear their views on the future of North Korea. The experts agreed that regime succession was fully underway and that the North Korean people had accepted the process. Kim Sung-min, Representative for Free North Korea Radio, a VOA-style broadcast station run by North Korean refugees, said a North Korean diplomat based in Beijing had told him over the phone that morning that the DPRK Foreign Ministry had instructed all of its overseas missions to "lay the foundation for leadership change in Pyongyang." Most of the experts believed the challenge for Kim Jongil's youngest son and designated heir, Kim Jong-un, would most likely come after his father died. Former Prime Minister Chang Sang recalled the Chosun Dynasty's 500 year history in which political intrigue and tension might simmer for years, but tended to erupt only after the king died. 3. (C) The group agreed that Kim Jong-il's brother-in-law and right-hand man Jang Song-taek was spearheading the succession drive and would be a rival for power once Kim Jong-un's father died, but the group was split on the younger Kim's prospects for holding onto power. Kim Sung-min believed it would be difficult for Jang to wrest power from the younger Kim once the succession process was complete. National Assemblywoman Park Sun-Young suggested it was unclear whether Jang would be content to control the younger Kim from behind the curtain, or would challenge him directly for outright control. Park is a member of the right-of-center Liberty Forward Party and was formerly the Director of the North Korea Human Rights Studies Center at Korea's Catholic University.

Doubts About Younger Kim's Experience
— — — — — — — — —

4. (C) There were many reasons to doubt that Kim Jong-un would be able to successfully fend off challenges to his control after his father died, according to

Han Ki-Hong, President of DailyNK, an NGO focused on democratizing North Korea and disseminating information about conditions within the country. Han noted that Kim Jong-il had twenty years of experience as an official of the Korean Workers' Party before his father died. Furthermore, Kim Jong-il had the benefit of years of guidance from his father after he had been officially anointed in 1980 to eventually succeed him. By contrast, Kim Jong-un had very limited experience and might not get much direct guidance before Kim Jong-il dies. Even now, Han said, it was not clear that Kim Jong-il's health was good enough to exercise the faculties necessary for day-to-day management of state affairs. Given the limited opportunity the younger Kim had to gain experience, Han doubted his ability to solidify his position in the Party and win the unwavering support of Pyongyang's power elites. Han recalled the tumultuous state of affairs in the ROK following the death of President Park Chung Hee in 1979 and suggested the DPRK succession would be "100 times more troublesome." Han is a veteran of the ROK student democratization movement that emerged in the post-Park era.

Tight Control and Aid Kept Regime Afloat

5. (C) Kim Heung-kwang, Representative for North Korea Intellectuals Solidarity, an NGO formed by intellectuals who had defected from the North, opined that brutal repression and international aid had been the secrets of Kim Jong-il's ability to fend off challenges. After three separate coup attempts in the 90s, Kim Jong-il had implemented very strict controls and sent a stern warning to would-be plotters by executing anyone who had been even remotely involved in the plots. Therefore, only the military could even dare consider rising up, but the Security Services had successfully kept the military in check. Kim Heung-kwang went on to suggest that the "indulgence" of the international community over the past ten years had also helped sustain the

regime. The large-scale assistance provided to the regime by the ROK, China, the U.S., Japan and others had been intended in part to avoid a hard landing, and indeed had kept the regime afloat, he said. Park Sun-Young suggested that North Korea had skillfully played Washington and Beijing off one another. She believed that the DPRK had exploited large amounts of assistance from China, taking advantage of a situation in which Beijing was presumed by Washington to have significant influence over Pyongyang. China Complicates the Endgame

— — — — — — — — — — — — — —

6. (C) The experts agreed that China's obsession with DPRK stability at all costs, was clearly and fundamentally at odds with U.S. and ROK interests. Given a choice between reaching out to Seoul or Beijing, Park believed that Pyongyang elites would reflexively look to China for support if they believed they needed help in maintaining stability. The Seoul option would be unacceptable because of the U.S.-ROK alliance and concerns over becoming subservient to Seoul. China, on the other hand, would gladly provide support with few or no strings attached, just to maintain the DPRK as an independent entity, she maintained.

7. (C) Han Ki Hong noted that although Washington had a keen interest in both denuclearization and human rights, the U.S. stake in North Korea was minimal compared to that of China by virtue of its proximity to the North. China did not share American perspectives on these two key issues, considering them somewhat abstract. Rather, Beijing was concerned about what it considered to be more concrete issues, such as a potential flood of "economic migrants" and broader social unrest on its immediate border. Reaching the People and Close Cooperation are Key

— — — — — — — — — — — — — —

8. (C) Negating Chinese influence over the long term, Park Sun-Young observed, would involve close U.S.-ROK cooperation in winning the hearts and minds of the North

Korean people. Park said that while she understood the importance of the nuclear issue for Washington, she urged more focus on human rights issues that would convince the populace that "we are on their side."
STEPHENS

Profile of the Libyan Leader

This 2009 cable offers a colorful profile of the Libyan leader, Col. Muammar el-Qaddafi, by the American ambassador to Libya, Gene A. Cretz.

DATE 2009-09-29 17:21:00

SOURCE Embassy Tripoli

CLASSIFICATION SECRET//NOFORN

S E C R E T SECTION 01 OF 02 TRIPOLI 000771

NOFORN SIPDIS

STATE FOR NEA/MAG AND INR.

E.O. 12958: DECL: 9/29/2019 TAGS: PREL, PGOV, LY, PINR SUBJECT: A GLIMPSE INTO LIBYAN LEADER QADHAFI'S ECCENTRICITIES

CLASSIFIED BY: Gene A. Cretz, Ambassador, U.S. Embassy Tripoli, Department of State. REASON: 1.4 (b), (d)

1. (S/NF) Summary: Recent first-hand experiences with Libyan Leader Muammar al-Qadhafi and his staff, primarily in preparation for his UNGA trip, provided rare insights into Qadhafi's inner circle and personal proclivities. Qadhafi appears to rely heavily XXXXXXXXXXXX, and reportedly cannot travel with his senior Ukrainian nurse, Galyna Kolotnytska. He also appears to have an intense dislike or fear of staying on upper floors, reportedly prefers not to fly over water, and seems to enjoy horse racing and flamenco dancing. His recent travel may also suggest a diminished dependence on his legendary female guard force, as only one woman bodyguard accompanied him to New York. End Summary.

QADHAFI'S PERSONALITY REFLECTED IN HIS PHOBIAS

2. (S/NF) Muammar al-Qadhafi has been described as both mercurial and eccentric, and our recent first-hand experiences with him and his office, primarily in preparation for his UNGA trip, demonstrated the truth of both characterizations. From

the moment Qadhafi's staff began to prepare for his travel to the United States, XXXXXXXXXXXX of his 40-year rule, various proclivities and phobias began to reveal themselves in every logistical detail. When applying for Qadhafi's visa, XXXXXXXXXXXX asked whether it was necessary for the Leader to submit a portrait of himself that fit consular application regulations, noting that his photo was displayed throughout the city and that anyone of hundreds of billboards could be photographed and shrunken to fit the application's criteria. When the rule was enforced, XXXXXXXXXXXX reluctantly conceded to take a portrait of the Leader specifically for the visa application.

3. (S/NF) When XXXXXXXXXXXX began to search for proper accommodations for Qadhafi, XXXXXXXXXXXX informed us that the Leader must stay on the first floor of any facility that was rented for him. (XXXXXXXXXXXX separately told U.S. officials in Washington that Qadhafi could not climb more than 35 steps.) XXXXXXXXXXXX cited this requirement as the primary reason that the Libyan residence in New Jersey was selected as the preferred accommodation site rather than the Libyan PermRep's residence in New York City. XXXXXXXXXXXX also sought to find accommodations with room to pitch Qadhafi's Bedouin tent, Qadhafi's traditional site for receiving visitors and conducting meetings, as it offers him a non-verbal way of communicating that he is a man close to his cultural roots.

4. (S/NF) Qadhafi's dislike of long flights and apparent fear of flying over water also caused logistical headaches for his staff. When discussing flight clearances with Emboffs, XXXXXXXXXXXX explained that the Libyan delegation would arrive from Portugal, as Qadhafi "cannot fly more than eight hours" and would need to overnight in Europe prior to continuing his journey to New York. XXXXXXXXXXXX also revealed in the same conversation that Qadhafi does not like to fly over water. Presumably for similar reasons, Qadhafi's staff also requested a stop in Newfoundland to break his travel from Venezuela to Libya on September 29. [Note: The Government of Canada recently confirmed that the Libyan delegation canceled plans to stop in Newfoundland. End Note.]

DEPENDENCIES: RELIANCE ON A SELECTIVE GROUP OF INDIVIDUALS

5. (S/NF) Qadhafi appears to be almost obsessively dependent on a small core of trusted personnel. This group includes XXXXXXXXXXXXcoordinate the logistics of Qadhafi's visit. XXXXXXXXXXXX balanced the UNGA preparations between equally frenetic preparations for the August 31 African Union (AU) Summit and September 1 celebration of Qadhafi's coup. XXXXXXXXXXXX At large events such as the August 31 AU Summit and September 1 celebrations, XXXXXXXXXXXX every last detail of these complex gatherings, ranging from the overall program to the position of the press pool. At UNGA, XXXXXXXXXXXX Qadhafi to the podium at the UNGA and XXXXXXXXXXXX his papers and props upon the conclusion of the Leader's remarks. Long-time Qadhafi Chief of Staff Bashir Salah appears to play an equally important role in Qadhafi's personal retinue, and XXXXXXXXXXXX via an old-fashioned green phone XXXXXXXXXXXX. It is next to a red phone, which presumably connects to Qadhafi himself. We constantly hear that National Security Adviser and son, Muatassim, also plays a key role as his father's confidante and handler during travel abroad. Muatassim also seems to have been tasked with insuring that the Leader's image is well-preserved through the full array of carefully-planned media events.

6. (S/NF) Finally, Qadhafi relies heavily on his long-time Ukrainian nurse, Galyna Kolotnytska, who has been described as a "voluptuous blonde." Of the rumored staff of four Ukrainian nurses that cater to the Leader's health and well-being, XXXXXXXXXXXX emphasized to multiple Emboffs that Qadhafi cannot travel without Kolotnytska, as she alone "knows his routine." When Kolotnytska's late visa application resulted in her Security Advisory Opinion being received on the day Qadhafi's party planned to travel to the U.S., the Libyan Government sent a private jet to ferry her from Libya to Portugal to meet up with the Leader during his rest-stop. Some embassy contacts have claimed that Qadhafi and the 38 year-old Kolotnytska have a romantic relationship. While he did not comment on such rumors, a Ukrainian political officer recently confirmed that the Ukrainian nurses "travel everywhere with the Leader."

PREFERENCES - FROM DANCING TO HORSEMAN

7. (S/NF) In addition to the personality quirks revealed through Qadhafi's travel to New York, the Qadhafi's preferences for dancing and cultural performances were displayed over the last month. The three-day spectacle of his 40th anniversary in power included performances by dance troupes from Ukraine, Tunisia, Algeria, Egypt, and Morocco, as well as musical performances by bands from Mexico, Russia, New Zealand, and a number of other nations. Qadhafi appeared particularly enthralled by Tuareg horse racing during two of the events, clapping and smiling throughout the races. The flamenco dancers that participated in his celebratory events appeared to spark a similar interest, as Qadhafi decided to stop in Seville (for a "personal trip" according to the Spanish Ambassador here) on his way back to Libya from Venezuela specifically to attend a flamenco dance performance. [Note: That stop has reportedly been scrapped for unknown reasons. End note.]

NO NEW YORK PHOTO OPS - QADHAFI LEAVES FEMALE GUARDS AT HOME

8. (S/NF) While Qadhafi's reported female guard force has become legendary, it played no role in his travels to New York. Only one female guard was included among the approximately 350-person strong Libyan delegation to New York. This is the same female bodyguard who sticks close to Qadhafi in his domestic and international public appearances and may, in fact, play some sort of formal security role. Observers in Tripoli speculate that the female guard force is beginning to play a diminished role among the Leader's personal security staff.

9. (S/NF) Comment: Qadhafi's state visits and appearances at various conferences and summits, both at home and abroad, have revealed greater details about his personality and character. While it is tempting to dismiss his many eccentricities as signs of instability, Qadhafi is a complicated individual who has managed to stay in power for forty years through a skillful balancing of interests and realpolitik methods. Continued engagement with Qadhafi and his inner circle is important not only to learn the motives and interests that drive the

world's longest serving dictator, but also to help overcome the misperceptions that inevitably accumulated during Qadhafi's decades of isolation. As XXXXXXXXXXXX told us, pointing to a larger-than-life portrait of Qadhafi, "When you have been isolated for so long, it is important to communicate." End comment.

CRETZ

U.S. Warns Germany on Bungled Rendition

The ambassador to Germany, William R. Timken Jr., reports on a meeting to caution German officials against trying to enforce an arrest warrant against C.I.A. officers implicated in the kidnapping of Khaled el-Masri, a German citizen with the same name as a suspected militant.

```
DATE 2007-02-06 17:48:00

SOURCE Embassy Berlin

CLASSIFICATION SECRET//NOFORN

S E C R E T BERLIN 000242

SIPDIS

NOFORN SIPDIS

FOR S/ES-O, EUR AND L

E.O. 12958: DECL: 02/06/2017 TAGS: KJUS, PTER, PREL, PGOV, GM
SUBJECT: AL-MASRI CASE -- CHANCELLERY AWARE OF USG CONCERNS

REF: A. BERLIN 230

B. BERLIN 200

Classified By: DCM John M. Koenig for Reasons 1.4 (b) and (d)
```

1. (S/NF) In a February 6 discussion with German Deputy National Security Adviser Rolf Nikel, the DCM reiterated our strong concerns about the possible issuance of international arrest warrants in the al-Masri case. The DCM noted that the reports in the German media of the discussion on the issue between the Secretary and FM Steinmeier in Washington were not accurate, in that the media reports suggest the USG was not troubled by developments in the al-Masri case. The DCM emphasized that this was not the case and that issuance of international arrest warrants would have a negative impact on our bilateral relationship. He reminded Nikel of the

repercussions to U.S.-Italian bilateral relations in the wake of a similar move by Italian authorities last year.

2. (S/NF) The DCM pointed out that our intention was not to threaten Germany, but rather to urge that the German Government weigh carefully at every step of the way the implications for relations with the U.S. We of course recognized the independence of the German judiciary, but noted that a decision to issue international arrest warrants or extradition requests would require the concurrence of the German Federal Government, specifically the MFA and the Ministry of Justice (MOJ). The DCM said our initial indications had been that the German federal authorities would not allow the warrants to be issued, but that subsequent contacts led us to believe this was not the case.

3. (S/NF) Nikel also underscored the independence of the German judiciary, but confirmed that the MFA and MOJ would have a procedural role to play. He said the case was subject to political, as well as judicial, scrutiny. From a judicial standpoint, the facts are clear, and the Munich prosecutor has acted correctly. Politically speaking, said Nikel, Germany would have to examine the implications for relations with the U.S. At the same time, he noted our political differences about how the global war on terrorism should be waged, for example on the appropriateness of the Guantanamo facility and the alleged use of renditions.

4. (S/NF) Nikel also cited intense pressure from the Bundestag and the German media. The German federal Government must consider the "entire political context," said Nikel. He assured the DCM that the Chancellery is well aware of the bilateral political implications of the case, but added that this case "will not be easy." The Chancellery would nonetheless try to be as constructive as possible.

5. (S/NF) The DCM pointed out that the USG would likewise have a difficult time in managing domestic political implications if international arrest warrants are issued. He reiterated our concerns and expressed the hope that the Chancellery would

keep us informed of further developments in the case, so as to avoid surprises. Nikel undertook to do so, but reiterated that he could not, at this point "promise that everything will turn out well." TIMKEN JR

Robbery in Yemen Aids Al Qaeda

A bank robbery in Yemen provides money for Al Qaeda's affiliate in the country.

DATE 2009-09-02 13:39:00

SOURCE Embassy Sanaa

CLASSIFICATION CONFI DENT IAL

C O N F I D E N T I A L SECTION 01 OF 02 SANAA 001632

SIPDIS

DEPT FOR NEA/ARP AMACDONALD AND INR SMOFFATT DEPT OF TREASURY FOR BRIAN MCCAULEY

E.O. 12958: DECL: 08/23/2019 TAGS: PTER, PGOV, KFIN, YM SUBJECT: AQAP LIFTS $500K IN ADEN HEIST?

Classified By: Ambassador Stephen Seche for reasons 1.4(b) and (d).

1. (C) SUMMARY: An armed robbery rocked Aden on August 17, in part due to the large amount stolen (100 million Yemeni riyals) and in part due to the belief of government and non-government sources that al-Qaeda in the Arabian Peninsula (AQAP) operatives are the culprits. The tactics utilized in the armed robbery bear a striking resemblance to AQAP methods used in previous attacks, and the sophistication of the attack discredits claims that ordinary robbers or bank officials acted alone. Given the ROYG's lack of follow-through investigating a similar 1998 armed robbery attributed to an Islamic extremist group and the potential for these monies to be used to fund terrorist activities, this bold, unusual operation, if truly attributable to AQAP, would provide the organization with a substantial financial infusion at a time when it is thought to be short of cash. END SUMMARY.

HIGHLY COORDINATED ATTACK POINTS TO AQAP
— — — — — — — — —

2. (C) Armed gunmen robbed an Arab Limited Bank truck carrying 100 million riyals (equivalent to $500,000) in Aden on August 17 in a highly coordinated attack that many suspect was the work of Al-Qaeda in the Arabian Peninsula (AQAP) operatives. The armed robbers were disguised as Yemeni policemen and conducted the robbery in a busy, downtown district in broad daylight, signaling a high level of operational sophistication uncommon among average Yemeni criminals. After hijacking the bank vehicle and transferring the money to a get-away car, they erased the serial number of a third car they used in the operation, which they abandoned outside Aden in order to delay authorities in tracing its ownership, according to press reports.

3. (C) According to independent and official sources, the precision of the attack and the tactics utilized during the armed robbery make it unlikely to be the work of ordinary criminals. Official government newspaper 26 September noted that a group of Islamic extremists are suspected to be behind the plot, though no confirmation of their affiliation or motives was published. XXXXXXXXXXXX told PolOff on August 18, "Al-Qaeda is responsible and I reiterate that the robbed money may be used for terrorist operations," underscoring the similarity to previous armed robberies by terrorist groups in the region. The attackers' use of police uniforms is reminiscent of al-Qaeda in the Arabian Peninsula (AQAP) tactics utilized during the attack on the U.S. Embassy in Sana'a on September 17, 2008.

4. (C) Rather than attack the bank itself, the robbers conducted the heist in broad daylight in a busy sector of Aden, suggesting a high degree of operational sophistication and access to bank routes and times. XXXXXXXXXXXX said, "There is no doubt that there were people who provided them with information about the amount of money and schedule of the movement." Several bank officials have been arrested by ROYG security forces for possible complicity in the robbery, according to press reports. Lieutenant Colonel Haider Haider

of the Political Security Organization in Aden told EmbOff, "Preliminary reports indicate that there was an insider involved in this case." Though no official word has been issued by the ROYG, Ministry of Defense-owned weekly 26 September noted on August 20 that security forces in Aden had arrested a group of Islamic extremists they believe were involved in the robbery. On August 22 the Yemen Observer, an English-language weekly owned by the President's secretary, quoted an anonymous security official claiming that the Islamic extremists were affiliated with Tariq al-Fadhli, former pro-Saleh jihadi turned Southern Movement leader. Interestingly, Free Aden, an anti-ROYG, openly secessionist web publication, also identified AQAP as the likely perpetrator but claimed the ROYG was attempting to frame the Southern Movement by highlighting the fact that the empty bank vehicle was found in a district of Aden populated by Southern Movement activists.

DJA VU?
— —

5. (C) XXXXXXXXXXXX highlighted the similarity between the recent attack and a 1998 armed robbery of a car carrying nine million Yemeni riyals of government salaries. The 1998 robbery was conducted by eight men dressed in military uniforms at a checkpoint where they ordered the vehicle to pull over, requested paperwork, and then shot two of the

SANAA 00001632 002 OF 002

passengers before hijacking the car with the stolen salaries. After the 1998 incident, the ROYG simply compensated the government employees whose salaries were stolen without investigating the robbery, according to XXXXXXXXXXXX. Though independent reporters tried to garner updated information from the ROYG on the whereabouts of the stolen money and the perpetrators, a follow-up was never published by independent or government press. A few weeks after the 1998 robbery, 16 western tourists were kidnapped in Abyan by the Aden-Abyan Islamic Army, an Islamic extremist group believed to have cooperated with al-Qaeda in the 2000 USS Cole bombing in Aden. (Note. The group was led by the late Abu al-Hassan al-Mihdar, who later confessed to the kidnapping and was summarily executed after a Yemeni court sentenced him and two of his men to death. End Note.) XXXXXXXXXXXX told PolOff that at the time, the robbery was widely believed by Adenis to have been carried out to fund the kidnapping operation, and he believes the same motives could be behind this recent robbery.

COMMENT

6. (C) It is unlikely that ordinary robbers were behind the August 17 attack, considering the precision of the attack and the sophisticated tactics used. The fact that the attackers conducted a coordinated attack requiring information on the specific routes and times of the bank vehicle suggests that they enjoyed good connections and access to sensitive information, both historical hallmarks of Islamic extremists in Yemen. The ROYG's lack of transparency regarding the 1998 armed robbery and its apparent failure to thoroughly investigate the whereabouts of the stolen monies does not inspire confidence that the perpetrators of this attack will be apprehended. If, in fact, they are affiliated with AQAP, $500,000 represents a significant influx of cash which could be used to fund future attacks. END COMMENT. SECHE

Secret Party Life of Saudi Elite

A 2009 cable from Saudi Arabia provided a fascinating behind-the-scenes look at the wild social life of elite Saudi youth and their "freedom to indulge carnal pursuits" away from the prying eyes of the religious police.

DATE 2009-11-18 16:58:00

SOURCE Consulate Jeddah

CLASSIFICATION CONFI DENT IAL

C O N F I D E NT I A L SECTION 01 OF 02 JEDDAH 000443

SIPDIS

DEPT FOR NEA/ARP, NEA/PPD

EO 12958 DECL: 10/31/2014

TAGS SA, SCUL, SOCI, ZR, KISL

SUBJECT: UNDERGROUND PARTY SCENE IN JEDDAH: SAUDI YOUTH

FROLIC UNDER "PRINCELY PROTECTION"

REF: A. JEDDAH 0292 B. JEDDAH 0079

JEDDAH 00000443 001.2 OF 002

Classified By: Consul General Martin R. Quinn for reasons 1.4 (b) and (d)

1. (C) Summary: Behind the facade of Wahabi conservatism in the streets, the underground nightlife for Jeddah's elite youth is thriving and throbbing. The full range of worldly temptations and vices are available -- alcohol, drugs, sex -- but strictly behind closed doors. This freedom to indulge carnal pursuits is possible merely because the religious police keep their distance when parties include the presence or patronage of a Saudi royal and his circle of loyal attendants, such as a Halloween event attended by ConGenOffs on. [DETAIL REMOVED] Over the past few years, the increased conservatism of Saudi

Arabia's external society has pushed the nightlife and party scene in Jeddah even further underground. End summary.

Elite party like the rest of the world,

— — — —

just underground

— — — —

2. (C) Along with over 150 young Saudis (men and women mostly in their 20's and early 30's), ConGenOffs accepted invitations to an underground Halloween party at PrinceXXXXXXXXXXXX residence in Jeddah on XXXXXXXXXXXX. Inside the gates, past the XXXXXXXXXXXX security guards and after the abaya coat-check, the scene resembled a nightclub anywhere outside the Kingdom: plentiful alcohol, young couples dancing, a DJ at the turntables, and everyone in costume. Funding for the party came from a corporate sponsor, XXXXXa U.S.-based energy-drink company as well as from the princely host himself.

Royalty, attended by "khawi," keep religious police at bay

— — — — — — — — — — — — — —

3. (C) Religious police/CPVPV (Commission for the Promotion of Virtue and Prevention of Vice) were nowhere to be seen and while admission was controlled through a strictly-enforced guest list, the partygoers were otherwise not shy about publicizing the affair. According to a young Saudi from a prominent Jeddah merchant family, the Saudis try to throw parties at princes' houses or with princes in attendance, which serves as sufficient deterrent to interference by the CPVPV. There are over 10,000 princes in the Kingdom, albeit at various levels and gradations --"Royal Highnesses" ("Saheb Al Sumou Al Maliki") signified by direct descent from King Abdulaziz, and mere "Highnesses" ("Saheb Al Sumou") from less direct branches of the Al Saud ruling family. Our host that evening, xxxxx (protect), traces his roots to Thunayan, a brother of Mohammad, Amir of Diriyyah and Nejd (1725-65), King Abdullah's direct ancestor, six generations back. Although PrinceXXXXXXXXXXXX is XXXXXXXXXXXX not in line for the throne, he still enjoys the perks of a mansion, luxury car, lifetime stipend, and security entourage. (Note: Most of the prince XXXXXXXXXXXX's security forces were young XXXXXXXXXXXX men.

It is common practice for Saudi princes to grow up with hired bodyguards from Nigeria or other African nations who are of similar age and who remain with the prince well into adulthood. They are called "khawi," derived from the Arabic word "akh," meaning "brother." The lifetime spent together creates an intense bond of loyalty. End note.)

Availability of black market alchol, prostitutes, and drugs
— — — — — — — — — — — — — —

4. (C) Alcohol, though strictly prohibited by Saudi law and custom, was plentiful at the party's well-stocked bar, well-patronized by Halloween revellers. The hired Filipino bartenders served a cocktail punch using "sadiqi," a locally-made "moonshine." While top-shelf liquor bottles were on display throughout the bar area, the original contents were reportedly already consumed and replaced by sadiqi. On the black market, a bottle of Smirnoff can cost 1,500 riyals when available, compared to 100 riyals for the locally-made vodka. It was also learned through word-of-mouth that a number of the guests were in fact "working girls," not uncommon for such parties.

JEDDAH 00000443 002.2 OF 002

Additionally, though not witnessed directly at this event, cocaine and hashish use is common in these social circles and has been seen on other occasions.

5. (C) Comment: Saudi youth get to enjoy relative social freedom and indulge fleshly pursuits, but only behind closed doors -- and only the rich. Parties of this nature and scale are believed to be a relatively recent phenomenon in Jeddah. One contact, a young Saudi male, explained that up to a few years ago, the only weekend activity was "dating" inside the homes of the affluent in small groups. It is not uncommon in Jeddah for the more lavish private residences to include elaborate basement bars, discos, entertainment centers and clubs. As one high society Saudi remarked, "The increased conservatism of our society over these past years has only moved social interaction to the inside of people's homes." End comment.

QUINN

Israeli Spy Scandal Touches New Zealand

This 2004 cable from New Zealand reports on the diplomatic dispute over a jail sentence for two Israelis suspected of being intelligence agents. They were charged with trying to obtain a false New Zealand passport.

DATE 2004-07-16 04:20:00

SOURCE Embassy Wellington

CLASSIFICATION CONFI DENT IAL

C O N F I D E N T I A L WELLINGTON 000605

SIPDIS

DEPT FOR EAP/ANP

NSC FOR GREEN, JONES

EO 12958 DECL: 07/15/2014

TAGS PGOV, PREL, PINR, NZ

SUBJECT: NEW ZEALAND IMPOSES "STRICT CONSTRAINTS" ON

DIPLOMATIC RELATIONSHIP WITH ISRAEL IN WAKE OF SPY SCANDAL

Classified By: DEPUTY CHIEF OF MISSION, DAVID R. BURNETT FOR REASONS 1. 5(B,D)

1. (U) In an escalating diplomatic row, two Israeli men were sentenced July 14 by the High Court of New Zealand to six months in jail on charges of trying to obtain a false New Zealand passport. The GoNZ has not pursued allegations that the men are agents of Israeli intelligence agency Mossad. While Prime Minister Helen Clark would not confirm which service employed the men, she noted "if one were to lay espionage charges, one would have to be prepared to offer the kind of evidence in court which our intelligence agencies don't like coming forward to display. We have very strong grounds for believing these are Israeli intelligence agents." Israeli

citizens Uriel Zoshe Kelman and Eli Cara were sentenced to six months in jail, and ordered to each make a NZ$50,000 (US35,000) donation to the Cerebral Palsy Society. (Note: In attempting to procure a passport, they had procured the birth certificate of a cerebral palsy sufferer.) The light sentence reflected the fact that the two men were not the principal actors in the plot, which was led by Israeli Zev William Barkan, who has fled New Zealand and is still wanted. Cara and Kelman pled guilty earlier this month to three charges, including attempting to obtain a New Zealand passport and participating in an organized crime group to obtain a false passport, and faced a maximum sentence of five years. The latter charge is a relatively new provision in the New Zealand Crimes Act, designed to counter transnational crime.

— — — — — — —

Fallout - "Strict Constraints"

— — — — — — —

2. (SBU) Prime Minister Helen Clark suspended high-level contact with Israel and announced a range of diplomatic sanctions, including placing Ministry of Foreign Affairs and Trade (MFAT) officials under "strict constraints" in their contact with Israelis. Clark justified her actions by stating "the Israeli agents attempted to demean the integrity of the New Zealand passport system. The Israeli Government was asked for an explanation and an apology three months ago. Neither has been received." Israeli Foreign Minister Silvan Shalom responded via radio, saying "we are sorry about this matter. It will be dealt with and all will be done to restore Israel's long history of good relations with New Zealand." Clark refused to accept this informal apology. She has announced New Zealand will continue plans to require Israeli officials to apply for visas, to postpone all Israeli consultations this year, and to delay the agrement for a new Israeli Ambassador, resident in Australia. Israel's president, Moshe Katsov, was expected to visit New Zealand in August, but the GoNZ will likely refuse his request.

3. (SBU) In a separate, but possibly related incident, a Jewish cemetery in Wellington was vandalized July 15, and

headstones were desecrated. Clark immediately condemned the attack.

4. (C) Comment: The GoNZ's public reaction is its strongest diplomatic retaliation in 20 years) since French spies bombed the Rainbow Warrior in Auckland harbor in 1985. Clark's limitations on diplomatic contact go further than the GoNZ reaction in 1985, however, and it was reported that she toughened the language of her response from that put forward by MFAT. The GONZ has little to lose by such stringent action, with limited contact and trade with Israel, and possibly something to gain in the Arab world, as the GoNZ is establishing an Embassy in Egypt and actively pursuing trade with Arab states. With Israeli Government officials eager to repair the relationship, and no time limit on the GoNZ's restrictions, it is possible the issue may be resolved in six months, when the Cara and Kelman have served their time, and leave the country. Swindells

Bahrain's King Says Iran Must Be Stopped

King Hamad of Bahrain tells Gen. David H. Petraeus that the United States must rein in Iran's nuclear program by whatever means necessary. "That program must be stopped," the king says. "The danger of letting it go on is greater than the danger of stopping it."

DATE 2009-11-04 06:44:00

SOURCE Embassy Manama

CLASSIFICATION SECRET//NOFORN

S E C R E T MANAMA 000642

NOFORN

E.O. 12958: DECL: 11/04/2019 TAGS: PREL, MARR, ENRG, BA, AF, IZ, IR, NATO SUBJECT: GENERAL PETRAEUS WITH KING HAMAD: IRAQ, AFGHANISTAN, IRAN, NATO AWACS, ENERGY

Classified By: Ambassador Adam Ereli, reasons 1.4(b) and (d).

1. (C) SUMMARY: In an hour-long meeting on November 1 with CENTCOM Commander General Petraeus, Bahrain's King Hamad said Arab states need to do more to engage Iraq, discussed Afghanistan and the positive role India could play, urged action to stop Iran's nuclear program, and reviewed regional plans for the peaceful use of nuclear energy. END SUMMARY.

2. (C) IRAQ: King Hamad fully endorsed General Petraeus's point that increased Arab engagement and influence would help frustrate Iranian designs in Iraq. He added that the Arabs need Egyptian and Saudi leadership in this matter and that he had tried to make this point to the Saudi government, but with little effect.

3. (C) AFGHANISTAN: General Petraeus praised Bahrain's commitment of a police company for internal security at FOB Leatherneck. King Hamad confirmed that he would personally see the force off at the airport on December 16. This date will be

the 10th anniversary of the King's assuming the throne, and General Petraeus said that U.S. air assets would be available on the 16th to transport the company to Afghanistan. King Hamad inquired about the extent of India's involvement in Afghanistan and noted that Bahrain saw India as very positive force in the region. "It's a new era," he said. "They can be of great help."

4. (C) IRAN: King Hamad pointed to Iran as the source of much of the trouble in both Iraq and Afghanistan. He argued forcefully for taking action to terminate their nuclear program, by whatever means necessary. "That program must be stopped," he said. "The danger of letting it go on is greater than the danger of stopping it." King Hamad added that in light of these regional developments, Bahrain was working to strengthen GCC coordination and its relations with allies and international organizations. He specifically mentioned NATO and confirmed that Bahrain had agreed to the Alliance's request to use Isa Airbase for AWACS missions, although the detail on numbers and timing have yet to be discussed.

5. (S/NF) BAHRAIN AIR SHOW AND NUCLEAR ENERGY: King Hamad asked General Petraeus for his help in encouraging U.S. aircraft manufacturers to participate in the inaugural Bahrain Air Show, scheduled for January 2010. He said that France was pushing the Rafale and would be there in force, although he agreed with Petraeus that the French fighter was yesterday's technology. Warming to the subject of French commercial diplomacy and referring to President Sarkozy, King Hamad said, "The UAE will give him a hard time soon," over France's proposed deal for nuclear reactors. "They're not happy with the project he's offered them." King Hamad also mentioned that Bahrain was studying options for using nuclear power to generate electricity. He said he had asked the Ministers of Foreign Affairs, Interior and Public Works to present him recommendations and invited the Ambassador to discuss with them possible U.S. involvement. Post will do so.

EREL I

An Inside Account of Tunisian Corruption

A 2009 cable, heavily redacted to protect American diplomats' sources, gives an inside account of corruption at the top, including a reported attempt by President Zine el-Abidine Ben Ali to obtain 50 percent of a private university.

DATE 2009-06-16 18:45:00

SOURCE Embassy Tunis

CLASSIFICATION CONFIDENTIAL//NOFORN

C O N F I D E N T I A L SECTION 01 OF 03 TUNIS 000372

NOFORN SIPDIS

STATE FOR NEA/MAG (NARDI AND HAYES)

E.O. 12958: DECL: 06/16/2019 TAGS: PGOV, PHUM, KCOR, SOCI, PREL, TS SUBJECT: TUNISIAN CRITICIZES REGIME IN FORTHCOMING BOOK; SHARES ANECDOTE OF BEN ALI CORRUPTION

REF: 07 TUNIS 1489

TUNIS 00000372 001.2 OF 003

Classified By: Ambassador Robert F. Godec for reasons 1.4 (b) and (d)

─── ───

Summary

─── ───

1. (C) XXXXXXXXXXXXX approached Ambassador and Pol/EconCouns XXXXXXXXXXXXX to share with us XXXXXXXXXXXXX the Ambassador gave him assurances that we would. XXXXXXXXXXXXX shared a rare first-hand account of corruption from several years ago in which Ben Ali himself was described as asking for a 50 percent stake in XXXXXXXXXXXXX private university. XXXXXXXXXXXXX End Summary.

─── ─── ─── ─── ─── ─── ───

XXXXXXXXXXXXX Book: XXXXXXXXXXXXX

─── ─── ─── ─── ─── ─── ───

2. (C) On the margins of a networking event for aspiring
and successful social entrepreneurs XXXXXXXXXXXX The book
is extremely critical of the Ben Ali regime for, among other
things, the "duality" between official discourse and the
reality on the ground. Specifically, XXXXXXXXXXXX points to
the "stifling" of political liberties and "omnipotent" controls
on the media. He also charges that freedom of association is
"illusory" and assesses that "the rule of law is more fiction
than reality." XXXXXXXXXXXX

— — —

XXXXXXXXXXXX
— — —

3. (C) XXXXXXXXXXXX asked that the US Embassy follow his case
XXXXXXXXXXXX; the Ambassador assured him that we would do
so. Pol/EconCouns reviewed XXXXXXXXXXXX some of the accounts
of life in prison that we have heard from released political
prisoners; XXXXXXXXXXXX

— — — — — — — — — —

Tale of Corruption I: The French Connection?
— — — — — — — — — —

4. (C/NF) Asked whether he had also been in touch with other
western embassies, XXXXXXXXXXXX said that he had not. He had
avoided reaching out to the French, in particular, arguing that
Ambassador Degallaix is seen as Ben Ali's Ambassador to French
President Sarkozy, not vice versa. In addition, XXXXXXXXXXXX
alleged that the GOT has improperly given Ambassador Degallaix
a villa, which is registered in his daughter's name, on rue
Sidi Dhrif, near the President's own residence. He did not
offer any evidence of this alleged corruption or explain how
this knowledge came to him.

TUNIS 00000372 002 OF 003
— — — — — — — — — — — —

Tale of Corruption II: Ben Ali Seeks 50 Percent Stake
XXXXXXXXXXXX
— — — — — — — — — — — —

5. (C) XXXXXXXXXXXX likened corruption to a dangerous cancer
that is spreading in Tunisia, spurred on by the corrupt
practices of President Ben Ali and his extended family.
When Pol/EconCouns responded by noting that most tales of

corruption that we hear concern "The Family" rather than
the President himself, XXXXXXXXXXXX recounted an incident
in which Ben Ali himself was involved. XXXXXXXXXXXX Ben Ali
came off as "very uneducated" in the meeting, failing to
grasp some of the key points XXXXXXXXXXXX about the virtues
XXXXXXXXXXXX Ben Ali abruptly told him that he wanted a
50-50 stake in the enterprise. Fearful of responding in the
negative, XXXXXXXXXXXX said he "played dumb," pretending not
to understand the President's proposition.

— — — — — — —

Other Run-ins with "The Family"
— — — — — — —

6. (C) XXXXXXXXXXXX also reviewed the difficulties that lead
to the closure XXXXXXXXXXXX

-- XXXXXXXXXXXX

-- XXXXXXXXXXXX

-- XXXXXXXXXXXX XXXXXXXXXXXX

— — — — — — — —

TUNIS 00000372 003 OF 003
How Suha Arafat Got Into Trouble
— — — — — — — —

7. (C) XXXXXXXXXXXX also offered a theory as to what was
behind the GOT's decision to revoke Suha Arafat's Tunisian
citizenship in 2007. (Note: Reftel also reports on this
incident.) He said that he had heard that Leila Ben Ali at
that time had been scheming to marry off an 18 year-old niece
(NFI) to UAE Prime Minister and Dubai Ruler Sheik Mohamed
bin Rashid al-Maktoum, one of whose wives is the half-sister
of the King of Jordan. According to this rumor, Suha Arafat
warned Jordanian Queen Rania about Leila Ben Ali's plans.
Word of Arafat's intervention got back to the Tunisian First
Lady, who turned against Arafat and soon forced her out of
Tunisia.

— — —

XXXXXXXXXXXX
— — —

8. XXXXXXXXXXXX

— — —

XXXXXXXXXXXX

— — —

9. (C) XXXXXXXXXXXX is extremely well respected and considered an upstanding member of the community. While we might doubt the veracity of some of the rumors that he shared with us, we have no reason to doubt his account of his conversation with President Ben Ali, in which he described the President as seeking a 50 percent stake in his private university. We routinely hear allegations of corruption, and such allegations are inherently difficult to prove. XXXXXXXXXXXX anecdote strikes us as credible. It is also significant in that it implicates Ben Ali himself, while so many other reported incidents of corruption involve his extended family.

10. XXXXXXXXXXXX

Please visit Embassy Tunis' Classified Website at: http://www.state.sgov.gov/p/nea/tunis/index.c fm Godec

A Wild Wedding in Dagestan, Russia

An American diplomat goes to a wedding in Dagestan, in the Caucasus region, and comes back with quite a tale.

DATE 2006-08-31 06:39:00

SOURCE Embassy Moscow

CLASSIFICATION CONFI DENT IAL

C O N F I D E N T I A L SECTION 01 OF 05 MOSCOW 009533

SIPDIS

SIPDIS

E.O. 12958: DECL: 08/30/2016 TAGS: PGOV, ECON, PINR, RS
SUBJECT: A CAUCASUS WEDDING

Classified By: Deputy Chief of Mission Daniel A. Russell.
Reason 1.4 (b, d)

Summary
—— ——

1. (C) Weddings are elaborate in Dagestan, the largest autonomy in the North Caucasus. On August 22 we attended a wedding in Makhachkala, Dagestan's capital: Duma member and Dagestan Oil Company chief Gadzhi Makhachev's son married a classmate. The lavish display and heavy drinking concealed the deadly serious North Caucasus politics of land, ethnicity, clan, and alliance. The guest list spanned the Caucasus power structure -- guest starring Chechen leader Ramzan Kadyrov -- and underlined just how personal the region's politics can be. End Summary.

2. (C) Dagestani weddings are serious business: a forum for showing respect, fealty and alliance among families; the bride and groom themselves are little more than showpieces. Weddings take place in discrete parts over three days. On the first day the groom's family and the bride's family simultaneously hold

separate receptions. During the receptions the groom leads
a delegation to the bride's reception and escorts her back
to his own reception, at which point she formally becomes
a member of the groom's family, forsaking her old family
and clan. The next day, the groom's parents hold another
reception, this time for the bride's family and friends, who
can "inspect" the family they have given their daughter to.
On the third day, the bride's family holds a reception for
the groom's parents and family.

Father of the Groom

3. (C) On August 22, Gadzhi Makhachev married off his 19 year-
old son Dalgat to Aida Sharipova. The wedding in Makhachkala,
which we attended, was a microcosm of the social and political
relations of the North Caucasus, beginning with Gadzhi's own
biography. Gadzhi started off as an Avar clan leader. Enver
Kisriyev, the leading scholar of Dagestani society, told us
that as Soviet power receded from Dagestan in the late 1980s,
the complex society fell back to its pre-Russian structure.
The basic structural unit is the monoethnic "jamaat," in this
usage best translated as "canton" or "commune." The ethnic
groups themselves are a Russian construct: faced with hundreds
of jamaats, the 19th century Russian conquerors lumped cantons
speaking related dialects together and called them "Avar,"
"Dargin," etc. to reduce the number of "nationalities" in
Dagestan to 38. Ever since then, jamaats within each ethnic
group have been competing with one another to lead the ethnic
group. This competition is especially marked among the Avars,
the largest nationality in Dagestan.

4. (C) As Russian power faded, each canton fielded a militia
to defend its people both in the mountains and the capital
Makhachkala. Gadzhi became the leader from his home canton
of Burtunay, in Kazbek Rayon. He later asserted pan-Avar
ambitions, founding the Imam Shamil Popular Front --named
after the great Avar leader of mountaineer resistance to the
Russians -- to promote the interests of the Avars and of
Burtunay's role within the ethnic group. Among his exploits
was a role in the military defense of Dagestan against the

1999 invasion from Chechnya by Shamil Basayev and al-Khattab, and his political defense of Avar villages under pressure in Chechnya, Georgia and Azerbaijan.

5. (C) Gadzhi has cashed in the social capital he made from nationalism, translating it into financial and political capital -- as head of Dagestan's state oil company and as the single-mandate representative for Makhachkala in Russia's State Duma. His dealings in the oil business --including close cooperation with U.S. firms -- have left him well off enough to afford luxurious houses in Makhachkala, Kaspiysk, Moscow, Paris and San Diego; and a large collection of luxury automobiles, including the Rolls Royce Silver Phantom in which Dalgat fetched Aida from her parents' reception. (Gadzhi gave us a lift in the Rolls once in Moscow, but the legroom was somewhat constricted by the presence of a Kalashnikov carbine at our feet. Gadzhi has survived numerous assassination attempts, as have most of the still-living leaders of Dagestan. In Dagestan he always travels in an armored BMW with one, sometimes two follow cars full of uniformed armed guards.)

6. (C) Gadzhi has gone beyond his Avar base, pursuing a multi-ethnic cadre policy to develop a network of loyalists. He has sent Dagestani youths, including his sons, to a military type high school near San Diego (we met one graduate, a Jewish boy from Derbent now studying at San Diego state. He has no plans to enter the Russian military).

MOSCOW 00009533 002 OF 005

Gadzhi's multi-ethnic reach illustrates what the editor of the Dagestani paper "Chernovik" told us: that in the last few years the development of inter-ethnic business clans has eroded traditional jamaat loyalties.

7. (C) But the Avar symbolism is still strong. Gadzhi's brother, an artist from St. Petersburg, ordered as a wedding gift a life-sized statue of Imam Shamil. Shamil is the iconic national symbol, despite his stern and inflexible character (portrayed in Tolstoy's "Hadji-Murat" as the mountaineers' tyrannical counterpart to the absolutist Tsar). Connection with Shamil makes for nobility among Avars today. Gadzhi

often mentions that he is a descendant on his mother's side
of Gair-Bek, one of Shamil's deputies.

The Day Before
— — — —

8. (C) Gadzhi's Kaspiysk summer house is an enormous structure
on the shore of the Caspian, essentially a huge circular
reception room -- much like a large restaurant --attached to
a 40-meter high green airport tower on columns, accessible
only by elevator, with a couple of bedrooms, a reception
room, and a grotto whose glass floor was the roof of a huge
fish tank. The heavily guarded compound also boasts a second
house, outbuildings, a tennis court, and two piers out into
the Caspian, one rigged with block and tackle for launching
jet skis. The house filled up with visitors from all over the
Caucasus during the afternoon of August 21. The Chair of
Ingushetia's parliament drove in with two colleagues; visitors
from Moscow included politicians, businessmen and an Avar
football coach. Many of the visitors grew up with Gadzhi in
Khasavyurt, including an Ingush Olympic wrestler named Vakha
who seemed to be perpetually tipsy. Another group of Gadzhi's
boyhood friends from Khasavyurt was led by a man who looked
like Shamil Basayev on his day off -- flip-flops, t-shirt,
baseball cap, beard -- but turned out to be the chief rabbi
of Stavropol Kray. He told us he has 12,000 co-religionists
in the province, 8,000 of them in its capital, Pyatigorsk.
70 percent are, like him, Persian-speaking Mountain Jews;
the rest are a mixture of Europeans, Georgians and Bukharans.

9. (C) Also present was XXXXXXXXXXXX He was reserved at the
time, but in a follow-up conversation in Moscow on August
29 (please protect) he complained that Chechnya, lacking
experts to develop programs for economic recovery, is simply
demanding and disposing of cash from the central government.
When we pressed him on disappearances, he admitted some took
place, but claimed that often parents alleged their children
had been abducted when in fact their sons had run off to
join the fighters or -- in a case the week before -- they had
murdered their daughter in an honor killing. We mentioned the
abduction of a widow of Basayev, allegedly to gain access to

his money. XXXXXXXXXXXX said he had not heard of the case, but knew that Basayev had had no interest in wealth; he may have been a religious fanatic, but he was a "normal" person. The fighters who remain are not a serious military force, in XXXXXXXXXXXX view, and many would surrender under the proper terms and immunities. He himself is arranging the immunity of a senior official of the Maskhadov era, whose name he would not reveal.

10. (C) During lunch, Gadzhi took a congratulatory call from Dagestan's president, Mukhu Aliyev. Gadzhi told Aliyev how honored he would be if Aliyev could drop in at the wedding reception. There was a degree of tension in the conversation, which was between two figures each implicitly claiming the mantle of leadership of the Avars. In the event, Aliyev snubbed Gadzhi and did not show up for the wedding, though the rest of Dagestan's political leadership did.

11. (C) Though Gadzhi's house was not the venue for the main wedding reception, he ensured that all his guests were constantly plied with food and drink. The cooks seemed to keep whole sheep and whole cows boiling in a cauldron somewhere day and night, dumping disjointed fragments of the carcass on the tables whenever someone entered the room. Gadzhi's two chefs kept a wide variety of unusual dishes in circulation (in addition to the omnipresent boiled meat and fatty bouillon). The alcohol consumption before, during and after this Muslim wedding was stupendous. Amidst an alcohol shortage, Gadzhi had flown in from the Urals thousands of bottles of Beluga Export vodka ("Best consumed with caviar"). There was also entertainment, beginning even that day, with the big-name performers appearing both at the wedding hall and at Gadzhi's summer house. Gadzhi's main act, a Syrian-born singer named Avraam Russo, could not make it because he was shot a few days before the wedding, but there

MOSCOW 00009533 003 OF 005

was a "gypsy" troupe from St. Petersburg, a couple of Azeri pop stars, and from Moscow, Benya the Accordion King with his family of singers. A host of local bands, singing in Avar

and Dargin, rounded out the entertainment, which was constant
and extremely amplified.

10. (C) The main activity of the day was eating and drinking
-- starting from 4 p.m., about eight hours worth, all told
-- punctuated, when all were laden with food and sodden
with drink, with a bout of jet skiing in the Caspian. After
dinner, though, the first band started an informal performance
-- drums, accordion and clarinet playing the lezginka, the
universal dance of the Caucasus. To the uninitiated Westerner,
the music sounds like an undifferentiated wall of sound. This
was a signal for dancing: one by one, each of the dramatically
paunchy men (there were no women present) would enter the
arena and exhibit his personal lezginka for the limit of his
duration, usually 30 seconds to a minute. Each ethnic group's
lezginka was different -- the Dagestani lezginka the most
energetic, the Chechen the most aggressive and belligerent,
and the Ingush smoother.

Wedding Day 1

11. (C) An hour before the wedding reception was set to begin
the "Marrakech" reception hall was full of guests --men taking
the air outside and women already filling a number of the
tables inside, older ones with headscarves chaperoning dozens
of teenaged girls. A Dagestani parliamentarian explained that
weddings are a principal venue for teenagers -- and more
importantly their parents -- to get a look at one another
with a view to future matches. Security was tight -- police
presence on the ground plus police snipers positioned on the
roof of an overlooking apartment block. Gadzhi even assigned
one of his guards as our personal bodyguard inside the
reception. The manager told Gadzhi there were seats for over
a thousand guests at a time. At the height of the reception,
it was standing room only.

12. (C) At precisely two p.m. the male guests started filing
in. They varied from pols and oligarchs of all sorts -- the
slick to the Jurassic; wizened brown peasants from Burtunay;
and Dagestan's sports and cultural celebrities. XXXXXXXXXXXX

presided over a political table in the smaller of the two
halls (the music was in the other) along with Vakha the
drunken wrestler, the Ingush parliamentarians, a member
of the Federation Council who is also a nanophysicist and
has lectured in Silicon Valley, and Gadzhi's cousin Ismail
Alibekov, a submariner first rank naval captain now serving
at the General Staff in Moscow. The Dagestani milieu appears
to be one in which the highly educated and the gun-toting
can mix easily -- often in the same person.

13. (C) After a couple of hours Dalgat's convoy returned with
Aida, horns honking. Dalgat and Aida got out of the Rolls
and were serenaded into the hall, and into the Makhachev
family, by a boys' chorus lining both sides of the red
carpet, dressed in costumes aping medieval Dagestani armor
with little shields and swords. The couple's entry was the
signal for the emcee to roll into high gear, and after a few
toasts the Piter "gypsies" began their performance. (The next
day one of Gadzhi's houseguests sneered, "Some gypsies! The
bandleader was certainly Jewish, and the rest of them were
blonde." There was some truth to this, but at least the two
dancing girls appeared to be Roma.)

14. (C) As the bands played, the marriageable girls came out
to dance the lezginka in what looked like a slowly revolving
conga line while the boys sat together at tables staring
intently. The boys were all in white shirts and black slacks,
while the girls wore a wide variety of multicolored but
fashionable cocktail dresses. Every so often someone would
shower the dancers with money -- there were some thousand
ruble notes but the currency of choice was the U.S. hundred
dollar bill. The floor was covered with them; young children
would scoop the money up to distribute among the dancers.

15. (C) Gadzhi was locked into his role as host. He greeted
every guest personally as they entered the hall -- failure to
do so would cause great insult -- and later moved constantly
from table to table drinking toasts with everyone. The 120
toasts he estimated he drank would have killed anyone,
hardened drinker or not, but Gadzhi had his Afghan waiter
Khan following him around to pour his drinks from a special

vodka bottle containing water. Still, he was much the worse for wear by evening's end. At one point we caught up with him dancing with two scantily clad Russian women who looked far from home. One, it turned out was a Moscow poet (later she recited an incomprehensible poem in Gadzhi's honor) who

was in town with a film director to write the screenplay for a film immortalizing Gadzhi's defense of Dagestan against Shamil Basayev. By 6 p.m. most of the houseguests had returned to Gadzhi's seaside home for more swimming and more jet-skiing-under-the-influence. But by 8 the summer house's restaurant was full once more, the food and drink were flowing, the name performers were giving acoustic renditions of the songs they had sung at the reception, and some stupendously fat guests were displaying their lezginkas for the benefit of the two visiting Russian women, who had wandered over from the reception.

The Wedding -- Day 2: Enter The Man
— — — — — — — —

16. (C) The next day's reception at the Marrakech was Gadzhi's tribute to Aida's family, after which we all returned to a dinner at Gadzhi's summer home. Most of the tables were set with the usual dishes plus whole roast sturgeons and sheep. But at 8:00 p.m. the compound was invaded by dozens of heavily armed mujahedin for the grand entrance of Chechen leader Ramzan Kadyrov, dressed in jeans and a t-shirt, looking shorter and less muscular than in his photos, and with a somewhat cock-eyed expression on his face. After greetings from Gadzhi, Ramzan and about 20 of his retinue sat around the tables eating and listening to Benya the Accordion King. Gadzhi then announced a fireworks display in honor of the birthday of Ramzan's late father, Ahmat-Hadji Kadyrov. The fireworks started with a bang that made both Gadzhi and Ramzan flinch. Gadzhi had from the beginning requested that none of his guests, most of whom carried sidearms, fire their weapons in celebration. Throughout the wedding they complied, not even joining in the magnificent fireworks display.

17. (C) After the fireworks, the musicians struck up the lezginka in the courtyard and a group of two girls and three boys -- one no more than six years old -- performed gymnastic versions of the dance. First Gadzhi joined them and then Ramzan, who danced clumsily with his gold-plated automatic stuck down in the back of his jeans (a houseguest later pointed out that the gold housing eliminated any practical use of the gun, but smirked that Ramzan probably couldn't fire it anyway) . Both Gadzhi and Ramzan showered the dancing children with hundred dollar bills; the dancers probably picked upwards of USD 5000 off the cobblestones. Gadzhi told us later that Ramzan had brought the happy couple "a five kilo lump of gold" as his wedding present. After the dancing and a quick tour of the premises, Ramzan and his army drove off back to Chechnya. We asked why Ramzan did not spend the night in Makhachkala, and were told, "Ramzan never spends the night anywhere."

18. (C) After Ramzan sped off, the dinner and drinking --especially the latter -- continued. An Avar FSB colonel sitting next to us, dead drunk, was highly insulted that we would not allow him to add "cognac" to our wine. "It's practically the same thing," he insisted, until a Russian FSB general sitting opposite told him to drop it. We were inclined to cut the Colonel some slack, though: he is head of the unit to combat terrorism in Dagestan, and Gadzhi told us that extremists have sooner or later assassinated everyone who has joined that unit. We were more worried when an Afghan war buddy of the Colonel's, Rector of the Dagestan University Law School and too drunk to sit, let alone stand, pulled out his automatic and asked if we needed any protection. At this point Gadzhi and his people came over, propped the rector between their shoulders, and let us get out of range.

Postscript: The Practical Uses of a Caucasus Wedding
— — — — — — — — — — — —

19. (C) Kadyrov's attendance was a mark of respect and alliance, the result of Gadzhi's careful cultivation --dating back to personal friendship with Ramzan's father. This is a necessary political tool in a region where difficulties

can only be resolved by using personal relationships to reach ad hoc informal agreements. An example was readily to hand: on August 22 Chechnya's parliamentary speaker, Dukvakha Abdurakhmanov, gave an interview in which he made specific territorial claims to the Kizlyar, Khasavyurt and Novolak regions of Dagestan. The first two have significant Chechen-Akkin populations, and the last was part of Chechnya until the 1944 deportation, when Stalin forcibly resettled ethnic Laks (a Dagestani nationality) there. Gadzhi said he would have to answer Abdurakhmanov and work closely with Ramzan to reduce the tensions "that fool" had caused. Asked why he took such statements seriously, he told us that in the Caucasus all disputes revolve around land, and such claims can never be

MOSCOW 00009533 005 OF 005

dismissed. Unresolved land claims are the "threads" the Russian center always kept in play to pull when needed. We asked why these claims are coming out now, and were told it was euphoria, pure and simple. After all they had received, the Chechen leadership's feet are miles off the ground. (A well-connected Chechen contact later told us he thought that raising nationalistic irredentism was part of Abdurakhmanov's effort to gain a political base independent from Kadyrov.)

20. (C) The "horizontal of power" represented by Gadzhi's relationship with Ramzan is the antithesis of the Moscow-imposed "vertical of power." Gadzhi's business partner Khalik Gindiyev, head of Rosneft-Kaspoil, complained that Moscow should let local Caucasians rather than Russians --"Magomadovs and Aliyevs, not Ivanovs and Petrovs" --resolve the region's conflicts. The vertical of power, he said, is inapplicable to the Caucasus, a region that Moscow bureaucrats such as PolPred Kozak would never understand. The Caucasus needs to be given the scope to resolve its own problems. But this was not a plug for democracy. Gadzhi told us democracy would always fail in the Caucasus, where the conception of the state is as an extension of the Caucasus family, in which the father's word is law. "Where is the room for democracy in that?" he asked. We paraphrased Hayek: if you run a family as you do a state, you destroy the family. Running a state as you do

a family destroys the state: ties of kinship and friendship will always trump the rule of law. Gadzhi's partner agreed, shaking his head sadly. "That's a matter for generations to come," he said.

BURNS

American Ambassador on Sarkozy

In this cable, the American ambassador, Charles Rivkin, reviews President Nicolas Sarkozy's domestic political situation ahead of regional elections in March 2009. He shares his perception of the French president as operating with "monarch-like impunity" after a string of scandals and notes his decision to promote his son Jean, then 23 years old, as the head of France's most prestigious business district.

DATE 2009-10-21 15:09:00

SOURCE Embassy Paris

CLASSIFICATION CONFI DENT IAL

C O N F I D E N T I A L SECTION 01 OF 02 PARIS 001416

SIPDIS

E.O. 12958: DECL: 10/21/2019 TAGS: PREL, FR SUBJECT: MARCH 2010 REGIONAL ELECTIONS PREVIEW SARKOZY'S STRENGTH AT MID-TERM

Classified By: POL M/C Kathy Allegrone for reasons 1.4 (b) and (d).

1. (C) Summary: French regional elections scheduled for March 2010 are shaping up as a measurement of President Nicolas Sarkozy's strength at the mid-point of his term. Despite rumors of malaise and dogged by a series of internal political tempests including the Clearstream trial, rumors of his Culture Minister's participation in sex tourism, and his son Jean's appointment to a coveted business position amidst charges of nepotism, no other political figure or party can match the dominance of Sarkozy on the French political scene. The opposition Socialists (PS) are in tatters, with Martine Aubry, as Party Chairman, vying for control of the left against her bitter rival, 2007 PS presidential candidate, Segolene Royale. With Sarkozy's UMP controlling only two of 22 regions, and following their impressive victory in the European elections last June, the center-right appears to have

nothing to lose. The debate has been how many more regions will tip their way -- and what will constitute victory. Regional councils play a role in the selection of French Senators, and by extension that body can take on a different complexion than the UMP-controlled National Assembly. As the only national vote before the 2012 presidential and legislative races, all eyes view this round of regional elections as a preview Sarkozy's reelection bid. End Summary.

2. (U) Regional elections will be held in France in mid-March 2010 to elect local leadership for the 22 regions of mainland France and four additional overseas regions. In 2005, Socialists overwhelmed the UMP in the regional elections, winning all but two regions. The huge Socialist victory was viewed widely as a repudiation of then-President Chirac's leadership. As the only nationwide elections before the 2012 presidential and legislative elections, "the regionals" are viewed as a referendum on Nicolas Sarkozy's leadership and a snapshot of parties' relative strength heading into 2012.

Mechanics
— — —

3. (U) As elsewhere in Europe, regional elections in France are a confusing system combining proportional and majority voting. Like other elections in France, voters choose a party list, or slate of candidates, representing various parties. Any list winning 10% of the vote in the first round of elections (likely to be on March 14 or 21, 2010), advances to a second round of elections (one week later, thus either March 21 or 28, 2010). Parties that win only 5% of the vote may join efforts with other parties to advance to the second round. If one party wins 25% of the votes, they win the right to form the regional council; the remaining seats are divided proportionally depending on the results of the second round.

Sarkozy's Dominance, Despite Governing Woes
— — — — — — — — — —

4. (C) Regional councils finance education, transport and other key infratructure, and are locked in a struggle with national authorities over taxation. They also participate,

along with other municipalities, in the selection process of French Senators, and will do so again in September 2011. With only two regions controlled by conservative majorities (in Alsace and Corsica), President Sarkozy would welcome extending his political dominance to regional councils, to match his lionized role in the executive and legislative branches. But Sarkozy faces his own challenges, and the press is abuzz about malaise in his administration, as well as Sarkozy's "monarchial tendencies." Concretely, Sarkozy first urged cabinet members to head the UMP ticket in various regions. He then flipped and decided it was incompatible to hold both jobs simultaneously. That decision forced three ministers to opt out of running in regional races, and has left the President's UMP party ill prepared for March, scrambling to find suitable candidates. Sarkozy has also been dogged by recent scandals, including his Culture Minister Frederic Mitterrand's dalliance in possible sex tourism. Mitterand chronicled his appetite for paying for sex with young men in a 2005 book (that Sarkozy described as "courageous") but subsequently publicly denied and condemned "sexual tourism," and vigorously denied that any of his actions extended to under-aged youth. Sarkozy has come in for withering criticism when news broke that his 23-year old son, Jean, an undergraduate law student, was to be named head of the regional business authority of France's premier business district, La Defense. Both the Mitterrand affair and the apparent favoritism enjoyed by the younger Sarkozy have given the president's opponents two potential campaign issues, that could damage his party's chances in the upcoming regionals.

PARIS 00001416 002 OF 002

Weakened Opposition Focused on Infighting
— — — — — — — — — —

5. (C) Despite the challenges facing Sarkozy, other parties are far from fighting shape. The opposition Socialists (PS) are locked in their own internecine struggle for dominance between party leader, Martine Aubry, and 2007 presidential candidate, Segolene Royal. Sarkozy confidant Alain Minc told Ambassador Rivkin in September, 2009 that he was a close friend

of Aubry's whom he had known since their days at France's Ecole Naitonale d'Administration (ENA), and that Aubry told him she ran for the PS leadership in order to clip Royale's wings. The PS is preoccupied with how to position the party for the 2012 presidential race, either by forming a broad left coalition, or moving into alliance with the centrist Mouvement Democratique (MoDem) party.

6. (SBU) The PS faces a real challenge from its left, with the Green party hoping to repeat their surprisingly strong showing in European parliamentary elections. The Greens have refused to run with PS in the first round of regional elections and are counting on the growing profile of their 34 year old leader, Cecile Duflot to win in Paris. A Green win in high-profile Paris would be a serious rebuke to the PS, and if repeated elsewhere in France could precipitate Aubry's ouster from her leadership role in the PS.

7. (SBU) MoDem will be challenged by a new group of centrists called Nouveau Centre, which is largely allied with Sarkozy's UMP. Neither party is expected to win any regional contest, but there is an open question of where MoDem will throw its support in a second round of elections. Their electoral results will be watched closely as a barometer for the 2012 presidential race, and whether MoDem will join forces with the PS to create a united coalition to oppose Sarkozy in 2012.

8. (C) The far right National Front (FN) will focus its efforts in the Provence Alpes Cote d'Azur (PACA) region in southern France, a traditional area of support. With his party's finances in tatters and its traditional themes co-opted by Sarkozy's UMP, this race likely represents Jean Marie Le Pen's final campaign. He has passed the torch to his daughter, Marine, who broke the Frederic Mitterrand story, largely to energize her flagging campaign. Fearing

association with the FN, other mainstream political parties were slow to criticize Mitterrand, although some PS leaders eventually joined the chorus calling for his resignation.

9. (C) Comment: Although the Mitterrand story has largely disappeared, it has been replaced since by the embarrassing

issue of Jean Sarkozy's likely election to head the La Defense
business district. Combined, these stories have bolstered the
impression that Sarkozy is operating in a zone of monarch-
like impunity, and his aides, according to an article in
Le Figaro, are unwilling to question the President's views.
UMP party leaders have turned to the traditional canard of
lashing out at the media for their unfair attention, but
they have just as quickly sought to lower expectations for
a strong conservative comeback in the March 2010 elections.
After losing 13 regions in 2005, UMP election expert Alain
Marleix said winning six back was a possibility, but that
estimate was lowered by UMP President Xavier Bertrand, who
said this week that a center-right win in four would "be
a miracle." Regardless of the result, Sarkozy will head
into 2012 enjoying an outsized role in the French political
firmament -- beloved by some, reviled by others -- and the
failure of the opposition to do anything other than bicker
amongst themselves spells a positive forecast as Sarkozy eyes
a re-election bid in two more years.

RIVKIN

Russian Corruption

A frank and bleak cable about the extent and nature of official corruption in Russia, which leaves little hope for improvement.

DATE 2009-11-19 15:07:00

SOURCE Embassy Moscow

CLASSIFICATION CONFIDENTIAL

C O N F I D E N T I A L SECTION 01 OF 02 MOSCOW 002823

SIPDIS

STATE FOR EUR/RUS, EEB NSC FOR MCFAUL

E.O. 12958: DECL: 11/18/2019 TAGS: ECON, PGOV, PINR, RS SUBJECT: EXPERTS REMAIN SKEPTICAL OF GOR'S ABILITY TO REDUCE CORRUPTION

REF: A. 08 MOSCOW 3775 B. 08 MOSCOW 3363 C. MOSCOW 1450

Classified By: Econ MC Matthias Mitman for reasons 1.4 (b. and d.)

—— ——

Summary

—— ——

1. (C) In a nod to President Medvedev's 2008 anti-corruption legislation, Transparency International's Corruption Perceptions Index ranked Russia at 146, up one spot from its 2008 147th ranking. This general lack of progress confirms what analysts have told us. Corruption in Russia remains a serious problem, despite Medvedev's public denouncements and efforts to reduce it. This presents a quandary for the GOR as it decides how to proceed. Dramatic steps might threaten the status quo, yet gradual steps so far have been ineffective. End Summary.

— — — — — — — — —

Russia's Corruption Rankings Stagnate

— — — — — — — —

2. (SBU) Transparency International released its 2009 Corruption Perceptions Index on 17 November. Russia was ranked

at 146 (it was ranked at 147 in 2008), which Transparency
International said reflected a "mildly positive" response to
Medvedev's 2008 anti-corruption legislation. Russia's 2009
rank, however, is still below its 2007 rank (143) and far
below its 2006 rank (121). These results echo the World Bank's
Worldwide Governance Indicators, with Russia's rankings on
"control of corruption" showing a steady annual decline since
2005.

3. (SBU) President Medvedev has repeatedly stated that
corruption is endemic to Russia and has made fighting it
a signature issue for his presidency. He has highlighted
consistently the damage corruption has done to Russia, most
recently in both his high-profile "Forward Russia" article in
September and his 12 November address to the Federal Assembly.
Beyond the anti-corruption legislation promulgated last year,
however, few practical steps have been implemented.

— — — — —

Elite Losing Control
— — — — —

4. (C) Furthermore, there is growing consensus among analysts
that even if the power elite wants to tackle corruption,
the economic crisis has exacerbated tendencies towards
unmanageability of corruption within the power vertical.
XXXXXXXXXXXX, told us that the GOR may have waited too long.
XXXXXXXXXXXX said that a few years ago, when only millions
had been "stolen" from the Russian people (as opposed to
today's billions), the GOR could have acted and not sparked
public outrage. XXXXXXXXXXXX said that the crisis had made
the GOR's task more difficult and the scope of corruption
has become unmanageable. As the crisis reduced the size
of the pot and the anti-corruption rhetoric increased,
some Russians felt that they had best grab as much as they
could while the going was good. XXXXXXXXXXXX, noted that
the tendency of corruption to evade control by the GOR was
not new. In 2006 -- at the height of Putin's control in a
booming economy -- it was rumored within the Presidential
Administration that as many as 60 percent of his orders were
not being followed.

— — — — — — — — — — — —

Do Changes At Interior Ministry Signal Progress?

— — — — — — — — — — — —

5. (C) XXXXXXXXXXXX noted that Minister of Interior Rashid Nurgaliev had recently fired or brought charges against a number of relatively low-ranking law enforcement officials for corruption. XXXXXXXXXXXX stated though, that it was too soon to judge whether this activity reflected real change. XXXXXXXXXXXX, argued that Nurgaliev's actions were not meaningful. He stated that action was required from higher up the power vertical and needed to affect the strata that average Russians would consider "untouchable".

— — — — — — — —

MOSCOW 00002823 002 OF 002

Can Russia's Trajectory Be Changed?

— — — — — — — —

6. (C) XXXXXXXXXXXX, said that only a "revolution" could change Russia's current trajectory. He argued that the system had become too sclerotic and too beneficial for too many to allow for change. XXXXXXXXXXXX noted that corruption had even become a positive factor for a substantial portion of society. By taking merit out of the equation for success, it was simply easier to pay for entrance to a university, for a contract, etc. XXXXXXXXXXXX, who has made a fortune in Russia's casino business, told us forthrightly that the "levels of corruption in business were worse than we could imagine" and that, after working here for over 15 years and witnessing first-hand the behavior of GOR officials at all levels, he could not imagine the system changing.

— —

Comment

— —

7. (C) Corruption in Russia remains pervasive and deep-rooted. While Medvedev's anti-corruption rhetoric is a step in the right direction, we have yet to see significant implementation of new measures. Russians appear to accept current levels of corruption and seem inclined to pay up or emigrate, rather than protest. Neither have Russians reacted to the sight of the connected few continuing to indulge in

luxurious lifestyles as the economic recession continues
to leave most Russians worse off than they were two to
three years ago. Nonetheless, the commentary on the GOR's
increasing inability to manage the scope of corruption bodes
ill for its stated effort to enhance corporate governance
and investor confidence. Beyrle

Airbus Wins Deal, Until U.S. Intervenes

In December 2007, Gulf Air, the government-owned airline of Bahrain, the small but wealthy island country in the Persian Gulf, announced that it intended to buy a new fleet of Airbus planes. Boeing officials alerted the State Department, which then intervened up to the highest levels of the government, urging them to buy American. The crown prince and king of Bahrain, preparing for the first visit by a sitting United States president, agreed to reverse the decision, ordering Gulf Air to reopen negotiations with Boeing, which ended up winning the deal, which was signed while then President Bush was visiting Bahrain.

DATE 2008-01-27 12:25:00

SOURCE Embassy Manama

CLASSIFICATION CONFI DENT IAL

C O N F I D E N T I A L SECTION 01 OF 03 MANAMA 000047

SIPDIS

SIPDIS

COMMERCE FOR 4520/ITA/MAC/ONE/HOFFMAN

E.O. 12958: DECL: 01/27/2018 TAGS: EAIR, EINV, ETRD, ECON, BA
SUBJECT: EMBASSY ADVOCACY HELPS WIN $6 BILLION BOEING DEAL

REF: A. 07 MANAMA 408

B. 07 MANAMA 338

Classified By: Ambassador Adam Ereli, reasons 1.4(b) and

SUMMARY

1. (C) Following months of heavy lobbying by the Ambassador, the Crown Prince and King rejected a Gulf Air proposal to buy Airbus and directed the airline to make a deal with Boeing. Gulf Air signed an agreement valued at $6 billion with Boeing

on January 13, in time to coincide with a POTUS visit. The agreement represents a significant Embassy commercial advocacy success. A last-minute French government push for Airbus included discussion of a visit to Bahrain by President Sarkozy. End Summary.

—   —   —   —

SMOOTH LANDING

—   —   —   —

2. (C) Post commercial advocacy efforts paid off handsomely on January 13 when Gulf Air signed a deal to buy 16 787s, valued at $3.4 billion, with options for an additional 8, valued at $2.6 billion. At a press conference following the signing, Gulf Air Board Chairman Mahmoud Kooheji said it was virtually assured that Gulf Air would exercise its options on all 8 additional planes. Boeing's stock opened sharply higher January 14, following the weekend announcement.

—   —   —

BUMPY RIDE

—   —   —

3. (C) Boeing first requested USG assistance in May 2006, when then Gulf Air president James Hogan announced plans to replace the carrier's aging fleet with a mix of medium-range and long-range aircraft. Under Hogan's business plan, Boeing would have supplied up to 25 787s and as many as 22 737s. Gulf Air was then still jointly owned by the Governments of Bahrain and Oman and Embassies Manama and Muscat each lobbied their respective host governments on Boeing's behalf. However, Hogan's managerial differences with Gulf Air's board subsequently led to his departure from Gulf Air and his ambitious plan was scrapped.

4. (C) With the Government of Oman's announced withdrawal from Gulf Air in May 2007, Minister of Finance Shaikh Ahmed Bin Mohammed Al Khalifa took personal oversight of Gulf Air's management with a view toward stemming Gulf Air's losses, which stood in excess of USD 1 million per day. Shaikh Ahmed stated that either the Airbus 320 or the Boeing 737 would fit Gulf Air's developing need for high-frequency regional traffic. "The long-term emphasis for the carrier is narrow-body instead

of wide-body." Andre Dose, Shaikh Ahmed's pick to replace James Hogan as Gulf Air CEO, soon confirmed to Emboffs that Gulf Air would downsize to an Airbus fleet (reftels).

5. (C) However, Dose's aggressive downsizing drive, which also led to cuts in routes and personnel, brought him into conflict with the Gulf Air board. In July 2007, after just four months on the job, he resigned his post, leaving Deputy CEO Bjorn Naff to succeed him.

6. (C) The Gulf Air board, now controlled entirely by the GOB, made clear to Naff its vision for Gulf Air as a robust, revitalized national carrier. The airline needed to grow rather than shrink. In October 2007, Gulf Air signed an MOU to purchase Boeing Dreamliners. However, the board reversed itself shortly thereafter, citing concern over being able to justify a decision for Boeing to the parliament in the face of a steeply discounted airbus quotation; the Airbus package was reportedly $400 million cheaper.

7. (C) On December 12 Gulf Air delivered bad news to Boeing -- the board had selected the Airbus package. Signaling that Boeing's prospects were finished, Gulf Air asked Boeing to return its deposit. Boeing executives promptly informed the Ambassador and Econoff that the deal was lost and Airbus had won. But from Post's perspective the contest remained far from over. Gulf Air's selection still needed to be endorsed by the government. The Ambassador directly queried senior

MANAMA 00000047 002 OF 003

GOB officials and learned that no formal decision had yet been reached. Accordingly, he advised Boeing of his recommendation -- it was too soon to walk away.

8. (C) Boeing renewed its request for advocacy. The Ambassador and Econoff persisted in lobbying Gulf Air management, board members, government officials and representatives of parliament. The Ambassador made the case repeatedly that Airbus, lower up-front costs would be eclipsed by Boeing's lower operating costs and product reliability. He made much

of the fact that the Airbus A-350 alternative was still on the drawing board.

—   —   —   —

COURSE CORRECTION

—   —   —   —

9. (C) Kooheji urgently requested a meeting with the Ambassador on December 30 to advise him that the Crown Prince and King had rejected Gulf Air's proposal to buy Airbus, and directed him to make a deal with Boeing in time to coincide with the January 12-13 POTUS visit. Kooheji said he would accordingly seek to come to terms with Boeing. However, if Boeing were to respond that its best deal was already on the table, Kooheji would be unable to justify a revised board recommendation. Boeing would need to show willingness to make some concession(s) that Kooheji could point to as equation-altering.

10. (C) The Ambassador notified Boeing that its representatives would need to return to Bahrain quickly and be ready to finalize an agreement. Somewhat skeptical, Boeing executives initially responded that their obligations precluded a return to Bahrain before January 14. The Ambassador pointed out that this would be too late. Boeing subsequently returned to Bahrain and called on the Ambassador January 3rd. The Ambassador shared that he had spoken directly to the Crown Prince on Boeing's behalf. The Crown Prince had assured him of the Government's sincerity in seeking a deal. This was not merely a last-minute maneuver to wring concessions from Airbus.

11. (C) Encouraged by such a high-level assurance of good faith, Boeing responded by shaving an additional five percent off its proposed sale price. This concession proved decisive in providing Kooheji with the justification he sought to advocate a board decision for Boeing.

12. (U) On January 13, Gulf Air and Boeing signed the $6 billion Boeing deal. Dreamliner delivery will start in 2016. In the meantime, Kooheji said Gulf Air will seek to meet its needs via the leasing market. The purchase will be supported via a blend of commercial and ExIm Bank financing with the sovereign backing of the GOB.

LAST-MINUTE FRENCH RECLAMA

13. (C) GOB officials tell Emboffs that French President Sarkozy, who was visiting the region at the time, made a last-minute call to King Hamad. Sarkozy reportedly said he would add Bahrain to his itinerary during the week of January 13 on the condition that he could sign a contract for 21 Airbus planes. French officials reportedly canceled the visit on news of the Boeing deal. Foreign Minister Sheikh Khalid told Ambassador that he would be calling in the local French Ambassador to tell her "we don't appreciate being dealt with this way."

COMMENT

14. (C) Although Gulf Air has just completed a major long-range aircraft purchase, it is not finished shopping. Kooheji has said Gulf Air still needs to replace eight of its mid-range aircraft. Gulf Air has already signed an MOU with Airbus for those planes, but Kooheji notes that bidding remains open. It seems likely that Gulf Air will choose to replace eight of its Airbus A-320s with newer planes from that manufacturer. But as Boeing's recent win illustrates, Airbus is in no position take Gulf Air's business for granted. Post will certainly continue to hail the advantages of a Boeing solution.

MANAMA 00000047 003 OF 003

15. (C) The Embassy's role in Boeing's success is noteworthy for advancing well beyond every-day advocacy. Gulf Air relied on the Embassy to not only communicate with Boeing, but to get the best possible deal; Boeing turned to us for an understanding of the true facts on the ground (which at times belied appearances) and as a force multiplier, conveying the Boeing advantage at all levels. These efforts resulted in a win-win solution. In a letter of thanks to the Ambassador Boeing stated, "Your continued effort to touch the right leaders and remain a strong advocate for Boeing in this process made an enormous difference in the final outcome. The

working together activity between you, your team, and Boeing
is a model that we should really aspire to replicate in other
countries." End Comment.

*** ********
Visit Embassy Manama's Classified Website:
http: //www. state. sgov. gov/p/nea/manama/

*** ********
EREL I

WAR LOGS

An archive of classified military documents offers an unvarnished view
of the wars in Afghanistan and Iraq. Some names and details have been
redacted (XXXXXXXXXXXX) by The Times to conceal suspects' identities, or because they might put people in danger or reveal key tactical
military capabilities. The ebook edition of *Open Secrets* includes a larger
selection of the original documents. A glossary of terms found in the war
logs appears on page 519.

Kidnapping and Murder

A man and his nephew were kidnapped by Afghan insurgents—just one of the methods they use to sow fear among the local population. The man was killed, and his body left in a village.

DATE 3/6/08

TITLE Report of Kidnapping and Murder of an Afghan Police Officer's Brother

On or about 06 MAR 08, INS kidnapped XXXXXXXXXXXX and his Nephew XXXXXXXXXXXX from their home in Tutakhel, Zormat District. On the night of 08 MAR 08, XXXXXXXXXXXX was killed. XXXXXXXXXXXX was blindfolded and he was shot in the chest approximately 16 times with an AK-47. The body along with AK-47 shells were dumped in the village of Chawni to make it look like XXXXXXXXXXXX was executed there. ANP assessed that the execution did not take place in Chawni because they interviewed all the personnel living in the area where the body was dumped and no one claimed to hear any gunfire. XXXXXXXXXXXX's nephew XXXXXXXXXXXX is still being held hostage by insurgents. No new information exists to XXXXXXXXXXXX's whereabouts and no ransom has been demanded by INS. XXXXXXXXXXXX and XXXXXXXXXXXX were reportedly kidnapped because XXXXXXXXXXXX's older brother, XXXXXXXXXXXX, is an AUP patrolman.NFTR.

Suicide Truck Bombs

The Taliban stole four Afghan National Army trucks, which the report says they planned to use for suicide bombings. The report provides an example of how the Taliban employ trickery as an effective weapon against a more technologically advanced foe.

DATE 11/20/06

TITLE Report of Use of Afghan National Army Trucks as Suicide Bombs

TB TO USE ANA TRUCKS AS SVBIEDS

Organization(s) Involved: TALIBAN

20061210-CJ2X INTSUM -(N/I C)

RC CAPITAL - TALIBAN captured Four ANA trucks to be used as SVBIEDs in KABUL City, KABUL Province. (B?2)

DOI: 20 Nov 06; OHR: CIINTREP-ADET-IX-480-06

(N/I C) 1. The TALIBAN has transported four captured ANA pick-up trucks to KABUL District, KABUL Province for use as SVBIEDs. They intend to use the pick-up trucks to target ANA compounds, ISAF and GOA convoys, as well as high-ranking GOA and ISAF officials. The four pick-up trucks are described as standard sand-coloured ANA FORD RANGER pick-up trucks; license plates are unknown. The four trucks were also accompanied by an unknown quantity of ANA uniforms to facilitate carrying out the attacks.

2. The four trucks were captured during an attack on an ANA convoy in SHAJOY District (GRID NOT AVAILABLE), ZABUL Province. The attack took place sometime during the week of 20 to 26 Nov 06, resulting in the deaths of two TALIBAN fighters. However, the remaining TALIBAN elements were able to capture a total of six ANA FORD RANGERs and some uniforms prior to fleeing. Four of the pick-ups were sent to KABUL

District while the remaining two were sent to PARWAN, KAPISA, or GHAZNI Province, no further information.

3. The Afghan Ministry of Defence (MOD) is aware of the vehicles capture and plate numbers. However, they are keeping all information related to the six vehicles quiet, while MOD and Afghan National Police (ANP) search for them. The four pick-ups supposedly entered KABUL District. This is not yet confirmed; however, the MOD and ANP are aggressively searching for them in KABUL City area.

4. In addition, on approximately 28 Nov 06, ANP forces seized 20 BM-1 rockets in the MOSAHI District (GRID NOT AVAILABLE), KABUL Province. The 20 rockets were set up and positioned to be fired at KABUL City; however, no one was found in the area, NFI. The area in which the rockets were found has been used in the past by HIG Commander DERVISH to conduct rocket attacks on KABUL City. It is possible that these rockets belonged to DERVISH, but this has not been confirmed.

This information MUST NOT be disseminated to AFGauthorities.

Suicide Training

This report suggests that a member of the Directorate for Inter-Services Intelligence is in charge of suicide bombing operations in Kabul, and that he is a graduate of the Haqqania madrasa near Peshawar. The report outlines the general process of preparing a suicide attack.

DATE 12/19/06

TITLE The Suicide Training Process

POSSIBLE IED ATTACKS IN KABUL

Organization (s) Involved:

24 DEC 2006, ISAF CJ2X INTSUM 06100, NIS

(XXXXXXXXXXXX) RC CAPITAL - Possible suicide attack in KABUL. (C?3)

DOI: 18 Dec 06; OHR: RO FHT/1929.

(XXXXXXXXXXXX) A network of both Afghani and Pakistani terrorists has been planning and executing suicide attacks in KABUL City starting with unknown date. They are carrying out these sorts of operations in present. The entire process runs cyclically.

The process includes: training of suicide attackers, reconnaissance of operation area, operation planning, transport and hosting of suicide attackers and the execution of the attacks.

Generally responsible (but in an unknown manner) for suicide operations in KABUL City is XXXXXXXXXXXX/ PAKISTAN. He is an ISI member in XXXXXXXXXXXX (Intelligence Service XXXXXXXXXXXX) office in XXXXXXXXXXXX and part of his job is XXXXXXXXXXXX. (OPR COMMENT: Source was unable to further specify this job function. ENDS.) He graduated DAR AL ULOM-E HAQQANIA (religious school) having XXXXXXXXXXXX as one of his teachers.

Training: The suicide attackers are trained in GHALANI CAMP MOHMAND GHAR and MAULANA Jalaluddin HAQQANI'S camp located in northern WALERISTAN.

Reconnaissance, planning and transportation: Responsible for reconnaissance of the area, planning and transporting the suicide attackers from PAKISTAN to AFGHANISTAN is XXXXXXXXXXXX. First, before bringing the attackers, XXXXXXXXXXXX travelled to KABUL in order to check the local situation and to get specific information from XXXXXXXXXXXX and XXXXXXXXXXXX, two police officers working in XXXXXXXXXXXX branch of KABUL City Police. After getting the necessary information, he returned to PAKISTAN and started making plans supervised by AL ZAWAHIRI, XXXXXXXXXXXX and XXXXXXXXXXXX. XXXXXXXXXXXX Village XXXXXXXXXXXX but presently he lives in XXXXXXXXXXXX.

Hosting: At the completion of the planning process, XXXXXXXXXXXX started bringing the suicide attackers to KABUL and delivering them to XXXXXXXXXXXX locals. These XXXXXXXXXXXX are: XXXXXXXXXXXX are involved in weapons and drug smuggling. They have links with PDXXXXXXXXXXXX police and PD XXXXXXXXXXXX and PD XXXXXXXXXXXX NDS and Anti-terrorism Department of MOI. These XXXXXXXXXXXX people harbour the suicide attackers inside their houses.

Execution: After arriving to KABUL, the suicide attackers reconnoitred the area in order to find a suitable place for their attacks. Once a suitable place is found the attackers perform their attacks.

This information MUST NOT be disseminated to the GoA.

Sectarian Killing

As early as 2005, sectarian killings in Iraq began to increase, reaching a fever pitch in December 2006. This report raises the suspicion that an Iraqi may have been killed for working for the Americans, a major reason for killings in 2005.

DATE 1/14/05

TITLE SEVERED HEAD THROWN FROM VEH IVO BAQUBAH: 1 CIV KILLED

AT 1637C, A SEVERED HEAD WAS THROWN FROM AN OPEL OMEGA AT THE MUFREK TRAFFIC CIRCLE. THE HEAD HAS BEEN IDENTIFIED BUT IT IS UNKNOWN IF THE PERSON WORKKED FOR COALTION.

Unchecked Torture

Another instance of prisoner abuse by the Iraqi police. In this case, American troops found evidence of "unchecked torture," including a wooden pallet and a rubber hose, implements that were often used to beat detainees on their backs and the soles of their feet. Unlike in other cases, in this case Americans officers took action, including ordering a soldier to spend the night in the prison to prevent further abuses.

DATE 6/26/06

TITLE SUSPECTED DETAINEE ABUSE BY IP IN HUSAYBAH: 0 INJ/ DAMAGE

THERE IS EVIDENCE OF TORTURE IN A HOLDING CELL AT THE IRAQI POLICE STATION IN HUSAYBAH

//MGRS: 37S FU 829 075//, IZ. THE FOLLOWING ITEMS AND PHYSICAL EVIDENCE WERE NOTED TO BE IN A HOLDING CELL AND ARE CLEAR INDICATIONS THAT HUMAN RIGHTS VIOLATIONS ARE OCCURRING.

EVIDENCE OF UNCHECKED TORTURE WAS NOTED IN THE IRAQI POLICE STATION IN HUSAYBAH, IZ. LARGE AMOUNTS OF BLOOD ON THE CELL FLOOR, A WIRE USED FOR ELECTRIC SHOCK AND A RUBBER HOSE WERE LOCATED IN THE HOLDING CELL. ENCLOSURES.

ELECTRICAL WIRES THAT HAVE BEEN SPLIT AT THE ENDS AND FIXED WITH MEDICAL TAPE WHERE NOTED ON THE FLOOR OF THE CELL. THE TAPED ENDS HAD THE PRESENCE OF BLOOD. AN UNHINGED METAL CELL DOOR WAS POSITIONED AGAINST THE BACK WALL OF THE CELL NEAR THE WIRES. LARGE AMOUNTS OF SPATTERED BLOOD WHERE NOTED ON THE FLOOR AND ON A WOODEN PALLET ALSO LOCATED IN THE CELL. A RUBBER HOSE WAS ALSO FOUND NEAR THE STATED ITEMS.

THE POLICE TRANSITION TEAM (PTT) AT CAMP AL QAIM, WHICH IS WORKING WITH THE IPS STATIONED AT THE IP-DHQ IN HUSAYBAH IS FULLY AWARE OF THIS MATTER HAVING REPORTED THE EVIDENCE AND IS TAKING THE APPROPRIATE MEASURES WITH THE IP LEADERSHIP TO DO EVERYTHING POSSIBLE TO PREVENT SUCH INCIDENTS FROM OCCURRING IN THE FUTURE.

THE PTT BELIEVES THAT MUCH OF THE BLOOD IS POTENTIALLY ATTRIBUTABLE TO THE SUICIDE VEST BOMBING THAT OCCURRED IN MAY AND AN INDIVIDUAL THAT WAS DRAGGED INTO THAT HOLDING CELL IMMEDIATELY AFTER THE INCIDENT. THE CELL DOOR HAS BEEN FIXED AND THE PTT HAS BEEN SLEEPING OVERNIGHT DURING EVERY PRISONER RELEASE TO ENSURE THAT EVERY PRISONER IS APPROPRIATELY RELEASED.

THE PITT TEAM IS CONDUCTING UNANNOUNCED VISITS TO THE IPDHQ, AND THE DETENTION CELLS HAVE BEEN CHECKED DURING EVERY SUBSEQUENT VISIT AND THE LOGBOOK ENTRIES ON EVERY PRISONER HELD ARE BEING DEMANDED. THE DETENTION CELL OFFICERS HAVE BEEN COUNSELED ON THE SEVERE NEGATIVE RAMIFICATIONS TO RELATIONS WITH THE COALITION FORCES IF HUMAN RIGHTS ARE NOT RESPECTED. THE HUMAN RIGHTS COURSE FROM THE POLICE ESSENTIAL TASK LIST (PETL) FROM CPATT IS ALSO BEING GIVEN TO THE IP OFFICERS THROUGHOUT AL QAIM. ADDITIONALLY, THE TASK FORCE MP DETENTION CELLS INSPECTION TEAM HAS PAID THE STATION A VISIT AND INSPECTED THE CELLS AND SPOKEN TO THE IP LEADERSHIP ON THE SUBJECT OF THEIR DETENTION CELLS OPERATIONS.

Firefight on the Iranian Border

This document describes a firefight between American and Iranian forces near Iraq's border with Iran. An American platoon accompanied Iraqi soldiers on a search for infiltration routes. The Americans soldiers were instructed to stay at least one kilometer away from the border. The report asserts that an Iranian with a rocket-propelled grenade launcher threatened the American troops, prompting an American soldier to shoot him with a .50-caliber machine gun.

DATE 9/7/06

TITLE *CROSS BORDER COMPLEX ATTK ON 5-73 CAV IVO BALAD RUZ: 1 IRANIAN ARMY KIA, 1 CIV

AT 1047D, TF 5-73 REPORTS A DIRECT ATTACK IN THE DIYALA PROVINCE, E OF BALAD RUZ, AT GRID 38SNC 8296 2128.

SUMMARY OF INCIDENT ALONG IRAQ-IRAN BORDER ON 7 SEP 06

THIS MORNING, A PLT/C/5-73CAV PARTICIPATED IN A PARTNERSHIP ROUTE RECON, LED BY DBE XXXXXXXXXXXX, AND AN IA SQD FROM 3RD CO, 2-1/5IA (IA SQD LEADER AND 5 SOLDIERS). CF LT ******** IS THE PLATOON LEADER. THE RECON WAS ALONG A KNOWN ROUTE WHICH LT XXXXXXXXXXXX HAD TRAVELED FREQUENTLY AND ESTABLISHED CHECKPOINTS ALONG THIS ROUTE. PLTS TASK AND PURPOSE WAS TO CONDUCT A ZONE/ROUTE RECON AS JOINT OPERATION WITH IA AND DBE IN ORDER TO IDENTIFY KEY INFILTRATION ROUTES INTO IRAQ AND TO ASSESS THE C2 CAPABILITY AND COOPERATION BETWEEN THE IA & DBE. XXXXXXXXXXXX RODE IN THE LEAD IA TRUCK WITH THE IA SQUAD, WHILE XXXXXXXXXXXX, THE IA SQD LEADER, ROAD IN A PLT VEHICLE.

SPECIAL INSTRUCTIONS GIVEN TO CF LT ******** WERE AS FOLLOWS: USE MAIN ROADS TO GET TO CASTLE ACCESS ROADS; THE DBE CASTLES ALONG THE BORDER. NO CROSS COUNTRY MOVEMENT FROM CASTLE TO CASTLE WAS AUTHORIZED DUE TO MINEFIELD DANGERS. THEY WERE ALSO TO NOT TO COME WITHIN 1KM OF BORDER. PATROL USED BFT AND GPS TO CONFIRM THEIR LOCATION AT ALL TIMES. FOCUS WAS NOT THE

IRANIANS THEMSELVES BUT INFILTRATION ROUTES AND THE MOVEMENT OF ACCELERANTS. ALL ACKNOWLEDGED SPECIAL SENSITIVITIES AROUND THE BORDER DUE TO UN SANCTIONS AND IRANIAN CONCERN THAT US WAS ATTEMPTING TO MOUNT AN INVASION. THEY ALSO NOTED A PREVIOUS ARTICLE ABOUT BRITISH WHO ALSO MOVED FORCES TOWARDS SOUTHERN IRANIAN BORDER.

AS THE PATROL APPROACHED THE IRAQI BORDER, XXXXXXXXXXXX, IN THE LEAD VEHICLE, STOPPED THE PATROL. HE AND THE IA SQUAD WERE 200M AHEAD OF PATROL MAIN BODY. XXXXXXXXXXXX IDENTIFIED THIS POINT AS A FREQUENT CROSSING POINT. XXXXXXXXXXXX IDENTIFIED 2 IRANIANS RUN FROM THE VICINITY OF THIS LOCATION BACK TO IRANIAN SIDE OF THE BORDER.

THE PATROL SCANNED THE AREA WITH THEIR LRAS. WHILE MOVING FORWARD TO THE IA VEHICLE AHEAD, AN ARMED IRANIAN SOLDIER RIDING A MOTORCYCLE APPROACHED THE IA VEHICLE. THAT THIS POINT THE IRAQI LEAD VEHICLE WAS 75M AHEAD OF US MAIN BODY. THE IA SOLDIERS STOPPED THE MOTORCYCLE, AND DISMOUNTED THEIR TRUCK AND WALKED APPROX 100M TO THE FRONT OF THEIR VEHICLE TO TALK TO IRANIAN SOLDIER.

WITH THEIR LRAS, THE PATROL SCANNED THE IRANIAN BORDER CASTLE APPROX 2200-2500M AWAY AND IDENTIFIED A FIGHTING POSITION WEST OF THE CASTLE CONTAINING 2 X T62S AND A DSKA. WITHIN APPROX. 2 MINUTES OF THE IA STOPPING THE MOTORCYCLE, TWO IRANIAN TRUCKS MOVED SOUTH DOWN THE WINDING ROAD FROM THE CASTLE AND 8 SOLDIERS DISMOUNTED EACH TRUCK (16 TOTAL). THE IRANIANS STARTED TO TALK TO THE IA PATROL, DRAWING THE SQUAD AWAY FROM THEIR VEHICLE, APPARENTLY TO SEPARATE THE TWO IN ORDER TO DENY THEIR ABILITY TO LEAVE EXPEDITIOUSLY. AN IRANIAN BORDER CAPTAIN LINKED UP WITH THE IA ELEMENT AT THE LEAD OF THE COLUMN, CLAIMING TO WANT TO DISCUSS BORDER CROSSING PROBLEMS. THE 2 GROUPS OF 8 IRANIAN SOLDIERS IMT D AND TOOK UP TACTICAL POSITIONS NORTH OF THE COLUMN ON THE EAST AND WEST SIDES OF THE ROAD. THE IRANIAN SOLDIERS WERE ARMED WITH SMALL ARMS WEAPONS.

CF LT *********** CALLED HIS LEAD TRUCK (100M TO HIS FRONT) TELLING THE SQUAD LEADER TO MOTION TO THE IA THAT THEY (THE IA) NEEDED TO GO. WHEN THAT DIDN'T WORK HE SENT HIS INTERPRETER,

XXXXXXXXXXXX(A TITAN LOCAL NATIONAL HIRED FROM FOB CALDWELL)
TO GO FORWARD TO TELL THE IA THAT THEY ALL NEEDED TO DEPART.
THE INTERPRETER DID SO, BUT RETURNED TO CF LT ********* TO
SAY THAT EVERYTHING WAS OK AND THE IRANIANS WANTED TO HAVE A
MEETING TO TALK ABOUT THE BORDER. CF LT *********** MOVED
FORWARD FAR ENOUGH TO SEE THE IA ALL OFF THEIR TRUCK, GUN
UNMANNED, WITH THEIR GEAR OFF, SHOWING PICTURES TO IRANIAN
SOLDIERS AND HAVING TEA WITH THE IRANIANS.

CF LT ********* HAD THE INTERPRETER ONCE AGAIN TELL THE IA THAT
THEY MUST LOAD UP AND GO. TWO MORE IRANIAN TRUCKS APPEARED
AND 8 SOLDIERS EACH (16 TOTAL) DISMOUNTED AND TACTICALLY
MANEUVERED INTO TACTICAL POSITIONS FURTHER SOUTH ON THE DIRECT
EAST AND WEST SIDES OF CF LT ************* PLATOON COLUMN.
WEAPONS CARRIED WERE AK47S, RPKS AND RPGS. THE IRANIANS WERE
CLEARLY INTENT UPON ENCIRCLING THE PATROL.

CF LT *********** HAD HIS PLT START TO SLOWLY BACK
THEIR TRUCKS UP (SOUTH). AT THIS POINT,
XXXXXXXXXXXX(INTERPRETER) WENT RUNNING BACK FROM THE LEAD
POSITION TELLING CF LT ******* NOT TO MOVE OR THE IRANIANS
WOULD ENGAGE THE COLUMN. CF LT *********** HELD HIS GUYS
AND THEN MOVED FORWARD TO TRY AND MOTION THE IA TO GET IN
THEIR TRUCK AND GO. HE THEN HAD XXXXXXXXXXXX GO ALL THE
WAY FORWARD TO TELL THE IA THAT HE WAS LOW ON GAS AND MUST
RETURN. XXXXXXXXXXXX RETURNED AND SAID THAT EVERYTHING WAS
OK – THE IRANIANS SAID THEY WOULD GIVE THEM GAS AND WANTED
TO CONTINUE THE MEETING. CF LT ********** THEN TOLD HIS GUYS
THEY WERE LEAVING.

THE IRANIANS TO THE NORTHWEST OF THE COLUMN STARTED TO
ENGAGE THE PATROL BEFORE CF LT ********** TRUCKS MOVED. CF
LT ********* GAVE THE COMMAND TO RETURN FIRE AND RETROGRADE
BACK TO THE CHECK POINT 14 (VIC NC 627243). THE ENTIRE COLUMN
WAS UNDER FIRE AND RETURNED FIRE AS THEY CONDUCTED U-TURNS TO
LEAVE THE AREA. AN RPG GUNNER WHO HAD MOVED TO THE SOUTHERN
END OF THE COLUMN AND WAS ON THE ROAD TRYING TO ENGAGE CF LT
*********** PLT WAS ENGAGED AND KILLED BY A .50 CAL GUNNER.
WHILE BREAKING CONTACT AND RETURNING TO CP14, THE PLT RECEIVED
RPG AND INDIRECT FIRE ALL THE WAY BACK TO CP 14 – WELL INSIDE
IRAQI TERRITORY AND WEST OF THE BORDER CASTLE. THE ENTIRE

ENGAGEMENT LASTED 1:30 TO 2:00 MINUTES. AS THE PLT BROKE
CONTACT - IRANIAN INDIRECT FIRE LANDED AROUND THEM FOR APPROX
5:00 MINUTES. TOTAL NUMBER OF IRANIAN CASUALTIES IS UNKNOWN,
MINUS THE RPG GUNNER WHO WAS KILLED IN THE .50 CAL ENGAGEMENT.

UPON ARRIVAL AT CP14, IT WAS OBVIOUS THAT THE IA SOLDIERS
HAD NOT FOLLOWED. WE ARE NOT SURE IF THE IA ATTEMPTED TO
REMOUNT THEIR VEHICLE OR NOT. PROBABLY NOT THOUGH, AS THE
IRANIANS APPEAR TO HAVE DELIBERATELY SEPARATED THEM FROM THEIR
VEHICLE. THROUGHOUT THE DAY WE CONTINUED TO TRY TO REESTABLISH
OBSERVATION OF THE IA SOLDIERS, VIA GROUND SURVEILLANCE,
SHADOW UAV AND GLOBAL HAWK, TO NO AVAIL.

COL ********** CDR 3/4ID, RECEIVED WORD THIS EVENING FROM
THE MANDALI POE JCC THAT THE IRANIANS HAVE INFORMED THEM
THEY HAVE 4 IA SOLDIERS AND A DBE LT IN DETENTION. THEY DID
NOT MENTION THE INTERPRETER, NOR A FIFTH IA SOLDIER. WE HAVE
SUBMITTED AN RTQ TO THE CORPS PAO, AND RECOMMEND RELEASING
TO TRY GETTING OUT AHEAD OF ANY IRANIAN CLAIMS OF CROSSING
THE BORDER (EXASPERATED BY US KILLING ONE OF THEIR SOLDIERS).

AS OF 081800D: MNC-I STILL CONSIDERS THE 7 PERSONNEL DUSTWUN
UNTIL WE HAVE PROOF OF THEIR STATUS. THERE WERE 19 US SOLDIERS
(1 OFFICER AND 18 ENLISTED) PRESENT IN THE PATROL IN 4 UAH'S.
ALL WERE FROM 5-73 CAV. CLOSED 171916JSEPT06

UPDATE: 041200C2006< 5 IA AND 1 BP RELEASED FROM IRAINIAN
CUSTODY, INTERPETER TO BE RELEASED WITH IN NEXT 48 HOURS.

GLOSSARY

AFG—Afghanistan

AH-64—Apache attack helicopter

ANA—Afghan National Army

ANP—Afghan National Police

ATT—At this time

CAV—Cavalry

CDR—Commander

CF—Coalition forces

CIV—Civilian

CP—Command post

DBE—Department of Border Enforcement

FOB—Forward operating base

GIRoA—Government Islamic Republic of Afghanistan

GoA—Government of Afghanistan

HIG—Hezb-e-Islami Gulbuddin, an Afghan Islamist faction

IA—Iraqi Army

IED—Improvised explosive device

INS—Insurgents

INTSUM—Intelligence summary

IP—Iraqi Police

ISAF—International Security Assistance Force

IVO—In the vicinity of

IZ—International Zone, also known as the Green Zone

KIA—Killed in action

LRAS—Long-range advanced scout surveillance system

MGRS—Military Grid Reference System

MOI—Ministry of Interior

NC—Noncombatant

NDS—Afghan National Directorate of Security

NFI—No further information

NOFORN—Do not share with foreign governments

POLAD—Political liaisons from the State Department

RC—Regional command

RPGS—Rocket-propelled grenades

RTB—Returned to base

SVBIED—A car or truck bomb

TB—Taliban

TF—Task force

UAV—Unmanned aerial vehicle

NOTES ON CONTRIBUTORS

Ellen Barry is a correspondent with the Moscow bureau of The New York Times.

Jo Becker is an investigative reporter with The New York Times.

Katrin Bennhold reports from Paris for The New York Times and The International Herald Tribune.

William J. Broad is a science reporter and senior reporter for The New York Times.

David Brooks is an op-ed columnist for The New York Times.

Elisabeth Bumiller is a correspondent with the Washington, D.C. bureau of The New York Times.

John F. Burns is chief foreign correspondent of The New York Times, based in the London bureau.

Jackie Calmes is a correspondent with the Washington, D.C. bureau of The New York Times.

David Carr is a media columnist and culture reporter for The New York Times.

C. J. Chivers is a foreign correspondent for The New York Times.

Nicola Clark, a Paris based reporter, writes for The New York Times and The International Herald Tribune.

Noam Cohen writes the Link by Link column for the business section of The New York Times.

Gail Collins is an op-ed columnist for The New York Times.

Helene Cooper is a correspondent with the Washington, D.C. bureau of The New York Times.

Alan Cowell is a senior foreign correspondent for The New York Times, based in Paris.

Judy Dempsey reports from Berlin for The New York Times and The International Herald Tribune.

Rachel Donadio is the Rome bureau chief of The New York Times.

Maureen Dowd is an op-ed columnist for The New York Times.

Celia Dugger is co-bureau chief of the Johannesburg bureau of The New York Times.

Dexter Filkins, a staff writer for The New Yorker, covered Afghanistan, Pakistan and Iraq for The New York Times.

Thomas L. Friedman is an op-ed columnist for The New York Times.

Carlotta Gall is a senior correspondent for The New York Times, covering both Afghanistan and Pakistan.

Jeffrey Gettleman is the East Africa bureau chief of The New York Times.

James Glanz is an investigative reporter with The New York Times.

Michael R. Gordon is a correspondent with the Washington, D.C. bureau of The New York Times.

Jack Healy is a correspondent with the Baghdad bureau of The New York Times.

Bill Keller is an executive editor for The New York Times.

Mark Landler is a correspondent with the Washington, D.C. bureau of The New York Times.

Andrew W. Lehren is a reporter on the computer-assisted reporting desk of The New York Times.

John Leland is a correspondent with the Baghdad bureau of The New York Times.

Eric Lichtblau is a correspondent with the Washington, D.C. bureau of The New York Times.

Eric Lipton is a correspondent with the Washington, D.C. bureau of The New York Times.

Robert Mackey writes "The Lede" blog for The New York Times.

Elisabeth Malkin reports for the Mexico bureau of The New York Times.

John Markoff writes for the science section of The New York Times.

Mark Mazzetti is a correspondent with the Washington, D.C. bureau of The New York Times.

Jane Perlez is a bureau chief for the Pakistan bureau of The New York Times.

Frank Rich is an op-ed columnist for The New York Times.

David E. Sanger is the chief Washington correspondent of The New York Times.

Charlie Savage is a correspondent with the Washington, D.C. bureau of The New York Times.

Scott Shane is a correspondent with the Washington, D.C. bureau of The New York Times.

Eric Schmitt is a correspondent with the Washington, D.C. bureau of The New York Times.

Michael Slackman is the Berlin bureau chief of The New York Times.

Ravi Somaiya reports for the London bureau of The New York Times.

Alexander Star is the senior editor of The New York Times Book Review.

Sabrina Tavernese, who covered Iraq, Turkey and Pakistan for The New York Times, is a national correspondent.

Ginger Thompson is a correspondent with the Washington, D.C. bureau of The New York Times.

Michael Wines is the Beijing bureau chief of The New York Times.

Robert Wright is editor in chief of Bloggingheads.tv and the author most recently of "The Evolution of God."

ACKNOWLEDGMENTS

Open Secrets could not have been published without the vital contributions of many people. At The New York Times, Archie Tse, David Furst, Scott Shane, Bill Horn, Jake Doherty, Tom Gaffney and Julia Cohn provided invaluable editorial support; and Gerald Marzorati, Jim Schachter, MZ Goodman, Alex Ward and John MacLeod oversaw its creation. Anne Leigh designed the digital edition and James Dunn and Marnee Muskal enabled that edition's distribution. Joshua Tallent and Chris Casey of Ebook Architects skillfully transformed the original manuscript into an ebook. At Grove/Atlantic, Jamison Stoltz applied equal skill to editing the ebook into a print book.